FOUNDATIONS
OF
CHRISTIANITY

Karl Kautsky

FOUNDATIONS
OF
Christianity

TRANSLATED BY HENRY F. MINS
PUBLISHED BY S·A·RUSSELL NEW YORK
1953

The title of this book, in the original German *Ursprung des Christenthums,* is more accurately translated as *Origins of Christianity.* This book, in fact, appeared in England under that title. However, an American edition, published in 1925, carried the title *Foundations of Christianity.* The present publishers have chosen to use the less accurate translation in order to avoid confusing American readers who may be familiar with the book under the latter title.

LIBRARY OF CONGRESS CATALOG NUMBER: 53-8294

COPYRIGHT, 1953, BY S · A · RUSSELL

MANUFACTURED IN THE U.S.A.

TRANSLATOR'S NOTE

As WE look back at it, the age in which Karl Kautsky wrote this book on the origins of Christianity seems like the youth of the world. Passports and immigration quotas, world wars and world-shaking depressions, were still to come. Western Europe was in the center of the world's spotlight and the rest of the globe were but supporting actors in the half-shadow surrounding it.

There is a certain tendency today to make an Arcadian idyll of that age, and to sigh nostalgically for that lost innocence. This is a mistake. The world was not as innocent as all that in the days of Otto, Prince Bismarck, and in any case wishing will not bring it back.

There are compensations for the loss of innocence, or growing up. Knowledge is, or can be, one of them. Yet, as we evaluate the tremendous changes in the world in the half century since this book was written, we find that Hegel was not altogether wrong in saying that the only thing we learn from history is that people learn nothing from history. Kautsky's time, before the first World War, may have been relatively youthful, and we now relatively adult, and still youth may see more clearly than age if experience has brought uneasiness and distraction rather than wisdom and mastery. *Foundations of Christianity* represents a type of book, and a type of scholarship, that we miss today.

Kautsky could still see what most of us today are too frightened and harried to make out, the forward movement of history. He could see the progress he was helping to make. The historical method he had learned from Marx and Engels led him to a vigorous optimism, based on that of his teachers, which is a refreshing change from the irrational or inhuman chthonic powers we worship. Kautsky was a rationalist: in the first place he saw that human work produces changes, and in fact that all changes in human society in the long run derive from the conscious and organized work of its members; and moreover his book assumes that coherent argument is the basis for convincing people. When he says propaganda he does not mean lying.

His faith in reason, his own and that of his fellow-men, is refreshing to our ears after the wry dissonances of modern techniques for influencing public opinion. When he went into what was for him the alien field of theology and religious history he did so for a rational reason and on a reasonable method. He took up the discussion of religious texts and institutions in order to give a historical explanation of them as they existed; for he knew (a piece of wisdom that the so-called New Criticism spends all its subtlety trying to obscure) that nothing makes sense apart from its history. To study that history, not being a specialist, he went to the works of the students of Christianity, and found rich veins to tap.

The Reformation had appealed from the infallible church to the infallible book. The next step was to examine the credentials and the origins of that authority. Throughout the nineteenth century theologians and critics, some because they wanted to and others in order to answer them, asked questions and compared texts, studied cuneiform inscriptions and got data from archeological diggings and the study of comparative religion. This work was preeminently under Protestant auspices, but it had strong echoes within Catholicism at that time in the form of the so-called Modernist movement, and among certain sectors of Jewish scholarship.

Now not all of this work had been done with an easy conscience. The rude attacks of English deists and French *philosophes* during the eighteenth century were still remembered; the search for the truth was often tempered by fear of losing received doctrine or fear of encouraging skepticism, or fear of reprisals by entrenched orthodoxy. But by and large the work was well and honestly done, even though some of the workers may not have drawn all the inferences they might, or may have shrunk back from touching this or that sacred cow.

By the end of the century there was a large number of conclusions that could be denounced, and were, but could not so easily be disputed. There still remained the task of making all this historical knowledge historical, by showing the connections of the individual results with each other and their relationship to the course of history. Until this was done, the subject remained to a great extent verbal and merely ideological.

Kautsky set himself the task of making these connections, and did his work so well that the half century since it appeared has not produced anything that can take its place. It is still the best volume on the subject.

It is some time since it has been available to the public. A previous translation (New York, 1925) has long been out of print.

A word about the author may be useful. Karl Kautsky was born in 1854 and as a young man became acquainted with Marx and Engels. For over thirty years he was editor of *Neue Zeit*, the theoretical organ of the German socialists. After Engels' death he published, as a fourth volume of *Capital*, Marx' economic manuscripts on the history of the theories of surplus value. Kautsky was one of the leading figures in the Second International, and a leader in opposing the revisionism that centered around such figures as Bernstein. He lived long enough to see Hitler take power in 1933, escaped to Czechoslovakia and died shortly thereafter.

CONTENTS

CHRISTIANITY and Bible criticism are themes I have long been concerned with. Twenty-five years ago I published an essay on the "Genesis of Biblical Primitive History" in *Kosmos,* and two years later one on the "Genesis of Christianity" in *Neue Zeit.* It is thus an old love that I come back to. The occasion was given when a second edition of my *Forerunners of Socialism* seemed needed.

The criticism made of that book, so far as I have seen it, found fault mainly with the introduction, in which I gave a brief account of the communism of primitive Christianity. It was held that this notion did not stand up in the face of the most recent results of research.

Soon after these criticisms it was announced further, especially by Comrade Göhre, that another conception in my book had been rendered obsolete. This was the notion, first upheld by Bruno Bauer and then accepted in essentials by Mehring and by me in 1885, namely that there is nothing certain we can say about the person of Jesus and that Christianity can be explained without introducing this person.

For these reasons I was unwilling to prepare a new edition of my book, which appeared thirteen years ago, without testing the ideas on Christianity in the light of the most recent literature.

In the process I arrived at the comforting conclusion that I had nothing to alter. However, the latest researches opened up to me so many new points of view and suggestions that checking my introduction to the *Forerunners* gave rise to a whole new book.

I do not of course claim to have exhausted the subject. It is too gigantic for that. I shall be content if I have succeeded in contributing to the understanding of those aspects of Christianity that seem to me to be the decisive ones from the point of view of the materialistic conception of history.

I certainly can not compare my learning in questions of religious history with that of the theologians who have devoted their lives to the subject, while I had to write this book in the free time left to me by editorial and political activity in an age when the present takes up all the attention of any man who takes part in modern class struggles, leaving him no time for the past.

But perhaps it was just my intensive involvement in the class struggle of the proletariat that made it possible for me to get insights into the essence of primitive Christianity that escape the professors of theology and religious history.

In his *Julie* J. J. Rousseau says:

"I think it is foolish to try to study society as a mere bystander. The man that wants only to observe observes nothing; as he is useless in business and a dead weight in amusements, he is not drawn into anything. We see others' actions only to the extent that we act ourselves. In the school of the world, as in love's school, we have to start by practicing what we want to learn" (Part II, Letter 17).

This proposition can be extended from the study of man, to which it is limited here, to the inquiry into all things. A man never gets far with mere looking-on, without entering into things practically. That holds true even for research into such distant things as the stars. Where would astronomy be if it confined itself to pure observation and did not link it with practice, with the telescope, spectral analysis, photography? And still more is this true of terrestrial things, for which our practice gets much closer under our skin than mere spectatorship. Just looking on is thin-blooded compared to what we learn by working on these things and with these things. We need only think of the tremendous importance of experiment in science.

In human society experiments are out of the question as methods of inquiry; but that does not mean that the practical activity of the inquirer plays a smaller role, given those conditions that are requisite to making an experiment, too, fruitful. These conditions are the knowledge of the most important discoveries made by previous investigators and acquaintance with a scientific method that sharpens the eye for what is essential in every phenomenon, that makes it possible to separate the essential from the unessential and to discover what different experiences have in common.

A thinker thus equipped who takes up the study of a field in which he is active, is likely to achieve results that would be impossible for him as a spectator. Not the last place in which this is true is history. A practical politician, if he has scholarly training, will understand political history better and find his way around in it better than a library scholar who lacks the least practical acquaintance with what makes politics go. The researcher will be helped by his practical experience particularly when he is studying a movement of the class in which he himself is active and with whose nature he is intimately at home.

Hitherto this has been of benefit almost exclusively to the propertied classes, who have monopolized scholarship. The movements of the lower classes have not had many discriminating students.

Christianity was in its initial stages undoubtedly a movement of the propertyless, of the most diverse sorts, whom we may lump together under the name of proletarians if we do not mean thereby only wage-workers. Any one who knows the modern movement of the proletariat and what it has in common in the various countries, and knows it by working with them; any one who has been a fellow-fighter of the proletariat and has learned there to share its feelings and aspirations, has a right to expect to penetrate into the beginnings of Christianity more easily, in many respects, than the men of learning that see the proletariat only from afar.

Now although the practical politician with scholarly training has many advantages over the mere bookish men when it comes to writing history, he often loses the advantage because he has stronger temptations, which interfere with his impartiality. There are two in particular: first, the attempt to put the past into the mold of the present; and then the effort to see the past in a way that corresponds to the needs of the politics of the present.

We socialists, to the extent that we are Marxists, feel ourselves insured against these dangers by the materialist conception of history that is directly connected with our proletarian point of view.

The traditional conception of history sees political movements as nothing more than the battle over definite political institutions —monarchy, aristocracy, democracy, etc.—which in turn are the result of definite ethical ideas and aspirations. If we go no further, and do not ask for the basis of these ideas, aspirations and institutions, we come easily to the conclusion that they change only externally in the course of the centuries, remaining basically the same; that the same ideas, aspirations and institutions keep recurring, that all history is a continuous striving toward freedom and equality that always comes up against oppression and inequality, is never realizable, but never altogether done away with.

If somewhere, sometime, fighters for freedom and equality have won, their victory turns into the basis of new oppression and inequality. Then new fighters for freedom and equality arise once more.

In this way all history appears as a circle, always returning upon itself, an eternal repetition of the same struggles, in which only the costumes change, but humanity makes no progress.

One who holds this view will always be inclined to paint the past in the likeness of the present; and the better he knows the men of the present, the more likely he is to fashion earlier times after their pattern.

On the other hand, there is a conception of history that does not confine itself to observing social ideas, but looks for their causes in the deepest foundations of society. In this search it always comes up against the mode of production, which in turn depends on the status of technology in the last analysis, although by no means exclusively.

As soon as we take up the technology and then the mode of production of antiquity, the notion disappears that the same tragicomedy keeps repeating itself on the stage of the world. Man's economic history shows a continual development from lower to higher forms, although one that is by no means a straight unbroken line. And when we have studied man's economic relationships in the various historical periods, we lose the illusion of the never-ending recurrence of the same ideas, aspirations and political institutions. We see that identical words change their meaning over the centuries, that ideas and institutions that resemble each other externally have a different content, because they arise out of the needs of different classes under different conditions. The freedom that the modern proletarian demands is different from the freedom that the representatives of the Third Estate strove for in 1789, and this in turn was basically different from the freedom the German Imperial knights fought for at the beginning of the Reformation.

Once one stops regarding political struggles as struggles for abstract ideas or political institutions, and shows their economic basis, he sees immediately that here, just as in technology and modes of production, there is a continual development toward higher forms; that no era is quite like any other; that the same battle-cries and the same arguments mean quite different things at different times.

Now if the proletarian point of view enables us to understand more easily than bourgeois scholars can, those aspects of primitive Christianity which it has in common with the modern proletarian movement, the emphasis on economic relationships that comes from the materialist conception of history helps us understand the peculiar characteristics of the ancient proletariat, characteristics that arose out of its particular economic situation and that made its strivings so basically different from those of the modern proletariat, for all the features they have in common.

The Marxist conception of history guards us against the danger of measuring the past with the yardstick of the present, and gives us a keener eye for the peculiar quality of each era and each people. At the same time it preserves us from the other danger, that of making our description of the past fit the practical interest we are upholding at the present time.

Of course an honest man, whatever his point of view may be, will not let himself be led into a conscious falsification of history. But nowhere is the scholar's impartiality more needed than in the social sciences, and nowhere is it harder to achieve.

The task of science is not simply to describe what exists, to furnish a photograph of reality that is true to life, so that any observer who is normally equipped will aim at the same picture. The task of science consists in getting at the general, the essential features in the bewildering "complex of features" or phenomena, and out of them to fashion a guiding thread that will enable us to find our way in the labyrinth of reality.

For the matter of that, the task of art is a similar one. It too does not simply furnish a photograph of reality; the artist has to reproduce what seems to him essential and characteristic in the reality he wants to depict. The difference between art and science lies in the fact that the artist presents the essential in a form that the senses can grasp, and that is the way he arrives at his effects, whereas the thinker presents what is essential as a concept or abstraction.

The more complicated a phenomenon is, and the fewer the phenomena it can be compared with, the harder it is to distinguish what is essential in it from what is accidental, and the more the subjective qualities of the researcher and expositor will come into play. The more vital, therefore, the clarity and impartiality of his view.

Now there is no more complicated phenomenon than human society, the society of men, each one of whom is already more complicated than any other being we know of. And at the same time the number of mutually comparable social organisms at the same stage of development is relatively very small. No wonder that the scientific study of society begins later than that of any other field of our experience; and no wonder that it is precisely in this domain that the views of scholars diverge more widely than anywhere else. But these difficulties are enormously magnified when, as is so often the case in the social sciences, different scholars have differing and often contrary practical interests in the outcome of their investigations, interests which need not be personal ones but may be a very matter-of-fact class interest.

It is obviously quite impossible to maintain impartiality when one is interested in any way in the social contradictions and battles of his time, and at the same time sees these phenomena of the present as a repetition of the contradictions and battles of the past. The latter become mere precedents entailing the justification or the condemnation of the former; our judgment of the present depends on our judgment of the past. Can any one to whom his cause is dear stay impartial? The more he is attached to it, the more importance he will attach to those facts of the past, and he will stress those, as the essential ones, that seem to support his own position, and relegate to the background, as unessential, the facts that seem to testify to the contrary. The researcher turns into a moralist or advocate who glorifies or stigmatizes certain phenomena of the past because he is a defender or an enemy of similar phenomena in the present—church, monarchy, democracy, etc.

The situation is quite different once it is realized, on the basis of economic insight, that nothing repeats itself in history, that the economic relationships of the past are gone beyond recall; that former class contradictions and struggles are essentially different from those of today; that hence modern institutions and ideas, for all their external coincidence with those of the past, have a totally different content. One realizes that every age must be measured with its own yardstick; that the strivings of the present must have their basis in present relationships; that past successes or failures have little relevance in the matter; that a mere appeal to the past to justify the demands of the present can but lead us astray. The democrats and proletarians of France found that out often enough in the last century when they relied more on the "theories" of the French Revolution than on insight into existing class relationships.

One who takes the standpoint of the materialist conception of history can look at the past with the most complete impartiality, even though he takes the most active part in the practical struggles of the present. His practical action can only make his view keener into many phenomena of the past; it can no longer becloud it.

So I too have proceeded to describe the roots of primitive Christianity without intending either to extol or stigmatize it, but merely to understand it. I knew that whatever results I might arrive at, the cause I was fighting for could not suffer thereby. No matter how I regarded the proletarians of the Empire, whatever their efforts and results may have been, they were totally different from the modern proletariat, which struggles and works in a quite different situation and with quite different methods. Whatever mighty deeds and successes, whatever miseries and defeats those proletarians may have had, they could not give any testimony as to the nature and the outlook of the modern proletariat, either favorable or unfavorable.

Now if that is the case, is there any practical purpose to busying oneself with history? The ordinary view looks upon history as a naval chart for mariners on the sea of political action; it should show the reefs and shallows where former seafarers were stranded, and enable their successors to get by unscathed. But if the channel of history is constantly changing and the shallows are always forming in new places, so that every pilot must find his way anew by constantly studying the channel; if mere steering by the old chart only too often leads astray, why still study history, except as a dilettante of antiques?

Anyone who took this position would throw out the baby with the bath.

To continue the image we have been using, history can not be used as a permanent chart for the pilot of a political vessel. But that does not signify that it is useless for him. He just has to make a different use of it. He has to use it as a sounding-lead, as a means of learning the channel he is in and finding his way in it. The only way to understand a phenomenon is to learn how it was formed. I can not understand today's society if I do not know how it arose, how its various phenomena—capitalism, feudalism, Christianity, Judaism, etc.—developed.

If I want to get a clear idea of the social status, the tasks and the outlooks of the class I belong to or have joined, I must get clarity as to the existing social organism; I must understand it from every aspect; and that is impossible if I have not followed it in its development. Without insight into the course of society's evolution it is impossible to be a conscious and far-sighted class fighter; one depends on the impressions received from one's immediate environment and the present moment, one is never sure that one is not going to be driven into a channel that seems to lead ahead but soon ends between cliffs from which there is no outlet. It is true that many class struggles succeeded even though those who took part in them were not always clearly aware of the nature of the society in which they lived.

But in present-day society the conditions for that sort of successful struggle are disappearing, just as in this society it is harder and harder to be guided merely by instinct and tradition in choosing one's food and enjoyments. They might be adequate in simple, natural conditions. The more artificial the conditions of life become as a result of the progress of technology and science, the more they depart from nature, the more the individual requires scientific knowledge to pick out what his organism needs from among the mass of artificial products offered him. So long as men drank only water, the instinct sufficed that made them seek out good spring water and reject foul swamp water. But instinct collapses completely as a guide to manufactured beverages. Scientific insight is needed here.

And it is precisely that way in politics, in social action in general. In the communities of antiquity with their simple and obvious relationships, which often remained unchanged for centuries, tradition and "sound common sense," that is the insight the individual had attained as a result of his personal experience, were enough to show him his place and his tasks in society. Today, in a society whose market is the entire globe, which is in constant motion, technical and social motion, in which the workers organize into armies of millions and capitalists concentrate in their hands sums amounting to billions: in such a society it is impossible that a rising class, that can not limit itself to the preservation of what exists, that must demand a complete renovation of society, could conduct its class struggle purposefully and successfully if it does not go beyond sound common sense and the practical man's skill. On the contrary, it becomes an urgent necessity for each fighter to broaden his horizon by scientific insight, to complete his knowledge of social connections in space and time, not in order to get along without practical skill or even to push it into the background, but in order to bring it into conscious connection with the total social process. What makes this even more necessary is that this same society, that increasingly encompasses the entire globe, carries the division of labor further and further, limits the individual more and more to a specialty, a single action, and tends to degrade him spiritually, making him less independent and less able to understand all the immensity of the entire process.

It is thus the duty of everyone who has made the rise of the proletariat his life's work to counteract this tendency to mental emptiness and narrowness, by interesting the proletarians in large views of history.

There is hardly any way in which this can be done better than by the study of history, by surveying and understanding the course of society's development over long periods of time, especially when this development contained powerful social movements that continue to operate in our own day.

In order to bring the proletariat to social insight, to self-consciousness and political maturity, to large-scale thinking, it is indispensable to study the historical process with the aid of the materialist conception of history. In this way the study of the past, far from being mere dilettante antiquarianism, will become a powerful weapon in the struggles of the present, in order to hasten the attainment of a better future.

Berlin, *September 1908*   K. Kautsky

FOUNDATIONS
OF
CHRISTIANITY

BOOK ONE: THE PERSON

OF JESUS

THE PAGAN SOURCES

WHATEVER one's position may be with respect to Christianity, it certainly must be recognized as one of the most titanic phenomena in all human history. One can not resist a deep feeling of wonder when one thinks of the Christian Church, now almost two thousand years old and still vigorous, more powerful than the governments of many countries. Anything that helps us to understand this colossal phenomenon, including the study of its origin, is of great and immediate practical significance, even though it takes us back thousands of years.

This makes researches into the beginnings of Christianity of far greater interest than any other historical question that goes back further than the last two hundred years; it also however makes finding the beginnings even more difficult than it would otherwise be.

The Christian Church has become a sovereign organisation serving the needs either of its own rulers or those of other, secular rulers who have been able to gain control over it. Any one who opposes these rulers must oppose the church as well. The struggle about the church and the struggle against the church have become matters of dispute bound up with the most important economic interests. It thus becomes only too easy to abandon impartiality in historical studies of the church and this long ago led the ruling classes to interdict the study of the beginnings of Christianity and to ascribe to the church a divine nature, standing above and outside all human criticism.

The bourgeois age of reason in the eighteenth century finally succeeded in getting rid of this halo. For the first time scientific study of the genesis of Christianity became possible. But it is remarkable how secular science avoided this field during the nineteenth century, acting as though it still belonged exclusively to the realm of theology. A whole series of historical works written by the most eminent bourgeois historians of the nineteenth century dealing with the Roman Empire quietly pass over the most important happening of the time, the rise of Christianity. For instance, in the fifth volume of his *Roman History* Mommsen gives a very extensive account of the history of the Jews under the Caesars, and in so doing can not avoid mentioning Christianity occasionally; but it appears only as something already existing, something assumed to be already known. By and large only the theologians and their adversaries, the propagandists of free thought, have taken an interest in the beginnings of Christianity.

It need not necessarily have been cowardice that kept bourgeois historians from taking up the origin of Christianity; it could also have been the desire to write history and not polemics. The hopeless state of the sources out of which we have to get our information in this field must alone have frightened them off.

The traditional view sees Christianity as the creation of a single man, Jesus Christ. This view persists even today. It is true that Jesus, at least in "enlightened" and "educated" circles, is no longer considered a deity, but he is still held to have been an extraordinary personality, who came to the fore with the intention of founding a new religion, and did so, with tremendous success. Liberal theologians hold this view, and so do radical free-thinkers; and the latter differ from the theologians only with respect to the criticism they make of Christ as a person, whom they seek to deprive of all the sublimity they can.

And yet, at the end of the eighteenth century the English historian Gibbon, in his *Decline and Fall of the Roman Empire* (written 1774 to 1788), had ironically pointed out how striking it is that none of Jesus' contemporaries mentions him, although he is said to have accomplished such remarkable feats.

"But how shall we excuse the supine inattention of the Pagan and philosophic world to those evidences which were presented by the hand of Omnipotence, not to their reason, but to their senses? During the age of Christ, of his apostles, and of their first disciples, the doctrine which they preached was confirmed by innumerable prodigies. The lame walked, the blind saw, the sick were healed, the dead were raised, daemons were expelled, and the laws of Nature were frequently suspended for the benefit of the church. But the sages of Greece and Rome turned aside from the awful spectacle, and, pursuing the ordinary occupations of life and study, appeared unconscious of any alterations in the moral or physical government of the world." At Jesus' death, according to the Christian tradition, the whole earth, or at least all Palestine, was in darkness for three hours. This took place in the days of the elder Pliny, who devoted a special chapter of his *Natural History* to eclipses; but of this eclipse he says nothing (Gibbon, Chap. 15).

But even if we leave miracles out of account, it is hard to see how a personality like the Jesus of the gospels, who according to them aroused such excitement in people's minds, could carry on his work and finally die as a martyr for his cause and yet not have pagan and Jewish contemporaries devote a single word to him.

The first mention of Jesus by a non-Christian is found in the *Jewish Antiquities* of Flavius Josephus. The third chapter of book 18 deals with the procurator Pontius Pilate, and says among other things:

"About this time lived Jesus, a wise man, if he can be called human, for he worked miracles and was a teacher of men, who received the truth gladly; and he found many followers among Jews and Greeks. This was the Christ. Although later Pilate sentenced him to the cross on the complaint of the nobles of our people, those who had loved him remained true to him. For he appeared again to them on the third day, risen to new life, as the prophets of God had prophesied this and thousands of other wonderful things about him. From him comes the name of the Christians, whose sect (*phylon*) has continued to exist ever since."

Josephus speaks of Christ again in the 20th book, ch. 9, 1, where the high priest Ananus is said in the time of the procurator Albinus to have brought it about that "James, the brother of Jesus, said to be the Christ (*tou legomenou christou*), together with some others, was brought to court, accused as a breaker of the law and delivered over to be stoned to death."

These pieces of evidence have always been highly prized by Christians; for they come from a non-Christian, a Jew and Pharisee, born in the year 37 of our era and living in Jerusalem, and so very well able to have authentic facts about Jesus. And his testimony was the more valuable in that as a Jew he had no reason to falsify on behalf of the Christians.

But it was precisely the exaggerated exaltation of Christ on the part of a pious Jew that made the first passage suspect, and quite early. Its authenticity was disputed even in the sixteenth century, and today it is agreed that it is a forgery and does not stem from Josephus.[1] It was insterted in the third century by a Christian copyist, who obviously took offense at the fact that Josephus, who repeats the most trivial gossip from Palestine, says nothing at all about the person of Jesus. The pious Christian felt with justice that the absence of any such mention weighed against the existence or at least the significance of his Savior. Now the discovery of his forgery has become testimony against Jesus.

But the passage concerning James is also dubious. It is true that Origen (185 to 254 A.D.) mentions testimony by Josephus concerning James; this occurs in his commentary on Matthew. He remarks that it is surprising that nonetheless Josephus did not believe in Jesus as the Christ. In his polemic against Celsus, Origen cites this statement of Josephus about James and again notes Josephus' unbelief. These statements by Origen constitute one of the proofs that the striking passage about Jesus in which Josephus recognizes him as the Messiah, the Christ, could not have been in the original text of Josephus. It follows at once that the passage

1. See e.g. Schürer, *Geschichte des jüdischen Volkes im Zeitalter Jesu Christi*, Vol. I, 3rd edn., 1901, p. 544 f.

about James that Origen found in Josephus was also a Christian forgery. For this passage he cites runs quite differently from what we find in the manuscript of Josephus that has come down to us. In it the destruction of Jerusalem is said to be a punishment for the execution of James; but this fabrication is not found in the other manuscripts of Josephus. The passage as it occurs in the manuscripts of Josephus that have come down to us is not cited by Origen, while he mentions the other version three times on different occasions. And yet he carefully assembled all the testimony that could be got from Josephus that had value for the Christian faith. It would seem likely that the passage of Josephus about James that has come down to us is also fraudulent, and was first inserted by a pious Christian, to the greater glory of God, some time after Origen, but before Eusebius, who cites the passage.

Like the mention of Jesus and James, the reference to John the Baptist in Josephus (*Antiquities*, XVIII, 5,2) is also suspect as an "interpolation."[2]

Thus Christian frauds had crept into Josephus as early as the end of the second century. His silence concerning the chief figures in the Gospels was too conspicuous, and required correction.

But even if the statement about James was genuine, it would prove at most that there was a Jesus, whom people called Christ, that is, the Messiah. It could not prove anything more. "If the passage actually had to be ascribed to Josephus, all that critical theology would get from it would be the thread of a web that could catch a whole generation. There were so many would-be Christs at Josephus' time and all the way deep into the second century, that in many of the cases we have only sketchy information left about them. There is a Judas of Galilee, a Theudas, a nameless Egyptian, a Samaritan, a Bar Kochba,—why should there not have been a Jesus among them as well? Jesus was a common Jewish personal name."[3]

The second passage of Josephus tells us at best that among the agitators in Palestine coming forward at that time as the Messiah,

2. Schürer, *op. cit.*, pp. 438, 548, 581.
3. Alb. Kalthoff, *The Rise of Christianity*, London 1907, pp. 20, 21.

the Lord's anointed, there was also a Jesus. We learn nothing at all about his life and work.

The next mention of Jesus by a non-Christian writer is found in the *Annals* of the Roman historian Tacitus, composed around the year 100. In the fifteenth book the conflagration of Rome under Nero is described, and chapter 44 says:

"In order to counteract the rumor [that blamed Nero for the fire] he brought forward as the guilty ones men hated for their crimes and called Christians by the people; and punished them with the most exquisite torments. The founder of their name, Christ, was executed by the procurator Pontius Pilate in the reign of Tiberius; the superstition was thereby suppressed for the moment, but broke out again, not only in Judea, the land in which this evil originated, but in Rome itself, to which everything horrible or shameful streams from all sides and finds increase. First a few were taken, who made confessions; then on their indications an enormous throng, who were not accused directly of the crime of arson, but of hatred of humanity. Their execution became a pastime; they were covered with the skins of wild beasts and then torn to pieces by dogs, or they were crucified, or prepared for burning and set on fire as soon as it was dark, to give light in the night. Nero lent his gardens for this spectacle and arranged circus games, in which he mingled among the crowd in the clothing of a charioteer or drove a chariot himself. Although these were criminals who deserved the severest punishments, sympathy arose for them as being sacrificed not so much for the general good but to satisfy the rage of an individual."

This testimony is certainly not something falsified by Christians in their favor. However its authenticity too is disputed, since Dio Cassius knows nothing of a persecution of Christians under Nero, although he lived a hundred years later than Tacitus. Suetonius, writing shortly after Tacitus, also speaks, in his biography of Nero, of a persecution of Christians, "men who had given themselves over to a new and evil superstition" (chap. 16).

But Suetonius tells us nothing at all of Jesus and Tacitus does not even hand down his name to us. Christ, the Greek word for "the anointed," is merely the Greek translation of the Hebrew word "Messiah." As to Christ's work and the content of his doctrine Tacitus says nothing.

And that is all that we learn about Jesus from non-Christian sources of the first century of our era.

BOOK ONE: THE PERSON

OF JESUS

THE CHRISTIAN SOURCES

BUT DO NOT the Christian sources gush forth all the more richly? Do we not have in the Gospels the most extensive descriptions of the teachings and deeds of Jesus?

It is true they are extensive; but as for credibility, there's the rub. The example of the falsification of Josephus showed us a character trait of ancient Christian historians, their complete indifference to the truth. It was not the truth, but effectiveness, that they were interested in, and they were not too delicate in the choice of their means.

To be fair, it must be granted that they were not alone in their age. The Jewish religious literature had no higher standards, and the "heathen" mystical tendencies in the centuries preceding and following the beginning of our era were guilty of the same sins. Credulousness on the part of the public, sensationalism together with lack of confidence in their own powers, the need to cling to superhuman authority, lack of a sense of reality (qualities whose causes we shall soon come to learn), infected all of literature at that time, and the more it left the ground of the traditional the more it was so infected. We shall find numerous proofs of this in the Christian and Jewish literature. But the same tendency appears in the mystical philosophy, which to be sure had an inner affinity to Christianity. We see this in the neo-Pythagoreans, a trend that began in the last century before our era, a mixture of Platonism and Stoicism, full of revelations and hungry for miracles, professing to be the doctrine of the old philosopher Pythagoras, who lived in the sixth century before our era—or before Christ, as they say—and of whom extremely little was known. That made it all the easier to attribute to him anything that needed the authority of a great name.

"The neo-Pythagoreans wanted to be considered faithful followers of the old Samian philosopher: in order to present their theories as the old Pythagorean ones, those countless forged documents were produced that put anything at all into the mouth of a Pythagoras or an Archytas, no matter how recent it was or how well known as stemming from Plato or Aristotle."[4]

We see exactly the same phenomenon in the early Christian literature, where it has produced such a chaos that for over a hundred years a series of the keenest minds have been working on it without getting very far in attaining any definitive results.

How the most discordant notions as to the origin of the early Christian writings still exist side by side can be shown by the case of the Revelation of St. John, an especially hard nut to crack anyway. Pfleiderer says of it in his book on *Early Christianity, Its Writings and Doctrines*:

"The book of Daniel was the oldest of such apocalypses and the model for the whole genus. Just as the key to the visions of Daniel was found in the events of the Jewish war under Antiochus Epiphanes, so the conclusion was correctly drawn that the apocalypse of John too must be explained by means of the conditions of its time. Now since the mystic number 666 in the eighteenth verse of the thirteenth chapter was interpreted almost simultaneously by various scholars (Benary, Hitzig and Reuss) as indicating the Emperor Nero in Hebrew letters, a comparison of chapters 13 and 17 led to the conclusion that Revelation was written soon after Nero's death in 68. This long remained the dominant view, in particular in the old Tübingen school, which still assumed that the book was written by the apostle John and thought it had the key to the whole book in the party battles between Judaists and Paulinists; this of course was not done without crass arbitrariness

4. Zeller, *Philosophie der Griechen*, Part 3, Sec. 2, Leipzig 1868, p. 96.

(especially in Volkmar). A new step toward the thorough study of the problem was made in 1882 by a student of Weizsäcker, Daniel Völter, who used the hypothesis of a repeated expansion and revision of a basic document between the years 66 and 170 (later up to 140), at the hands of various authors. The literary method thus introduced was varied in the extreme during the next fifteen years: Vischer would have it that an original Jewish document had been worked over by a Christian editor; Sabatier and Schön postulated a Christian document as the basis, into which Jewish elements had been inserted; Weyland distinguished two Jewish sources from the times of Nero and Titus, and a Christian editor in Trajan's reign; Spitta saw a Christian original of the year 60 and Jewish sources of 63 B.C. and 40 A.D., with a Christian editor in Trajan's time; Schmidt, three Jewish sources and two Christian; Völter, in a new work in 1893, an original apocalypse dating from the year 62 and four revisions under Titus, Domitian, Trajan and Hadrian. These mutually contradictory and competing hypotheses had the sole result that 'the unprejudiced got the impression that in the field of New Testament scholarship there was nothing sure and one could be sure of nothing' (Jülicher)."[5]

Pfleiderer believes none the less that "the strenuous researches of the last twenty years" have given a "definite result," but does not venture to say definitely what it is, but opines that it "seems" so to him. Almost the only definitive conclusions one can reach with respect to early Christian literature are negative ones; that is, we can find out definitely what is spurious.

It is certain that almost none of the early Christian writings are by the authors whose names they bear; that most of them were written in later times than the dates given them; and that their original text was often distorted in the crudest way by later revisions and additions. Finally, it is certain that none of the Gospels or other early Christian writings comes from a contemporary of Jesus.

The so-called Gospel according to St. Mark is now regarded as

5. Pfleiderer, *Urchristentum*, 1902, II, p. 282 f.

the oldest of the gospels, but was not in any case composed before the destruction of Jerusalem, which the author has Jesus predict, which, in other words, had already happened when the author began to write. It was probably written not less than half a century after the time assigned for the death of Jesus. What we see is thus the product of half a century of legend-making.

Mark is followed by Luke, then by the so-called Matthew, and last of all by John, in the middle of the second century, at least a century after the birth of Christ. The further we get from the beginning, the more miraculous the gospel stories become. Mark tells us of miracles, but they are puny ones compared to those that follow. Take the raising of the dead as an example. In Mark, Jesus is called to the bedside of Jairus' daughter, who is at the point of death. Everyone thinks she is dead already, but Jesus says: "the damsel . . . but sleepeth," reaches out his hand, and she arises (Mark, Chap. 5).

In Luke it is the young man of Nain who is waked. He is so long dead that he is being borne to his grave as Jesus meets him. Then Jesus makes him rise from the bier (Luke, Chap. 7).

That is not enough for John. In his eleventh chapter he shows us the raising of Lazarus, who has been in his grave for four days already and beginning to stink. That breaks the record.

In addition, the evangelists were extremely ignorant people, who had thoroughly twisted ideas about many of the things they wrote of. Thus Luke has Joseph leave Nazareth with Mary on account of a census in the Roman Empire, and go to Bethlehem, where Jesus is born. But there was no such census under Augustus. Moreover, Judea became a Roman province only after the date given for the birth of Jesus. A census was held in the year 7 A.D., but in the places where people lived, and thus did not require the trip to Bethlehem.[6] We shall have more to say on this topic.

The procedure of Jesus' trial before Pontius Pilate is not in conformity either with Jewish or with Roman law. Thus even where the evangelists do not tell of miracles, they often relate what is false and impossible.

6. Cf. on this point David Strauss, *Das Leben Jesu*, Tübingen 1840, I, 227 f.

And what was concocted as "Gospel" in this fashion later suffered all sorts of alterations at the hands of "editors," to the edification of the faithful.

For example, the best manuscripts of Mark close with the eighth verse of the sixteenth chapter, where the women seek the dead Jesus in the grave, but find a youth in a long white robe instead. Then they left the grave and "were afraid."

What follows in the traditional editions was added later. It is impossible however that the work ended with this eighth verse. Renan already assumed that the remaining portion had been stricken out in the interests of the good cause, since it contained an account that seemed obnoxious to later views.

From another angle Pfleiderer, after intensive studies, came to the conclusion, as did others, "that the Gospel of Luke said nothing of the supernatural conception of Jesus, that this story came up only later and was then inserted into the text by adding verse I, 34 ff.[7] and the words 'as was supposed' in III, 23.[8]" [9]

In view of all this it is no wonder that by the first decades of the nineteenth century many scholars had already recognized the complete uselessness of the gospels as sources for the history of Jesus, and Bruno Bauer could even go so far as to deny the existence of Jesus altogether. It is understandable nevertheless that the theologians can not dispense with the gospels, and even the liberals among them do all they can to maintain their authority. For what is left of Christianity if the person of Christ is given up? But in order to save this latter point, they have to go through some strange contortions.

Thus Harnack in his lectures on the *Wesen des Christentums* (1900) explains that David Friedrich Strauss thought he had succeeded in demolishing the reliability of the gospels as history; but the historical and critical work of two generations had succeeded in restoring it to a great extent. The gospels were not historical

7. "Then said Mary unto the angel, How shall this be, seeing I know not a man? And the angel answered and said unto her, The Holy Ghost shall come upon thee, and the power of the Highest shall overshadow thee," etc.
8. "being (as was supposed) the son of Joseph."
9. Pfleiderer, *Urchristentum*, I, p. 408.

works anyway; they were not written to report how things happened, but were works of edification. "Accordingly they are not useless as historical sources, especially since their purpose is not borrowed from outside, but coincides in part with the views of Jesus" (p. 14).

But all we know of these views is what the gospels tell us! Harnack's whole argument for the credibility of the gospels as sources for the person of Jesus only proves how impossible it is to offer anything solid and penetrating in that direction.

Later in his essay Harnack is compelled to abandon everything that the gospels say of Jesus' first thirty years as unhistorical, as well as everything regarding the following years that can be proved to be impossible or invented. But he would like to save the rest as historical fact. He thinks we still have left "a vivid picture of Jesus' teaching, the end of his life and the impression he made on his disciples" (p. 20).

But how does Harnack know that Jesus' teaching is so faithfully reported in the gospels? The theologians are more skeptical about the reproduction of other teachings of the time. Harnack's colleague Pfleiderer says in his book on early Christianity:

"It does not really make sense to argue over the historical reliability of these and other sermons in the apostolic history; we need only think of all the conditions required for a literally exact, or even an approximately correct, transmission of such a sermon: it would have had to be written down immediately by an auditor (properly speaking, it should be stenographic), and these records of the various sermons would have to be preserved for more than half a century in circles of hearers who were for the most part Jews and heathen and indifferent or hostile to what they had heard, and finally collected by the historian from the most scattered points! Any one who has realized how impossible all these things are will know once for all what to think of all these sermons: that is, in the stories of the apostles as in all the secular historians of antiquity these speeches are free compositions, in which the author has his heroes speak in the way that he himself thinks they could have spoken in the given situation" (p. 500 f.).

Right! But why should not all this apply to the sermons of Jesus too, which were still further in the past for the authors of the gospels than the sermons ascribed to the apostles? Why should Jesus' sermons in the gospels be anything more than speeches that the authors of the reports wished Jesus had made? Actually, we find all sorts of contradictions in the sermons that have come down to us, for example both rebellious and submissive speeches, which can only be explained by the fact that divergent tendencies existed among the Christians, each group composing and handing down speeches for Christ in accordance with its own requirements. How free and easy the evangelists were in such matters can be seen from an example. Compare the Sermon on the Mount in Luke and in Matthew, which is later. In the first it is still a glorification of the poor and a damning of the rich. By Matthew's time this had become a touchy subject for many Christians, and the Gospel according to Matthew baldly turns the poor who are blessed into the poor of spirit, and leaves the damning of the rich out altogether.

That is the sort of manipulation that went on with sermons that had already been written down; and then we are asked to believe that sermons that Jesus is said to have given half a century before they were written down are faithfully reported in the gospels! It is clearly impossible to keep the words of a speech straight merely by oral tradition for fifty years. Anyone who writes down such a speech at the end of such an interval shows thereby that he feels justified in writing down what suits him, or that he is credulous enough to take at face value everything he hears.

What is more, it can be shown that many of Jesus' sayings do not originate with him, but were in circulation previously.

For instance, the Lord's Prayer is regarded as a specific product of Jesus. But Pfleiderer shows that an Aramaic Kaddish prayer going far back into antiquity ended with the words: "Exalted and blessed be His great name in the world that He created according to His will. May he set up His kingdom in your lifetime and the lifetime of the whole house of Israel."

As we see, the beginning of the Lord's Prayer is an imitation.

But if nothing is left of Jesus' sermons, nothing left of the story of his youth, certainly nothing left of his miracles, then what is left of the gospels altogether?

According to Harnack there is left the impression Jesus made on his disciples, and the story of his Passion. But the gospels were not written by disciples of Christ, they do not reflect the impression made by the person of Christ, but that made by the story of the person of Christ on the members of the Christian community. Even the strongest impression does not testify to the historical truth of any story. The story of an imaginary person is capable of producing the deepest impression on society, if historical conditions for it are present. Goethe's *Werther* made a tremendous impression. Everyone knew that it was only a novel, nevertheless he had many disciples and followers.

In Judaism, and precisely in the centuries directly before and after Jesus, fictitious personalities had tremendous influence when the deeds and doctrines attributed to them corresponded to the deeply-felt needs of the Jewish people. This is shown for example by the figure of the prophet Daniel, of whom the book of Daniel reports that he lived under Nebuchadnezzar, Darius and Cyrus, that is in the sixth century B.C., worked the greatest of miracles and made prophecies that were fulfilled later in the most amazing way, ending with the prediction that great afflictions would come to Judaism, out of which a savior would rescue them and raise them to new glory. This Daniel never lived; the book dealing with him was written about 165, at the time of the Maccabean uprising; and it is no wonder that all the prophecies that the prophet ostensibly made in the sixth century were so strikingly confirmed up to that year, and convinced the pious reader that the final prediction of so infallible a prophet must come to pass without fail. The whole thing is a bold fabrication and yet had the greatest effect; the belief in the Messiah, the belief in a Savior to come, got its strongest sustenance from it, and it became the model for all future prophecies of a Messiah. The book of Daniel also shows, however, how casually fraud was practiced in pious

circles when it was a question of attaining an end. The effect produced by the figure of Jesus is therefore no proof at all of its
historical accuracy.

Hence the only thing left of what Harnack thought could still
be rescued from the gospels as an historical nucleus is the Passion
of Christ. But this is so filled with miracles from beginning to
end, up to the Resurrection and Ascension, that even here it is
virtually impossible to get any kind of reliable historical nucleus.
We shall look further into the credibility of this story of the
Passion later on.

Matters are in no better shape with the rest of early Christian
literature. Everything that ostensibly comes from contemporaries
of Jesus, as from his apostles for instance, is known to be spurious,
at least in the sense that it is a production of some later time.

And as for the letters that are attributed to the apostle Paul,
there is not one whose authenticity is not in dispute, and
many of them have been shown by historical criticism to be
altogether false. The baldest of these forgeries is the second letter
to the Thessalonians. In this counterfeit letter the author, using
the name of Paul, warns: "That ye be not soon shaken in mind,
or be troubled, neither by spirit, nor by word, nor by letter as
from us" (2, 2). And at the end the forger adds: "The salutation
of Paul with mine own hand, which is the token in every epistle:
so I write." It was just these words that betrayed the forger.

A number of other letters of Paul are perhaps the earliest literary evidence of Christianity. About Jesus however they tell us
virtually nothing, except that he was crucified and rose again.

It will not be necessary, at least for our readers, to go into details as to what to think about the Resurrection. In a word, there
is hardly anything left in the Christian literature that can be said
to be a solidly established fact about Jesus.

BOOK ONE: THE PERSON
OF JESUS

3

THE DISPUTE OVER THE CONCEPT
OF JESUS

THE factual core of the early Christian reports about Jesus is at best no more than what Tacitus tells us: that in the days of Tiberius a prophet was executed, from whom the sect of Christians took their inspiration. As to what this prophet taught and did, we are not yet able, even today, to say anything definite. Certainly he could not have made the sensation the early Christian reports describe, or Josephus who relates so many trivialities, would certainly have spoken of it. Jesus' agitation and his execution did not get the slightest attention from his contemporaries. But if Jesus really was an agitator that a sect honored as its champion and guide, the significance of his person must have grown as the sect grew. Now a garland of legends began to form around this person, pious minds weaving into it anything they wished their model had said and done. The more this idealization went on, the more each of the many currents within the sect tried to put into the picture those features that were dearest to it, in order to lend them the authority of Jesus. The picture of Jesus, at it was painted in the legends that were first passed from mouth to mouth, and then put down in writing, became more and more the picture of a superhuman person, the epitome of all the ideals the new sect developed; but in the process it became an increasingly contradictory picture, whose several features no longer harmonized.

When the sect achieved firm organization and became a comprehensive church in which one definite tendency prevailed, one of its tasks was the formation of a fixed canon, a list of all the early Christian writings that it recognized as genuine. Naturally this included only works in agreement with the prevailing tendency. All the gospels and other writings that gave a different picture of Jesus were rejected as "heretical," as spurious, or as "apocryphal," not quite trustworthy; they were no longer disseminated, in fact they were suppressed so far as that was possible, and copies of them were destroyed, so that only a few of them have come down to us. The works received into the canon were then "edited," to get them into as much concordance as possible; but fortunately the job was done so clumsily that traces of earlier, divergent accounts may be seen here and there and betray the course of development.

The aim of the Church, namely to assure the unity of opinions within it by this process, was not attained and could not be. The development of social relations kept producing new diversities of views and endeavors in the Church. And thanks to the contradictions that remained in the picture of Jesus recognized by the Church despite all the editing and expurgating, these variations could always find something in that picture they could use as a point of attachment. Thus the clash of social contraditions came to appear within the framework of the Christian Church as a mere dispute over the interpretation of the words of Jesus, and superficial historians think that all the great (and so often bloody) battles that were fought in Christendom under the flag of religion were nothing but battles over words, a sad sign of mankind's stupidity. But wherever a social mass phenomenon is reduced to the mere stupidity of the men involved, this alleged stupidity merely shows lack of understanding on the part of the observer and critic, who has not been able to orient himself in a way of thinking that is strange to him, and to penetrate to the material conditions and forces that underlie it. As a rule it was very real interests that were at grips when the various Christian sects fell out over the interpretation of Christ's words.

It is true that with the rise of the modern way of thinking and the eclipse of the clerical mode of thought the conflicts over the conception of Jesus have lost more and more of their practical importance and sunk to mere hair-splitting on the part of theologians, who are paid precisely to keep the clerical mode of thought alive as long as possible, and have to do something for their money.

Recent Bible criticism, which applies the methods of historical research and analysis of sources to the biblical writings, has given the dispute over the personality of Jesus a new fillip. It shook the traditional picture of Jesus; but since it was carried on, for the most part, by theologians, it stopped short of the position first formulated by Bruno Bauer and later by others, in particular by A. Kalthoff: this was the position that, in view of the condition of the source materials, no new conception of Jesus could be formulated. The new Bible criticism keeps searching for such a new conception, always with the same result that the Christendom of previous centuries had produced: each theologian painted into the picture of Jesus his own private ideals and spirit. Like second-century descriptions of Jesus, twentieth-century ones do not show what Jesus really taught, but what the makers of these descriptions wish he had taught.

Kalthoff points up these vagaries keenly:

"From the standpoint of social theology the conception of Christ is the most sublimated religious expression of every active social and ethical force in an epoch; and in the transformations that this conception has constantly undergone, in the fading of its old features and its illumination in new colors, we have the most delicate instrument for measuring the changes in contemporary life, from the heights of its spiritual ideals to the depths of its most material actions. This picture of Christ some times has the lineaments of a Greek thinker, then those of the Roman Emperor, then those of the feudal lord of the manor, of the guild master, of the tormented villein and of the free citizen; and these traits are all true, all living, so long as the theologians of the school do not undertake to prove that the single traits of their time are just the ones which are the original and historical traits of the Christ of the gospels. At most these traits acquire an appearance of being historical from the fact that at the time when Christian society was developing and taking form the most divergent and even contradictory forces collaborated, each one having a certain similarity with forces operating today. Now the picture of Christ we have today seems very contradictory at first glance. It still has some of the traits of the old saint or the heavenly monarch, together with the modern features of the friend of the proletariat, or even of the labor leader. But that is only the expression of the innermost contradictions that our time is shot through with." And earlier he says:

"Most representatives of so-called modern theology use the scissors on their excerpts in accordance with the critical method dear to David Strauss: the mythical part of the gospels is cut away, and what is left is supposed to be the historical nucleus. But finally even this nucleus got to be too thin in the hands of the theologians. . . . In the absence of all historical precision, the name of Jesus has become an empty vessel for Protestant theology, into which every theologian pours his own thoughts. One of them makes Jesus a modern Spinozist, another makes him a socialist, while the official professorial theology naturally looks at him in the religious light of the modern state and recently has come to present him more and more as the religious representative of all those efforts that today claim a leading place in the State theology of Greater Prussia."[10]

It is no wonder then that secular historiography feels no great need for investigating the origins of Christianity if it starts from the view that Christianity was the creation of a single person. If this view were correct, we could give up studying the rise of Christianity and leave its description to our poetic theologians.

But it is a different matter as soon as we think of a world-wide religion not as the product of a single superman but as a product

10. Kalthoff, *Das Christusproblem*, 1902, pp. 80 f., 15, 17.

of society. Social conditions at the time of the rise of Christianity are very well known. And the social character of early Christianity can be studied with some degree of accuracy from its literature.

To be sure, the historical value of the gospels and the Acts of the Apostles can not be set as any higher than that of the Homeric poems or the *Nibelungenlied*. They may deal with historical personages, but their actions are related with such poetic freedom that it is impossible to get anything like a historical description of those personages, quite apart from the fact that they are so mixed up with fabulous creatures that on the basis of these stories alone it can never be determined which of the characters are historical and which are invented. If we knew nothing about Attila but what the *Nibelungenlied* says about him, we should have to say, as we must about Jesus, we do not even definitely know whether he lived or not, or whether he is just as mythical a character as Siegfried.

But such poetical accounts are invaluable for the understanding of the social conditions under which they arose, and of which they give a true reflection no matter how freely their authors may have invented individual facts and personages. The extent to which the story of the Trojan War and its heroes rests on a historical basis is obscure, perhaps for ever. But as for the nature of social conditions in the Heroic Age, we have two first-class historical sources in the *Iliad* and the *Odyssey*.

Poetical creations are often far more important for understanding a period than the most faithful historical accounts. For the latter merely communicate the personal, the striking, the unusual, which has the least permanent historical effect; the former furnish us with a look into the daily life and labor of the masses, which works continually and lastingly and has the most permanent effect on society, but which the historian does not take note of because it seems to him to be so obvious and well-known. Thus in Balzac's novels we have one of the most important historical sources for the social life of France in the first decades of the nineteenth century.

And out of the gospels and the acts of the apostles, similarly, we can not learn anything definite as to the life and doctrine of Jesus, but very valuable things about the social character, the ideals and aspirations of the primitive Christian communities. When Bible criticism uncovers the different layers that lie one on top of the other in these writings, it enables us to follow the development of these communities, at least to a certain extent, while the "heathen" and Jewish sources make possible an insight into the social driving forces that were acting upon primitive Christianity at the same time. So we are able to see and understand it as the product of its time, and that is the basis of any historical knowledge. Individuals can influence society too, and the portrayal of outstanding individuals is indispensable for a complete picture of their time. But in terms of historical epochs, their influence is only transitory, merely the outer ornament which strikes the eye first in a building but says nothing about its foundations. But it is the foundations that determine the character of the structure and its permanence. If we can lay them bare, we have done the most important part toward understanding the whole edifice.

BOOK TWO: SOCIETY IN THE

ROMAN EMPIRE

1

THE SLAVE ECONOMY

LANDED PROPERTY

IF WE WISH to understand the ideas that are characteristic of an era as distinct from the ideas of other ages, the first thing we must look into is that era's special requirements and problems, which are based in the last analysis on its particular mode of production, in the way the society of that time made its living.

First, we shall trace the economic system on which the society of the Roman Empire rested as it developed from its beginnings. Only in that way can we understand its nature at the end of this development, under the emperors, and the special trends it manifested at that time.

The basis of the mode of production of the countries comprising the Roman Empire was agriculture; crafts and trading were much less important. Production for self-consumption still predominated; commodity production, production for sale, was still slightly developed. Craftsmen and merchants often had farms as well that were in close connection with their domestic establishments; their work went principally toward producing for their households. The farm supplied provisions for the kitchen and raw materials such as flax, wool, leather, wood, from which the members of the family themselves made clothes, house furnishings and tools. It was only the surplus, if there was any, over and above the needs of the household that was sold.

This mode of production required private property in most of the means of production, all such in fact as contain human labor, including arable land but not forest and pasture, which could still be common property. It would include domestic animals but not game, and finally tools and raw materials as well as the products made from them.

With private property the possibility of economic inequality arises. Fortunate accidents could favor and enrich one farm and hurt and impoverish another. The first group grew and got more land and cattle. A special kind of labor question arises for the larger farms, the question as to where the additional labor power is to come from that is needed to care properly for the larger herds and suitably cultivate the more extensive fields.

Class differences and class contradictions now appear. The more productive agriculture is, the greater the surplus it furnishes over and above the needs of the husbandman. This surplus serves to feed craftsmen who devote themselves to producing many useful objects, for instance smiths and potters, but the surplus may also be used in exchange for useful objects or raw materials that can not be produced in the locality, either because nature does not furnish them or because the skill is lacking. Such products are brought from other regions by merchants. The rise of crafts and trade helps increase inequalities in land ownership. The inequality between larger and smaller properties is now supplemented by the difference in proximity to the points in which craftsmen and merchants congregate and exchange their goods for the farmers' surpluses. The worse the means of transportation are, the harder it is to bring the products to market and the more the man who lives near the market is favored.

Those who are favored by all or some of these factors become a class of landholders obtaining larger surpluses than the mass of peasants, exchanging them for more products of trade and craft, having more leisure than the average husbandman, having at their disposal more technical aids in work and in warfare, receiving more intellectual stimulation by living together with artists or merchants or having frequent contact with them and so having their intellectual horizon broadened. This class of favored landholders now has the time, opportunity and means to carry on affairs that go beyond the limits of peasant narrow-mindedness. It gets the time and strength to unite several communities into a state, and to rule and define that state, as well as to settle its relations with nearby and even distant states.

All these classes, bigger farmers, merchants, craftsmen live on the surplus created by labor on the land, soon increased by the surpluses from craft and industry. Merchants take more and more of these surpluses for themselves, in the measure that their functions in society become more important. Soon the big landowners make use not only of their economic superiority but also of their powerful position in the state to take the surpluses of the work of peasants and craftsmen away from them. In this way they gain wealth far beyond the scale of peasant and craftsman, make their power in society even stronger and increase their ability to get more surplus for themselves and win new riches.

So peasants and craftsmen are overtopped by various layers of big exploiters, large landowners and merchants, with the addition of usurers, of whom we shall speak in another connection. The more their wealth increases, the greater is their need to expand their business, which is still in close connection with agriculture. At that time anyone who wanted a business of his own still had to control his own farm, and the surest way to that was owning it. Everybody strove to get land, including craftsmen, usurers and merchants. And they all tried to add to their land, for it was still production for self-consumption that prevailed; if one wanted more comfort, a more prosperous household, he had to have more acres.

The drive to obtain and extend landed property is the ruling passion of this period, which extends from the establishment of settled society on the basis of agriculture to the time of the formation of industrial capital. Ancient society, even at its acme during the Empire, never got beyond this stage. That step had to wait for modern times, after the Reformation.

DOMESTIC SLAVERY

But owning land is nothing without labor power to work it. We have already referred to the peculiar labor problem that followed upon the formation of the larger estates. Even in prehistoric times we find among the wealthy the quest for labor forces, over and above the members of the family, that could be incorporated into the conduct of the estate and that could always be counted on.

Such labor forces could not be obtained directly by wage labor. We find cases of wage labor early, but they are always exceptional and temporary, like help at harvest time. An active family could easily procure the few means of production required for an independent farm. And the family and community bonds were still strong, so that the occasional misfortunes which might render a family landless were mitigated through the aid of relatives and neighbors.

If there was only a meager supply of wage laborers, there was only a meager demand for them. Household and occupation were still closely linked. If additional workers were to be incorporated into the farm, they would have to be incorporated into the household as well; they would have to be not only without a place of their own to work in, but also without a family of their own. Free workers would not serve the purpose. Even in the middle ages the journeymen accepted membership in the master's family only as a temporary phase, a step toward being masters themselves and starting their own families. Permanent labor forces for a strange family could not be obtained at this stage of history in the form of free wage laborers. Only compulsion could supply the necessary labor for the larger landed estates. The answer was slavery. The stranger had no rights, and with the small size of the communities of that time the term "stranger" had a wide denotation. In war not only the captured soldiers, but often the entire population of the conquered land were enslaved and either divided among the victors or sold. But even in peacetime there were ways of catching slaves, for example, sea trading, which was frequently linked up with piracy at the outset; and one of the prizes that was most sought after was able-bodied and handsome people, who were snatched by the coasting sailors when found defenceless on the shore. In addition, male and female slaves mated and their off-spring were slaves.

From the material point of view the situation of these slaves was not too hard to start with; they sometimes found themselves well enough off. As members of a prosperous household, often serving convenience or luxury, they were not taxed unduly. When they did productive work, it was often—in the case of the wealthy peasants—in common with the master; and always only for the consumption of the family itself, and that consumption had its limits. The position of the slaves was determined by the character of the master and the prosperity of the families they belonged to. It was in their own interest to increase that prosperity, for they increased their own prosperity in the process. Moreover the daily association of the slave with his master brought them closer together as human beings and, when the slave was clever, made him indispensable and even a full-fledged friend. There are many examples, in the ancient poets, of the liberties slaves took with their masters and with what intimacy the two were often connected. It was not rare for a slave to be rewarded for faithful service by being freed with a substantial gift; others saved enough to purchase their freedom. Many preferred slavery to freedom; they would rather live as members of a rich family than lead a needy and uncertain existence all by themselves.

"It should not be thought," says Jentsch, "that the shocking legal conception of slavery was taken literally in private life and that the slave was not considered or treated as a human being; up to the end of the First Punic War the slaves were not too badly off. What was said with respect to the legal power of the master of the house over his wife and children applies to slaves too. His power was legally unlimited, but religion, custom, reason, feeling and interest put limits to it; and the man that the law regarded as a saleable object, subject to his master's caprice without any protection, was valued on the farm as a faithful fellow-worker and at home as a member of the household, with whom one chatted cozily after work before the fireplace."[1]

This comradely relationship was not limited to peasant establishments. Princes too worked with their hands in the Heroic Age. In the *Odyssey* the daughter of King Alcinous washes clothes with her female slaves; Odysseus challenges a rival not to a duel but to a competition in mowing and ploughing, and when he comes home to his country he finds his father in the garden busy with his shovel. Odysseus and his son Telemachus have the warm love of Eumaeus, the "godlike swineherd," who is grimly convinced that as a reward for his faithful service his master, if he were home, would long ago have given him freedom, a farm and a wife.

This kind of slavery was one of the mildest known forms of exploitation. But it changed in aspect when it came to serve moneymaking, as labor on great enterprises distinct from the master's household.

SLAVERY IN COMMODITY PRODUCTION

The first such enterprises must have been mines. The very nature of the extraction and refining of minerals, especially metallic ores, hardly suits it to be carried on only for the self-consumption of the single household. As soon as it is at all developed, it furnishes a large surplus above the individual's needs; and it can only come to some sort of perfection when it is aimed at the regular production of large quantities, for only in that event do the workers acquire the requisite skill and experience and the necessary structures and works become profitable. Even in the stone age we find large sites at which stone tools were produced professionally on a mass scale and then circulated by exchange from village to village or tribe to tribe. These mineral products were the first commodities; and certainly the first to be produced intentionally as commodities, for the purpose of exchange.

As soon as mining had developed at a place where valuable

---

1. Karl Jentsch, *Drei Spaziergänge eines Laien ins klassische Altertum,* 1900, Third *Spaziergang,* "Der Römerstaat," p. 237. Cf. the second *Spaziergang* in the same book: *Die Sklaverei bei den Dichtern.*

minerals are found, and gone beyond the most primitive surface work, it called for larger and larger working forces. The need could easily exceed the number of free workers that could be recruited from the village community to which the mine belonged. Wage-labor did not permanently supply a large number of workers; they could only be slaves or condemned criminals.

These slaves no longer produced consumption objects for the limited personal use of their master; they worked to make money for him. They did not work so that he might use marble or sulphur, iron or copper, gold or silver in his household, but so that he might sell the products of the mine and get money for it, that commodity with which one can buy everything, all the pleasures, all the power that one can never have enough of. Now as much work was squeezed out of the miners as was possible, for the more work they did the more money their owner got. Moreover, they were fed and clothed as badly as possible, for their food and clothing had to be bought, money had to be given up for the purpose, since the slaves in the mines did not produce those things themselves. The proprietor of a rich household had no other outlet for his surplus food and consumption-goods than to provide them for his slaves and guests; but now, under commodity production, the more money the enterprise earned, the less the slaves consumed. The bigger the enterprise became, the worse their lot was; increasingly they were detached from the household, kept in barracks that contrasted sternly with the luxury of the master's dwelling. All personal relationships between master and slaves were lost, not only because of the separation of their place of work from his residence, but also because of the numbers involved. In Athens at the time of the Peloponnesian War Hipponikos is said to have had 600 slaves working in the Thracian mines, and Nikias 1000. The slave's total absence of rights was now a fearful scourge. The free wage-worker could still choose his master to a certain extent and, at least under favorable circumstances, use quitting work as a means of putting pressure on his master and avoiding the worst effects; but the slave who escaped from his master or refused to work would be put to death immediately.

There was only one motive for sparing the slave, the same as for sparing an ox: the cost of buying the slave. The wage-worker does not cost anything. If he dies at work, another will take his place. The slave has to be bought. If he died too soon, his master would lose his purchase-price. But this motive was of less importance when slaves were cheap. And there were times when their price fell enormously, when unending wars, civil and foreign, brought numerous captives on the market.

In the Romans' third war against Macedonia in 169 B.C. seventy cities in Epirus alone were sacked and 150,000 of their inhabitants sold as slaves.

According to Böckh the ordinary price of a slave in Athens was from 100 to 200 drachmas (20 to 40 dollars). Xenophon says the price varied between 50 and 1000 drachmas. Appian tells us that on one occasion in Pontus war prisoners were sold at 4 drachmas (less than a dollar) apiece. Joseph, who was sold into Egypt by his brothers, brought only 20 shekels ($3.50).[2]

A good saddle-horse was much dearer than a slave; in Aristophanes' time it cost some 12 minae, about $240.

The wars that furnished slaves cheap also ruined many peasants, for at that time the peasant militias made up the core of the army. If the peasant had to go to war, his farm was likely to run down for want of care. There was nothing left for the ruined farmer but to take to banditry, if he could not find refuge in a nearby city as craftsman or lumpenproletariat. Crimes and criminals abounded, something unknown in earlier times, and the hunt for criminals furnished new slaves, for prisons were unknown since they are products of the capitalist mode of production. At that time those that were not crucified were sentenced to forced labor.

Thus from time to time there were large numbers of extremely cheap slaves, whose situation was most miserable. This is shown for example by the Spanish silver mines, among the most productive of antiquity.

"In the beginning," says Diodorus of these mines, "ordinary private citizens were occupied in the mining and got great riches,

2. Herzfeld, *Handelsgeschichte der Juden des Altertums,* 1894, p. 193.

because the silver ore did not lie deep and was present in great quantity. Later, when the Romans became masters of Iberia (Spain), a crowd of Italians appeared at the mines, who won great riches through their greed. For they bought a throng of slaves and handed them over to the overseer of the mines. . . . Those slaves that have to work in these mines bring incredible incomes to their masters: but many of them, who toil underground in the pits day and night, die of the overwork. For they have no rest or pause, but are driven by the blows of their overseers to endure the hardest exertions and work themselves to death. A few, that have enough strength and patience to endure it, only prolong their misery, which is so great it makes death preferable to life."[3]

If patriarchal domestic slavery is perhaps the mildest form of exploitation, slavery in the service of greed for profits is surely the most ghastly.

In the mines large-scale operations with slaves were indicated by the technology of the industry under the given circumstances. But with time other branches of production as well give rise to the need for commodity production on a large scale by means of slaves. There were commonwealths that far surpassed their neighbors in military power, and derived such advantages from war that they never had enough of it. Waging wars constantly provided new hordes of slaves, whom they tried to employ at a profit. But such commonwealths were connected with large cities. A city that was favored by its position and became the marketplace for a vigorous trade attracted many men merely in the course of trade; and if it was not too niggardly in granting citizenship to foreigners, soon became richer in men and means than the other communities around it, which it brought into subjection. Plundering and exploiting the surrounding territory increased the wealth of the city and its population still more. This wealth produced the need for big constructions, some sanitary like sewers, aqueducts; some esthetic and religious such as temples and theaters; some military such as city walls. The quickest way to erect such struc-

3. Diodorus Siculus, V, 36, 38. Cf. the passage, III, 13, on the Egyptian gold mines to which Marx refers in *Capital* Vol. I, chap. 8, 2, Note 43.

tures was to use huge troops of slaves. Building contractors came into being who bought many slaves and did all sorts of construction for the state. The metropolis also gave rise to an extensive market for large quantities of foodstuffs. With low prices for slaves, the most significant surpluses came from large landed estates. There could be no question at that time of any technical superiority of large-scale agriculture; on the contrary, slave labor was less productive than the labor of the free peasants. But the slave, whose labor power did not have to be spared and who could be sweated to death without a second thought, produced a greater surplus over the cost of his subsistence than the peasant, who at that time knew nothing of the blessings of overwork and was used to a high standard of living. There was the further advantage that in such a commonwealth the peasant was constantly being taken from the plough to defend his country, while the slave was exempt from military service. Thus the sphere of economic influence of such large and warlike cities saw the rise of large-scale agricultural production with slaves. The Carthaginians developed it to a significant extent. The Romans learned it in their wars with Carthage; along with the provinces which they took from their great rival they also took over the large-scale farm, which they further developed and extended.

In large cities where masses of slaves of the same craft were assembled and there was a good market for their production, it was an easy next step to buy up a number of such slaves and set them to work together in a single workshop, producing for the market as wage-workers do today in factories. Such slave manufacturing was of importance only in the Hellenic world, not in the Roman. Everywhere however there developed a special kind of slave industry in large-scale farming, whether in factory-like plantations producing a single crop, like grain, for the market, or devoted primarily to the consumption of the family or household and supplying it with all the diverse products it required.

Agricultural work has the property of requiring much labor only at certain times of year, but only little at others, namely in winter. That is a problem for modern large-scale agricultural enterprises; it was still a greater problem under the system of slave labor. For it is always possible to let the wage-worker go when he is not needed and fetch him back when he is. In between he must take care of himself. At that time, though, the big land-holder could not sell his slaves every autumn and buy new ones in the spring. That would have come too dear, for the slaves would have been worth nothing in the fall and been dear in the spring. The owner therefore had to try to keep them busy in the season when there was little work to be done on the land. The traditional ties between agriculture and industry were still alive; the peasant still made up flax, wool, leather, wood and other products of his farm into clothing and equipment. Likewise the slaves of the large-scale farms were set to industrial work in the slack times for farmwork: weaving, tanning and leather working, making wagons and ploughs, pottery making of all sorts. But commodity production was so far advanced that they produced not only for the individual farm and household, but for the market too.

If the slaves were cheap, their industrial products would be cheap too. They required no outlay of money. The farm, the lati-fundium provided the workers' foodstuffs and raw materials, and in most cases their tools too. And since the slaves had to be kept anyway during the time they were not needed in the fields, all the industrial products they produced over and above the needs of their own enterprise were a surplus that yielded a profit even at low prices.

In the face of this slave-labor competition it is no wonder that strong free crafts could not develop. The craftsmen in the ancient world, and particularly so in the Roman world, remained poor devils, working alone for the most part without assistants, and as a rule working up material supplied to them, either in the house of the client or at home. There was no question of a strong group of craftsmen such as grew up in the Middle Ages. The guilds re-mained weak and the craftsmen were always dependent on their clients, usually the bigger landowners, and very often led a parasitic existence on the verge of sinking into the *lumpenproletariat* as the landowner's dependents.

But the big enterprise with slaves was only able to prevent any strengthening of the artisanate and any development of their techniques, which remained on a low level throughout antiquity, corresponding to the poverty of the craftsman: his skill could rise to unusual heights under certain circumstances, but his tools remained wretchedly primitive. But the same was true of the big enterprises themselves; there too slavery had a crippling effect on their technological development.

THE TECHNOLOGICAL INFERIORITY OF THE SLAVE ECONOMY

In agriculture large size was not yet a condition of high productivity, as it was in mining. The increase in commodity production did produce an expansion of social division of labor in agriculture as well; many estates took to grain growing, others to raising livestock, and so forth. In the case of a large estate there was the possibility of having its direction in the hands of scientifically trained men who rose above peasant routine. Actually we find in countries with large landed estates, as among the Carthaginians and then among the Romans, a theory of agriculture that was as advanced as in eighteenth-century Europe. The labor force was lacking however that could apply this theory and raise the large estate above the level of the peasant holding. Even wage labor is inferior to the work of the free farmer-owner with respect to interest and care, so that it is profitable only where the large estate is considerably superior to the small farm in technology. But the slave on the large estate, no longer a member of the patriarchal family, is a still more indifferent worker, in fact one that would like to do his master harm. Even in domestic slavery the slave's work was not thought to be as productive as the work of the free landholder. Odysseus remarks: "Slaves, when their master's control is loosed, do not even wish to work well. Ah, the day a man's enslaved, Zeus robs him of half his virtue!" (*Odyssey*, xvii, 320 f., Lawrence's translation).

How much more so with slaves that were savagely beaten every day and were full of desperation and hatred toward their master! The large estate would have to be enormously superior in technology to the small farm to obtain the same results with the same number of workers; but it was not only not superior, but in many ways inferior. The slaves, mistreated themselves, vented all their spite on the ox, who did not thrive. It was just as impossible to put fine tools into their hands.

Marx had pointed this out. He says of "production by slave power":

"To use an expressive phrase of the ancients, the slave is merely a vocal instrument, distinguished only as vocal from the beast as semivocal instrument, and from the inanimate tool as dumb instrument. But he himself is careful to let both beast and tool know that he is of a different order from them, that he is a man. He has the self-satisfaction of convincing himself that he is different, by misusing the beast and damaging the tool. Consequently, it is a universal principle in production by slave labour that none but the rudest and heaviest implements shall be used, such tools as are difficult to damage owing to their sheer clumsiness. In some of the slave states of the American Union, those bordering on the Gulf of Mexico, the only ploughs used were constructed upon an old Chinese model; ploughs which burrowed into the soil like a pig or a mole, but did not cut a furrow and turn the earth over. . . . In *A Journey in the Seaboard States*, Olmsted writes: 'I am here shown tools that no man in his senses, with us, would allow a labourer, for whom he was paying wages, to be encumbered with; and the excessive weight and clumsiness of which, I would judge, would make work at least ten per cent greater than those ordinarily used with us. And I am assured that, in the careless and clumsy way they must be used by the slaves, anything lighter or less rude could not be furnished them with good economy, and that such tools as we constantly give our labourers and find our profit in giving them, would not last out a day in a Virginia cornfield—much lighter and more free from stones though it be than ours. So, too, when I am asked why mules are so universally substituted for horses on the farm, the first reason given, and confessedly the most conclusive one, is that horses cannot bear the treatment that they must always get from the Negroes; horses are always soon foundered or crippled by them, while mules will bear cudgelling, or lose a meal or two now and then, and not be materially injured, and they do not take cold or get sick if neglected or overworked. But I do not need to go further than to the window of the room in which I am writing, to see at almost any time treatment of cattle that would ensure the immediate discharge of the driver by almost any farmer owning them in the North.' " (*Capital*, Vol. I, Eden and Cedar Paul translation, London, 1928, p. 191).

Unintelligent, half-hearted, malicious, glad of any chance to do harm to their hated tormentor, the slave labor of the latifundia produced far less than peasant farms. In the first century A.D. Pliny was already pointing out how fruitful the fields of Italy had been when generals were not ashamed to do their own farming, and how refractory Mother Earth became when she was turned over to chained and branded slaves to mistreat. This sort of agriculture might give a greater surplus than peasant farms in some cases, but it could not by any means support as many men in well-being. Meanwhile, all through the wars during which Rome kept the whole Mediterranean world in constant unrest, the slave economy kept expanding and the peasant class kept sinking; for war brought rich booty to the great landowners who conducted it, new tracts of land and countless cheap slaves.

Thus we find in the Roman Empire an economic evolution that externally bears a striking resemblance to modern developments: decline of small enterprise, advance of large enterprises and still quicker growth of large landed estates, the latifundia, which dispossesses the peasants and, where they do not replace him by plantations or some such extensive form of cultivation, at least reduce him from a free landholder to a dependent tenant.

Pöhlmann in his *Geschichte des antiken Kommunismus und Sozialismus* cites among other things "The Complaint of the Poor Man against the Rich Man" from the pseudo-Quintilian's collection of declamations; in it the spread of the latifundia is well depicted. An impoverished peasant wails:

"I was not always the neighbor of a rich man. Round about there was many a farm with owners alike in wealth, tilling their modest lands in neighborly harmony. How different is it now! The land that once fed all these citizens is now a single huge plantation, belonging to a single rich man. His estate has extended its boundaries on every side; the peasant houses it has swallowed up have been razed to the ground, and the shrines of their fathers destroyed. The old owners have said farewell to their tutelary gods and gone far away with their wives and children. Monotony reigns over the wide plain. Everywhere riches close me in, as if with a wall; here there is a garden of the rich man's, there his fields, here his vineyard, there his woods and stacks of grain. I too would gladly have departed, but I could not find a spot of land where I would not have a rich man for my neighbor. Where does one not come up against the rich man's private property? They are not content any longer to extend their domains so far that they are bounded by natural boundaries, rivers and mountains, like whole countries. They lay hold even of the furthest mountain wildernesses and forests. And nowhere does this grasping find an end and a limit until the rich man comes up against another rich man. And this too shows the contempt the rich have for us poor, that they do not even take the trouble to deny it when they have used violence on us." (II, p. 582 f.).

Pöhlmann sees in this a picture of the tendencies of "extreme capitalism in general." But the similarity of this development with modern capitalism and its concentration of capital is purely external; it is thoroughly misleading to equate the two. If we go deeper into the matter, we shall find a complete contradiction between them. First, the tendency towards concentration, the drive to replace smaller enterprises by larger ones and have the small business depend on the owners of great wealth, is most conspicuous in industry today, and much less so in agriculture; in ancient times, it was the reverse. Today the victory of big business over small business is done through competition, which brings out the greater productivity of enterprises with powerful machines and equipment. In antiquity it took place through the crippling of the free peasants, who were crushed by military service, and by the greater cheapness of the labor power that large-scale importation of slaves made available to those who had money; and finally by means of usury (which we shall come back to)—all factors that decreased the productivity of labor instead of raising it. The prerequisites for the development and application of machine production were lacking in antiquity. Free craftsmanship had not yet developed to the point where it could provide large numbers of free skilled labor, ready to hire themselves out for wages on a permanent basis; but these are the only labor forces capable of producing machines and making their application possible. There was therefore no incentive for thinkers and inventors to create machines, which would not have been applied in practice. But once machines have been invented that can be used successfully in production, and large free labor forces appear, pressing to be employed in the production and application of machines, the machine becomes one of the most powerful weapons in the competition of the entrepreneurs against each other. As a consequence machines are constantly perfected and enlarged, the productivity of labor rises, and with it the surplus over wages that it produces; but also so does the need rise to collect, to accumulate, a part of this surplus in order therewith to obtain new and better machines, and the need to expand the market continually, since the improved machinery keeps supplying a larger production to be disposed of. The result is that capital grows continually. The production of means of production occupies a larger and larger place in the capitalist mode of production. In order to dispose at a profit of the increased quantity of consumption goods that the increased means of production create, capitalism must constantly find new markets; and it can be said to have conquered the entire world in the course of a single century, the nineteenth.

The course of developments in antiquity was quite different. As we have seen, only the crudest tools could be put into the hands of the slaves on the large estates, and only the roughest and least

intelligent workers used there. It was only by having slaves extremely cheap that the large estates could realize any profit at all.
This created constant pressure for war, on the part of the owners
of large estates, as the most effective way to get cheap slaves, and
toward the constant expansion of the state's territories. From the
time of the Punic Wars this was one of the most powerful incentives of the Roman program of expansion, which in two centuries
conquered all the lands on the Mediterranean and at the time of
Christ was proceeding from the conquest of Gaul to subjugate
Germany, whose vigorous people furnished such fine slaves.

It is true that the large enterprises of antiquity resembled those
of modern times in this insatiability, in this constant pressure to
extend the field of exploitation, but there is no resemblance at all
in the application of the surplus which the growing troops of
slaves furnished. The modern capitalist, as we have seen, must put
aside a large part of his profit for improving and expanding his
concern if he is not to be overtaken and beaten by his competitors.
This was unnecessary for the ancient slave-owner. The technical
basis on which he produced was not higher, but rather lower, than
that of the small peasants he was supplanting. He could therefore,
without being a spendthrift, use all his surplus, over the fixed costs
and replacements of tools, cattle and slaves, for his personal consumption.

It was possible of course to invest money in trade and usury or
put it into new lands, and so get more gain, but this too could not
be applied in any other way than in consumption. The accumulation of capital for the purpose of producing new means of production beyond a certain point would have been senseless, for these
new means of production could not have been used.

The more the latifundia supplanted the peasants, and the
greater the quantities of land and slaves that were held by individuals, the greater were the surpluses, the treasures that those individuals had at their disposal and could use for no other purpose
than their individual consumption. The modern capitalist is
marked by the drive to heap up capital; the noble Romans of the
Empire, the time at which Christianity arose, were marked by love

of pleasure. The modern capitalists have accumulated capital to an extent that dwarfs the riches of the richest ancient Romans. The Croesus of all of these was said to be Nero's freedman Narcissus, with a fortune of some twenty million dollars. What is that compared to the billions of a Rockefeller? But the expenditures of the American billionaires, no matter how reckless they are, are not to be compared with those of their Roman predecessors who served dishes of nightingales' tongues and dissolved precious pearls in vinegar.

Increasing luxury meant a corresponding increase in the number of house slaves used for personal service, and the more so the cheaper slaves were. Horace says in one of his satires that ten slaves were the fewest someone living in moderate circumstances could get along with. In a noble household the number could go up into thousands. The barbarians were driven into the mines and plantations, but the well-educated slaves, especially the Greeks, were taken into the "city family," the city household. Not only cooks, clerks, musicians, teachers and actors, but doctors and philosophers as well were held as slaves. In contrast to the slaves who were engaged in production, these had only light services to render. Most of them were as big loafers as their masters. But the two factors which in former times had more or less guaranteed the family slaves good treatment no longer existed: their high price, and the comradely relationship with the master, who worked alongside the slave. Now, given the great wealth of the master and the low price of the slaves, there was not the slightest restraint in the treatment of the slaves. Moreover, for the vast majority of the house slaves there was not the slightest personal relationship with the master; he hardly knew most of them. And when master and servant came together, it was no longer at work, which gave rise to mutual respect, but in revelry and depravity, arising out of idleness and arrogance and causing mutual contempt in master and servants alike. The slaves were idle and often pampered, and yet defenceless against any malicious caprice or fit of rage. The crime of Vedius Pollio is well known. A slave of his had broken a crystal dish, and he had him thrown to the lampreys to be eaten, as a tidbit for the voracious fish he kept in a pool.

These house slaves constituted a notable addition to the unproductive elements in society. Another increase came from among troops of the urban lumpenproltetarians to which the majority of the displaced peasants sank. And this took place at a time when the replacement of free labor by slave labor in many productive activities sharply reduced the productivity of labor.

The more members a household had, however, the easier it was for it to have things made for it by its own workers which a small household would otherwise have had to buy, such as clothing and furniture. This led to a renewed extension of production for the family's own consumption. This later form of family economy on the part of the rich must not be confused with the original simple family economy that was based on the almost total absence of commodity production and produced the most important and necessary goods, buying only tools and luxuries. The second form of production for self-consumption in the family, as we see it at the end of the Roman republic and during the Empire in rich households, was based on commodity production, the production of mines and latifundia for the market, and itself was aimed primarily at luxury production.

This sort of extension of production for self-consumption did damage to the free crafts, which the industries run by gangs of slaves in the cities and on the latifundia had already undermined. Relatively the free crafts had to retreat, that is the proportion of free workers to slave workers decreased even in the crafts. Absolutely the number of free workers might increase in some trades, because of the increase of expenditure brought about by an increasing demand for paintings and statues and objects of art, but also for luxuries and extravagances, like salves and pomades.

Those who judge the prosperity of a society by its spending, and take the narrow point of view of the Roman Caesars and land owners with their trains of courtiers, artists and literary men, will think of the social situation at the time of the Emperor Augustus as brilliant. Colossal wealth poured into Rome for the sole purpose of increasing pleasure; rich pleasure-loving rakes reeled from party to party, throwing their surplus wealth around by handfuls, since by themselves they were unable to spend it all. Many artists and men of learning received substantial sums from patrons like Maecenas; huge buildings sprang up, whose tremendous size and artistic balance we still admire; the whole world seemed to sweat riches at every pore—and yet this society was already doomed to death.

THE ECONOMIC DECLINE

An indication that the trend was downward could be seen early in the ruling classes, who stood apart from all activity and let slaves take care of all work, even in science and politics. In Greece slave labor had served at first to leave the masters full leisure for governing the state and reflecting on the weightiest problems of life. But the bigger the surpluses grew and the more they were concentrated in the hands of a few by means of the concentration of land ownership, the extension of the latifundia and the growth of the masses of slaves, the more the enjoyment and expenditure of these surpluses became the foremost social function of the ruling classes, and the more intense was the competition in extravagance, brilliance, arrogance and idleness. This process was even briefer in Rome than in Greece, since Rome reached this mode of production while she was still on a low cultural level. The Greek power had spread principally at the expense of barbarous peoples, having come up against strong resistance in Asia Minor and Egypt. Their slaves were barbarians, from whom the Greeks had nothing to learn and to whom they could not entrust the administration of the state. And the wealth they were able to extract from the barbarians was relatively small. The Roman rule, on the other hand, spread soon over all the age-old civilized regions of the East up to Babylonia (or Seleucia) and beyond; from these newly conquered provinces the Romans took not only infinite riches but also slaves far superior to their masters in knowledge, from whom they had to learn and to whom they could easily leave the administration of the government. During the Empire the large landholding aristocracy were more and more replaced by slaves of the Imperial household and former slaves, freedmen who remained under obligation to their former master.

The only function left the owners of the latifundia and their numerous parasites was pleasure. But man becomes indifferent to any stimulus that works on him constantly, to joy and to pain, to pleasure and to the fear of death. Mere unbroken enjoyment, uninterrupted by any work or struggle, produced at first a constant pursuit of new pleasures that would surpass the old ones and stimulate the jaded nerves once more. This led to the most unnatural vices, the most intricate cruelties, as well as to extravagance on the largest and most senseless scale. Everything has its limits however, and once the individual has come to the point of financial or physical exhaustion, to being without means or strength, so that he can not increase pleasure any further, he falls into a dreadful depression, an aversion to all enjoyment, to the point of being fed up with life and feeling that all earthly scheming and striving are useless—*vanitas, vanitatum vanitas.* Despair and longing for death appeared, but along with them the longing for a new and higher life; yet the aversion to work was so deeply rooted in people that even this new, ideal life was not thought of as a life of happy work but as a thoroughly passive blessedness that got its joy only from being freed from the sorrows and disappointments of bodily needs and enjoyments.

In the best individuals among the exploiters there arose too a feeling of shame at the fact that their comfort was built on the destruction of many free peasants, on the abuse of thousands of slaves in the mines and the latifundia. The state of depression also gave rise to sympathy with the slaves—a strange contrast to the unthinking brutality with which masters disposed of the slaves' lives, as in the gladiatorial shows. Finally this morning-after feeling produced an aversion to the greed for gold and money that even in those times ruled the world.

"We know," says Pliny in the thirty-third book of his *Natural History,* "that Spartacus (the leader of a slave uprising) did not allow gold or silver in his camp. How our runaway slaves tower above us in largeness of spirit!"

Under this ruling class, some of which went to rack and ruin in the mad pursuit of pleasure, money and cruelty, while another section felt sympathy for the poor, aversion to money and pleasure and even longing for death: under this ruling class there was a numberless horde of working slaves, worse treated than our beasts of burden. These men and women had been swept together from all sorts of nations and coarsened and brutalized by constant mistreatment and labor in chains under the crack of the whip. They were embittered, desperate with thirst for revenge and hopelessness, always inclined to violent rebellion; but unable, because of the low intellectual level of the barbarian elements that formed the majority among them, to overthrow the existing order of the state and found a new one, even though some outstanding minds among them looked forward to some such goal. The only kind of liberation they could attain was not the overthrow of society but flight from society, flight either into crime, into the ranks of the bandits, or flight over the borders of the Empire to join its enemies.

Above these millions of the most wretched of mankind stood hundreds of thousands of slaves, often in comfort and luxury, always the witnesses and objects of the wildest and most insane sensuality, accomplices in all imaginable sorts of corruption and either caught up in this corruption and perverted like their masters, or else, like many of their masters, and even sooner than they, since they tasted the bitterness of a life of pleasure much earlier, deeply revolted by the perversion and pleasures and full of longing for a new, purer, higher life.

Along with all these there were the crowds of hundreds of thousands of free citizens and freed slaves, numerous (but impoverished) remains of the peasantry, beggared tenant farmers, the miserable city craftsmen and porters, and finally the urban lumpenproletariat, with the rights and the pride of the free citizen and yet economically superfluous in society, homeless, with no security, completely at the mercy of chance gifts thrown to them by the mighty out of their surplus, out of liberality or fear, or just to have peace and quiet.

When the Gospel according to St. Matthew has Jesus say (8, verse 20): "The foxes have holes, and the birds of the air have nests; but the Son of man hath not where to lay his head," that expresses for the person of Jesus a thought that Tiberius Gracchus had expressed for the whole proletariat of Rome 130 years before Christ: "The wild beasts of Italy have their holes and their lairs, in which they rest, but the men that fight and die for Italy's power have nothing but air and light, because this they can not be robbed of. They roam with their wives and children without house and home."

Their poverty and the constant insecurity of their existence must have embittered them even more because of contrast with the shameless luxury of the wealthy. A grim class hatred of the poor against the rich arose, but it was a class hatred of a different kind from that of the modern proletarian.

Today all society is based on the labor of the proletarian. All he need do is to stop that labor, and the foundations of society tremble. The ancient lumpenproletarian did not work, and even the work of what few free peasants and craftsmen were left was not indispensable. Society did not live off the proletariat then; the proletariat lived off society. It was quite superfluous and could have disappeared altogether without hurting society; it would have done it good instead. The labor of slaves was the foundation on which society was based.

The opposition between the capitalist and the proletarian is worked out today in the factory, the place of work. The question is who shall control production, the owner of the means of production or the owners of labor power. It is a battle over the mode of production, an effort to replace the existing mode of production by a higher one.

The ancient lumpenproletarian had no such aim in mind. He did no work and did not want to work. What he wanted was a share in the pleasures of the rich, redistribution of the means of enjoyment, not of the means of production; he wanted to plunder the rich, not to change the mode of production. The sufferings of the slaves in the mines and the plantations left him as cold as the sufferings of the packhorses.

Thus, there were tremendous social contradictions, great class hatred and class struggles in the Roman society of the end of the Republic and during the Empire; there was an infinite longing for a different, better life, for going beyond the existing organization of society; there were no efforts to introduce a new, higher mode of production.[4]

The moral and intellectual conditions for such a movement were not present. There was no class that had the knowledge, the vigor, the joy in labor and the unselfishness to be able to make a real drive for a new mode of production. In addition the material conditions were lacking that could even permit such an idea to arise.

The slave economy, we have seen, did not denote a technical advance, but a step backward. Not only did it make the masters impotent and incapable of working, and increase the number of unproductive workers in society, but it also cut down the productivity of the productive workers and checked the progress of technology, with the possible exception of some luxury trades. If the new mode of production of the slave economy were compared with the free peasant economy it had supplanted, it would have to be considered a backward rather than a forward step. So men came to the idea that the old times were better, a golden age, and that each generation was worse than the one before. The age of capitalism, with its constant drive to improve the means of production, is marked by the concept of the unlimited progress of mankind and tends to see the past as black as possible and the future as rosy as possible. In the Roman Empire the prevailing

4. Pöhlmann in his *Geschichte des antiken Kommunismus und Sozialismus* (*op. cit.*) meaninglessly identifies the class struggles of the ancient proletarians, even of the debt-ridden agrarians, the debt cancellations of the landholders, the plunderings and land reforms of the propertyless, with modern socialism. The object of this absurdity on the part of the Erlangen professor is to prove that the dictatorship of the proletariat never under any circumstances can produce anything but burning and looting, murder and rape, pillage and debauchery; lacking facts and arguments, he showers us with Greek citations.

view was the opposite, the steady decline of mankind and perpetual longing for the good old times. To the extent that the
social reforms and social ideals of the time denoted making the
productive relations sounder, they aimed merely at restoring the
old mode of production, the old peasantry and rightly so, for it
was the higher mode. Slave labor led into a blind alley. Society
had to be put back on the basis of the peasant economy before it
could recommence its upward path. But Roman society was no
longer capable of doing that, for the peasants themselves had been
lost. Many nations of free peasants had to flood the entire Roman
Empire in the great migrations before the remains of the culture
the Empire had created could provide the basis for a new social
development.

Like every mode of production that is founded on contradictions, the ancient slave economy dug its own grave. In the form it
finally took in the Roman world empire, it was based on war. It
was only continual victorious wars, continual subjugation of new
nations, continual extension of the territory of the Empire that
could supply the masses of cheap slave material it required.

But war can not be waged without soldiers, and the best material for soldiers was the peasant. Accustomed to steady hard
work in the open, in cold and heat, in sun and rain, he was the
best fitted to endure military hardships. The city lumpenproletarian, unaccustomed to labor, and even the nimble-fingered
craftsman, the weaver or goldsmith or sculptor, were less well
adapted to war. When the peasants disappeared, so did the
soldiers needed for the Roman army. It became increasingly necessary to fill out the ranks of the citizen militia with voluntary en-
listments, professional soldiers serving beyond their term of con-
scription. Soon this too proved inadequate, if restricted to Roman
citizens. Tiberius was already declaring in the Senate that there
was a shortage of high-grade volunteers, and recourse would have
to be made to all sorts of riff-raff and vagabonds. The Roman
armies had more and more barbarian mercenaries from the conquered provinces; and finally in order to fill the ranks they had

to recruit foreigners, enemies of the Empire. Even in Caesar's times we find Germans in the Roman armies.

As the army became less and less able to draw its recruits from the master nation, and soldiers became fewer and costlier, Rome's love of peace grew, not because of an ethical change, but for very material reasons. It had to conserve its soldiers and, instead of extending the frontiers of the Empire, be grateful if there were enough soldiers to guard the existing boundaries. Just at the time in which Jesus's life is placed, in the reign of Tiberius, the Roman offensive basically came to a standstill. From that point on the Empire was primarily concerned with warding off the enemies that were pressing in on it. This pressure kept increasing too because the more foreigners, especially Germans, there were serving in Rome's armies, the better Rome's barbarian neighbors got to know its wealth, its art of war, and its weakness as well; and the more they desired to enter the Empire not as mercenaries and servants but as conquerors and masters. Instead of carrying on manhunts against the barbarians, the masters of Rome were soon compelled to retire before them or purchase their favor. So in the first century of our era the flow of cheap slaves came to a speedy end, and they had to rely more and more on slave-breeding.

This was an expensive procedure. Slave-breeding paid only in the case of house slaves of a superior sort who could do skilled work. It was impossible to continue the latifundia economy with home-bred slaves. The use of slaves in agriculture kept decreasing; mining too declined, for many mines became unprofitable as soon as there were no more droves of cheap slaves coming from the wars.

The decline of the slave economy did not give rise to a renaissance of the peasant economy. There did not exist the requisite full generation of numerous, economically powerful peasants; and private property in land was another obstacle. The owners of the latifundia had no inclination to give up their property. They merely cut down the extent of their operations. They turned a part of their lands into small farms, which they let out to tenants, *coloni*, on condition that the tenant devote part of his labor power to the master's house estates. This was the origin of that system of cultivation to which the large landowners resorted more and more in feudal times, until capitalism replaced it by capitalistic rental farming.

The labor forces from which the *coloni* were recruited were partly country slaves and ruined peasants, partly proletarians, free craftsmen and slaves of the big cities, who could no longer earn a living there once the incomes from the slave economy in mine and plantation had fallen off and cut down the liberality and the extravagance of the wealthy. Later there must have been added inhabitants of the border provinces, driven from their lands by the advancing barbarians and taking refuge in the internal provinces, where they found places as *coloni*.

But this new mode of production could not avert the economic decline arising out of the end of slave importation. It too was technically inferior to free peasant agriculture and was an obstacle to further technical development. The work that the *colonus* had to do on the manor remained forced labor, with the same reluctance, the same lack of care for cattle and tools as was the case with slave labor. The *colonus* got a farm for himself, to be sure, but it was stingily measured out to him so that he could just keep body and soul together. In addition, the rent in kind was set so high that everything above the barest subsistence was delivered to the master. The poverty of the *coloni* is something like that of the small tenants of Ireland or the peasants of Southern Italy, where a similar mode of production still persists. But the agrarian regions of today at least have a safety valve open in the form of emigration to rising industrial regions. There was nothing like that for the *coloni* of the Roman Empire. Industry was only to a very small extent devoted to the production of means of production, principally to producing luxury consumption goods. As the surpluses of the owners of latifundia and mines shrank, the urban industries declined and their population fell rapidly.

At the same time the rural population fell as well. The tenants on their diminutive farms could not support large families. Their yield was normally barely enough to support themselves. Bad harvests found them without reserves or money to make up the deficit. Hunger and poverty must have taken a heavy toll and thinned the ranks of the *coloni,* especially among the children. Just as the population of Ireland has been decreasing for a century, so did that of the Roman Empire.

"It is easily understandable that the economic causes that led to a decrease of population all over the Roman Empire should be felt especially in Italy, and there most strongly in Rome. If figures must be given, it may be assumed that the city had about a million inhabitants at the time of Augustus and stayed more or less at that level for the first century of the Empire, falling to about 600,000 at the time of the Severi (about 220 A.D.), and declining rapidly thereafter."[5]

In has excellent book on *Die wirtschaftliche Entwicklung des Altertums* (1895), Eduard Meyer gives in an appendix the description that Dio Chrysostom (born about 50 A.D.) sketches in his seventh oration with respect to conditions in a small city in Euboea, which he does not name. Here we see in harsh colors the depopulation of the Empire.

"The whole region belongs to the city and owes it taxes. For the most part, if not exclusively, the land is owned by rich men, whose extensive estates are partly in pasture and partly cultivated fields. But it is completely deserted. 'Almost two-thirds of our region,' says a citizen in the town meeting, 'lies desert, because we take no care of it and have too small a population. I myself have as many acres as anyone else, not only in the mountains but in the plain as well, and if I could find anybody to work it, I would not only let him have it free, but would gladly give him money too. . . .' The waste land, he says, begins right outside the city gates, 'the country is completely uninhabited and has a dreary look, as if it lay deep in the wilderness and not at the gates of a city. Within the city walls most of the land is plowed or turned into pasture. . . . The exercise grounds have been planted so that in summertime Hercules and the other statues of gods and heroes are hidden in the standing grain, and the orator who spoke

5. Ludo M. Hartmann, *Geschichte Italiens im Mittelalter,* 1897, Vol. I, p. 7.

before me has his cow driven into the marketplace every morning to graze in front of the government buildings, so that strangers who come to us mock the city or pity it.'

"Likewise there are many empty houses in the city; obviously the population is falling steadily. There are some fishers of the murex to get the purple dye out at the Kapharian cliffs; otherwise the whole region is uninhabited for wide stretches. Formerly this whole section belonged to a rich citizen, 'who possessed many herds of horses and cattle, many pastures, many fine fields and other important property.' He was killed for his money at the command of the Emperor, his herds were driven off, including the cow that belonged to his herdsman, and since that time all the land lies unused. There are only two cowherds, free men and citizens, left; they live by hunting and a little farming and gardening and dairying. . . .

"The conditions that Dio pictures here—and all over Greece things looked like that even at the beginning of the Empire—are the same that developed during the next few centuries in Rome and its surroundings and have left their mark on the Campagna down to the present day. Here too it came to the point that the country towns disappeared, the land lay fallow for miles around and was used only for grazing (and here and there on the mountain slopes for vineyards), until finally Rome itself was deserted, the houses were unoccupied and collapsed, as did the public buildings; and cattle grazed in the Forum and on the Capitol. These conditions have begun to develop in Ireland in our century (the nineteenth) and strike any visitor that comes to Dublin or travels in the country." (*Op. cit.*, pp. 67-69).

At the same time the fertility of the soil decreased. Stall feeding was poorly developed, and must have fallen off still further under the slave economy, which entailed bad handling of the cattle. But without stall feeding there was no manure. Without copious manuring and intensive cultivation, only the best lands will give any kind of profitable yield. And the quantity of such lands kept shrinking the longer the cultivation lasted, the longer the land was sucked dry.

Something similar was to be seen in America in the nineteenth century, where in the Southern states with their slave economy the ground was not fertilized and was quickly exhausted, while at the same time the use of slaves was profitable only on the best lands. The slave economy could exist only by constant westward expansion, by constantly putting new lands under cultivation, leaving the exhausted land abandoned behind it. We find the same phenomenon in the Roman Empire, and that too was one of the causes of the constant land hunger of its masters, and their drive to conquer new lands by war. By the beginning of the Empire Southern Italy, Sicily and Greece were already desolate.

Soil exhaustion and increasing shortage of labor power, coupled with the irrational use of what labor power there was, could have no other result than a steady decrease in the crops.

At the same time the ability of the country to buy food stuffs from abroad decreased. Gold and silver became rarer and rarer. For the mines ran dry for want of labor, as we have seen. The gold and silver on hand kept flowing out, partly to India and Arabia to buy luxuries for the wealthy, but especially tribute to the neighboring barbarian tribes. We have seen that that is where the soldiers were recruited to an increasing extent; there was a constantly increasing number who took their pay, or what was left of it at the end of their service, abroad with them. The more the military power of the Empire sank, the more the attempt was made to appease their dangerous neighbors and keep them in good humor; the simplest way was to pay rich tribute. Where this failed, the enemy hordes all too often invaded the Empire to plunder it; and this too deprived it of a part of its wealth.

What was left was finally frittered away in the effort to guard it. The more the military power of the inhabitants of the Empire sank, the fewer the recruits that came from within it, the more they had to be brought in from over the borders and the stronger the pressure of the barbarian enemies; the more the demand for mercenaries rose while the supply fell, the higher the wages that had to be paid them. "Since Caesar, the pay had been 225 denarii per annum ($40.) and in addition each man received two-thirds a medimnus of grain monthly (a medimnus was 54 liters or 1.44 bushels), or four modii, a ration later raised to five modii. That was as much grain as a slave received who lived on nothing else. With the sobriety of the Southerner, the largest part of his needs in food was met by the grain ration. Domitian raised the pay to 300 denarii (one-third more). Under the later Caesars arms were supplied free of charge. Septimius Severus and later Caracalla raised the pay even further."

The purchasing power of money was then of course much higher than it is today. Seneca thought in Nero's time that a philosopher could live on half a sesterce (2¢) a day. Forty liters of wine cost six cents, a lamb ten to twelve cents, a sheep 36 cents.

"With prices such as these, the pay of the Roman legionary was something considerable. But in addition he got an inauguration gift from the new emperor; in times when a new Caesar was installed by the soldiers every month or two, that came to a good deal. When his time of service was up he received a separation bonus which was 3000 denarii ($510.) in the time of Augustus, halved by Caligula, then raised by Caracalla to 5000 denarii ($850.)." (Paul Ernst, "Social Conditions in the Roman Empire before the Barbarian Invasions," *Neue Zeit,* vol. XI, No. 2, p. 253 f.)

Along with this, the size of the standing army must have increased constantly as the attacks on the frontiers from all sides mounted. In Augustus' time it consisted of 300,000 men, and later was more than twice as many.

These are enormous figures when we consider that in keeping with the state of the development of agriculture the population of the Empire was very thin and the surplus that their labor produced very meager. Beloch calculates the population of the whole Roman Empire, that was something like four times the size of the present German Empire, as in the neighborhood of 55 million at the time of Augustus. Italy, that has 33 million inhabitants today, had only 6 million then. These 55 million with their primitive technology had to maintain an army as large as the army which is an oppressive burden for the German Empire today (1908) despite the enormous technical progress that has

been made since then, and this was an army of enlisted mercenaries, far better paid than the German conscript of today.

And while the population became smaller and poorer, the
burdens of militarism kept growing greater and greater.

This had two causes, which made the economic collapse complete.

The state had two basic outlays: the military establishment
and public building. If it wanted to raise the expenditures for
one without raising taxes, it would have to neglect the other. And
that is what happened. At the time of wealth and the great surpluses
arising out of the labor of masses of slaves, the state was rich too
and in a position to erect huge edifices not only for luxury, religion and hygiene, but for economic life as well. With the enormous human masses at its disposal the state built those colossal
works that still astound us today, temples and palaces, aqueducts
and sewers, and also a network of magnificent roads that linked
Rome with the furthest corners of the empire and constituted a
powerful means of economic and political unity and international
communication. In addition, great irrigation and drainage
works were constructed. Thus for instance the Pontine Marshes
gave an enormous stretch of fertile land; when they were
drained, 100,000 hectares were brought under the plough. Once
there were no fewer than 33 cities there. The construction and
maintenance of drainage canals in the Pontine marshes were a
constant concern of the rulers of Rome. These works fell into
such complete decay that today the whole region of the marshes
and its surroundings is a barren waste land.

As the financial might of the Empire weakened, its rulers let
all these structures go to pieces rather than put a limit to militarism. The colossal constructions became colossal ruins, which
fell apart all the sooner because as labor power became scarcer
it was easier to get materials for unavoidable construction by
tearing down the old edifices instead of getting them from the
quarries. This method did more harm to the ancient works of art
than the devastations of the invading Vandals and other barbarians.

"The spectator who casts a mournful view over the ruins of ancient Rome is tempted to accuse the memory of the Goths and Vandals for the mischief which they had neither leisure, nor power, nor perhaps inclination, to perpetrate. The tempest of war might strike some lofty turrets to the ground; but the destruction which undermined the foundations of those massy fabrics was prosecuted, slowly and silently, during a period of ten centuries. . . . The monuments of consular or Imperial greatness were no longer revered as the immortal glory of the capital: they were only esteemed as an inexhaustible mine of materials, cheaper, and more convenient, than the distant quarry."[6]

Not only works of art decayed, but the public works that served commerce or hygiene, roads and aqueducts; this decay, a consequence of the general economic decline, now contributed to accelerate that decline.

The military burdens increased none the less, and must have become still more unendurable, completing the general ruin. The total of public burdens—taxes in kind, labor services, money taxes —remained the same or even increased while the population and its wealth grew smaller. The burden of the government on the individual became heavier and heavier. Everyone tried to shift it to weaker shoulders; the wretched *coloni* got most of it unloaded on them, and their already bad position became a desperate one, as is shown by the numerous rebellions, for example that of the Bagaudae, *coloni* in Gaul, who rose under Diocletian, 285 A.D. and after successful beginnings were beaten down, but showed the scale of their misery by new disorders and attempts at uprisings for over a hundred years thereafter.

The other classes of the population were also being depressed, if not as hard as the *coloni*. The fisc took everything it could find; the barbarians were no worse plunderers than the state. A general breaking-up of society began, an increasing unwillingness and inability on the part of the individual members of society to perform even the most necessary services for the commonwealth and for each other. Things that had formerly been regulated by custom

6. Gibbon, *Decline and Fall of the Roman Empire*, Chap. 36.

and economic necessity now had more and more to be enforced by the power of the state. These coercive laws spread after Diocletian. Some fastened the *coloni* to the soil, thus transforming them legally into bondsmen; others forced the landowners to participate in the city government, a task consisting chiefly in the collection of taxes for the state. Still others organized the craftsmen into compulsory guilds and obliged them to furnish their services and wares at set prices. The state bureaucracy, that had the task of enforcing these coercive laws, grew larger.

The bureaucracy and the army, that is the power of the state, thus came into an ever stronger opposition not only to the exploited classes, but even to the exploiters. Even for these latter the state changed more and more from the function of protection and fostering to that of plundering and devastating. Hostility to the state grew; even the rule of the barbarians was looked on as a deliverance. The barbarians were free peasants to whom the inhabitants of the border regions more and more took flight, regarding them as saviors and rescuers from the ruling order in state and society, inviting them and receiving them with open arms.

Salvian, a Christian author of the dying Roman Empire, said on this subject in his book *De gubernatione dei:*

"A large part of Gaul and Spain is already Gothic, and all the Romans who live there have only one wish, not to become Romans again. I should only wonder that there were any poor and needy people that did not go over to them, were it not that they can not leave their possessions and families behind. And we Romons wonder that we can not defeat the Goths, when we Romans prefer living under them to living with each other."

The great migrations, the flooding of the Roman Empire by the swarms of savage Germans did not mean the premature destruction of a flourishing high culture, but merely the conclusion of the dissolution of a dying civilization and the formation of the basis for a new upswing of civilization; it is sure that this last took place slowly and unsteadily over centuries.

Christianity took form in the four centuries from the founding of the Imperial power by Augustus to the barbarian invasions; in an era which began with the greatest brilliance that the ancient world attained, with the most colossal and intoxicating accumulation of wealth and power in a few hands; with the most abundant accumulation of the greatest misery for slaves, ruined peasants, craftsmen and lumpenproletarians; with the crudest class contradictions and the bitterest class hatred—and ended with the complete impoverishment and despair of the entire society.

All of this left its mark on Christianity. But it also shows the traces of other influences, arising out of the political and social life that grew in the soil of the mode of production we have described above.

BOOK TWO: SOCIETY IN THE ROMAN EMPIRE

2

THE STATE

STATE AND COMMERCE

ALONG WITH slavery there were two other important methods of exploitation in ancient society; these also reached their high point at the time Christianity arose; they sharpened class oppositions to an extreme and speeded the decline of society and of the state. These two were usury and the plunder of the conquered provinces by the conquering central power. Both were intimately related to the nature of the state at that time, and that in turn was so closely connected with economics that we must take it into account even when dealing with the basis of state and society, namely, the mode of production.

First we must briefly describe the ancient state.

Ancient democracy never got beyond the limits of the municipality or the *Markgenossenschaft* [group of villages sharing common land], which was made up of one or more villages that owned and ruled a region in common. This was done through direct legislation by the people, by the assembly of all the members with the right to vote. In such an arrangement the community could not be very extensive. Its territory could be only so large that every member could get from his house to the assembly without too much trouble and loss. Antiquity was unable to develop a democratic organization beyond this framework, for want of the necessary technical and economic prerequisites. It was only modern capitalism with printing and post-offices, its newspapers, railroads and telegraphs that was able to create the modern nation, not merely as a linguistic unity but as a durable political and economic organization. Basically this was not accomplished until the nineteenth century. Special conditions made it possible for England and France, and no others, to become nations in the modern sense earlier, and set up a national parliament, the foundation of a democracy in a wider framework than that of the commune. But this achievement was possible only because of the leading role played by two great communes, London and Paris, and even in 1848 the national and democratic movement was mainly the movement of single outstanding communes—Paris, Vienna, Berlin.

In antiquity, with its much more primitive means of communication, democracy was confined within the limits of the commune. At last, in the first century of our era, commerce among the countries on the Mediterranean did achieve a respectable scope, so much so that it brought two languages into international use there, Greek and Latin. Unfortunately this took place right at the time when democracy and political life in general were declining—unfortunately, but not by an unfortunate accident. The development of communication among the communes was of necessity tied up at that time with conditions that were fatal to democracy.

It is not our purpose to show how this was the case in the Oriental countries, where democracy limited to the commune became the basis for a particular kind of despotism. We shall consider only the special course of development taken by the Hellenic and Roman world, using a single example, the commune of Rome. This shows the tendencies of the ancient course of development most acutely, since things went more quickly and on a more gigantic sale here than in any other community of the ancient world. The tendencies at work in all of them, however, were the same, although often more petty and less dramatic.

The extension of every *Markgenossenschaft* and commune had narrow limits beyond which it could not go. As a result, the various villages and communes remained more or less on the same level so long as they had a peasant economy pure and simple. At this stage there were few incentives to greed and strife among them, since each community produced virtually everything it needed. At most increasing population might produce a shortage of land; it could not however lead to an extension of its territory, for the commune could not become so large that each member could not attend the legislative assembly without excessive loss of time and effort. If actually all the cultivable land of the commune were in use, the excess young men of military age took themselves off to found a commune of their own, either expelling other elements that were weaker or by settling in regions where a lower mode of production still prevailed, and hence the population was thin enough to make room.

Thus the various communes or *Markgenossenschaften* were pretty much on the same level; but this changed when commerce arose alongside of the peasant economy.

We have seen that trading in commodities began very early. Its origins go back to the Stone Age. In regions where it was easy to obtain many sought-after raw materials which were scarce or non-existent elsewhere, the inhabitants would be likely to get more than they needed, as well as becoming more skillful in obtaining and processing them. They traded the excess to their neighbors for other products, and much of what they traded was again traded to places further removed. By means of this process of barter from tribe to tribe many products traveled incredible distances. The prerequisite for this trade was a nomadic form of life for some hordes, who frequently encountered one another in their wanderings and traded surplus objects on such occasions.

These occasions came to an end when men settled down in fixed dwelling places, but the need for exchange of goods did not cease therewith. In particular the need grew for tools or the materials they were made from, and that were to be found only in certain places, and so as a rule could only be obtained through trade. To supply this need a special class had to come into being, the merchants. These were either nomadic tribes of herdsmen who now took to carrying goods on their beasts of burden from a district where they were in surplus, and therefore cheap, to other districts where they were scarce and dear, or else they were fishermen who ventured along the coast or from island to island in their little boats. The more trade throve, the more it would induce peasants as well to take it up. In general landholding looked down with scorn on trade; the Roman aristocracy considered usury, but not trade, as an honorable profession. That did not prevent many landowners from getting large profits from trade.

Trade takes to definite routes, on which traffic becomes heavier. Communities that lie on such routes get their wares more easily than others, and find customers for their products in the merchants. At many points it is not possible to deviate from the route; such points can not be got around; and if they are also natural fortifications, that makes it possible for their inhabitants and lords, that is the landowners, to hold up the traders and lay them under contribution, tax them. There were other points that became warehouse points or depots, where goods had to be transshipped, such as harbors and crossroads, where merchants came in large numbers from various points and often stored goods for long periods.

It was inevitable that communities thus favored by nature for trade should grow beyond the size of a peasant commune. The population of a peasant commune soon finds its limit in the extent and fertility of its territory, but the population of a commercial state does not depend on the productivity of its territory and can increase far beyond it. For, in the goods it owns it has the means to buy whatever it needs, including foodstuffs. In addition to trade in tools for agriculture, in raw materials and tools for industry and in luxury products of industry, there develops trade in foodstuffs for the cities.

The extension of trade has no set limits and by its very nature tends to overcome any barriers, always looking for new clients and new producers, for new lodes of scarce metals, for new industrial districts, for new purchasers for their products. Thus the Phoenicians early emerged from the Mediterranean and went as far as

England in one direction and south around the Cape of Good Hope in the other.

"We find them at an incredibly early date in Cyprus and Egypt, in Greece and Sicily, in Africa and Spain, even in the Atlantic Ocean and the North Sea. Their sphere of trade reaches from Sierra Leone in West Africa and Cornwall in England in the West, eastward to the Malabar Coast in the East Indies; through their hands pass the gold and the pearls of the East, the Tyrian purple, the slaves, ivory, lion and leopard skins from the heart of Africa, Arabian frankincense, Egypt's linen, Greece's pottery and fine wines, Cyprian copper, Spanish silver, English tin, the iron of Elba." (Mommsen, *Römische Geschichte,* 6th edn., 1874, vol. I, p. 484).

Craftsmen like to settle in commercial cities. For many crafts such a city constitutes the market without which they could not come into being: on the one hand the merchants looking for goods, and on the other the country people from the surrounding villages, who come to town on market days to sell their produce and buy tools, arms and finery in exchange. In addition the trading town assures the craftsmen of the supply of raw materials he needs to practice his craft.

Alongside the merchants and craftsmen a class of rich land-holders arises in the city community. The members of the rural community of this city, those who had a share in its rural districts, now become wealthy, since the newcomers seek land, which rises steadily in value. The same people also profit from the fact that among the wares the merchant brings there are slaves, as we have seen. Individual families of landowners, who for one reason or another have risen above the level of ordinary peasants and obtain more land or greater wealth, now find it possible to extend their farming operations by the use of slaves, and even to have them carried on exclusively by slaves, while they settle in the city and devote themselves to business in town, to municipal affairs or to war. Such a landowner, who hitherto had lived exclusively in his farmhouse in the outskirts, could now build himself a town house to live in. Such landlords still derived their economic power and social position from the ownership of land and agriculture, but were city-dwellers as well and augmented the city population with their households, which in time came to considerable dimensions including the luxury slaves.

In this way the commercial city kept growing richer and more populous. With its power, its warlike spirit and its greed for plunder increased as well. For trade is by no means so peaceable a thing as bourgeois economics says it is, and least of all at the outset. Commerce and transportation were not distinct in those days. The merchant could not stay in his office, as he can today, get his orders by mail and send them out by road and ship and mail. He had to bring the goods to market himself, and that took strength and courage. Through the trackless wilderness on foot or on horseback, or over stormy seas in small open boats he had to find his way, away from home for months or even years. The hardships of such a life were no less than those of a military campaign; and only a strong man could endure them.

But the dangers too of travel were not less than those of a war. It was not only nature that threatened the trader at every moment, here with wave and cliffs, there with sandstorms, thirst or starvation, icy cold or pestilential heat. The treasures he carried with him were a booty to tempt anybody who had the strength to take them away from him. Originally trade had been carried on from tribe to tribe; later too it was a group activity, caravans on land and trading fleets at sea. And every member of such a party had to be armed and ready to defend his goods sword in hand. Trade became a school of war.

The wealth of goods that the merchant carried along with him compelled him to acquire military power to defend them; this military power in turn became a temptation to use it aggressively. The profit in trade was obtained by getting cheap and selling dear. The cheapest way to get things however was undoubtedly to take without payment what one wanted. Robbery and trade have been closely linked from the beginning. Where the merchant felt stronger, it was easy for him to turn into a robber, when there was something valuable to steal—and not the least valuable booty was man himself.

The merchant had need of his skill in arms not merely to procure his goods and gains as cheaply as he could, but also to keep competitors from the markets he frequented; for, the more buyers there were the higher would be the prices of the goods he had to buy, and the more sellers, the lower the prices on what he had to sell, and hence the lower the difference between the purchase and selling prices, the profit. As soon as several great commercial cities arose, wars soon arose between them, in which the victor not only gained the advantage of driving his competitor out of the market but also that of turning the competitor from a factor unfavorable to profit to a favorable one. This could be done either in the most radical way, which to be sure can not be repeated, by totally looting the opponents' city and selling its inhabitants into slavery; or less radically, but repeating itself every year, by taking the conquered city in as an "ally" that has to furnish troops and tribute and refrain from doing any damage to the competitor that has become its master.

Some commercial cities especially favored by their situation or other conditions were thus able to combine many other cities with their territories into a single state. A democratic constitution could continue to exist in each city, but the totality of the cities, the state as a whole, would not be democratically governed, since only the single victorious city ruled and the others had to obey without the slightest influence on the legislation and administration of the state as a whole.

In Greece we find many such city states. The mightiest among them was Athens. But none of the victorious cities was strong enough to subjugate all the others permanently, to get rid of all its rivals. So the history of Greece shows nothing but the unending war of the single cities and city states with each other, with only the occasional interruption of a common defence against a common enemy. These wars contributed enormously to hastening the decline of Greece, once the consequences of the slave economy we have spoken of began to make themselves felt. But it is ridiculous to view this with moral indignation, as so many of our professors do. Fighting against competitors is a natural concomitant of trade. The forms of this conflict vary, but it inevitably takes on the form of war where the opponents are sovereign trading cities. It was inevitable that Greece should tear itself to pieces as soon as trade began to make her cities big and powerful.

The goal of every war of competition is to shut out or suppress the competitor: that is, monopoly. No Greek city had the strength for that, not even powerful Athens. It was an Italian city that accomplished it. Rome became the ruler of the entire civilized world around the Mediterranean.

PATRICIANS AND PLEBEIANS

Competition with rivals is not the only source of war for a great commercial city. When it has vigorous peasants for neighbors, especially cattle-raising peasants in the mountains, who are as a rule poorer than the ploughmen of the fertile plains, but also less tied down to the soil and more used to bloodshed and the hunt, that school of war, the wealth of the great city is likely to excite the peasants to plunder. They could pass by and disregard small country towns that only served the local trade of a limited region and a few artisans; but the treasurers of a great commercial center must have tempted them sorely to collect into bands for a raid on the rich community. Meanwhile the city was trying to extend its territory and the number of its vassals. We have seen how the growth of the city creates in it an extensive market for agricultural products and the land that produces goods for the city increases in value. In this way the hunger grows for more land and for more labor power to work the newly-won fields for the conquerors. All this leads to constant war between the big city and the rural peoples round about it. If the latter win, the city is looted and its city must start over again from the beginning. If the city wins, it turns a part of the peasants' lands over to its own landowners, who sometimes settle their own landless sons there, but for the most part cultivate the newly-won lands by means of forced labor, whether in the form of tenants or serfs or slaves. Sometimes things are done more gently; the conquered people is not only not enslaved but incorporated into the citizenry of the victorious city; not however as full citizens, whose assembly rules the city and the state, but as second-class citizens, who have full freedom and all the protection of the laws of the state, but have no share in its government. The city needed such new citizens all the more as its military burdens rose with the growth of its wealth; for the families of the old citizens no longer sufficed now to supply the needed number of citizen soldiers. Now, military service and citizenship are closely linked from the outset. If the number of warriors was to be increased quickly, new citizens would have to be taken into the body politic. One of the most important causes of Rome's rising to greatness was the fact that it was very liberal with citizenship toward immigrants as well as toward the inhabitants of near-by conquered communities.

The number of these new citizens could be extended indefinitely. They were not limited by the factors which kept down the number of old citizens. In part these limits were technical. The city government was as a rule governed by the assembly of the old citizens, and this assembly could not be so unwieldy as to make action impossible. Moreover, the citizens had to live near enough the place of assembly to be able to reach it at stated times without hardship and harm to their affairs. These considerations did not apply in the case of the new citizens. Even when they were granted certain political rights, even in some cases the right to vote in the citizen assemblies (something which seldom happened), it was not at all necessary, at least from the point of view of the old citizens, for them to be able to take part in these assemblies. The more the old citizens remained a caste apart, the better they liked it.

Thus the factors limiting their number did not apply to the new citizens.

The number of the latter could grow indefinitely, limited only by the size of the state and its needs for trustworthy soldiers. For even when troops could be obtained from the conquered provinces, the army needed a nucleus it could rely on, and that could only be made up of a strong contingent of citizen soldiers.

In this way the growth of the city gives rise to a second form of undemocratic organization in the state. On the one hand the great city community becomes absolute ruler of many communes and provinces; on the other, within the citizenry of the community, which now extends far beyond the territory of the old city district, there arises the opposition between full or old citizens (patricians) and new citizens (plebeians). In both ways democracy turns into aristocracy, not by restricting the group of full citizens nor by raising some of them to a privileged position above the others, but in virtue of the fact that the state grows while that group remains unchanged, so that all the new elements added to the old community or *Markgenossenschaft* lack some or all of the rights of full citizenship.

These two ways of evolving aristocracy out of democracy follow different paths. One form of the exploitation and domination of the state by a privileged minority, the rule of a community over a whole empire, can always increase in size, as the example of Rome shows; and it must increase, so long as the state is vigorous and does not break against some superior power. It is different with the lack of political rights on the part of the new citizens. As long as they are almost exclusively peasants, they take the absence of rights more or less calmly. Most of them live so far from the city that they are not in a position to leave their houses in the morning, be present at noon in the assembly in the city's marketplace and return home in the evening. Moreover, as the state grows, its internal and external relationships become more and more complicated. Politics and warfare become trades requiring special knowledge which the peasant can not obtain. He had no understanding of all the personal and factual questions that are decided in the political assemblies of the city, and so feels no great urge to demand the right to participate in them.

But the new citizenry does not remain confined to peasants only. Foreigners who come to the city and are useful to it receive citizenship. The regions that have been conquered and given citizenship contain not only villages, but cities with craftsmen and merchants, and large landholders as well, who have a city house in addition to their country estate. As soon as they get Roman citizenship, they have a strong incentive to move from the smaller city to the larger one, to which they now have a right to go, and in which they can have better earnings and more leisure. At the same time there are more and more peasants who have lost their property through war and the slave economy in the way we have described. The best refuge for such elements, left hanging in the air, is the big city, whose citizens they are; there they try to get along as craftsmen or porters, tavern keepers, shopkeepers, or hangers-on of some rich lord, to whom they attach themselves as clients, to perform all sorts of services—genuine lumpenproletarians.

These elements have much more time and opportunity than the peasants to concern themselves with city politics, whose consequences they feel much more clearly and directly. It is in their most vital interests to have some influence in politics, to replace the assembly of the old citizens by the assembly of the entire citizenry, to win for the latter the election of officers and the passage of laws.

As the state grew there came to be more and more of these elements, while the number of old citizens remained more or less the same. The latter gradually became relatively weaker, and especially so since they did not have any military power apart from the general citizenry; the new citizens were in the militia just as the old citizens were, in possession of arms and familiar with their use. Hence there flares up in all the cities of this sort a bitter class warfare between old citizens and new citizens, which usually ends sooner or later with the triumph of the latter, that is of democracy; this is really however only a broadening of the aristocracy, since the provinces continue to be exploited and do not have the rights of citizens. In fact, the extent and sometimes the intensity of the exploitation of the provinces is often increased at the same time that the democracy makes progress within the ruling community.

THE ROMAN STATE

All these conflicts, which characterize every flourishing commercial city of antiquity, are to be found fully developed in Rome at the time that city first appears in history.

Rome's position is very well suited to making it a trading center. It lies on the Tiber a little distance from the sea, but at that time this was no obstacle to ocean commerce, ships were so small; it was even an advantage, because being inland they were safer from pirates and storms. It is no accident that so many of the great older commercial cities were not directly on the sea, but on navigable rivers at some distance from their mouths—Babylon and Bagdad, London and Paris, Antwerp and Hamburg.

The city of Rome grew up at a spot where the Tiber, still navigable, is flanked by two easily fortifiable hills that afforded security for the goods entering and leaving. The country around was still rough, solidly peasant, but north and south of it were economically advanced regions, Etruria and Campania, with strong industries, extensive trade, and an agriculture already based on unfree labor. From Africa came the Carthaginians with their wares, standing on the same level of development as the Etruscans and the South Italian Greek colonies.

This geographical situation put Rome into a peculiar double position. Compared to its immediate neighbors, the Latins and the Volscians, the trading city appeared as the representative of a higher civilization; compared to their more distant neighbors, the Etruscans and the Italian Greeks, the Romans seemed to be a crude peasant folk. Actually, for all the growth of commerce, agriculture remained the fundamental occupation. Far from the sea, they had no understanding of seafaring and shipbuilding. They left it to foreign merchants and seamen to come to them and do business. This trait did not change. It is a partial explanation of the fact that at the time of Caesar and his first successors, that is at the time of the rise of Christianity, the Jews had so large a colony in Rome. At that time they had got into their hands a part of Roman commerce. So today in Constantinople trade is principally in the hands of non-Turks.

The more Rome flourished through her trade, the more she came into conflict with her neighbors. The market for foodstuffs that was opened up by commerce produced in the Roman land-owners a drive to increase their landholdings at the expense of their neighbors, who in turn hankered for the riches of the city. Then too conflicts arose out of the competition with the Etruscan cities. The young community had to endure many long hard wars, but emerged victorious from them thanks to the double position we have spoken of. The peasants were beaten by the more advanced technology and the firm organization of the big city; the Etruscans, who had already gone down in military strength because of the supplanting of the free peasantry by forced labor, lost to the tenacity and endurance of the Roman peasants.

As soon as Rome had become strong enough to subdue the Etruscans, it learned what an excellent business war can be. There is much more wealth to be got in successful wars than in trade, which mostly was carried on by foreigners anyway, or in agriculture which yielded only meager surplus under the conditions of small-scale farming; and especially so when the wars were waged against rich cities and nations that could be plundered and laid under tribute. Commerce and robbery are related to each other in any event; but no other commercial city put robbery in the foreground and raised it to a government institution, in fact made it the basis of the city's greatness, as did Rome.

As soon as Rome has conquered the Etruscan cities, plundered them and made them tributaries, it turned on its rich neighbors to the south whose growing wealth had brought with it a decline in their military power, in accordance with the process described above; the booty was thus easier to get in the measure that it was more valuable. This wealth however attracted another peasant nation, the Samnites, at the same time. They had to be driven out of the competition before the Greek cities in Southern Italy could be conquered. Peasant nation fought peasant nation, but the Samnites had no great city like Rome to give the peasant fighting forces a centralized organization. They lost, and then the way was open for Rome to the rich cities of South Italy, which were now plundered and subjugated.

From Southern Italy it was but a step to Sicily, which was just as rich as Greek Italy and had an equal attraction for the Roman robber hordes. There however they came up against a dangerous enemy, the Carthaginians. Carthage, a powerful commercial city near present-day Tunis, had conquered the western part of the north coast of Africa, following the same robber drive as Rome, and was now trying to do the same thing in Sicily. It was a colony of the Phoenecians, who had early been led to seafaring by the very nature of their country and in that domain had attained a marked superiority. Carthage too achieved its greatness and its wealth through seafaring. It bred seamen, not peasants. Instead of a peasant economy it developed a latifundia economy with cheap captured slaves and, along with that, mining. It therefore had no peasant national army. As soon as they had to leave the coast and go inland to hold their controlling position, they needed an army and had to use mercenaries.

The struggle between Rome and Carthage, known as the three Punic Wars, began in 264 B.C. and ended in 146 with the complete destruction of Carthage. It had been decided when Hannibal was defeated, after which the second Punic War ended, in 201. These were wars between mercenary armies and peasant armies, between professionals and a militia. The former often won; Rome was on the brink of being defeated by Hannibal; but in the end the militia army, defending its own hearths, proved to be more tenacious and forced its opponent to the ground. Carthage was razed and its inhabitants wiped out. Its enormous wealth in latifundia, mines, and subject cities fell as booty to the victor.

With this the most dangerous enemy of Rome had fallen, and Rome ruled unchallenged in the Western Mediterranean, and soon in the Eastern basin as well. The countries of that region were in decline, going the way of ancient civilization—the supplanting of the free peasants by forced labor by slaves or serfs and their ruin by endless wars, and the replacement of the militias by mercenaries; they had gone so far on this road and become so weak in military strength that they could no longer offer any significant opposition to Rome's armies. One city after another, one country after another fell almost of its own weight, to be plundered and put under perpetual tribute. From now on Rome remained the ruler of the old civilized world until the Germanic barbarians dealt out the same fate to it that it had to the Greeks, despite the fact that the Greeks were far more advanced than the Romans in science and art. As in economics and politics, Rome was in philosophy and art too merely a plunderer of the Greeks. Its great thinkers and poets were almost entirely plagiarists.

The richest lands of the world at that time, in which the untold treasures of centuries, or as in Egypt thousands of years, of culture had been accumulated, were delivered to the looting and extortions of Rome.

It was only as a democracy that Rome could develop the enormous military effort that brought this brilliant result, only as a city in whose existence all the classes of its population were interested although not in the same way. In a long and bitter struggle from the sixth to the fourth centuries B.C. the new citizens, the plebeians, had succeeded in wresting one privilege after another from the old citizens, the patricians, until finally every legal distinction between the two orders had disappeared and the assembly of all the citizens made the laws and elected the highest officials, the consuls, praetors and aediles; on the expiration of their terms these officials entered the Senate, which actually ruled the whole state.

These conquests however did not give the Roman people mastery in the state, but only the right to choose its masters. The more the lumpenproletariat came to predominate in Rome, the more the right of democracy became a means of extorting money and entertainments from the candidates, a means of getting handouts.

We have already become acquainted with the clients, who were at the service of the rich lords, for all sorts of services. If they had the right to vote, there was no more important service they could render than to vote as their protector, the patron, wanted them to. Every rich Roman, every rich family, had many votes in the assembly at its disposal to give to the clique they belonged to. A few cliques of rich families thus held control of the state in their hands by getting their members elected to the higher offices and thus into the Senate. The only change that democracy introduced was to allow the rich plebeian families to push their way into this circle, which formerly under aristocratic rule had been limited to patricians only.

The newly elected consuls and praetors had to spend their first year of office in Rome. In their second year each of them took over the government of a province, where he tried to get back the money he had spent on getting elected and if possible something over for himself. For he had no salary. The offices were "offices of honor." On the other hand, the hope of getting rich in the provinces by extortion and bribery, and sometimes even by direct robbery, was one of the reasons for seeking office, so that the various candidates, vying for popular favor, kept raising the scale of gifts and offerings.

But the more the various methods of buying votes improved the lumpenproletarian's chances of gaining some advantage by selling his civic rights, the more the peasants, who possessed Roman citizenship, must have felt tempted to give up their hard poor existence on the land and come to Rome. This further increased the size of the voting lumpenproletariat and the corresponding demands on the candidate's purse. In Caesar's time there were in Rome no less than 320,000 Roman citizens receiving free grain from the state; the number of votes for sale must have been something on the same order. It can be imagined what sums an election required.

In the year 53 B.C. the buying of votes caused such a demand for coin that the interest rate rose sharply and there was a money crisis.[7]

"The nobility (office-seeking nobles) had to pay dear," says Mommsen. "A gladiatorial show cost 720,000 sesterces [$35,000].

7. Salvioli, *Le capitalisme dans le monde antique,* 1906, p. 243.

But they paid willingly, because by it they shut political careers off from the propertyless."[8]

And they had to pay often, since there were new elections every year; but they paid not out of idealistic motives but because they knew that they were just buying the opportunity for more profitable plundering of the provinces; they were doing good business.

"Democracy," that is the rule of the population of the whole Roman Empire of about 50 to 60 million people by a few hundred thousand Roman citizens, thus became one of the most powerful means of raising the looting and exploitation of the provinces to an extreme, because it increased the number of those sharing in it. And it was not only the governors who carried on these extortions, but each took with him a crowd of "friends," who had helped in his election and now went out in order to steal and rob under his protection.

But that was not all; in addition, Roman usury capital was loosed on the provinces, where it had a devastating influence and grew to a scale reached nowhere else in the ancient world.

USURY

Usury itself is age-old, almost as old as trade. It can not be traced back to the Stone Age, but it is surely older than money. As soon as there were distinct households with definite family property, there was the possibility of having one family richer than another in cattle, land or slaves, while others became poor. Peasants in difficulties would be likely to borrow something from their better-off neighbors, for example some of their surplus cattle or grain, pledging to return it with something added or to perform some labor for the loan—the beginning of debt slavery. Such usurious transactions are possible under a natural economy, without the use of money. Large landholding and usury are closely interwined from their beginnings, and usury capital— known today as high finance—and large landholding have often got along very well together. In Rome too the large landowners

8. *Römische Geschichte*, vol. I, p. 809.

were usurers as far back as we can trace their history; the clash between patricians and plebeians was not merely a conflict between aristocracy and democracy over political rights, not merely a conflict between large landholders and peasantry over the public lands, but also a conflict between usurers and debtors.

Meanwhile the productivity of peasant labor and hence the surplus it produced were so small that it required the exploitation of great masses of men to assure the exploiters any considerable wealth. So long as the Roman aristocrats only despoiled the peasants of the areas around Rome, there was not too much to be got no matter how hard they squeezed the victims. Their affairs flourished much more brilliantly and brought in much more wealth through access to the new empire, the then entire civilized world.

Here a division of labor took place. Taking usurious interest from neighbors was not a business that required particular attention. The aristocrats could easily take care of that while farming their lands and governing the state. But it was hard to manage the usurious exploitation of Spain and Syria, Gaul and North Africa, and at the same time carry on the affairs of so enormous a state. The business of usury became more and more something distinct from the business of the state. Along with the high officials who robbed the provinces in the course of their functions as generals and governors, without disdaining a profitable piece of business here and there, a special class of usury capitalists arose, organized into a separate social order of "knights." As the number of these moneyed capitalists increased, the variety of their enterprises grew as well.

One of the principal ways of plundering the provinces was the farming of the taxes. As yet there was no bureaucracy to whom tax collection could be entrusted. The easiest way was to hand the function over to a wealthy Roman, who turned over the amount of the tax to the state and saw to it that he did not lose in the transaction. It was a system like the one that still prevails in many parts of the Orient and serves to devastate them. For the tax farmer of course does not stop with the sum that is coming to him. The provincials are handed over to him and are bled white without mercy.

It often happened however that single cities or tributary kings could not pay the sums imposed on them. Here again the Roman men of money were prepared to advance the needed sums, naturally at a suitable rate of interest. For example, Junius Brutus, the great republican, made "excellent speculations by lending money to the King of Cappadocia and the city of Salamis; with the latter he made a loan at the rate of 48% interest." (Salvioli, *op. cit.*, p. 42). This was not an exceptionally high rate. Loans to cities were made, as Salvioli shows, at as high as 75%. In risky cases it was even higher. Thus in Caesar's time the great banking house of Rabirius lent its entire fortune and that of its friends to the exiled king Ptolemy of Egypt at 100% interest. Rabirius miscalculated, for when Ptolemy regained his throne, he did not pay his debt, and jailed the importunate creditor, who tried to treat all Egypt as his own domain. The financier managed to escape to Rome, and Caesar gave him the chance of making a new fortune in contracts for supplies for the African war.

This was still another method of making money. The tribute of the subject provinces that flowed into the Roman treasury was enormous. But the perpetual wars cost money too. They were one way in which the financiers got their hands on large sums out of that part of the loot of the provinces that did not go directly to them but was delivered to the state. They contracted for war supplies—still a method for making large fortunes today. They also took interest from their own state itself, when it was caught short of funds, something that happened often enough, for the more it took from the provinces, the more parasites of all sorts there were to share in the profits. Sometimes the state needed such large sums that no individual could furnish them, and joint stock companies were formed for the purpose. Just as usury is the first form of capitalist exploitation, it forms the first function of corporations.

The moneyed men of Rome "founded societies, corresponding to our banking corporations, with directors, cashiers, agents, etc.

At the time of Sulla there was the company of the *Asiani* [the Asia Company] with a large enough capital to lend the state 20,000 talents [$25,000,000]. Twelve years later they had run this debt up to 120,000 talents. . . . Small capital sums were invested in shares of the big companies, so that as Polybius says (VI, 17) the whole city (of Rome) was interested in the various financial enterprises of a few prominent firms. The smallest savings had their share in the undertakings of the *publicani,* that is in the farming of the taxes and the public domains, which yielded extraordinary profits." (Salvioli, *op. cit.,* p. 40 f.).

All this sounds very modern to us; and it does show that Roman society had reached the threshold of modern capitalism at the time of the rise of Christianity; and yet the effects of that old capitalism were quite different from those of the modern variety.

The methods we have described here are roughly the same as those by which modern capitalism was founded, which Marx denoted as those of "primary accumulation": expropriation of the peasantry, plundering the colonies, slave trading, trade wars and government debts. In modern times as in antiquity we find the same destructive and devastating effects of these methods. But the difference is that antiquity was able to develop only the destructive effects of capitalism, while modern capitalism derives from these destructions the conditions for the construction of a new and higher mode of production. To be sure the method of modern capitalism's development is no less barbaric and gruesome; but it creates the basis for rising above this bloody destruction, while ancient capitalism could not.

We saw the basis for this in the previous chapter. Only a minute fraction of what modern capitalism scrapes together by plunder and extortion and all sorts of acts of violence is used for enjoyment; most of it goes to create new, higher means of production and increases the productivity of human labor. The capitalism of the ancient world did not possess the conditions for any' such process. In so far as it entered into the mode of production at all, it could only replace the labor of the free peasants by that of slaves; in the decisive branches of production this meant a technical regression, a decline in the productivity of social labor, an impoverishment of society.

That part of the gains of the Roman financiers and of the booty of Roman generals and officials that did not go into new usurious deals, that is into further plunderings, could have only two outlets: one in pleasures and the creation of means of enjoyment—including not only palaces but temples as well; and the other, except for the acquisition of a mine or two, was the purchase of landed property, that is the expropriation of free peasants and their replacement by slaves.

The plundering and devastation of the provinces only served to give the wealthy men of Rome means of reducing the productivity of social labor even more quickly by spreading slavery than would have been possible otherwise. The devastation was not compensated for by an economic advance elsewhere, as happens at least occasionally with modern capitalism; instead devastation in once place only hastened the decline elsewhere. And so thanks to Rome's world domination the general impoverishment of the ancient world after the beginning of our era took place even sooner than it would have otherwise.

For a long time however the signs of economic bankruptcy were masked by the glamour arising from the fact that in a few decades there was brought to Rome everything that hundreds or thousands of years of diligent artistic work had produced in all the centers of civilization around the Mediterranean. The political bankruptcy of the system came to light much sooner than the economic bankruptcy.

ABSOLUTISM

Rome killed political life in all the regions it conquered breaking their power of resistance and depriving them of all independence. All the politics of the enormous empire was concentrated in the one city of Rome. But in whom was the political life vested there? Moneyed men, whose only concern was how to pile interest on interest; aristocrats, reeling from one pleasure to another, to whom any regular work or effort, even government or making war, was repulsive; and lumpenproletarians, whose only means of support was selling their political power to the highest bidder.

For example, in his biography of Caesar, Suetonius reports the leader's expenditures after the civil wars: "He distributed to the people, in addition to ten modii of grain and the same number of pounds of oil, the 300 sesterces he had previously promised, and 100 more as interest for the delay. [That is, twenty dollars at a time when a man could get by on two cents a day.—K.K.] He also undertook [for those renting dwellings in Rome.—K.K.] to pay a year's rent up to 2000 sesterces [$100] in Rome and up to 500 in Italy [$25]. To this he added a great banquet [for 250,000 people. —K.K.] and a distribution of meat, and after the victory in Spain two breakfasts into the bargain. Because the first breakfast seemed miserly to him and unworthy of his liberality, he had a second one prepared five days later, very sumptuous" (chap. 28).

In addition, he gave entertainments of unheard-of splendor. An actor, Decimus Laberius, received 500,000 ($25,000) sesterces for a single performance.

And about Augustus, Suetonius says: "He often distributed bounties to the people, but not always in the same amount, sometimes 400 sesterces [$20], sometimes 300, often only 250 per man. And once he did not omit young boys, although as a rule they only received the bounty from the age of eleven on. Likewise he often had grain sold at a very low price in scarcity years, sometimes even given away free, and at those times doubled the amount to be distributed in money" (*Octavius*, chap. 41).

Obviously a proletariat that let itself be bought in this way, that made a system out of venality right out in the open, had lost all political independence. It was no longer anything more than a tool in the hands of the highest bidder. The struggle for power in the state became a competition among a small number of robbers who had been able to amass the largest booty and therefore had the best credit with the financiers.

This factor was enormously strengthened by the rise of the

mercenary soldiery. The army became more and more the master of the republic. As the mercenary soldiery increased, the fighting capacity of the Roman citizens fell; or rather, the decline of their fighting capacity conditioned the growth of the mercenary soldiery. All the elements of the people that were capable of fighting were in the army; the part of the people outside of it kept losing both its ability and its desire to bear arms.

There were however two special factors tending to make the army deteriorate more and more into a willing tool of any general who gave or promised them enough pay and loot, and to make the soldiers indifferent to political considerations. The first cause was the increasing number of non-Romans, of provincials, and finally of foreigners in the army, elements that had no civic rights and were thus completely excluded from the political life of Rome; the second was the increasing unwillingness of the pleasure-seeking, flabby aristocracy to do military service. Heretofore they had furnished the officers; now their place was more and more taken by professional or career officers, who were not economically independent, like the aristocrat, and moreover had not the slightest interest in the party struggles in Rome, which were really struggles among aristocratic cliques.

The more non-Romans there were in the army and the more the aristocratic officers were replaced by career men, the more willing the army was to sell itself to the highest bidder and make him the ruler of Rome.

In this way the foundations were laid for Caesarism, by having the richest man in Rome buy up the republic by purchasing its political power. It was also the basis for having a successful general with an army at his back try to make himself the richest man of Rome; the simplest way to do this was to expropriate his opponents and confiscate their property.

The political life of the last century of the republic consists basically in nothing but "civil wars,"—a most misleading term, since the citizens had nothing whatsoever to say about these wars. They were not wars of citizens, but wars between individual politicians, who were for the most part as greedy for money as they were successful as generals; they murdered and robbed each other until finally Augustus succeeded in overcoming all competition and setting up a permanent monarchy.

To a certain extent Caesar had succeeded in doing this before him. Caesar, an aristocratic adventurer, had conspired to take over the state with two of the richest Roman financiers, Pompey and Crassus. The latter is described by Mommsen in this way: "His fortune had been founded on the buying up of confiscated estates during the revolution; but despised no means of gain; he carried on building operations in the capital carefully and on a large scale; he went into partnership with his freedmen in the most diverse enterprises; he acted as banker in and out of Rome, himself and through agents; he advanced money to his colleagues in the Senate and undertook to do public works on their accounts or bribe the courts, as the case might be. He was not choosy in making profits. . . . He did not refuse to take an inheritance for the mere reason that the will in which his name occurred was notoriously a forged one."[9]

But Caesar was no better. No means to acquire money were too foul. Suetonius, whom we have often cited, tells in his biography of Caesar of this man whom Mommsen later glorified: "He did not show unselfishness either as general or as statesman. As many witnesses have testified, when he was proconsul in Spain he took money for the allies, in fact begged it, to pay his debts, and looted several cities of Lusitania as though they were enemy cities, although they had submitted and opened their doors at his approach. In Gaul he robbed the temples and shrines with their stores of offerings; he destroyed cities more for the sake of the booty than on account of any offences they had committed. By these means he got gold in such quantities that he had it put up for sale and sold in Italy and the provinces at 3000 sesterces the pound [$150.].[10] During his first consulate he stole three thousand pounds of gold from the Capitol and replaced it by the same amount of

9. *Römische Geschichte,* III, 14.
10. Ordinarily gold was worth 4000 sesterces the pound. Caesar's Gallic lootings brought its price down in Italy by fully one-fourth.

gilded copper. He sold alliances and kingdoms for money; for example he took almost 6000 talents [$7,500,000] from Ptolemy, King of Egypt, in his own name and Pompey's. Later on he met the crushing costs of civil wars, triumphs and festivities by the crudest extortions and temple robberies" (*Julius Caesar*, chap. 54).

It was primarily in order to gain money that Caesar undertook the war against Gaul, which hitherto had been free of Roman rule and so unplundered. The rich booty he stole there enabled him to stand on his own feet and break off his friendship with Pompey, with whom he had shared the business of mastery up to then. The third partner, Crassus, had fallen in a robber expedition against the Parthians in Asia, in which, as Appian says, "he hoped to gain not only much fame but also stores of money"[11]— in the same way that Caesar had been doing in Gaul at the same time.

After Crassus' death only Pompey stood in Caesar's way; and around Pompey the remainder of the politically active aristocracy rallied. The great Julius finished them off in a series of campaigns, which once more brought him rich loot.

"It is said that in his triumph [at the end of the civil war] he carried 60,000 talents of silver, together with 2822 golden crowns, weighing 2414 pounds. Immediately after his triumph he used these treasures to satisfy his army; going beyond his promises, he gave every soldier 5000 Attic drachmas [$1000], every non-commissioned officer twice as much and every higher officer twice as much again."[12] What he gave the proletariat of Rome as largess, we have already reported from Suetonius.

From that time on Caesar's one-man rule was not publicly contested, and it was only by assassination that the republicans could protest. Caesar's heirs, Antony and Augustus, then disposed of the republicans.

Thus the Roman Empire became the domain, the private property of a single man, the Caesar or Emperor. All political life came

11. *History of the Civil Wars*, Book II, chap. 3. Appian testifies that the Parthians had not shown the slightest hostility. The war against them was therefore nothing more than a robber expedition.
12. Appian, *History of the Civil Wars*, Book II, chap. 15.

to an end. The administration of this domain became the private affair of its proprietor. Like any other property, it was under all sorts of attacks; robbers, that is successful generals with a strong army to support them often menaced the current possessor, who was sometimes killed by his own bodyguard so that they could sell the vacant throne to the highest bidder. But this was a business deal no worse than many another that was going on at the same time; it was not a political action. Political life came completely to an end. In fact there appeared, first among the lower classes and then among the upper classes too, not merely indifference towards the state, but hate towards it and its officials, against its judges, its tax collectors, its soldiers, against the very emperors, who no longer protected anyone and were a torment even to the wealthy classes who had to defend themselves against the emperors as they did against the barbarians.

After Caesar's victory there were only a few spots in the Roman world empire which still retained remnants of a political life. These remnants were soon wiped out by Caesar's successors. The last place in which a vigorous political life survived was the capital of Palestine, Jerusalem. It required the most violent efforts to destroy this last fortress of political freedom in the Roman Empire. After a long and obstinate siege Jerusalem was razed to the ground in the year 70 A.D., and the Jewish people were robbed of their homeland.

BOOK TWO: SOCIETY IN THE
ROMAN EMPIRE

3

THOUGHT AND SENTIMENT IN THE
AGE OF THE ROMAN EMPIRE

INSECURITY

As WE HAVE seen, the age in which Christianity arose was a time of utter decomposition of traditional forms of production and government. Correspondingly, there was a total breakdown of traditional ways of thinking. There was a general search and groping for new ways of thinking. In this task the individual felt himself all alone, for all the social support he had found hitherto in his commune or *Markgenossenschaft* and their traditional moral views had now disappeared. Thus one of the predominant traits of the new way of thinking is individualism. This can never signify that the individual is completely isolated from social relationships. This is impossible. The human individual can only exist in society and through society. But individualism does mean that the social context in which the individual had grown up and which had heretofore seemed the natural and obvious way of life loses its power, and the individual is now faced with the task of making a way for himself outside this old context. He can do so only by combining with others with like needs and like interests to form new social organizations. The nature of these organizations is, to be sure, determined by the existing conditions and does not depend on the caprice of individuals. But the individual is not confronted

by some ready made and completed institutions, as he is in the
case of traditional organizations; they have to be created by him
together with others striving in the same direction. Many errors
and tremendous differences of opinion can and must occur until
finally out of the strife of opinions and experiments new organisms arise that best answer to the new conditions, that can endure
and so furnish future generations with the same firm support as
the old organizations they have supplanted. In such transitional
times there is the illusion that society does not condition the individual, but rather vice versa, as though social forms, tasks and
purposes depended entirely on his whim.

A similar individualism, a similar individual search and groping for new ways of thinking and new social organizations marked
the age of liberalism that followed the breakup of the feudal organizations without putting new social organizations at once in
their stead, until gradually the new organizations of workers and
employers came more and more to constitute the decisive elements
of capitalist society.

The decomposition of old and formation of new social organizations lend the first centuries of the Roman Empire a great
resemblance to the nineteenth century. They have the further
resemblance that in both periods the collapse of the old organizations took place earliest and most spectacularly in the big cities,
and that social life was more and more determined by these cities.

Social life gave the peasant few occasions for reflection in the
days of their strength and complacency, since that life was rigidly
fixed for him by use and custom. He did have to reflect on nature,
with which he was in constant conflict, which always had new
surprises for him and with which he had to cope if he was to exist.
The question of why the various natural phenomena came into
being was very close to him. He looked naively for the answer at
first in personification of the single forces of nature, by assuming
numerous gods as active in nature; but this way of putting the
question implicitly included the beginnings of natural science,
which asks for the why, for the causes of all things. As soon as men
began to realize that the connection between cause and effect is

regular and necessary, and does not depend on the caprice of personal divinities, they had entered on the road of scientific knowledge.

Such an accomplishment could not come from peasants who were in total dependence on nature. They bowed down meekly before the forces of nature, which they did not try to master by knowledge, but to mollify by prayer and sacrifice. Scientific knowledge of nature is possible only in cities, where man is not so immediately and intensely aware of his dependence on nature, so that he can start to observe it dispassionately. It was only in cities too that there arose a ruling class that had leisure enough to observe and did not succumb to the desire to use its leisure for merely bodily pleasures, as the landowners did on their estates in the country, where physical strength and endurance play such a large part in production and leisure and surplus give rise only to coarse pleasures like feasting and riding to hounds.

Natural philosophy began in the cities, but gradually many of these cities grew so large that their inhabitants began to get out of touch with nature and lose interest in her. More and more the cities took the leading role in the spiritual and economic life of extensive regions; and this development, as we have seen, dissolved all the social support that the individual had previously found in traditional organizations and ways of thought. In addition, it intensified the class contradictions and gave rise to bitterer class conflicts, leading sometimes to the overthrow of all hitherto accepted social relationships. It was now society, rather than nature, that kept bringing new surprises to men in the great cities and setting them new tasks every day, every day raising the question: what is to be done?

It was not the reasons why things happened in nature that were uppermost in men's minds now, but the question of what they ought to do in society: not the knowledge of necessary natural connections, but the apparently free postulation of new social purposes. Ethics replaced natural philosophy, and took the form of the quest for the supreme happiness of the individual. This had already been so in the Hellenic world after the Persian wars. The Roman world, we have seen, was but a plagiarist of the Greeks in art and science; they got their treasures by plunder, not by work, in the intellectual realm as well as the material. The Romans got to know Greek philosophy at a time when the ethical interest outweighed the interest in the knowledge of nature. Accordingly Roman thought too did not concern itself much with natural philosophy and turned its attention immediately to ethics.

In the first centuries of the Empire two tendencies in the wisdom of life dominated philosophical thought: the doctrine of Epicurus and Stoicism.

Epicurus called philosophy an activity that brings about a happy life by means of concepts and proofs. He believed this would be achieved by striving for pleasure, but only for rational lasting enjoyment, not for transitory sensual dissipations, which lead to the loss of health and wealth, and hence to pain.

This was a philosophy very well suited to a class of exploiters that found no other employment for their wealth than to consume it. What they needed was a rational regulation of the life of enjoyment. But this theory gave no consolation to those, and their number kept growing, who had already suffered bodily, spiritual or financial shipwreck; nor to the poor and wretched, nor to the satiated, those who were revolted by pleasures. And not to those who still had an interest in the traditional forms of the community and still followed goals beyond their own personality, those patriots who grieved to see the decline of state and society, without being able to prevent it. For all these groups the pleasures of this world seemed stale and vain. They turned to the Stoic doctrine, which valued not pleasure but virtue as the highest good, as the only blessedness, and held external goods, health, wealth, etc. to be matters just as indifferent as external evils.

This ended by leading many people to turn away from the world altogether, to despise life, even to long for death. Suicide became common in Imperial Rome; it actually became fashionable.

But it was remarkable that, along with the longing for death, a real terror of death grew up in Roman society.

A citizen of a commune of classical antiquity felt himself to be a member of a great entity that survived him when he died, that was immortal compared to him. He continued to exist in his community; it bore the traces of his work, and he needed no other immortality. Actually, we find in the peoples of antiquity, who did not have a long cultural development in back of them, either no ideas at all as to life after death, or else the idea of a shadowy existence, arising out of the need for explaining the appearance of the dead in dreams: a miserable life that one had rather be without. We are familiar with the complaint of Achilles' shade: "Would that I were on earth a menial, bound to some insubstantial man who must pinch and scrape to keep alive! Life so were better than King of Kings among the dead men who have had their day and died." (*Odyssey*, xi, 489-491 Lawrence's translation).

The assumption of a shadowy life after death was, as we have said, a naive hypothesis aimed at explaining certain dream phenomena. It did not arise from a need of the soul.

It was a different matter when the community was dying and the individual was breaking away from it. He no longer had the feeling that his actions lived on in the state, to which he was in fact indifferent or even hostile; and yet he could not bear to think of complete annihilation. There arose a fear of death such as antiquity had never known before. Cowardice took root; death became a bugbear, instead of the brother of sleep that he had been.

More and more men felt the need of a doctrine that would assert the immortality of the individual, not as an unessential shadow but as a blissful being. Soon bliss was no longer sought in earthly pleasure, not even in earthly virtue, but in the attainment of a better world beyond, for which this wretched life is but a preparation. This conception found strong support in Plato's doctrine, and that was the way in which the Stoic school too developed.

Plato had already taught of a life beyond, in which the souls, freed from their bodies lived on and received rewards and punishments for their deeds on earth. In the thirteenth chapter of the tenth book of his *Republic* he tells of a Pamphylian who had fallen in war. On the twelfth day after his death, as he was about to be cremated, he suddenly awoke and related how his soul, after leaving his body, had come to a wondrous place where there were fissures, part leading to heaven, part to the inner parts of the earth. There judges sat in judgment on the souls that came, showing the just the way to the right to heaven, where inconceivable beauty holds sway, and pointing out to the unjust the way down on the left into the bowels of the earth, into a subterranean abyss, where they must make good their earthly sins tenfold. The incurably wicked are seized by wild men, fiery to behold, and chained and tortured. For the others, however, in the abyss, and for those in heaven, a new life begins after a thousand years. The Pamphylian, who had seen all this, had been charged to relate it and brought to life again by a miracle.

Who can help thinking here of heaven and hell in the Christian sense, the sheep on the right hand and the goats on the left, the everlasting fire prepared in Hell (Matthew, 25, verses 33 and 41), and the dead who lived again "until the thousand years were finished" (Revelation, 20, verse 5), and so forth? And yet Plato lived in the fourth century B.C.

It sounds equally Christian when we read the following: "The body is the soul's burden and punishment. It weighs down on the soul and keeps it in bonds." It was not a Christian who wrote this, however, but the Stoic philosopher Seneca, teacher and minister of Nero, the persecutor of Christians.

Another passage has a similar sound: "By this carcass the soul is hidden, varnished over, contaminated, separated from what is true and its own, cast into deception; its whole battle is against the burdensome flesh. It strives thither, to the place from which it was sent forth: there eternal rest awaits it; there, after this massive and confused world it beholds the pure and clear."

There are a surprising number of other expressions to be found in Seneca which also appear in the New Testament. Thus Seneca says, for example: "Put on the spirit of a great man." Bruno

Bauer is right in comparing this expression with that of Paul's Epistle to the Romans: "Put ye on the Lord Jesus Christ" (13, verse 14) and the Epistle to the Galatians: "For as many of you as have been baptized into Christ have put on Christ" (3, verse 27). The inference has been drawn from these coincidences that Seneca borrowed from Christian sources, even that he was a Christian. This is a product of Christian fantasy. Seneca wrote before the various parts of the New Testament were composed; if there was any borrowing, it should rather be assumed that the Christians dipped into the widely circulated writings of the fashionable philosopher of the period. One is tempted to assume that both parties independently made use of expressions that were on everybody's tongue at the time.

As to the expression "to put on Christ," etc., Pfleiderer points out that it derives from the Persian cult of Mithras, which was very popular in Imperial Rome. He says, of the influence of this cult on Christian ideas: "The Mithraic sacraments also included the sacred meal, in which the consecrated bread and a chalice with water or wine served the believers in Mithras as the mystic symbol of the communication of the divine life; the faithful appeared at this festival in animal masks, in order to suggest that the celebrants had 'put on' their god, that is, had entered into an inmost community of life with him. This has its close parallel in the Pauline doctrine of the sacramental meal as a communication of the blood and body of Christ (I Corinthians, 10, verse 16), whom the baptized have 'put on' (Galatians, 3, verse 27)" (Pfleiderer, *Die Entstehung des Christentums*, 1907, p. 130).

Seneca is not the only philosopher of his time who formulated or used expressions that sound Christian to us.

In the particular, the ideas we are now dealing with, the immortality of the soul and the beyond, had any number of adherents in the era of the origin of Christianity. Thus for example, the Alexandrian Jew Philo, who lived at the beginning of our era, ended his first book on the allegories of the holy laws with the sentence: "True, Heraclitus has said, 'We live their (the gods') death, and die their life'; when we are alive, the soul is dead and buried in the body as in a funeral mound, while the soul lives its own life when we are dead, and is freed from the evil and the corpse of the life tied to the body."

More and more, preparation for the life to come seemed far more important than the fight for the goods of this world. The kingdom of God replaced the kingdom of this world. But how was it to be found? Formerly the citizen had had three clear and reliable guides to action in tradition, the will of the people and the needs of the community. These were gone now. Tradition had become an empty shadow; the people no longer felt it had a common will; the needs of the community had become a matter of indifference. The individual stood helpless, abandoned to himself, in the stream of new ideas and new relations pouring into society, and looked around for a new firm point of support, for teachings and teachers that would teach truth and the right wisdom of life, and show him the right way to the kingdom of God. As always, when a new need arises, there were many men who sought to satisfy it. They began to preach an individual morality, a morality by means of which the individual, without any change in society, would rise out of and above this world and become a worthy citizen of a better one.

What else could rhetorical and philosophical ability resort to? All political activity had come to an end; interest in the study of the causes of things, scientific activity had broken down. What other outlet was left for the energy of orators and philosophers than to try cases for the winning of property or teach the morality of despising property, to become a preacher or a jurist? And in fact both of these fields were well cultivated in the days of the Empire, and the Romans made notable contributions in the form of declamations on the nullity of the goods of this world as well as in paragraphs on the defence of these same goods. It became the fashion to make edifying speeches and make up and compile edifying sayings and anecdotes. At bottom the gospels are nothing more than a reworking of this sort of collections of sayings and anecdotes.

Naturally this era should not be judged only by its moralizing rhetoric. The new morality, with its contempt of the world, did, it is true, answer strong spiritual needs arising out of very real social conditions. But in reality it was impossible to escape from the world; it always proved to be the stronger. Thus there arose the contradiction between moral theory and moral practice that is inevitable in this sort of morality.

Seneca, whom we have often mentioned, is a classic example. This noble Stoic moralized against participation in politics and blamed Brutus for violating the basic precepts of Stoicism by such a participation. But this same Seneca, who reproached the republican Brutus for taking part in political strife, was a party to all the crimes of Agrippina and Nero and acted as bawd for them just to remain minister. The same Seneca thundered in his writings against riches, greed and the love of pleasure. In the year 58 of our era he had to hear Suilius denounce him in the Senate for having amassed his millions through legacy-hunting and usury. According to Dio Cassius one of the causes of the rebellion of the Britons under Nero was that Seneca had forced on them a loan of ten million denarii ($1,700,000) at a high rate of interest and then called it all in at once with the utmost severity. The orator who praised poverty left a fortune of 300 million sesterces (15 million dollars), one of the greatest of the age.

Compared to this imposing example of genuine hypocrisy it has almost an air of futility when the satirist Lucian a hundred years later, in his *Hermotimus,* mocks an imaginary Stoic philosopher who teaches contempt of money and pleasures and promises that his doctrine will give one noble equanimity in all the vicissitudes of life, and sues his pupils in court when they fail to pay the school fee agreed upon, who gets drunk at banquets and argues so heatedly that he throws a silver cup at the head of his opponent.

Moralizing became fashionable in the Empire. But people were looking not merely for moral theories for dependent helpless spirits to lean on, once they had lost all contact with common public activity and tradition; they felt the need of a personal support. Epicurus had already said: "We must pick out a noble man to have always in our mind's eye, so that we may live as though he were looking on, and act as though he saw our actions." Seneca cites this passage and continues: "We need a protector and tutor. A great many sins will be avoided if there is a witness alongside the one who is making the false step. The spirit must have someone whom it honors with a reverence that touches its inmost essence. Even the thought of such helpers has power to regulate and improve. He is a watchman, model and rule, without which what is twisted can not be restored to order."

People fell into the habit of choosing a dead great man as patron saint. They went further than that, and submitted their actions to the control of men still living, moral preachers who made pretensions that their lofty morality raised them above the rest of mankind. Stoicism had already declared that the philosopher was free from errors and weaknesses. Now, along with sanctimoniousness and hypocrisy, there developed the Pharisaical arrogance of the moral teachers—qualities that were totally alien to classical antiquity, that arose from a time of social dissolution and necessarily came to the foreground more as science was replaced by ethics in philosophy, that is the study of the world was subordinated to the making of demands on the individual.

There were now moral preachers for every class, undertaking to raise men to greater moral completeness on the pattern of their own sublime personality. For the proletariat, philosophers of the Cynic school presented themselves, disciples of the notorious Diogenes; these men preached in the streets, lived by begging and saw happiness in dirt and freedom from needs, which liberated them from any work; work they hated and despised as grevious sin. Christ and his apostles too are presented as begging street preachers. None of the gospels has anything to do with work. For all their contradictions they are in accord on that point.

The nobles however had their own house moralists, belonging to the Stoic school for the most part.

"After the fashion of the powerful since the time of the Scipios, Augustus had his own philosopher around in the person of Areus, a Stoic from Alexandria; to him he intrusted Livia to derive consolation after the death of her son Drusus. Augustus had Areus in his suite when he entered Alexandria after the battle of Actium and told his fellow-citizens, in the speech in which he pardoned the Alexandrians for their support of Marc Antony, that Areus was one of the reasons for his mildness. Spiritual guides of the same sort in other palaces and houses cared for the spiritual needs of the mighty. Formerly teachers of a new theory, they were for the Romans, after the civil wars, practical shepherds of souls, spiritual directors, consolers in misfortune, confessors. They accompanied the victims of the Emperor's arbitrary will to their deaths, and gave them the last cheering words. Canus Julius, who received his death sentence by the Emperor Caligula with thanksgiving and died with calm and composure, was accompanied by 'his philosopher' on his last march. When Thrasea went into the room in which he had his veins opened, he was accompanied by his son-in-law Helvidius and by the Cynic Demetrius, as chaplain, and in the torments of the slow death kept his eyes on Demetrius" (B. Bauer, *Christus und die Cäsaren*, p. 22 f.).

Thus even before the rise of Christianity we see the father confessor appear on the stage and a new historical factor enter into the countries of Europe, theocracy, not because of the teachings of a single man, but in virtue of the new conditions. There had long been priests among the Romans and Greeks, of course, but they had small importance in the state. It was only under the Empire that there arose in the countries of Europe the conditions for a theocracy such as was known in early antiquity in many lands of the Orient. Now there took form in the West as well the preconditions for a spiritual caste, a priestly order as ruler of men, already marked by the presence in so many of its members of the sanctimoniousness and arrogance which are characteristic of the priesthood and which from that day to this have earned it the enmity of any elements of society with strength enough not to need a guardian.

Plato had declared that the state would only be well-ordered when philosophers ruled it and the rest of the citizens had nothing to do with it. Now his dream was realized, in a way which would not have been much to his taste.

But these moral preachers and father confessors were not enough for this unstable generation. The state was in uncontrollable decline. The barbarians were knocking more and more loudly at the doors of the Empire, which was often torn by the bloody rivalries of its generals. And the misery of the masses grew; depopulation increased. Roman society saw its own decline, but it was a generation too corrupt, too sick in body and mind, too cowardly, too much at odds with itself and its surroundings to make an energetic attempt to free itself from its intolerable conditions. It had lost faith in itself, and the only support that kept it from total desperation was hope in help from a higher power, from a savior.

At first this savior was seen in the Caesars. At the time of Augustus a prophecy, of the Sibylline books, circulated, which predicted a savior in the near future.[1] People saw Augustus as a prince of peace who would lead the Empire, torn by the civil wars, into a new epoch of glamour and prosperity, where there would be "peace on earth to men of good will."

But the Caesars brought neither lasting peace nor an economic or moral uplift, despite all the confidence men had in their divine powers. And that was not a little.

People regarded them as gods; even before the doctrine of God's becoming man arose, the doctrine of a man's becoming a god was accepted, and yet this second procedure must obviously be much more difficult than the first.

Where all political life has been wiped out, the head of the state rises so high above the populace that he is a sort of superman, compared to them, since he unites in his own person the entire power and might of society and directs it wherever he desires. On the other hand, the deities were regarded as very human in antiquity. Thus the leap from superman to god was not too violent.

1. Merivale, *The Romans under the Empire*, 1862, VII, 349.

The corrupt Greeks of Asia and Egypt had already begun some centuries before our era to consider their despots as gods or sons of gods. But their philosophers too were similarly honored. A story had arisen about Plato even in his lifetime, mentioned in the funeral oration of his nephew Speusippus, to the effect that his mother Periktione had conceived him not by her husband but by Apollo. As the kingdom of Hellas became Roman provinces, they carried over the divine honors paid their kings and philosophers to the Roman governors.

Julius Caesar however was the first who dared to demand of the Romans what the hireling Greeks gave him: divine honors. He proclaimed himself to be of divine descent. No less a goddess than Venus was his ancestor, something that his nephew Augustus' court poet Virgil later recorded in detail in a long heroic poem, the *Aeneid*.

When Caesar returned to Rome from the civil war as triumphant victor, it was decided in Rome "to erect several temples to him as a god, one of the temples being devoted to him in conjunction with the goddess of mercy, showing him as hand in hand with the goddess."[2] This shrewd maneuver was aimed at evoking the mercy of the victor. After his death the "divine Julius" was formally taken into the list of the Roman deities, by a decree of the people and Senate of Rome. And that took place, says Suetonius, "not merely externally, by decree, but also by the inner conviction of the people. For during the games which his heir Augustus devoted to his honor, the first after his apotheosis, a comet appeared, seven days in a row, at about the eleventh hour [between 5 and 6 in the evening]; this was thought to be the soul of Caesar in Heaven. That is why he is represented with a star over his head" (chap. 89).

Who can help thinking here of the star that showed the wise men of the East the divinity of the Christ child!

After Augustus, it went without saying that every emperor was translated among the gods after his death. In the eastern portions

2. Appian, *Roman Civil Wars*, II, 16.

of the Empire he received, as such, the Greek title of Soter, that is, savior.

But such deifications (apotheoses) were not restricted to dead Emperors, but were also distributed to their relatives and favorites. Hadrian had fallen in love with a pretty Greek youth named Antinous, who "became the favorite of the Emperor on every side," as Hertzberg delicately says it in his *Geschichte des Römischen Kaiserreichs* (p. 369). When his favorite drowned in the Nile, Hadrian at once had him set among the gods, in memory of his services before and after; he built a noble city near the place of the disaster and named it Antinoopolis and in it a lordly temple for his remarkable saint. The cult of Antinous soon spread over the whole Empire; in Athens there were even solemn games and sacrifices in his memory.

Even of Augustus, Suetonius reports: "Although he knew that temples were devoted even to proconsuls [governors], he would not accept this honor in any province, if the temple were not devoted in common to himself and to Roma. In Rome itself he always firmly rejected this honor" (chap. 52).

Augustus was relatively modest. The third emperor of the Julian dynasty, Gaius, nicknamed Caligula (little boot), had himself honored in Rome, and in his lifetime, not only as a demi-god but as a full god, and felt himself to be one.

He said on one occasion, "Just as those who have to guard sheep and oxen are neither sheep nor oxen, but have a higher nature, so those who are set as rulers over men are not men like the others, but gods."

Actually it is the sheep's nature of men that produces the divinity of their rulers. This sheep's nature was uncommonly well developed under the Empire. The divine honors paid to emperors and their favorites were taken just as earnestly as many people today take a bit of ribbon in their buttonhole seriously and expect wonderful things of it. Naturally this divine worship contained an enormous portion of servility; in this point the Empire has not yet been surpassed, and that is saying a good deal. But along with the servility, credulity played a great role.

CREDULITY

Credulity too was a child of the new conditions.

It has always been vital to man to observe nature exactly, not to deceive himself about any of its phenomena and clearly to conceive causes and effects. That is the basis of his whole existence; and when he fails to do so, it is only too easy for him to perish.

All his action has its basis in the knowledge that definite causes evoke definite effects, that the stone with which he hits a bird kills it, that the flesh of this bird satisfies his hunger, that two sticks rubbed together produce fire, that fire warms, but consumes wood, etc.

Man judges the impersonal phenomena of nature after the pattern of his own actions. He sees in them too the effects of the acts of individuals endowed with superhuman powers, deities. Their first role is not that of miracle-workers, but as those who cause the ordinary natural course of events, the blowing of the wind, the waves of the sea, the destructive power of lightning, as well as many of men's notions, wise or foolish. The gods are known to make blind those they would destroy. The operation of such processes remains the chief function of the gods in naive natural religion.

The charm of this religion lies in its naturalness, in its keen observation of things and men, the qualities that still make the Homeric poems today a matchless work of art.

This keen observation and inquiry into natural philosophy and into the causes of events was refined, as we have seen, as cities arose. The urban observers were now able to discover impersonal events in nature, so simple and yet so rigorously regular that they could easily be recognized as necessary, beyond the realm of the capriciousness that is bound up with the notion of personal deities. Above all it was the motions of the heavenly bodies that gave rise to the concept of regularity and necessity. Natural science begins with astronomy. Then these concepts are extended to all of nature; men begin to look for necessary, regular connections everywhere. The regularly recurring experience is the basis of this activity.

The picture changes when, for the reasons mentioned, interest in scientific study of nature wanes and is replaced by ethical interest. The human spirit is now no longer concerned with such simple motions as the paths of the stars, which he could take as his starting point; he deals exclusively with himself, with the phenomenon which is most complicated, most variable, most elusive, which most resists scientific study. And then ethics no longer has to do with knowing what is and has been, what is present in experience, and for the most part in regularly repeated experience; instead it deals with desires and duties for the future, which lies before us not yet experienced and hence seemingly in complete freedom. Here wishing and dreaming have full scope, and fantasy runs wild, rising above all the confines of experience and criticism. Lecky is right in saying in his *History of the Rise and Influence of Rationalism in Europe* (New York, 1866, I, 43): "The philosophy of Plato, by greatly aggrandizing the sphere of the spiritual, did much to foster the belief (in sorcery); and we find that whenever, either before or after the Christian era, that philosophy has been in the ascendant, it has been accompanied by a tendency to magic."

At the same time life in the large city robs the inhabitants, who are now the intellectual leaders, of contact with nature, and the need and possibility of observing and understanding nature. The notion of what is natural and what is possible becomes weaker for them; they lose their measuring-rod for the absurdity of the impossible and unnatural or supernatural.

The more helpless the individual feels, the more desperately he gropes for solid support in some personality standing out beyond the ordinary; the more desperate the conditions and the greater the need for miracles, the more he will be inclined to lay miracles to the account of that personality, whom he regards as his rescuer and savior: in fact he will demand miracles as the touchstone which proves that the savior is genuine.

In this connection points of contact with divine myths of old times will easily be found, and themes from them will eagerly be taken up into the new myths. But the new ones have an entirely

different character. Superhuman powers were attributed to the
old gods in order to explain very exactly and correctly observed
real events. Now superhuman powers were attributed to men, in
order to have them perform deeds that no one had ever observed,
that were quite impossible. It was possible now and then for an
over-powerful imagination to evolve such miraculous events out
of the old legends of the gods, even in primitive times; but such
was not the origin of those legends. But for new myths miracles
are the starting point and origin.

One of the points in which the old and the new legend met
most frequently was the begetting of their hero by a god. In primitive times men loved to magnify the glory of their ancestors to
the maximum by making the man from whom their clan stemmed
appear as tremendous, as a superman, a demigod. Naturally, in
a mode of thinking that saw a god behind every event, the hero
could receive the requisite power only from a god. And since
these gods, for all their divinity, were thought of in very human
terms and with very human feelings, it was easy to assume that
the mother of the progenitor inspired a tender feeling in some
god and the stout hero was the fruit thereof.

In the same way the new legend had the saviors of the world
come from mortal mothers but divine fathers. So Suetonius says,
for example:

"I read in the book of Asclepiades of Mendes on the deities,
that Atia, the mother of Augustus, once attended a solemn sacrifice to Apollo at midnight and fell asleep in her sedan chair while
waiting for the other women to arrive. Then suddenly a snake
glided in to her and left her soon; when she woke she had the
feeling as if her husband had slept with her and so purified herself. At once a spot showed on her body in the shape of a snake,
and could not be got off, so that from then on she never went to
the public baths. In the tenth month Augustus was brought into
the world, and was taken as a son of Apollo" (*Octavius*, chap. 94).

A love affair with a god seems to have been considered something both possible and attractive among Roman ladies at that
time. Josephus tells an edifying story in that connection. There

lived in Rome at the time of Tiberius a lady named Paulina, whose beauty was as great as her chastity. A rich knight, Decius Mundus, fell hopelessly in love with her, offering her 200,000 drachmas for a single night, but was refused. A freedwoman found a way, however. She had learned that the fair Paulina was a diligent worshipper of the goddess Isis, and founded her plan on that. With 40,000 drachmas she bribed the priests of the goddess to inform Paulina that the god Anubis longed for her. "The woman was glad and boasted to her friends of the great honor Anubis was paying her. She also told her husband that she had been invited by Anubis to eat and to sleep with him. The husband willingly consented, knowing his wife's chastity. She came to the temple, and after she had dined and it was time to go to sleep, the priests put out all the lights and closed the door. Mundus, who had previously hidden in the temple, now came to her not at all unwillingly. She was his all night, for she thought he was the god. After he had had his pleasure, he left early in the morning, before the priests came into the temple, and Paulina went back to her husband and related how the god Anubis had been with her, and boasted of it to her acquaintances." But the noble knight Mundus went so far in shamelessness as to mock the lady a few days later in the street for having given herself to him for nothing. Great indignation on the part of the crestfallen worshipper of the god; she ran post-haste to Tiberius and had the priests of Isis crucified, their temple destroyed and Mundus exiled.[3]

What gives this little anecdote a specially piquant flavor is the fact that it comes immediately after the passage we have spoken of, in which the praise of the miracle-worker Christ is sung in inspired tones. Pious commentators early occupied themselves with this sequence, linking the adventure of Madame Paulina with Christ, and seeing in it a hidden sneer on the part of the malicious Jew Josephus at the virginity of the Virgin Mary and the credulity of her fiancé Joseph, a sneer that to be sure would not go very well with the recognition of the miracles of Christ immediately preceding it. However, since Josephus ac-

3. *Jewish Antiquities*, XVIII, 3.

tually had no suspicion of Christ's miracles, and the passage dealing with them is a later Christian interpolation, as we have seen, the sneer at the Virgin and her devoted bridegroom is a very unintentional one. It only proves the dulness of the Christian forger, who chose just this passage as the best place to introduce testimony as to the son of God.

Being a son of God's was a part of the stock in trade of a savior at that time, whether he was a Caesar or a street preacher. And so was miracle-working, the miracles being made up on the same pattern in either case.

Even the sober Tacitus reports of Vespasian (*Histories*, IV, chap. 81) that he worked many miracles in Alexandria, proving the approbation of Heaven for the emperor: he put spittle on the eyes of a blind man and made him see, and stepped on the hand of a man lame in that member and healed him.

Later the power to perform such miracles passed from the heathen emperors to the Christian monarchs. The kings of France had the remarkable gift of healing scrofula and goiter by touch at their coronation. As late as 1825, at the crowning of Charles X, the last Bourbon on the French throne, this miracle was produced according to schedule.

Similar cures were of course often told of Jesus. The pious Merivale assumed that Vespasian's miracles were patterned after the Christian ones—which is not very likely if we consider how insignificant and unknown Christianity was in Vespasian's time. Bruno Bauer, on the other hand, explains in his *Christus und die Cäsaren:* "I will present the theologians of today with the theorem that the late author of the fourth gospel and after him the revisers of the original gospel contained in Mark all borrowed from Tacitus the application of spittle in Christ's miraculous cures" (John 9, 6; Mark 7, 33 and 8, 23).

In our opinion this borrowing need not necessarily be accepted. Every age that believes in miracles has ideas of its own as to how they occur. Just as at the time of the dying middle ages it was generally assumed that a pact with the devil must be signed with warm blood, so that two authors can bring the same detail into their tales in the same manner without one having borrowed from the other, likewise it is possible that at Vespasian's time and later spittle was considered a common means of miraculous cures, so that it was equally natural for the sober reporter of the mundane savior on the throne of the Caesars as for the enthusiastic reporter of the savior on the throne of the millennial kingdom to attribute such a cure to the person they were glorifying, without one author having made use of the other. Moreover, Tacitus certainly did not invent this detail but found the legend already in fashion.

But it was not only the Caesars who worked miracles at that time, but a great number of their contemporaries. Stories of miracles were something so common that finally they no longer attracted any particular attention. The evangelists do not show the miracles and signs of Jesus as having the profound effect they should have according to our way of thinking. The miraculous feeding of the five thousand for example leaves even the disciples still of little faith. Moreover, besides Jesus, his apostles and disciples too worked many miracles. Indeed, men were so credulous that for example the Christians never thought of doubting the miracles worked by people they held to be rogues. They got out of it very simply, by ascribing such miracles to the power of devils and evil spirits.

Miracles were as cheap as blackberries; every founder of a religious sect or philosophical school performed them to show his ability. Thus we have the example of Apollonius of Tyana, a contemporary of Nero's.

Naturally his birth too is miraculous. When his mother was pregnant, the god Proteus appeared to her, the wise god no one can understand; she asked him unafraid what she would give birth to. He answered, "Me."[4] The young Apollonius grows up, a miracle of wisdom, and preaches a pure, moral life, distributes his property among his friends and poor relations and goes into the world as a begging philosopher. But even more imposing than his abstemiousness and morality are his miracles. These often

4. *Apollonius von Tyana*, translated by Baltzer, 1883, I, 4.

seem strikingly similar to the Christian ones. Thus, it is told of him during his stay in Rome:

"A maiden had died on the day of her marriage; at least she was thought to be dead. The bridegroom followed her bier lamenting and Rome mourned with him, for the maiden belonged to a very noble house. Now as Apollonius met the funeral procession he said: 'Put down the bier, I will dry your tears for the maiden.' Then he asked her name, and the crowd thought he would give one of the usual funeral orations. However, he touched the dead girl, spoke some unintelligible words and waked her from her seeming death. She raised her voice and returned to her father's house."[5]

According to the legend, Apollonius boldly braves the tyrants, Nero and Domitian, is thrown into prison, casts off his fetters without any effort, but does not escape, waiting instead in prison for the trial; he delivers a long speech in his defence, but before sentence is pronounced disappears mysteriously from the courtroom in Rome and comes some hours later to Dikaearchia near Naples, whither the gods had transported him with the speed of an express train.

Apollonius has a highly developed gift of prophecy, a gift which at that time was essential in the trade of savior, along with clairvoyance. When Domitian was murdered in his palace in Rome, Apollonius in Ephesus saw the event as clearly as if he had been present, and at once imparted it to the Ephesians, a system of wireless telegraphy that puts Marconi to shame.

His end came in this way: he disappeared in a temple whose doors flew open for him and flew shut behind him. "From within was heard the song of maidens sounding as though they were inviting him to ascend into heaven: Come from earthly darkness, come into heaven's light, come."[6]

His body however was never found. Therefore this savior too obviously ascended into Heaven.

Between the supporters of the belief in Christ and those of

5. *Ibid.*, IV, 45.
6. *Ibid.*, p. 378.

Apollonius a lively competition in miracles soon arose. Under Diocletian one of his governors, Hierocles, wrote a book against the Christians, in which he maintained that Christ's miracles were nothing in comparison with those of Apollonius and badly attested into the bargain. Eusebius of Caesarea answered in a refutation which did not express the slightest doubt as to the reality of Apollonius' miracles, but sought to minimize them as being not God's work but witchcraft, the work of dark demons.

Thus even when miracles had to be criticized the idea of doubting them did not arise.

This credulity increased as society deteriorated; the scientific spirit faded and was replaced by moral preaching. With credulity the thirst for miracles grew as well. A sensation ceases to operate when it is too often repeated. Stronger and stronger means must be used to make an impression. This we saw in the first chapter, where we examined the gospel treatment of wakings from the dead; they are simpler in the older gospels than in the later ones.

The most recent gospel, John, adds to the old miracles reported in the earlier gospels, the turning of water into wine at the marriage in Cana; an invalid that Jesus heals must have been sick for 38 years in John; a blind man whom he causes to see must have been born blind; in general, the miracles are carried to an extreme.

Exodus, 17, verses 1 to 6, tells us that Moses struck water from a rock in the desert to give the thirsting Israelites to drink. That was not miraculous enough in the time of the Christians. The first letter of the apostle Paul to the Corinthians, 10, verse 4, informs us that the rock from which the Jews got water followed them through the desert so that they should never lack water—a mobile spring.

Especially crude are the miracles that appear in the so-called *Acts of the Apostle Peter*. In a miracle competition with Simon the magician the Apostle brings a salt herring to life.

In addition, the men of that era considered quite natural occurrences as miracles, as signs of God's arbitrary interference in the course of events: not merely healings and deaths, victories and defeats, but the most common pastimes, like bets. "In Gaza at a horse race between the horses of a zealous Christian and a zealous pagan, 'Christ beat Marnas' and many pagans had themselves baptized."[7]

The natural event regarded as a miracle was not always so unequivocal. "In Marcus Aurelius' war against the Quadi in 173-74 the Roman army once found itself surrounded by a superior force of the enemy in the burning heat of the sun, parched with thirst and threatened with imminent annihilation. Suddenly thick clouds came together and poured down in a heavy rainfall, while on the enemy's side a fearful storm caused confusion and ruin; the Romans were saved, victory went to their side. The effect of this event was overpowering. It was preserved in pictorial representations, as the custom was then, and counted generally as a miracle which was remembered down to the end of antiquity and to which hundreds of years later Christians and pagans alike referred as a proof of the truth of their faith. . . . Apparently the miraculous deliverance was ascribed by most people to the emperor's prayer to Jupiter; others however asserted that it was thanks to the craft of an Egyptian magician in his suite, who brought about the downpour by conjuring the gods, notably Hermes. But according to the story of a Christian contemporary the miracle was brought about by the prayers of Christian soldiers in the twelfth (Melitenian) legion. Tertullian tells this as something well known, and refers to a letter of Marcus Aurelius."[8]

This letter must have been a forgery. It was a time as rich in forgeries as in miracles. Credulity and the need for miracles directly produced the forgeries.

The need for miracles and the credulity took on ever larger dimensions, until finally in the fourth and fifth centuries, the ages of the greatest decay, the monks worked wonders compared to which Jesus' miracles as related by the gospels seem insignificant.

". . . a believing age was easily persuaded that the slightest

7. Friedländer, *Sittengeschichte Roms*, 1901, II, p. 534.
8. *Ibid.*, II, p. 475.

caprice of an Egyptian or a Syrian monk had been sufficient to in-
terrupt the eternal laws of the universe. The favourites of Heaven
were accustomed to cure inveterate diseases with a touch, a word,
or a distant message; and to expel the most obstinate demons
from the souls or bodies they possessed. They familiarly accosted,
or imperiously commanded, the lions and serpents of the desert;
infused vegetation into a sapless trunk; suspended iron on the
surface of the water; passed the Nile on the back of a crocodile;
and refreshed themselves in a fiery furnace." (Gibbon, *op. cit.*,
ch. 37).

An excellent description of the state of mind of the time in
which Christianity arose is furnished by the character sketch
Schlosser gives in his *Weltgeschichte* of Plotinus, the most famous
neo-Platonist philosopher (3rd century A.D.).

"Plotinus, who was born in 205 in Lykopolis in Egypt and died
in 270 in Campania, was for eleven years an ardent disciple of
Ammonius, going so deep in his delving into the nature of god
and man that, unsatisfied by the Egyptian-Greek secret doctrine
of his predecessor and teacher, he craved for Persian and Indian
wisdom too and attached himself to the army of the younger
Gordianus in order to go with him to Persia. . . . Later Plotinus
went to Rome, where he found the prevailing tendency toward
Oriental mysticism much to his purpose, and played the role of
a prophet for twenty-five years, until shortly before his death. The
Emperor Gallienus and the Empress honored him with such fanatical zeal that they are even said to have had the intention of
founding a philosophical state on Plotinus' lines in some city of
Italy. Equally great was the applause that Plotinus found in the
most noble families of Roman citizens; some of the first men of
the state were enthusiastic supporters of his and received his
teachings as a message from heaven.

"The spiritual and moral exhaustion of the Roman world and
the generally prevalent tendency to fanaticism, to monastic morality and to the supernatural and prophetic were nowhere so clearly
in evidence as in the impression made by Plotinus and in the

respect his doctrine received precisely because it was incomprehensible.

"The methods Plotinus and his disciples used to spread the new wisdom were the same as those which at the close of the eighteenth century in France won corrupt notables to the mystical nonsense of Mesmer and Cagliostro, and in Germany won a pious Prussian king for Rosicrucians, exorcists and such people. Plotinus practiced magic, called up spirits and even descended to the business, now practiced only by the riff-raff of society, of solving petty thefts at his friends' request.

"Plotinus' writings too were prophetically composed; for according to his best-known disciple he wrote down his alleged inspirations without deigning to look at them afterwards or even correct slips of the pen. That is not how the masterworks of the ancient Greeks were composed! The ordinary rules of thought, or what we call method, were not to be found in the writings or the lectures of a man who required everyone who wished to arrive at philosophical knowledge to renounce himself or to abandon the natural state of thinking and feeling, as the first condition.

"To get an idea of the character of his theory and its effects, we need only a few remarks on the contents of his writings. He always represents life with and among men as sinful and perverse; for him true wisdom and holiness consist only in total divorce from the sensible world, in brooding and a sombre hermetic absorption in oneself and the contemplation of higher things. . . . This theory of life, which undermines all activity and scorns all experience and any human relationships, and moreover is preached with the greatest contempt for any one who thinks otherwise, is complemented by a purely theoretical conception of nature and its laws, based on fantastic notions. Aristotle had based his ideas of nature on experience, observation and mathematics; but there is no trace of such things in Plotinus. He considered himself a divinely enlightened philosopher, who knew everything from internal inspiration and needed no scaffolding to arrive at knowledge; his wings bore him above the earth and through all the spaces of heaven. . . .

"Plotinus had three disciples who brought into passable style what he had pronounced as oracles, and then, as his apostles, spread his doctrine. These were Herennius, Amelius and Porphyrius. All three had decided talent, and of the last two Longinus says, although in general he would have none of a wisdom hostile to life and sound reason, they were the only philosophers of his time whose writings were readable.

"How feeble their love of truth was, however, is best seen from the life of Plotinus composed by Porphyry. Porphyry tells the silliest stories about his lord and master, and since he had far too much sense to believe them, he must purposely and consciously have invented them to make Plotinus' oracular sayings more impressive."[9]

UNTRUTHFULNESS

Untruthfulness is the natural complement of credulity and hunger for miracles. Thus far we have only adduced examples in which informants told miraculous things about the dead. But people were not lacking who reported the greatest marvels about themselves, like Apion of Alexandria, the Jew-hater, "the world-bell, as the emperor Tiberius called him, full of big words and bigger lies, of loudest omniscience and unconditional self-confidence, knowing men, or if not men at least their worthlessness, a veteran master of oratory and betrayal, quick-witted, clever, shameless and implicitly loyal."[10]

Loyal—that is, servile—is usually applicable to this kind. The loyal rascal was bold enough to conjure Homer up out of the underworld to ask him his ancestry. He asserted that the poet's spirit had appeared to him and answered his question, but bound him not to reveal it to anyone!

A still cruder fraud was practiced by Alexander of Abonoteichos (born about 105, died about 175 A.D.). He used the grossest methods for his hocus-pocus, like trained animals and hollow statues of the gods in which men were concealed. Alexander

9. *Weltgeschichte*, 1846, IV, p. 452 f.
10. Mommsen, *Römische Geschichte*, V, 517 f.

founded an oracle that gave its predictions for something like twenty-five cents in our money. Lucian values the profit of this enterprise at about $15,000 per annum.

Alexander gained influence over the "philosophical" emperor Marcus Aurelius through the consular Rutilianus. The swindler died at seventy, rich and honored. A statue that was erected in his honor was supposed to give predictions even after his death.

The following was another well-staged fraud:

"Dio Cassius relates that in the year 220 A.D. a spirit, on its own confession the spirit of Alexander the Great, with his well-known form, features and clothing, went with a train of four hundred men dressed as Bacchantes from the Danube to the Bosphorus, where he disappeared: no magistrate dared detain him; rather, he received food and lodging everywhere at the public expense."[11]

In the face of performances like that our table-lifting heroes of the fourth dimension, and the more material captain of Köpenick, are not in it. However, these practices were not merely conscious fraud and deception on the part of sharpers and prestidigitators; they emanated from serious thinkers and honest men.

Ancient historical writing was never distinguished for over-rigorous critical faculty. It was still not a science in the narrow sense of the word, and still served pedagogical or political purposes rather than the study of the laws of social development. It aimed at edifying the reader or proving the correctness of the political tendencies professed by the writer. The great deeds of ancestors were to elevate future generations and inspire them to similar deeds; in this sense the historical work was but the echo in prose of the heroic epic. But future generations should also learn from their forefathers' experience what should be done and what should not. Naturally, since many a historian, especially when the purpose of edification and inspiration got the upper hand, was not too strict in the choice and criticism of his sources, it is understandable that he would also take the liberty of filling in gaps by means of his imagination, in the interests of the artistic effect.

11. Friedländer, *op. cit.*, II, 626.

In particular every historian considered it his prerogative to make up the speeches he set in the mouths of his characters. Nevertheless, the classical historian strictly avoided any consciously or intentionally false treatment of the actions of the personages they dealt with. They were under the greater necessity of avoiding any such procedures in that they were dealing with public political actions, in which their reports could be checked.

But as ancient society decayed, the function of historical writing changed. Men no longer desired political instruction, for politics became more and more a matter of indifference, and even repugnance, to them. They no longer demanded examples of manly courage and devotion to the fatherland; what they wanted was diversion, new titillations for their jaded nerves, tittle-tattle and sensations, marvels. A little precision more or less made no difference here. In addition, test and verification became much more difficult, since private occurrences now held the center of the stage, occurrences that did not take place in public. History-writing turned more and more into scandalous chronicle on the one hand, or tall tales on the other.

This new trend in history-writing appears in Greek literature from the time of Alexander the Great; Alexander's courtier Onesicritus wrote a book about his deeds that teems with lies and exaggerations. From lying to forgery is but a step. The step was made by Euhemerus who brought back inscriptions from India in the third century that were supposed to be age-old, but which he had fabricated himself.

But this convenient method was not confined to history-writing alone. We have seen how in philosophy interest in this world faded away and interest in the other world increased in strength. But how was a philosopher to persuade his students that his ideas of the other world were anything more than mere fantasies? The simplest way was obviously to find or invent a witness who came with a report from the bourne whence no traveler returns. Even a Plato did not disdain a trick like that, as we saw with his famous Pamphylian.

Furthermore, as interest in natural science shrank and was replaced by ethics, the critical spirit that tries to test the truth of every statement by factual experience disappeared; as the individual became more insecure, he felt a greater need to find support in some great man. It was not factual proofs but authorities that were decisive for men now; and anyone who wanted to make an impression had to try to get the necessary authorities on his side. If they were lacking, then the facts had to be improved upon and the authorities fabricated. We have seen such authorities in the cases of Daniel and Pythagoras. Jesus belonged to the same category, as did his apostles, Moses, the Sibyls, and so forth.

People did not always take the trouble to write a whole book under a false name. Frequently it was enough to insert a suitable sentence into a genuine work of a recognized authority, and in this way win this authority for oneself. This was all the easier because printing had not yet been invented. Books circulated only in copies made either by the writers themselves or by a slave, if they were rich enough to have competent slaves. There were business men who kept slaves busy copying books, which were then sold at a high profit. How easy it was to falsify such a copy, to leave out a sentence one had no use for or add a sentence one needed, especially when the author was already dead, so that there would be no protest in that negligent and credulous age. Further copyists then took care of preserving the forgery for the future.

For the Christians this was very simple. Whoever the first teachers and organizers of Christian communities may have been, they certainly came from the lowest classes of society, were illiterate and left no written notes. In the beginning, their teachings were handed down only by word of mouth. Anyone of their supporters who appealed in a dispute to the first teachers of the community could hardly be convicted of falsehood unless he flew too crassly in the face of tradition. Soon divergent versions of the words of "the Lord" and his apostles must have taken form. And in view of the heated conflicts that took place within the Christian communities from the outset, these different versions must have been from the first put forward not so much for the sake of objective history but in order to win a polemical victory, and then later written down and assembled in the gospels. It was primarily polemical ends too that inspired the later copyists and revisers to strike out an inconvenient sentence here and add one there, in order to adduce it all as proof that Christ or his apostles supported this or that opinion. We meet with this polemical tendency at every step in testing the gospels.

Soon however the Christians were not satisfied with thus improving their own sacred scriptures for their purposes by falsifications and forgeries. It was too convenient a method not to tempt imitation in the case of other, "heathen" authors, as soon as there were elements among the Christians educated enough to attach some value to the testimony of eminent authors outside of Christian literature, and numerous enough to make it worth the trouble to have their own falsified copies made for these educated Christians, which they would gladly receive and circulate. Many of these forgeries have been preserved down to the present time.

We have already mentioned Josephus' testimony as to Jesus as one such forgery. The next writer after Tacitus who mentions the Christians is the younger Pliny, who, as propraetor of Bithynia (probably 111 to 113), sent a letter about them to Trajan, which has come down to us in the collection of his letters (*C. Plinii Caecilii Epistolarum libri decem*, Book X, letter 97). In it he inquires what to do with the Christians of his province, of whom he hears nothing but good, but who are emptying the temples. This idea of the harmlessness of the Christians does not go well with the view of his friend Tacitus, who stresses their "hate for the whole human race." It is equally striking that by Trajan's time Christianity should already have been so widespread that it was able to empty the temples of Bithynia, "which were already all but deserted, their ceremonies long neglected, their sacrificial animals seldom finding a purchaser." One should expect that facts like these would invite general attention (as if shall we say only Social Democratic votes were cast in Berlin). People in general would be excited. Pliny however first learns of the existence of the Christians through a denouncement. These and other considerations suggest that this letter is a Christian forgery. Already in 1788 Semler assumed that the whole letter of Pliny was invented by a later Christian to glorify Christianity. On the other hand Bruno Bauer thinks the letter is Pliny's, but originally did not sound very complimentary to the Christians and was suitably "edited" later by a Christian copyist.

The forgeries became still bolder when the Germanic barbarians overflowed into the Roman Empire during the great migrations. The new masters of the world were simple peasants, with their peasant shrewdness to be sure, sober and cunning enough in all the things they understood. For all their simplicity they proved to be less hungry for miracles, less credulous, than the heirs of ancient culture. Reading and writing, however, were unknown arts to them. These became the privilege of the Christian clergy, which alone now represented the educated class, and now no longer needed to fear any criticism of their forgeries in the interest of the church. They went at it with a will. The fabrications were no longer confined to the domain of doctrine, as they had thus far; they did not only aim at winning theoretical, tactical or organizational conflicts, but were a source of gain or legal justifications of appropriations that had been carried out. The most monstrous of these falsifications were the Donation of Constantine and Pseudo-Isidorian Decretals. Both were fabricated in the eighth century. In the first document Constantine (306-337) leaves to the popes absolute and eternal rule over Rome, Italy, and all the provinces of the West. The Pseudo-Isidorian Decretals are a collection of church laws, allegedly by the Spanish bishop Isidore in the beginning of the seventh century, reinforcing the autocratic rule of the popes in the church.

These countless forgeries are one of the principal factors in making the history of the origin of Christianity so obscure to this day. Many of these documents are readily detected as spurious; many were exposed centuries ago, as for instance Laurentius Valla proved the Donation of Constantine to be false as early as 1440. But it is not so easy to find out whether there is a kernel of truth hidden in the fabrication and to dig it out.

This is not an attractive picture that we have to paint here.

Decadence in every nook and corner, economic, political and hence also scientific and moral decay. The old Romans and Greeks regarded virtue as being the full, harmonious development of manliness in the best sense of the words. *Virtus* and *arete* denote courage and steadfastness, but also manly pride, willingness to make sacrifices, and selfless devotion to the community. But the lower society sank in slavery, the more slavishness became the highest virtue, out of which and by means of which grew all those estimable qualities we have seen emerging: withdrawal from the community into oneself, cowardice and lack of self-confidence, longing for salvation by an emperor or a god, not by one's own strength or the strength of one's class; self-abasement toward those above, priestly arrogance toward those below; lassitude and tedium, and at the same time a passion for sensations and marvels; exaggeration and ecstasy along with flattery, lying and forgery. That is the picture the Imperial age presents us with and the picture whose features are reflected in Christianity, the product of that time.

HUMANENESS

But, the defenders of Christianity will say, this description is one-sided and therefore untrue. It is true that Christians were only men and could not avoid the degrading influences of their environment. But that is only one side of Christianity. We also find that it develops a morality that rises far above that of antiquity, a sublime humaneness extending to everything that has a human figure, low as well as high, foreigner as well as fellow-countryman, enemy as well as friend; that it preaches the brotherhood of men of all classes and races. This morality is not to be explained by the times in which Christianity arose; it is all the more remarkable for the fact that it was preached in an era of the deepest moral decadence; here, they say, is where historical materialism breaks down, here we have a phenomenon that is explicable only in terms of the sublimity of a person rising above the condition of space and time, of a divine man, or to use the modern jargon, a superman.

That is what our "idealists" say.

How does that fit with the facts? First take charity toward the poor and humaneness toward slaves. Are these two phenomena really confined to Christianity? It is true that we do not find much charity in classical antiquity. The reason is very simple: charity presupposes poverty on a mass scale. The mental life of antiquity, however, had its roots in communistic conditions, in the common property of the *Markgenossenschaft,* the community, the household, which gave their members a right to the common products and means of productions. It was rare that there was any occasion for alms.

We must not confuse hospitality with charity. Hospitality was a universal practice in antiquity. It represents however a relationship between equals whereas charity presupposes social inequality. Hospitality cheers both guest and host. Charity elevates the man who gives it, and lowers and mortifies the man that receives it.

In the course of history a mass proletariat began to form in some large cities, as we have seen. But this group possessed or obtained political power and used it to get a share in the means of enjoyment that came to the wealthy and to the state from slave labor and the plunder of the provinces. Thanks to democracy and their political power these proletarians did not need charity; for this requires not only mass poverty but also the absence of political rights and power on the part of the proletariat, and these conditions were present for the first time to any great extent in the time of the emperors. It is no wonder that it was just then that the idea of charity began to prevail in Roman society. But it did not come from any supernatural higher morality of Christianity.

At the beginning of their rule the Caesars still found it advisable to buy off not only the army but the proletariat of the capital as well with bread and circuses. Nero in particular did wonders in this respect. In many large cities of the provinces as well the effort was made to keep the lower classes quiet in this way.

This did not last long. As the society grew poorer, government expenditures had to be cut down, and the Caesars began, naturally, with the proletarians, whom they no longer feared. There was also the need to cope with the growing shortage of labor power. If bread was no longer distributed, the able-bodied proletarians would have to look around for work, perhaps by binding themselves to the great landholders as *coloni,* hereditary tenants.

But it was precisely the need for labor power that now gave rise to new forms of subsidies.

Under the emperors all the old social organizations distintegrated, not only the *Markgenossenschaften* but the households and the enlarged families as well. Everyone thought only of himself; blood relationships went by the board with political ones; readiness to make sacrifices for relatives disappeared along with public spirit. Orphan children suffered especially. Without parents they were now defenceless in the world, with nobody to take them in. Another factor increasing the number of waifs was the fact that, as everyone became poorer and self-sacrifice decreased, people tended more and more to get away from the burden of a family. Some managed this by staying single, by relying on prostitution, the male branch of which flourished enormously; others sought at least to avoid having children from their marriages. Both methods contributed mightily to depopulation and the lack of labor power, and so to the further impoverishment of society. Many who had children found it the most convenient thing to get rid of them by exposure. This exemplary practice became widespread, despite repeated prohibitions. It became more and more urgent on the one hand to take care of the waifs and on the other to take care of the children of poor parents at home. These tasks occupied the early Christians to a great extent. The care of orphans was constantly on their minds. Both sympathy and the need for workers and soldiers contributed to insuring the upbringing of orphans, foundlings and proletarian children.

Even in the time of Augustus we find efforts in this direction; in the second century of our era these efforts become practical. The emperors Nerva and Trajan were the first who initiated foundations, at first in Italy, on the basis of having estates either bought by the state and rented out, or given out on mortgages.

The proceeds from the rents and mortgages were to go for the rearing of poor children, especially orphans.[12]

At Hadrian's coronation he expanded this institution, which had been organized for 5,000 children under Trajan. Later emperors went still further. In addition to this, a municipal institution came into existence. The oldest private orphanage we know of dates from the time of Augustus. Helvius Basila, a former praetor, left the citizens of Atina in Latium $22,000 to provide bread for children (unfortunately the number is not given).[13] By Trajan's time many such foundations are mentioned. A rich lady, Caelia Macrina of Tarracina, whose son had died, contributed a million sesterces ($50,000) so that a hundred boys and a hundred girls could be supported on the interest; in the year 97 Pliny the Younger founded an asylum in his native city Comum (now Como), in which the yearly revenues of an estate worth 500,000 sesterces were devoted to the support of poor children. He founded schools, libraries and so forth.

All these foundations however, were not able to counteract the depopulation of the Empire. That had its basis deep in economic conditions, and increased with the decay of the economy. The general impoverishment finally took away the means of continuing the care of the children; along with the state the charitable institutions went bankrupt.

Müller reports on this development:

"Their existence can be traced for almost 180 years. Hadrian saw to it that the children should be better covered. Antoninus Pius appropriated more money for this purpose. Inscriptions giving thanks were devoted to him in 145 by the boys and girls in question in Cupramontana, a city in Picenum, and in 161 by the children of Sestinum in Umbria. To attest Marcus Aurelius's activity in the same field there is a similar dedication from Ficulea in Latium. In the first years of his reign this foundation seems to have been at its height; then it went steeply down with the decline

12. See B. Matthias, "Römische Alimentarinstitutionen und Agrarwirtschaft," *Jahrbuch für Nationalökonomie und Statistik*, 1885, VI, p. 503 f.
13. A. Müller, *Jugendfürsorge in der römischen Kaiserzeit*, 1903, p. 21.

of the Empire. As the result of his constant military needs, which led him to auction off the crown jewels, ornaments and other valuables, he seems to have withdrawn the capital funds of the institutions and transferred the payment of the interest to the government treasury. Under Commodus, however, the treasury was for nine years unable to meet its obligations, and Pertinax was not able to pay the arrears and had to cancel them. However the position of the foundations seems to have been improved later. At the end of the third century we still find official references to these institutions. That, however, is the end. Under Constantine they no longer existed."[14]

The increasing poverty destroyed the foundations, but not the idea of charity, which increased along with the growing misery. This idea is by no means peculiar to Christianity or confined to it; Christianity shared it with its era, and was led to it not by moral elevation but by economic decline.

With the sense of charity and the respect for it there came another less attractive quality, ostentation of the alms one gave. An example is Pliny, just mentioned. We know of his benevolent institutions only through himself; he has described them at length in writings, meant to be published. When we see how Pliny peddles his feelings and what admiration he has for his own nobility, it does not seem to us a proof of the ethical grandeur of the "golden age" of the Roman Empire, its happiest time, as Gregorovius, with most of his colleagues, calls it, but rather a proof of the vain frivolity of the period, an edifying addition to its priestly arrogance and pious hypocrisy.

Niebuhr condemns Pliny most sharply, for his "childish vanity" and "dishonorable baseness."

As for humaneness towards slaves, which is supposed to be another quality peculiar to Christianity, the situation is quite the same as in the case of charity.

To begin with it must be noted that Christianity, at least in the form in which it became the official religion, never had any notion of opposing slavery in principle. It in no way tended

14. *Op. cit.,* p. 7 f.

towards its abolition. The fact that under Christianity the exploitation of slaves for money profit came to an end had reasons that had nothing to do with any religious ideas. We have already seen these reasons. The basic one was the military decline of Rome, which cut off the supply of cheap slaves and took the profit out of exploiting them. Slavery for luxury however outlasted the Roman Empire; in fact, along with Christianity there arose a new sort of slaves in the Roman world, the eunuchs, who played a great part under the Christian emperors from Constantine on. We find them already at the court of Claudius, Nero's father (Suetonius, *Tiberius Claudius Drusus,* chaps. 28, 44).

The idea of putting an end to slavery never occurred to the free proletarians. They tried to improve their lot by milking the rich and the government without doing any work themselves, and this was possible only by means of exploiting slaves.

It is significant that, in the communistic state of the future which Aristophanes ridicules in his *Ecclesiazusae,* slavery continues. The distinction between rich and poor disappears, but only for the freemen; for them everything becomes common property, including the slaves, who carry on production. This is only a joke, but it is an accurate reflection of the way the ancients thought.

We find similar notions in a pamphlet on the reasons for the prosperity of Attica, dating from the fourth century B.C., to which Pöhlmann refers in his *Geschichte,* previously cited.

As Pöhlmann puts it, this pamphlet demands "a vast extension of the government's economic activity to commerce and production." Above all government purchase of slaves for the silver mines. The number of these government slaves should be increased so much that finally there would be three slaves to every citizen. Then the state would be able to assure each of its citizens at least a minimum subsistence.[15]

Professor Pöhlmann is of the opinion that this brilliant proposal is typical of the "collectivist radicalism" and "democratic socialism" that wants to nationalize all the means of production

15. Pöhlmann, *Geschichte des Antiken Kommunismus,* II, p. 252 f.

in the interests of the proletariat. Actually what it is typical of is the nature of the ancient proletariat and the interest it had in maintaining slavery; but Pöhlmann's conception and presentation of it is typical of the shallowness of bourgeois scholarship, for whom any nationalization of property, even property in men, is "collectivism," every step taken in the interests of the proletariat is "democratic socialism," no matter whether this proletariat belongs to the exploiters or the exploited.

The interest which the Roman proletariat had in slavery is shown by the fact that even in the revolutionary actions they never showed opposition to the principle of property in human beings. Hence we occasionally find even the slaves ready to crush a proletarian uprising. It was slaves, led by aristocrats, that gave the death-blow to the proletarian movement of Caius Gracchus. Fifty years later Roman proletarians under the leadership of Marcus Crassus crushed the rebellious slaves led by Spartacus.

Nobody thought seriously of a general abolition of slavery; but the way in which slaves were handled was another matter. Here it must be granted that under Christianity the attitude toward slavery became much more humane and the human rights of slaves came to be recognized, in sharp contrast to the wretched state of the slaves at the beginning of the Empire, when, as we have seen, the body and the life of the slave were at the mercy of any whim of his master, who often made the most atrocious use of his rights.

There is no doubt that Christianity firmly opposed this sort of treatment of slaves. But that is not to say that in this it went against the spirit of its time, that it was alone in its defence of the slaves.

What class claimed the right to unrestricted misuse and murder of slaves? Naturally, the class of rich landholders, above all the aristocracy.

But the democracy, the common people, who owned no slaves, did not have the same interest in the right to mistreat slaves as the great slave-owners did. At any rate, so long as the order of small farmers (who too held slaves) or at least the traditions of this order were predominant in the Roman people, it felt no urge to defend the slaves.

Gradually a swing in public opinion was built up, not because of the ennoblement of morality but because the composition of the Roman proletariat had changed. There were fewer and fewer free-born Romans and especially small farmers in their ranks, and more and more freedmen, who too shared in Roman citizenship and under the Empire ended by constituting the majority of Rome's population. There were many reasons for emancipation. Many a man who was childless (and that was often the case in those days, when people were more and more afraid of the burdens of marriage and children) was impelled by caprice or kindness to liberate his slaves after his death by a clause in his will. Often an individual slave was freed during the master's lifetime as a reward for special services, or out of vanity, for a man who manumitted many slaves got the reputation of being wealthy. Other slaves were liberated out of political considerations, since in most cases the freedman remained in dependence on his master as a client, but had political rights. Thus he increased his master's political influence. Finally slaves might be allowed to save up and buy their liberty, and many a master did good business in this way by having a slave he had worked to the bone buy himself free for a price that would enable the master to buy a fresh slave with full strength.

With the growth of the number of slaves in the population the number of freedmen grew as well. The free proletariat was now recruited not so much from the farmers but from slaves, and stood in political opposition to the slave-holding aristocracy, from which it wanted to win political rights and political power which could lead to such tempting economic gains. It is no wonder that a fellow-feeling with the slaves began to spring up in the Roman democracy just at the time that the excesses of the slaveholders against their human beasts of burden were at their height.

There was another circumstance tending in the same direction.

When the Caesars came to power, their household, like that of every noble Roman, was run by slaves and freedmen. No matter how deep the Romans might have sunk, a free-born citizen would have held it beneath his dignity to descend to personal service even for the most powerful of his fellow-citizens. The household of the Caesars however now became the Imperial court, and their house servants became officials of the Imperial court, who began to form a new administrative apparatus alongside the traditional republican one. It was the new government which more and more took care of the actual business of the business and rule of the state, while the offices that had come down from republican times became more and more empty titles that gratified vanity but gave no real power.

The slaves and freedmen of the emperor's court became the rulers of the world, and hence, by means of embezzlement, extortion and bribery, the world's most successful exploiters. Friedländer's excellent *Sittengeschichte des kaiserlichen Rom,* which we have often cited, well says: "The riches that came to them because of their privileged position were a principal source of their wealth. At a time when the freedmen's opulence was proverbial, few could compete with these servants of the emperor. Narcissus owned 400 million sesterces [$20,000,000], the greatest fortune known in antiquity; Pallas 300 million [$15,000,000]. Callistus, Epaphroditus, Doryphorus and others had treasures not much smaller. When the emperor Claudius once complained about the low level of the imperial treasury, it was said in Rome he would have more than enough if he were to be taken into partnership by his two freedmen, Narcissus and Pallas."

In actual fact one of the sources of income of many emperors was forcing rich slaves and freedmen to share the proceeds of their frauds and extortions with them.

"The emperor's freedmen, owning so much money, surpassed the Roman magnates in pride and pomp. Their palaces were the most splendid in Rome; Juvenal says that the palace of Claudius's eunuch Posides outshone the Capitol; the rarest and most precious objects were piled up extravagantly there. . . . However the imperial freedmen adorned Rome and other cities of the monarchy with splendid and useful structures. Cleander, the powerful freedman of Commodus, devoted a part of his tremendous fortune to building houses, baths and other edifices useful to individuals and to whole municipalities."

This rise of many slaves and liberated slaves seemed all the more startling compared with the financial decline of the old landowning aristocracy. And just as today the bankrupt hereditary aristocrats hate and despise the rich Jews in their hearts, and yet flatter them when they have to, so also was the case with the imperial slaves and freedmen.

"The highest aristocracy of Rome vied in honoring and courting the all-powerful servants of the emperor, no matter how deeply these scions of old and famous houses despised and abhorred men who came from hated stocks and were indelibly stained with the shame of servitude, and in more than one respect were legally beneath the free-born beggar."

Externally the position of the emperor's servants was very modest, completely subordinate to the high-born title-bearers.

"Actually the relationship was quite different, often quite the opposite, and the utterly despised 'slave' had the satisfaction of seeing 'the free and noble admire them and call them fortunate,' of having the greatest men of Rome humble themselves before them; few dared to treat them as serving-men. . . . In crude flattery a family tree was invented for Pallas which traced his ancestry back to the king of Arcadia of the same name; and a descendant of the Scipios proposed an address of thanks in the Senate because this scion of a royal house had put aside his age-old nobility for the good of the state and condescended to become the servant of a prince. On the motion of one of the consuls (52 A.D.) the praetorian insignia and a considerable gift of money (15 million sesterces) were awarded to him." Pallas accepted only the former.

For this the Senate voted Pallas a resolution of thanks. "This decree was set up on a bronze tablet next to a statue of Julius Caesar in armor, and the possessor of 300,000,000 sesterces praised as a model of strict unselfishness. L. Vitellius, the father of the emperor of the same name, a man of very high position and of a rascallity which even in that time caused astonishment, honored gold statues of Pallas and Narcissus among his domestic deities. . . .

"But nothing shows the position of these former slaves so well as the fact that they could marry the daughters of noble houses, even houses related to the emperor, and this in an era when the pride of the nobility in their ancient origin and a long series of noble ancestors was tremendous."[16]

In this way the Roman citizens, the masters of the world, came to be ruled by slaves and erstwhile slaves and bow the knee before them.

It is clear what a tremendous effect this must have had on the attitude of the time toward slavery in general. The aristocrats may have hated the slaves all the more, the more they had to bow down before some of them; the mass of the people began to respect the slave, and the slave to respect himself.

In addition, Caesarism had come to the fore in the struggle of the democracy, itself largely made up of former slaves, against the aristocracy of the great slave-owners. The latter were not so easy to buy off as the propertyless masses, and formed the only considerable rival to the newly founded Caesarian government; the great slave-owners constituted the republican opposition in the Empire, so far as one existed. Slaves and freedmen on the other hand were the emperor's most faithful supporters.

The effect of all this was the formation, not only in the proletariat but also in the imperial court and in the circles in which the court set the tone, of an attitude favorable to the slaves; this attitude was strongly expressed by court philosophers as well as by proletarian street preachers.

Without taking the space to cite such statements, we give only one case: the favor the bloody Nero showed toward slaves and freedmen. This kept him in constant conflict with the aristocratic Senate which, no matter how servile it was toward particular powerful freedmen, in general wanted the most rigorous regulations against slaves and freedmen. Thus in the year 56 the Senate de-

16. Friedländer, *Sittengeschichte Roms,* I, pp. 42-47.

sired to break the "arrogance" of the freedmen by giving the former owner the right to take liberty from freedmen who proved to be "worthless," that is not slavishly obedient enough, toward him. Nero opposed this proposal in the most vigorous way. He pointed out how important the order of freedmen had become and how many knights and even senators had been recruited from their midst, and recalled the old basic Roman principle that whatever differences there might exist among the different classes of the nation, freedom must be the common good of all. Nero offered a counter-proposal, that the rights of the freedmen should not be abridged, and forced the cowardly Senate to accept it.

The situation was more difficult in the year 61. The city prefect Pedanius Secundus was murdered by one of his slaves. The expiation of such a deed required, according to the old aristocratic law, the execution of all the slaves who were in the house at the time of the murder, in this case no fewer than 400 people, including women and children. Public opinion called for milder treatment. The masses of the people stood firmly for the slaves; it semed as though the Senate itself would be carried away by the general attitude. Then Caius Cassius came forward, the leader of the republican opposition in the Senate, and a descendant of one of the murderers of Caesar. In a fiery speech he warned the Senate not to let itself be cowed and yield to gentleness. It was only through fear that the dregs of humanity were to be held in check. This agitator's speech had an overwhelming effect; no one in the Senate contradicted him. Nero himself was intimidated and thought it best to remain silent. The slaves were all executed. But when the republican aristocrats, emboldened by this success, introduced a bill in the Senate to have the freedmen who had lived under one roof with the condemned slaves deported from Italy, Nero got up and declared that even if sympathy and pity were not to soften the old custom, at least it should not be made more rigorous; and the bill was defeated.

Nero also appointed a special judge who, as Seneca tells us, "was to inquire into cases of abuse of slaves by their masters and set bounds to the savagery and caprice of the masters as well as

their stinginess with food." The same emperor restricted the gladiatorial games and sometimes, as Suetonius relates, would not let
any gladiator be killed, not even if he was a condemned criminal.

Similar tales are told of Tiberius. Facts like these show clearly
the fruitlessness of writing history with a moralistic or political
bias with the aim of measuring men of the past with the moral
or political standards of today. Nero, the murderer of his mother
and wife, who out of kindness grants slaves and criminals their
lives; the tyrant who defends freedom against the republicans; the
debauched maniac who practices the virtues of humanity and
charity to the saints and martyrs of Christianity, who feeds the
hungry, gives the thirsty to drink, clothes the naked—recall his
princely generosity toward the Roman proletariat—, who stands
up for the poor and the wretched: this historical figure defies
any attempt to judge him by an ethical standard. Difficult and
senseless as it is to try to decide whether Nero was a good fellow
at bottom or a rascal, or both, as is generally held to be the case
today; it is just as easy to understand Nero and his actions, those
we sympathize with and those that revolt us, as results of his times
and his position.

The mildness of the imperial court and the proletariat alike
toward the slaves must have been strongly supported by the fact
that the slave was no longer a cheap commodity. This led, on the
one hand, to an end of that aspect of slave labor that had always
given rise to the worst brutalities, namely their exploitation for
profit. There remained only luxury slavery, which had always
been milder. Moreover, the scarcer and dearer slaves became, the
greater the loss caused by the early death of a slave, the harder he
was to replace.

A final factor in the same direction was the increasing disin-
clination to military service, which made many cities shrink more
and more from bloodshed, together with internationalism, which
taught that every man should be held as equal without distinction
of descent, and thus tended to destroy national differences and
oppositions.

INTERNATIONALISM

We have already pointed out the extent to which world commerce spread under the Empire. A network of magnificent roads linked Rome with the provinces and one province with another. The movement of trade was especially favored by the peace that existed within the Empire after the perpetual wars of the cities and states against one another and then the civil wars that had occupied the last centuries of the republic. As a result the navy could be entirely used against the pirates; piracy in the Mediterranean, which had never really ended, was now over. Weights, measures and coinage were uniform over the entire Empire: all these factors considerably helped commerce among the various parts of the Empire.

This commerce was primarily a personal matter. Postal service, at least for private messages, was not well-developed, and anyone who had business abroad had to go there and do it in person much more frequently than is the case today.

All this brought the nations living around the Mediterranean closer together and smoothed out their differences. It never to be sure got to the point where the whole Empire formed a completely uniform body. Two halves could always be distinguished, a Western, Romanized, Latin-speaking half and an Eastern, Hellenized, Greek-speaking half. As the forces and the traditions of world-ruling Rome died away and Rome was no longer the capital of the Empire, these two parts separated in politics and religion.

At the beginning of the Empire, however, there was no question of any impairment of the unity of the empire. At that time too the difference between the conquered nations and the ruling community began to disappear. The more the people of Rome degenerated, the more the Caesars thought of themselves as rulers of the whole Empire, as masters of Rome and the provinces, not as rulers of the provinces in the name of Rome. Rome got itself fed by the provinces, aristocracy and people alike, but was not able to furnish enough soldiers and officials for governing the provinces; thus Rome constituted an element of weakness, not of strength, for the empire of the Caesars. What Rome took from the provinces was so much lost for the Caesars, and with nothing in exchange. Thus in their own interests the emperors were driven to counteract the privileged position of Rome in the Empire and finally to put an end to it.

Roman citizenship was now freely given to the provincials. We see them entering the Senate and filling high offices. The Caesars were the first to put the principle of the equality of all men irrespective of origin into practical application: all men were equally their slaves and were valued by them only to the extent they could be made use of, whether they were senators or slaves, Romans, Syrians or Gauls. Finally, at the beginning of the third century the fusion and levelling of the nations had gone so far that Caracalla could venture to confer Roman citizenship on all the inhabitants of the provinces and thus do away with the last formal distinction between the former masters and the former subjects, after all actual differences had long since ceased to exist. It was one of the most contemptible emperors who thus gave such open expression to one of the noblest ideas of the time, an idea that Christianity would like to claim for itself; and contemptible too was the motive that drove the despot to his action: need of money.

Under the republic the Roman citizens had been free from taxes from the time conquered provinces began to yield booty and good profits. "Aemilius Paullus brought 300,000,000 sesterces into the treasury from the Macedonian booty after defeating Perseus, and from this time on the Roman people were free of taxes."[17] But from Augustus on growing financial stringency had led to reimposing more and more tax burdens on the Roman citizens. The "reform" of Caracalla now made Roman citizens out of the provincials so that in addition to the taxes they had been paying they would be subject to those of Roman citizens, which the imperial financial wizard immediately thereafter doubled. In return he increased the military budget by 15 million dollars. No wonder that he could not make ends meet with only one financial "reform"

17. Pliny, *Natural History*, XXXIII, 17.

and needed others, the most important among them being debase-
ment and counterfeiting of the coinage on the most shameless
scale.

The general decadence got worse so fast that the Romans, having ceased to furnish soldiers, soon were unable to furnish competent officials. We can trace this in the emperors themselves.
The first emperors were still descendants of old Roman aristocratic families of the Julian and Claudian gens. But by the time
the Julian dynasty had come to its third emperor, he was a mad-
man, Caligula; and with Nero the Roman aristocracy showed the
bankruptcy of its ability to govern. Nero's successor Galba came
from a Roman patrician clan, but he was followed by Otho, of
a noble Etruscan family and by Vitellius, a plebeian from Apulia.
Finally, Vespasian, who founded the Flavin dynasty, was a plebeian of Sabine origin. But the Italian plebeians soon proved themselves to be as corrupt and incapable of rule as the Roman aristocrats, and the miserable Domitian, Vespasian's son, was followed,
after the brief interregnum of Nerva, by the Spaniard Trajan.
With him there begins the rule of the Spanish emperors which
lasted almost a hundred years, until it too, with Commodus,
showed its political bankruptcy.

After the Spaniards came Septimius Severus, the founder of an
African-Syrian dynasty; after the murder of the last emperor of
this dynasty, Alexander Severus, Maximinus, a Thracian of
Gothic origin, took the crown the legions offered him, a fore-
boding of the time when Goths were to rule in Rome. More and
more the provinces were involved in the general decomposition,
and more and more new barbarian, non-Roman blood was needed
to infuse new life into the dying Empire; not only the soldiers,
but the emperors, had to be found further and further away from
the centers of civilization.

Above, we saw slaves as court officials rule over free men; now
we see provincials and even barbarians set over the Romans as
emperors, as beings honored with divine worship. All the race and
class prejudices of pagan antiquity had to disappear, and the

feeling of the equality of everyone come more and more to the forefront.

This feeling appeared in many minds early, before the conditions we have been depicting became a commonplace. Cicero was already writing (*De officiis*, 3, 6): "Anyone who asserts that fellow-citizens must be taken into consideration but not foreigners breaks the general bond of the human race, and with it destroys charity, liberality, kindness and justice." Our ideological historians, naturally, here too take the cause for the effect and the effect for the cause, and look for the cause of the humanization of manners and the broadening of the nation into the concept of humanity in sentences like the above, which the "pious" find in the gospels and the "advanced" in heathen philosophers; the trouble is merely that at the apex and peak of the "noble and sublime" spirits that are supposed to have brought about this revolution in men's minds we find such bloodthirsty degenerates and tyrants as Tiberius, Nero and Caracalla. along with a line of frivolous, pretentious, fashionable philosophers and frauds, of the kind we have come to know in the younger Pliny, Apollonius of Tyana and Plotinus.

The nobler Christians, by the way, had no trouble in adapting themselves to this fine society. Just one example. Among the many concubines, male and female, that the emperor Commodus (180-192) kept (a harem of 300 girls and as many boys is spoken of), Marcia had the honor of the first place. Marcia was a pious Christian and foster-daughter of Hyacinthus, an elder in the Christian community in Rome. Her influence was so great that she was able to have a number of deported Christians freed. Nevertheless, little by little she got tired of her imperial admirer; perhaps his bloodthirstiness made her fear for her own life. At any rate, she took part in a conspiracy against his life and undertook to execute the murderous plan; on the night of December 31, 192 the upright Christian gave her unsuspecting lover a poisoned drink. When this did not take effect soon enough, the emperor, already unconscious, was strangled.

As typical as this episode is the story of Calixtus, a protege of Marcia:

"This Calixtus had an special knack for business and in an earlier period of his life had been a banker. At first he was the slave of a noble Christian who entrusted a large sum of money to him to use in a banking business. After the slave had misappropriated the many deposits that widows and other believers had made in the bank on the strength of the solid reputation of the master, and the bank was on the brink of failing, the master asked for an accounting. The unfaithful servant fled, was captured and sent by his master into the treadmill. Released at the entreaty of Christian brethren and then sent by the prefect to the Sardinian mines, he won the favor of Marcia, the most influential mistress of the emperor Commodus; he was released on her recommendation and soon was chosen bishop of Rome."[18]

Kalthoff thinks it possible that the gospel stories of the unjust steward who "made himself friend of the mammon of unrighteousness" (Luke, 16, verses 1 to 9) and of the woman sinner to whom "her sins, which are many, are forgiven, for she loved much" (Luke, 7, verses 36 to 48) were taken into the evangels in order to "lend churchly explanation and sanction" to the dubious personalities of Marcia and Calixtus, who played such a role in the Christian community at Rome.

Another contribution to the history of the origin of the gospels.

Calixtus was not the last bishop and pope who owed his office to a courtesan, just as the murder of Commodus was not the last act of Christian violence. The savagery and bloodthirstiness of many popes and emperors since the "sainted" Constantine is well known.

The "softening and ennoblement of manners" that came in with Christianity was therefore of a peculiar kind. To understand its limitations and contradictions, we must look at its economic roots. The fine moral doctrines of the time do not explain it.

And the same is true for the internationalism of the period.

18. Kalthoff, *Die Entstehung des Christentums*, p. 133.

PIETY

World trade and political levelling were two great causes of
the growth of internationalism; and yet it would have been impossible, in the same degree, without the dissolution of all the
ties that held the old communities together, but also kept them
apart from each other. The organizations that had determined
the entire life of the individual in antiquity, and given him support and direction, lost all importance and vigor under the Empire: both those which were based on ties of blood, like the gens
or even the family, and those which were based on territorial
links, on living together on a common ground, like the *Markgenossenschaft* and the commune. This was the reason, as we have
seen, why men, now without such moral support, looked to models
and leaders, even to saviors. It also provided the incentive for men
to create new organizations better adapted to their new needs
than the traditional forms, which became more and more of a
burden.

At the end of the republic the trend to form clubs and associations, mainly for political purposes but also for mutual aid, was
conspicuous. The Caesars dissolved them; despotism is afraid of
nothing so much as social organizations. Its power is greatest when
the state is the only social organization and the citizens stand to
it only in the relation of isolated individuals.

Caesar "suppressed all societies except those which came down
from the remotest antiquity," says Suetonius (*Caesar*, chap. 42).
Of Augustus he says: "Many parties (*plurimae factiones*) were
organized under the name of a new college and practiced all sorts
of misdeeds. . . . He dissolved the colleges, with the exception of
those that were age-old and recognized by law."[19]

Mommsen finds these measures very praiseworthy. He sees
Caesar, the tricky and unscrupulous conspirator and gang-leader,
as a "true statesman," who "served the people not for reward,
not even for the reward of their love," but "for the blessings of
the future and above all for permission to save and rejuvenate

19. *Octavianus Augustus*, Chapter xxxii.

his nation."[20] To understand this conception of Caesar, it must be remembered that Mommsen's work was written in the years after the June massacres of 1848 (the first edition appeared in 1854), when Napoleon III was being hailed by many liberals, especially German ones, as the savior of society and Napoleon had brought the Caesar cult into fashion.

After the end of political activity and the suppression of the political clubs, the urge towards organization turned to more innocent unions. Guilds and mutual aid societies for cases of sickness, death and poverty, voluntary fire companies, but also plain social clubs, dining clubs, literary societies and the like sprang up like mushrooms. But Caesarism was so suspicious that it could not tolerate even such organizations; they might serve to cover up more dangerous associations.

In the correspondence between Pliny and Trajan there are letters in which Pliny recounts a conflagration that devastated Nicomedia, and recommends the formation of a voluntary fire company of not more than 150 men; these would be easy to watch. Trajan found this too dangerous however, and refused his assent.[21]

We see from later letters (117 and 118) that even gatherings at marriages or other festivals of the wealthy, where money was distributed, seemed to Pliny and Trajan to be dangerous to the state.

Hence our historians praise Trajan as one of the best emperors.

Under these conditions the urge to organize was driven into forming secret societies. If they were found out, however, the members faced the death penalty. It is clear that mere enjoyment or even advantages that only benefited the individual or gave him a better personal status could not be enough to make anybody risk his neck. Only those associations could survive that had a goal beyond the individual, a goal that remained even when the individual disappeared. And associations like this could gain strength only when this goal met a strong, generally felt social

20. *Römische Geschichte*, III, 476.
21. Pliny, *Letters*, X, 42 and 43.

interest and need, a class or general interest, an interest strongly felt by large masses and capable of making the strongest and most unselfish members of the masses risk their lives to satisfy it. In other words, the only organizations that could exist under the Empire were those that had a broad social goal, a high ideal. It was not the desire for practical advantage or immediate interests but only the most revolutionary or the most ideal of motives that could give an organization the strength to live.

This idealism has nothing in common with philosophical idealism. Large social goals can be set on the basis of the materialist philosophy too; in fact, it is only the materialist method, proceeding from experience and studying the necessary causal connections of our experiences, that can lead to the formulation of great social aims that are free of illusions. But under the Empire all the social prerequisites for such a method were absent. It was only by way of a moralistic mysticism that the individual of that time could rise above himself and set himself goals beyond personal and momentary well-being, or in other words, that way of thought that is known as religious. The only societies that maintained themselves under the Empire were religious ones, but it would be taking a mistaken view of them to let the religious form, the moralistic mysticism obscure the social content underlying all these associations which gave them their strength: the desire for a solution to the hopeless existing conditions, for higher forms of society, for close cooperation and mutual support on the part of the individuals lost in their isolation who drew new joy and courage from their coming together for high purposes.

These religious associations introduced a new division in society just at the time when the Mediterranean world was shifting from the concept of nationality to that of humanity. The purely economic organizations, aimed at helping the individual in one particular respect, did not free him from existing society or give his life new content. It was different, however, with the religious associations, which under religious garb strove toward a great social ideal. This ideal was in completest contradiction to existing society, not in one point only but in every jot and tittle. The

defenders of this ideal spoke the same language as their com-
patriots and yet were not understood by them; at every step the
two worlds, the old and the new, collided at their boundaries, although they lived in the same country. A new opposition arose
among men. Just as Gauls and Syrians, Romans and Egyptians,
Spaniards and Greeks were beginning to lose their national in-
dividuality, there arose the great opposition between believers
and unbelievers, saints and sinners, Christians and heathen that
soon split the world in two down to its foundations.

The sharper the strife, the greater the intolerance and fanaticism which are naturally involved in any conflict; these are
necessary elements of progress and development, when they inspire and strengthen the progressive forces. We do not mean by
intolerance here the forcible suppression of propaganda for any
inconvenient opinion, but energetic rejection and criticism of
every other view and energetic defence of one's own. Only cowards
and idlers are tolerant in this sense, when the large general interests of life are at stake.

It is true that these interests are constantly changing. What was
a vital question but yesterday may be a matter of indifference
today, not worth fighting over. On such a point the fanaticism
that was a necessity only yesterday is today a waste of energy, and
so very harmful.

The religious intolerance and religious fanaticism of many of
the growing Christian sects was one of the forces that made social
development go forward, as long as large social aims could get
to the masses only in religious garb, that is from the time of the
Empire down to the Reformation. These qualities become reactionary and nothing more than a means to block progress once
the religious way of thinking has been replaced by the methods
of modern investigation, so that it is no longer cultivated
except by backward classes, levels and regions, and is no longer
capable of cloaking new social goals.

Religious intolerance was quite a new trait in the way of thinking characteristic of ancient society. Though they were intolerant
nationalistically and disliked the foreigner or enemy, whom

they enslaved or killed even if he had not fought in battle against them, it never occurred to them to think less of anyone because of his religion. Cases that seem to be religious persecution can be reduced to complaints of a political nature.

It was the new way of thinking, arising in the era of the Emperors which brought religious intolerance with it, and on both sides, Christians as well as pagans; in the latter case, of course, not against every strange religion but only against that which propagandized a new social idea under the cloak of religion, an idea in complete contradiction to the existing social order.

Apart from that the pagans remained true to the religious tolerance they had been used to; indeed, the international trade of the Empire led to internationalism in religious rites as well. The foreign merchants and other travelers brought their gods with them everywhere. And strange gods were more highly thought of at that time than the home-grown sort, which had shown they were of no use. The feeling of desperation, arising out of the general rack and ruin, led to doubting the old gods as well and brought many of the bolder and more independent spirits to atheism and scepticism, to doubting all divinity and even all philosophy. The fainter-hearted and weaker however were driven, as we have seen, to look for a new savior in whom they could find support and hope. Many thought they had found saviors in the Caesars, and raised them to the status of gods. Others thought it safer to turn to gods who had counted as such for a long time but had not been tested in the locality as yet. Outlandish cults came into fashion.

In this international competition of the gods the Orient defeated the West, partly because the oriental religions were less naive and had more urban philosophical depth, for reasons that we shall have occasion to discuss later; and partly because the East was industrially superior to the West.

The old civilized world of the Orient was industrially far superior to the West when it was conquered and plundered, first by the Macedonians and then by the Romans. It might be thought that the international exchanges that took place thereafter might have brought about industrial exchange as well and brought the West up to the Eastern level. The contrary was the case. We have seen that from a certain point on there sets in a general decline of the ancient world, a consequence in part of the predominance of forced labor over free, and in part of the plundering of the provinces by Rome and usury capital. But this decline went forward more rapidly in the West than in the East, so that the relative cultural superiority of the latter increased rather than diminished from the second century of our era up to the year 1000, more or less. Poverty, barbarism and depopulation progressed faster in the Occident than in the Orient.

The cause of this phenomenon is to be looked for mainly in the industrial superiority of the East and the steady increase in the exploitation of the working classes all over the Empire. The surpluses they produced flowed chiefly from the provinces to Rome, the center of the great exploiters. But to the extent that the surplus accumulated there took the form of money, the lion's share went back to the Orient; for the East alone produced the luxury goods desired by the exploiters. It furnished the slaves, but also industrial products like glass and purple in Phoenicia, linen and textiles from Egypt, fine woolens and leather goods from Asia Minor, rugs in Babylonia. And the decreasing fertility of Italy made Egypt the granary of Rome, for, thanks to the floods that covered its fields every year with fresh fertile mud, the farms of the Nile valley were inexhaustible.

A large part of what the Orient supplied, it is true, was taken from it by force in the form of taxes and usurious interest, but there still remained a considerable part that had to be paid with the proceeds of the exploitation of the Occident, which grew poorer in the process.

Commerce with the East extended beyond the borders of the Empire. Alexandria grew rich not only through dealing in Egyptian industrial products but also through acting as middleman for the trade with Arabia and India, while from Sinope on the Black Sea a trade route to China was opened up. Pliny estimates in his *Natural History* that each year about a hundred million sesterces ($5,000,000.) left the Empire for Chinese silks, Indian jewels and Arabian spices. Without any equivalent worth mentioning in the form of goods, and without any debts on the part of foreign countries in the form of tribute or interest, the whole sum had to be paid in precious metals.

With the oriental wares, the oriental merchants too pressed toward Rome, and with them their cults. These cults were suited to the needs of the West in view of the fact that they had arisen in the Orient in similar social circumstances, although not of such a desperate degree as those that now prevailed over the entire Empire. The notion of salvation through a deity whose favor is gained by the sacrifice of earthly pleasures was common to most of these cults now rapidly spreading through the Empire, especially the Egyptian worship of Isis and the Persian cult of Mithra.

"The worship of Isis had entered Rome in Sulla's time and won imperial favor under Vespasian. She had spread to the far West and gradually won enormous popularity and importance, first as a goddess of health, and more narrowly of healing. . . . Her cult was full of pompous processions, along with self-mortifications, penitences and rigorous observances, and above all mysteries. Religious longing, hope for atonement, craving for violent penance, and hope to win blessed immortality by devotion to a deity were the factors that favored the acceptance of such strange cults into the world of Graeco-Roman gods, which had hitherto had little in common with these mysterious ceremonies, fanatical ecstasy, magic, self-renunciation and boundless devotion to the deity, resignation and penance as preliminary conditions to purification and consecration. Still more powerful, however, especially in the armies, was the secret cult of Mithra, likewise with the promise of salvation and immortality. It first became known under Tiberius.[22]

Indian ideas too entered the Roman empire. For example, Apollonius of Tyana, whom we have mentioned, travelled to India only to study the philosophical and religious teachings

---

22. Hertzberg, *Geschichte des römischen Kaiserreichs*, p. 451.

there. We have heard of Plotinus, too, who, in order to make a closer study of Persian and Indian wisdom, went to Persia.

All these ideas and cults did not go unnoticed by the Christians struggling for salvation and exaltation; they had a powerful influence in the origin of the rites and legends of Christianity.

"The Church Father Eusebius contemptuously spoke of the Egyptian cult as 'scarab wisdom'; and yet the myth of the Virgin Mary is only an echo of the myths that were native to the banks of the Nile.

"Osiris was represented on earth by the bull Apis. Now as Osiris himself had been conceived by his mother without the assistance of a male god, so his earthly representative had to be born of a virgin heifer without the assistance of a bull. Herodotus tells us that the mother of Apis was impregnated by a sunray; according to Plutarch it was a moonray.

"Like Apis, Jesus too had no father, but was conceived by a heavenly ray of light. Apis was a bull, but represented a god; Jesus was a god that was represented by a lamb. Now Osiris too was often represented with a ram's head."[23]

In the third century, when Christianity was already very strong, a scoffer was of opinion that there was no great difference in Egypt between Christians and heathen: "A man that worships Serapis in Egypt is also a Christian, and those that call themselves Christian bishops worship Serapis as well; every Grand Rabbi of the Jews, every Samaritan, every Christian priest is also a magician, a prophet, a quack doctor (*aliptes*). Even when the patriarch comes to Egypt, some ask him to pray to Serapis, others ask that he pray to Christ."[24]

The story of the birth of Christ, as we find it in Luke, shows Buddhist traits.

Pfleiderer remarks that the author of the gospel did not invent this story, no matter how apocryphal it is; he rather took it from legends "that had come to him in some way or other," perhaps

23. Lafargue, "Der Mythus von den unbefleckten Empfängnis," *Neue Zeit*, XI, No. 1, p. 849.
24. Cited in Mommsen, Römische Geschichte, V, 585.

primeval legends common among the peoples of the Near East. "For we find the same legends, sometimes with amazingly similar traits, in the story of the childhood of the Indian savior Gautama Buddha [fifth century B.C.—K.K.]. He too is born miraculously of the virgin queen Maya, into whose spotless body the heavenly luminous essence of Buddha entered. At his birth too heavenly spirits appeared and sang this song of praise: 'A wonderful hero is born, one without compare. Weal of the world, full of pity, today thou spreadest thy good-will over all the universe. Let joy and contentment come to all creatures, that they may be calm, masters of themselves, and happy.' He too is brought to the temple by his mother to learn to perform the rites of the law; there he is found by the old hermit Asita, whom an intuition had sent down from the Himalaya; Asita foretells that this child will become Buddha, the savior from all evils, he who leads to freedom and light and immortality. . . . And finally the brief description of the way in which the royal child increased daily in spiritual perfection and bodily beauty and strength—quite in the way that the Jesus child is described in Luke 2, verses 40 and 52."[25]

"And of Gautama too as an adolescent instances of early wisdom are recounted, among others that once he was separated from his family at a festival and later after a feverish search found by his father in the midst of a circle of holy men, deep in pious contemplation; he admonished his amazed father to seek for higher things."[26]

Pfleiderer lists further elements that had been taken up into Christianity from other cults, for example from the Mithra worship. We have already spoken of his reference to the prototype of the last Supper that was "one of the Mithra sacraments" (*op. cit.*, p. 130). The doctrine of the Resurrection too contains pagan elements.

"Here perhaps may be traced the effects of popular notions of the god dying and reborn, as they were prevalent at that time in the Near Eastern cults of Adonis, Attis, Osiris, under various names

25. Pfleiderer, *Urchristentum*, I, 412.
26. Pfleiderer, *Entstehung des Christentums*, 198 f.

but generally basically similar. In the Syrian capital of Antioch, where Paul labored for a long time, the main holiday was the festival of Adonis in spring; first death of Adonis ('the Lord') and the burial of his body, represented by a picture, were celebrated to the wild laments of women. On the next day (in the Osiris festival it was the third day and in the Attis festival the fourth day after the death) the news was broadcast that the god lived, and he (a picture) was brought to light, etc."[27]

But Pfleiderer points out, correctly, that Christianity did not merely absorb these heathen elements but adapted them to its unitary world view. For Christianity could not accept strange gods just as they came; its monotheism, if nothing else, stood in the way.

MONOTHEISM

But monotheism, the belief in a single god, was not something peculiar to Christianity alone. And here too it is possible to get at the economic roots from which this idea came. As we have seen, the inhabitants of the big cities had lost contact with nature; all the traditional organisations, in which the individual had previously found moral support, had disappeared; and preoccupation with the ego became the main object of thought, which turned from study of the external world into grubbing around inside one's personal feelings and needs.

The gods had originally served to explain what happened in nature, whose laws were not understood. These events were extremely numerous and of all kinds. To explain them all sorts of gods had to be postulated, dreadful and cheerful, brutal and tender, male and female. As knowledge of the regular causal connections in nature progressed, the individual deities became more and more superfluous. But they had struck too deep roots in people's ways of thought over the centuries and entered too deeply into their every-day concerns, and knowledge of nature was still too fragmentary, for it to be able fully to put an end to the belief in gods. The gods merely kept being shifted from one

27. *Op. cit.*, p. 147.

sphere of activity to another; they changed from being constant comrades of men to extraordinary marvelous phenomena, from dwellers on earth to dwellers in supermundane regions, in heaven; from being active, energetic workers and fighters, tirelessly moving the world, to contemplative onlookers of the world theatre.

In the end, the progress of natural science would have completely done away with them, had not the formation of the large cities and the economic decline, which we have described, caused men to turn away from nature and thrust the study of spirit through spirit into the foreground of thought; that is, instead of scientific study of mental experience and events as a whole the individual's own mind became the source of all wisdom about himself, and this in turn the source of all wisdom generally. No matter how variegated and changeable the movements and needs of the soul might be, the soul itself seemed to be something simple and indivisible. The souls of others proved to be just like one's own soul. A scientific view would have concluded from all this that all mental activity followed regular laws. But just at that time there began the collapse of the old moral supports, and that lack of support that appeared to men as freedom, freedom of the will for the individual. The unity of mind in all men seemed explicable only on the hypothesis that it was everywhere a portion of the same mind, the one mind whose emanation and copy forms the indivisible and incomprehensible soul in each individual. This general soul or world soul is not in space, and neither is the individual soul. But it is present and active in all men, and hence present everywhere and all-knowing. Even the most secret thoughts are known to it. The predominance of the moral interest over the natural, which was the basis for assuming this world soul, gave it a moral character. The world soul became the totality of all the moral ideals that then concerned men. In order to achieve this, it had to be freed from the corporeality that adheres to the soul of man and clouds its morality. In this way the concept of a new deity arose. This could only be a single one, corresponding to the unity of the soul of the individual, in contrast to the plurality of the gods of antiquity, which corresponded to the multiplicity of the natural events outside us. And the new deity was outside of nature and above nature, and existed before nature, which it had created, whereas the old gods had been a part of nature and no older than nature.

But no matter how purely psychic and moral the new spiritual interest of men appeared, they could not abstract from nature altogether. And since natural science declined at the same time, the assumption of super-human personal intervention was resorted to once more. The higher beings that interfered in the course of nature were now no longer sovereign gods, as before; they were subordinate to the world soul in the same way as, according to the ideas of that time, nature was under God and the body under the soul. They were beings intermediate between God and men.

The course of political development gave support to this way of thinking. The downfall of the republic of gods in heaven went hand in hand with the downfall of the republic in Rome; God became the omnipotent emperor of the other world, and like Caesar he had his court, the saints and angels, and his republican opposition, the devil and his legions.

In the end the Christians came to divide God's heavenly bureaucracy, the angels, into ranks and classes just as the emperors classified their terrestrial bureaucracy; and the same pride of place seems to have ruled among the angels as among the emperor's officials.

Since the time of Constantine the courtiers and officials of the state had been classified in various degrees, each with a distinctive title: Thus we have 1. the *gloriosi*, the glorious ones, as the consuls were called. 2. The *Nobilissimi*, the most noble; this name was given to princes of the blood. 3. The *patricii*, or barons. After these ranks of the nobility came the higher grades of the bureaucracy. 4. The *illustres*, the famous. 5. The *spectabiles*, the eminent. 6. The *clarissimi*, the notable. Below these again: 7. The *perfectissimi*, the most perfect. 8. The *egregii*, the outstanding. 9. The *comites*, or companions.

The heavenly court is organized in exactly the same manner. Our theologians have precise information on this subject.

Thus, for example, the *Kirchenlexicon der katholischen Theologie* (published by Wetzer and Welte, Freiburg i.B., 1849) tells in its article *"Angel"* of the large number of angels, and continues: "Many doctors believe, after the example of St. Ambrose, that the number of angels is to the number of man as 99:1; for the lost sheep in the parable of the good shepherd (Luke 15, verse 7) signifies the human race, and the 99 sheep that were not lost represent the angels. In this innumerable multitude the angels constitute various classes, and the church also pronounced against Origen's opinion, according to which all spirits are equal with respect to substance, power, etc., at the second council of Constantinople in the year 553, strongly asserting the diversity of angels. The church knows nine choruses of angels, each three in turn constituting another chorus. They are: 1. *Seraphim,* 2. *Cherubim,* 3. *Thrones,* 4. *Dominations,* 5. *Virtues,* 6. *Powers,* 7. *Principalities,* 8. *Archangels,* 9. *Angels.*"[28]

"This much seems to be beyond all doubt, that the angels, in the narrow sense of the word, are the lowest but most numerous class, while the Seraphim are the highest in rank but the fewest in number." And so it goes on earth as well. There are only a few Excellencies, but whole masses of ordinary letter-carriers.

We read further:

"In relation to God the angels live in intimate and personal communion with him; and their relationship to him is shown in unending homage, in humble submission, in a love that knows no exception and renounces everything outside of God, in full and joyful dedication of their entire being, in unceasing thanks and inward adoration, as well in perpetual praise, in constant glorification, in reverential exaltation, in holy jubilation and enraptured rejoicing."

This joyful obsequiousness is precisely what the emperors required of their courtiers and officials. It was the ideal of Byzantinism.

28. The word *angelus* originally meant nothing more than "messenger."

We see that the picture of a single God, that took form in Christianity, received as large a contribution from imperial despotism as from philosophy, which had been tending towards monotheism more and more ever since Plato.

This philosophy conformed so closely to the general longings and way of feeling, that it soon passed into the consciousness of the masses. Thus in Plautus, a writer of comedies of the third century B.C. who only put very popular wisdom into the best possible form, we find passages like the following pleas of a slave asking for a favor:

> "There is, you know, a God who hears and sees
> All that we do; and as you treat me here,
> He'll see your son is likewise treated there.
> If you do well, 'twill be to your advantage;
> If ill, he'll deal impartially with you."
> (*The Captives*, Act II, Scene 2. Allison's translation)

This is a quite Christian conception of God. But it is still a naive monotheism, one that unreflectingly leaves the old gods still existing. It never occurred even to the Christians to deny the existence of the old gods, just as they accepted so many heathen miracles without question. Yet their God suffered no other god along with him; he wanted to be sole ruler. If the heathen gods would not submit to him and become part of his court, the only role left them was that played by the republican opposition under the first emperors, for the most part a pretty shabby one. All it consisted of was trying to play some trick or other on the omnipotent ruler now and then and stir up honest subjects against him, without any hope of overthrowing the ruler but merely of irritating him.

But even this intolerant and peremptory monotheism, never for an instant doubting the superiority and omnipotence of its God, was something that Christianity found all ready to its hand, not among the pagans to be sure but in a little nation of a peculiar sort, the Jews, who had developed the belief in a savior and the duty of mutual aid and strong cohesiveness far more strongly than any other nation or class of the population of its time, and thereby gave far more satisfaction to needs strongly felt in that period. Judaism therefore gave powerful impetus to the new doctrine which was growing out of those needs, and furnished it with some of its most important elements. It is only after we have gone forward from our general treatment of the Roman-Hellenic world of the Empire to consider Judaism in particular that we shall have traced all the roots from which Christianity grew.

BOOK THREE: THE JEWS

1

ISRAEL

MIGRATIONS OF THE SEMITIC PEOPLES

THE BEGINNINGS of the Jewish history are as obscure as those of Greek or Roman history, or even more so. For many centuries these beginnings were preserved only orally and when the old legends were finally collected and written down, they were distorted in the most one-sided and partisan manner. Nothing could be more mistaken than to take the Bible story as an actual historical account. The stories have a historical core, but it is extremely difficult to get at.

It was only long after the return from Babylonian exile, in the fifth century, that the "holy" scriptures of the Jews were given the form in which we know them today. All the old traditions were ceremoniously refurbished and added to, in order to help the pretensions of the rising theocracy. In the process all of early Jewish history was turned topsy-turvy. This is especially true of everything that is related of the religion of Israel before the Exile.

When, after the Exile, Judaism founded a community of its own in Jerusalem and the surrounding territory, the other nations were struck by its singularity, as we learn from many sources. On the other hand, no such testimony has come down to us with respect to pre-Exile times. Down to the destruction of Jerusalem by the Babylonians the Jews were regarded by the other nations as a people like any other, with no special characteristics. And we have every reason to assume that up to that time the Jews actually were not odd or unusual in any way.

It is impossible to outline a picture of ancient Israel with any certainty, given the scarcity and the unreliability of the sources that have come down to us. Bible criticism by Protestant theologians has already shown that a great deal of it is spurious and fictitious, but tends far too much to take as gospel truth everything not yet proved to be obviously counterfeit.

Basically we are reduced to hypotheses when we try to form an idea of the course of the development of Israelite society. We can make good use of the stories of the Old Testament to the extent that it is possible for us to compare them with descriptions of peoples in similar situations.

The first authentic appearance of the Israelites on the stage of history is their invasion of the land of the Canaanites. All the stories of their nomadic era are either old tribal legends and tales reworked for propaganda purposes, or later fabrications. They come into history as participants in a great Semitic migration.

The migrations played a role in the ancient world comparable to today's revolutions. In the last book we became acquainted with the decline of the Roman Empire, and saw the way in which its inundation by the Germanic barbarians, an event called a migration, was built up and prepared. It was not an unprecedented event. It had repeatedly occurred in the old Orient on a smaller scale, but from similar causes.

In the fertile basins of many of the great rivers of the Orient there early arose an agriculture that produced considerable surpluses of foodstuffs which not only supported the peasants but enabled a numerous supplementary population to live and work. Crafts, arts and sciences flourished there; but an aristocracy too was formed, which could devote itself exclusively to the trade of arms and was all the more needed because the wealth of the river-basin tempted warlike nomadic neighbors to robber raids. If the farmer wanted to cultivate his field in peace, he needed the protection of such aristocrats and had to buy it. As the aristocracy became stronger, it was natural for it to attempt to use its military power to increase its revenues, particularly since the flourishing of the arts and crafts gave rise to all sorts of luxury, which required great wealth.

The oppression of the peasants begins at this point, together with slave-hunting campaigns by the better-armed aristocrats and their vassals against the neighboring peoples. Forced labor begins and drives society into the same blind alley in which the society of the Roman Empire was later to end up. The free farmer is ruined and replaced by forced laborers. But that means that the basis of the empire's military power disappears; the aristocracy, despite its highly-developed military technique, loses its military superiority, unmanned by growing luxury.

They lose the qualities they need to perform the function on which their social status was based: that of defending the community against the inroads of plundering neighbors. These neighbors see the growing weakness of the rich and tempting prey; they press harder and harder on its borders and finally overflow it, unchaining a movement that extends to more and more nations pressing onward and continues for a long period. A part of the invaders takes possession of the land and creates a new free peasant class. Others who are stronger form a new military aristocracy. At the same time the old aristocracy can still maintain a superior status as guardian of the arts and sciences of the old civilization, no longer as a caste of warriors, but only as a caste of priests.

Once the migration has come to rest, the development of the cycle begins all over again, more or less comparable to the cycle of prosperity and crisis in capitalist society—although not a ten-year cycle, but one that takes many centuries, a cycle that was first eliminated by the capitalist mode of production.

This course of events went on for thousands of years in the most diverse regions of Asia and North Africa, most strikingly in regions where broad fertile river valleys are next to steppes or deserts. The valleys produce mighty riches, but in the end they produce deep-reaching corruption and effeminacy as well. This makes it possible for poor but warlike nomad nations to develop who are always ready to change their location when there is a chance of booty, and can come together quickly in countless hordes from distant regions to make a devastating assault on a single district.

Such river valleys were those of the Yellow River and Yangtze-kiang, in which the Chinese community took form; of the Ganges, in which India's wealth was concentrated; of the Euphrates and Tigris, where the mighty empires of Babylonia and Assyria arose; and finally of the Nile, in Egypt.

In contrast Central Asia on the one hand and Arabia on the other constituted inexhaustible reservoirs of warlike nomads who made life miserable for their neighbors and from time to time took advantage of their neighbors' weakness to make mass invasions.

Out of Central Asia from time to time, in such periods of weakness, floods of Mongols and occasionally of so-called Indo-Germans overflowed the banks of civilization. Out of Arabia there came those peoples to whom we give the common name of Semites. Babylonia, Assyria, Egypt and the Mediterranean coast in between were the goals of the Semitic invaders.

Toward the end of the second millennium before Christ another great Semitic migration sets in, driving toward Mesopotamia, Syria and Egypt, and coming to an end roughly in the eleventh century B.C. Among the Semitic stocks that conquered neighboring civilized countries at that time were the Hebrews. In their Bedouin-like wanderings they may previously have been at the Egyptian border and on Sinai, but it was only after they had succeeded in establishing themselves in Palestine that they take on a fixed character and emerge from the stage of nomadic instability, in which no durable national unities are formed.

PALESTINE

From now on the history and character of the Israelites was determined not only by the qualities they had acquired on the Bedouin stage and retained for some time thereafter, but also by the nature and situation of Palestine.

The influence of the geographical factor in history should not of course be exaggerated. The geographical factor—position, contour, climate—remains more or less the same in most countries over the course of history; it is there before history and certainly has a tremendous effect on that history. But the way in which that effect is produced depends in turn on the level to which technology and social relations have developed in the country in question.

Thus the English would certainly never have reached their position of world dominance during the eighteenth and nineteenth centuries without the special nature of their country, without its wealth in coal and iron and its insular position. But so long as coal and iron did not have that dominant role in technology that they acquired in the era of steam, these natural riches of the soil had only slight significance. And until America and the sea route to India had been discovered, the techniques of sailing highly developed, and Spain, France and Germany highly cultivated; so long as these countries were inhabited by mere barbarians, England's insular position was a factor shutting it off from the civilization of Europe and keeping it weak and barbarous.

Under different social conditions the unchanging nature of the land can have a quite different significance; even where the nature of the country is not altered by the change in the modes of production, its effect does not necessarily remain the same. Here too we always come up against the totality of economic relationships as the decisive factor.

It was not therefore the absolute nature and position of Palestine, but that nature and position under determinate social relationships, that determined the history of Israel.

The peculiarity of Palestine was that it was a border region, where hostile elements collided and fought. It lay in a place where on one side the Arabian desert came to an end and the Syrian civilized country began, and on the other the spheres of influence of the two great empires clashed: the Egyptian empire in the valley of the Nile, and the Mesopotamian on the rivers Euphrates and Tigris, with its capital now at Babylon and now at Nineveh.

Finally, Palestine was crossed by very important trade routes. It controlled traffic between Egypt on the one side and Syria and

Mesopotamia on the other, together with commerce between Phoenicia and Arabia.

Let us consider the effects of the first factor. Palestine was a fertile land; its fertility was nothing out of the ordinary, but it seemed sumptuous compared with the deserts of sand and stone nearby. For the inhabitants of those wastelands it seemed a land flowing with milk and honey.

The Hebraic clans came as nomadic herdsmen; their settling down took place in constant battle with the native inhabitants of Palestine, the Canaanites, from whom they took one city after another, forcing them into submission. But what they had won in constant war they had to keep by constant warfare, for other nomads came after them who were just as eager as they were to own the fruitful land, Edomites, Moabites, Ammonites and others.

Even after conquering the land the Hebrews remained herdsmen for a long time, although they were now sedentary. However they gradually took over from the original inhabitants their mode of agriculture, the growing of grain and wine, the culture of olive and fig trees, etc., and intermixed with them. But they kept for a long time the character traits of the nomadic Bedouin tribes from which they came. Nomadic cattle-raising in the desert seems to be particularly unfavorable to technological progress and social development. The way of life of the Bedouins of Arabia today still reminds us strongly of that described in the old legends of Abraham, Isaac and Jacob. Out of the centuries there came down from generation to generation eternal repetition of the same activities and sufferings, the same needs and views, ending in a bitter conservatism, which is even stronger in the nomad herdsman than in the peasant, and favors the preservation of old customs and institutions even in the presence of great changes.

As an example of this tendency, the hearth had no fixed position in the house of the Israelitish peasant, and no religious significance. "In this point the Israelites come close to the Arabs and differ from the Greeks, to whom they are much closer in the other aspects of daily life," says Wellhausen, adding: "Hebrew hardly has a word for the hearth; the name 'aschphot' has significantly taken on the meaning of 'rubbish heap.' That shows the difference from the Indo-European hearth, the house altar; instead of the hearth fire that never goes out, the Hebrews had the eternal lamp."[1]

Among the qualities that the Israelites carried over from their Bedouin period should be included the inclination for trading. Above, in studying Roman society, we pointed out how early trade among peoples developed. Its first agents must have been nomadic herdsmen of the desert. Their way of earning a living compelled them to wander ceaselessly from one pasture to another. The meager nature of their land must very early have aroused in them the need for products of other richer countries bordering on their own. They traded, perhaps, their surplus cattle for grain, oil, dates, or tools of wood, stone, bronze and iron. Their mobility enabled them however not merely to get products for themselves from distant parts, but also to barter desirable and easily transportable products for other people; that is, not for the purpose of keeping them and consuming or enjoying them for themselves, but for the purpose of surrendering them against compensation. They were thus the first merchants. So long as there were no roads and sea travel was poorly developed, this form of commerce must have predominated, and could lead to great riches for those who carried it on. Later, as sea travel increased and safe and practicable roads were built, this sort of trade through nomads must have decreased, and the nomads, reduced to the products of their deserts, must have grown poor. That must be at least in part the reason why the old civilization of Central Asia has declined so since the discovery of the sea route to the East Indies. Earlier, Arabia became poor for the same reason; at the time the Phoenician cities flourished the Arabian nomads carried on a very profitable trade with them. They delivered the valued wool of their sheep to the city looms working for export to the West; they also brought the products of the rich and fertile Arabia Felix to the south, frankincense, spices, gold and precious stones. In addition, they brought from Ethiopia, which is separated from Arabia Felix only by a

1. Wellhausen, *Israelitische und jüdische Geschichte*, p. 87 f.

narrow body of water, precious goods like ivory and ebony. The trade with India too passed chiefly through Arabia; to its coasts on the Persian Gulf and the Indian Ocean goods came by ship from Malabar and Ceylon and then were taken across the desert to Palestine and Phoenicia.

This trade brought considerable wealth to all the tribes through whose hands it passed, partly through the merchant's profit, partly through the duties imposed on the wares as they passed through.

"It is common to find very rich tribes among these peoples," says Heeren. "Among the Arabian nomads none seem to have carried on caravan trade with more profit than the Midianites, who used to rove near the northern border of this land, near Phoenicia. It was a caravan of Midianite merchants loaded with 'spicery and balm and myrrh,' going from Arabia to Egypt, to whom Joseph was sold (Genesis 37, verse 28). The Israelites got so much booty in gold from this people when Gideon drove back an invasion of the Midianites into Gilead that it caused amazement; the metal was so common among them that it was used not only for personal adornment but even for the camels' collars." The eighth chapter of Judges tells us: "And Gideon arose, and slew Zebah and Zalmunna, and took away the ornaments (or, ornaments like the moon) that were on their camels' necks. . . . And Gideon said unto them (the men of Israel), I would desire a request of you, that ye would give me every man the earrings of his prey. (For they had golden earrings, because they were Ishmaelites.) . . . And the weight of the golden earrings that he requested was a thousand and seven hundred shekels[2] of gold, beside ornaments, and collars, and purple raiment that was on the kings of Midian, and beside the chains that were on their camels' necks."

Heeren then discusses the Edomites and continues: "The Greeks include all the nomadic tribes wandering in northern Arabia under the name of Nabataean Arabs. Diodorus, who beautifully describes their way of life, does not forget their caravan trade

2. A shekel of gold was 16.8 grams, or about $11.

with Yemen. 'Not a small part of them,' he says, 'makes a business of transporting frankincense, myrrh and other costly spices, which they get from those who bring them from Arabia Felix, to the Mediterranean.' (Diodorus, II, p. 390).

"The riches that some of the desert tribes acquired in this way was great enough to excite the greed of Greek men of war. One of the depots for the wares that went through the district of the Edomites was the fortified place of Petra, from which Northwest Arabia gets the name of Petraean. Demetrius Poliorcetes tried to surprise and plunder this town."[3]

We must imagine the Israelites during the time of their wanderings as resembling their neighbors the Midianites. It is already reported of Abraham that he was rich not only in cattle but also in silver and gold (Genesis 13, verse 2). The nomadic herdsmen could obtain these only by trade. Their later situation in Canaan could not weaken the trading spirit they had acquired when they were nomads. For the position of this country enabled them to take part in the trade between Phoenicia and Arabia, between Egypt and Babylon, just as before, and to get profit from it, partly by acting as middlemen and forwarders, partly by interfering with it, falling on trading caravans from their mountain fastnesses and plundering them or taking tribute. We must not forget that at that time commerce and robbery were closely related professions.

"Even before the Israelites came to Canaan, the trade of this country was highly developed. In the Tel-el-Amarna letters (fifteenth century B.C.) caravans are spoken of as passing through the land under convoy."[4]

But even by the year 2000 we have evidence of the close commercial relationships between Palestine and Egypt and the lands on the Euphrates.

Jeremias (the *Privatdozent* at Leipzig, not the Jewish prophet) gives the substance of a papyrus of that period as follows:

"The Bedouin tribes of Palestine were thus closely linked with

3. Heeren, *Ideen über die Politik, den Verkehr und den Handel der vornehmsten Völker der alten Welt,* 1817, I, 2, p. 84-86.
4. Franz Buhl, *Die sozialen Verhältnisse der Israeliten,* 1899, p. 76.

the civilized land of Egypt. According to the papyrus, their sheikhs occasionally visit the court of the Pharaoh and understand events in Egypt. Ambassadors go with written commissions between the Euphrates region and Egypt. These Asiatic Bedouins are not barbarians at all. The barbarian peoples whom the Egyptian king combatted were expressly distinguished from them. The Bedouin sheiks later allied themselves to wage large campaigns against 'the princes of the nations.' "[5]

Herzfeld, in his *Handelsgeschichte der Juden des Altertums*, gives an extensive account of the caravan routes that crossed Palestine or passed near it. He is of the opinion that such trade routes were "perhaps of even greater commercial importance in antiquity than the railroads are today."

"One such route led from Southwestern Arabia parallel to the coast of the Red Sea and the Gulf of Akaba. On it the products of Arabia Felix, Ethiopia and some Ethiopian hinterlands came to Sela, later called Petra, some 70 kilometers south of the Dead Sea. Another caravan route brought the wares of Babylonia and India from Gerrha on the Persian Gulf across Arabia to Petra. From here three other routes diverged: one to Egypt, with forks to the right leading to Arabian ports on the Mediterranean; a second to Gaza, with a very important extension northwards; a third along the eastern shore of the Dead Sea and the Jordan to Damascus. Moreover, Ailat, in the inner corner of the Gulf of Akaba (the ancient Sinus Aelanites) was already a depot for the goods of the countries to the south; it was connected with Petra by a short route. The road north from Gaza, mentioned above, led through the lowlands of Judaea and Samaria, and in the plain of Yisreel ran into another road going to Acco from the east. The wares brought in these diverse ways were put aboard ship in the Arabian Mediterranean ports or in Gaza and Acco, if they were for Phoenicia; for the stretch from Acco to Tyre and Sidon was very rocky and usable for land transport only at a much later date. The much-travelled caravan route from the east led from Babylon on the middle Euphrates through the Arabian-Syrian

5. Jeremias, *Das alte Testament im Lichte des alten Orients*, 1906, p. 300.

desert in which Palmyra later flourished, and after a short stretch along the eastern bank of the upper Jordan crossed that river and ran down to the sea through the plain of Yisreel. Shortly before it reached the Jordan, it joined the road from Gilead, which as we have seen was used even in Joseph's times, and into which ran the road from Gaza; apparently Gaza was also the starting-point of the road from Palestine to Egypt (Genesis 37, verses 25, 41, 57). That these trade routes and the fairs, which formed at their nodal points, had a commercial influence on the Jews cannot be shown from historical facts for some time after this; but on internal grounds cannot be doubted; and by assuming it many an ancient reference is elucidated for the first time."[6]

Luxury and export industries and art flourished far less than did trade among the Israelites. The reason is probably that they became sedentary at a period when all around them craftsmanship had reached a high point of perfection. Luxury articles were better and cheaper when obtained through trade than when prepared by home industry, which was limited to the production of the simplest goods. Even among the Phoenicians, who became civilized much earlier, the advance of their industry was held back by the competition of Egyptian and Babylonian goods. "In early times the Phoenicians were hardly superior to the inhabitants of the rest of Syria in the field of industry. It is more likely that Herodotus is right when he says that the first Phoenicians that landed on the coasts of Greece were peddling goods that were not produced in their own country, but in Egypt and Assyria, that is the countries inland from Syria. The great cities of Phoenicia first became industrial cities after they had lost their political independence and a large part of their commercial connections."[7]

It may have been the eternal state of war, too, that interfered with the development of crafts. In any case it is certain that they did not develop very far. The prophet Ezekiel gives a detailed account of the trade of Tyre in his lamentation for that city, including the trade with Israel, whose exports are exclusively agri-

6. *Handelsgeschichte der Juden*, p. 22-25.
7. R. Pietschmann, *Geschichte der Phönizier*, 1889, p. 238.

cultural: "Judah, and the land of Israel, they were thy merchants: they traded in thy market wheat of Minnith, and Pannag, and honey, and oil, and balm" (Ezekiel 27, verse 17).

When David made Jerusalem his capital, King Hiram of Tyre sent him "cedar trees, and carpenters, and masons: and they built David an house" (II Samuel, 5, verse 11). The same thing happened when Solomon was building the temple, and paid Hiram twenty thousand measures of wheat and twenty of oil every year.

Without highly developed luxury crafts, that is without artistic handicrafts, there is no fine art in which to portray the human person, going beyond the outline of the human type to individualize and idealize it.

Such an art presupposes a high level of trade to bring the artist all sorts of materials of all sorts of qualities, thus enabling him to choose those best fitted for his purposes. It also presupposes intensive specialization and generations of experience in the handling of the various materials, and finally a high esteem for the artist, which sets him above the level of forced labor and gives him leisure, joy and strength.

All these elements combined are to be found only in large commercial cities with vigorous and well-established handicrafts. In Thebes and Memphis, in Athens, and later, after the Middle Ages, in Florence, Antwerp and Amsterdam, the fine arts reached their high points on the basis of a healthy craftsmanship.

This was lacking among the Jews, and had its effect on their religion.

THE CONCEPTION OF GOD IN ANCIENT ISRAEL

Ideas about divinity are extremely vague and confused among primitive peoples, and by no means as clear-cut as we see them presented in the mythology books of the learned. The individual deities were not clearly conceived nor distinguished from one another; they are unknown, mysterious personalities affecting nature and men, bringing men good luck and bad luck, but as shadowy and indefinite, at least at first, as visions in a dream.

The only firm distinction of the individual gods one from the other consists in their localization. Every spot that particularly arouses the fantasy of primitive man seems to him to be the seat of a particular god. High mountains or isolated crags, groves in special places and also single giant trees, springs, caves—all thus receive a sort of sanctity as the seats of gods. But also peculiarly shaped stones or pieces of wood may be taken to be the seats of a deity, as sacred objects the possession of which assures the aid of the deity that inhabits them. Every tribe, every clan tried to obtain such a sacred object, or fetish. That was true of the Hebrews as well, for their original idea of God was quite on the level we have just described, far from monotheism. The sacred objects of the Israelites seem to have been nothing more than fetishes at first, from the images or idols (teraphim) that Jacob steals from his father-in-law Laban to the ark of the covenant in which Jehovah is located and which brings victory and rain and riches to the man who possesses it justly. The sacred stones that the Phoenicians and Israelites worshipped bore the name of Bethel, God's house.

The local gods and the fetishes are not distinctly individual on this stage; often they have the same names, as for example among the Israelites and Phoenicians many gods were called El (plural, Elohim) and others were called by the Phoenicians, Baal, the lord. "Despite the identity of names all these Baals counted as quite distinct beings. Often nothing more was added to distinguish them than the name of the place in which the god in question was worshipped."[8]

It was possible to keep the separate gods distinct in the minds of the people only when the plastic arts had developed enough to individualise and idealise human forms, to present concrete forms with a character of their own, but also with a charm, a majesty or a size or fearsomeness that raised them above the form of ordinary men. At this point polytheism got a material basis; the invisible became visible and so imaginable by all; now the individual gods were permanently distinguished from each other and confusion among them became impossible. From then on men

8. Pietschmann, *Geschichte der Phönizier*, p. 183 f.

could choose individual figures out of countless numbers of spiritual beings that danced about in the fantasy of primitive man, and give them particular forms.

We can clearly trace how the number of the particular gods in Egypt increases with the development of the fine arts. In Greece too it is certainly no accident that the highest point of the art industry and human representation in the plastic arts coincided with the greatest diversity and sharpest individualization in the world of the gods.

Because of the backwardness of the industry and art of the Israelites, they never carried to completion the progress of the industrially and artistically developed peoples, the replacement of the fetish, the dwelling place of the spirit or god, by the image of the god. In this respect too they remained on the level of the Bedouin mode of thought. The idea of representing their own gods in pictures or images never came into their heads. All the images of gods they knew were images of foreigners' gods, gods of the enemy, imported from abroad or imitated after their model; and hence the hate of the patriots against these images.

This had an element of backwardness; but it made it easier for the Jews to advance beyond polytheism once they learned of the philosophical and ethical monotheism that had arisen in various great cities on the highest level of development of the ancient world for causes we have already mentioned. Where the images of the gods had struck root in the minds of the people, polytheism received a firm basis that was not so easily overcome. The indefiniteness of the images of the gods and the identity of their names in different localities on the other hand, opened the way for popularizing the idea of one god, compared to whom all the other invisible spirits are but lower beings.

At any rate it is no mere chance that all the monotheistic popular religions came from nations that were still in the nomadic mode of thought and had not developed any notable industry or art: along with the Jews, these were the Persians and later the Arabians of Islam, who adopted monotheism as soon as they came into contact with a higher urban civilization. Not only Islam but the Zend religion is monotheistic; this recognizes only one lord and creator of the world, Ahuramazda. Angromainju (Ahriman) is a subsidiary spirit, like Satan.

It may seem strange that backward elements will adopt an advance more easily and carry it further than more developed elements will; it is a fact, however, that can be traced even in the evolution of organisms. Highly developed forms are often less capable of adaptation and die out more easily, whereas lower forms with less specialized organs can more easily adapt to new conditions and hence be capable of carrying progress further.

In man the organs do not merely develop in an unconscious way; he also develops other artificial organs whose manufacture he can learn from other men. With respect to these artificial forms, individuals or groups can leap over whole stages of development when the higher stage has already been prepared for them by others from whom they can take it over. It is a well-known fact that many farm villages took to electric lighting more easily than the large cities which already had large capital investments in gas lighting. The farm village could jump directly from the oil lamp to electricity without passing through the phase of gas; but only because the technical knowledge required for electric lighting had already been gained in the big cities. The farming village could never have developed this knowledge on its own account. Similarly, monotheism found easier acceptance among the Jews and Persians than among the mass of Egyptians, Babylonians or Hellenes; but the idea of monotheism had first to be developed by the philosophers of these more advanced civilizations.

However at the time with which we are dealing, before the Exile, things had not yet gone so far; the primitive cult of the gods still prevailed.

TRADE AND PHILOSOPHY

Trade gives rise to a way of thinking different from that based on handicrafts and art.

The specific productive activity that produces specific use values is of interest primarily to the consumer, who wants specific use values. If he needs cloth, he is interested in the labor that goes into making the cloth, precisely because it is this particular cloth-producing work. But for the producer of the commodities as well —and on the stage we are speaking of this includes, as a rule, not only wage workers but independent farmers, craftsmen and artists, and the slaves of any of these—labor enters into the picture as the specific activity that enables him to produce specific products.

It is different with the merchant. His activity consists in buying cheap in order to sell dear. What specific commodities he buys or sells is basically a matter of indifference to him, as long as they find a purchaser. He does have an interest in the· quantity of labor socially necessary at the times and places of purchase and of sale to produce the goods he deals in, for that has the decisive influence on their prices, but this labor interests him only as value-giving, general human labor, abstract labor, not as concrete labor producing specific use values. The merchant is not consciously aware of all this; for it is a long time till men come to discover the determination of value by general human labor. The discovery was first completely reached by the genius of a Karl Marx under conditions of highly-developed commodity production. But, many thousands of years before that, abstract general human labor, as contrasted with concrete forms of labor, finds its tangible expression in money,[9] which does not need the slightest powers of abstraction to comprehend. Money is the representative of the general human labor contained in every commodity; it does not represent a particular kind of labor, like the work of weavers, potters or blacksmiths, but all and every kind of labor, one kind today

9. Before money is used as a means of circulation it appears as a standard measure of value. It is used for that purpose while barter is still the prevailing form of trade: Thus, it is said of Egypt that the custom prevailed there "of utilizing copper bars (uten) weighing 91 grams not as real money, for which all other commodities can be exchanged, but as the measure of value in barter, by means of which the goods bartered for each other are evaluated. Thus on one occasion in the New Empire an ox whose value is set at 119 uten of copper is paid for by a staff with work on it amounting to 25 uten, another at 12 uten, 11 jars of honey at 11 uten, and so forth. Out of this there arose later the Ptolemaic copper standard of coinage." (Ed. Meyer, Die wirtschaftliche Entwicklung des Altertums, 1895, p. 11.)

and another kind tomorrow. The merchant however is interested in the commodity only as it represents money; he does not care for its specific usefulness but for its specific price.

The producer—peasant, craftsman, artist—is interested in the particular nature of his work, the particular nature of the stuff he has to work on; and he will increase the productivity of his labor power in the measure that he specializes his labor. His specific work ties him down to a specific place, to his land or his workshop. The determinateness of the work that occupies him thus produces a certain narrowness in his way of thinking, which the Greeks called banausic (from *banausos,* workman). "It may well be that smiths, carpenters and shoemakers are skilled in their trades," said Socrates in the fifth century B.C., "but most of them are slavish souls; they do not know what is beautiful, good and just." The same opinion was expressed by the Jew Jesus son of Sirach about 200 B.C. Useful as crafts are, he holds, the craftsman is useless in politics, jurisprudence, or the dissemination of moral education.

Only the machine makes it possible for the mass of the working class to rise above this narrowness, but it is only elimination of capitalist commodity production that will create the conditions under which the machine can fully fulfill its noble mission of freeing the laboring masses.

The activity of the merchant on the other hand has quite a different effect on him. He need not confine himself to the knowledge of a specific branch of production in a specific locality; the wider his view, the more branches of production he takes in, the more regions with their special needs and conditions of production, the sooner he will find out which commodities it is most profitable to deal in at a given time; the sooner he will find the markets where he can buy most profitably and those in which he can sell most profitably. For all the diversity of products and markets he is involved in, basically his interest is only in the relationship of prices, that is the relationships of various quantities of abstract human labor, that is of abstract numerical relationships. The more trade develops, the more buying and selling are separate in space and time, the greater the differences of the coins and coinages the merchant has to deal with, the further apart the acts of selling and payment are and systems of credit and interest develop: the more complex and diversified these numerical relationships become. Thus trade must develop mathematical thinking and, along with that, abstract thinking. As trade broadens horizons beyond local and professional narrow-mindedness and opens up to the merchant knowledge of the most widely differing climates and soils, stages of culture and modes of production, it stimulates him to comparisons, enables him to see what is general in the mass of particulars, what is regular in the mass of fortuities, what always repeats itself under given conditions. In this way, as well as by mathematical thinking, the power of abstraction is highly developed, while handicrafts and art develop the sense for the concrete, but also for the superficial aspects, rather than the essence of things. It is not the "productive" activities like agriculture and handicrafts, but "unproductive" trade that forms those mental capacities that constitute the basis of scientific research.

But that is not to say that trade as such gives rise to research itself. Disinterested thought, the quest for truth rather than for personal advantage, is the last thing to characterize a merchant. A peasant and a craftsman live only by the work of their hands. The well-being they can attain is confined within narrow limits; but within those limits it is assured to every healthy average individual under primitive conditions, if war or natural catastrophes do not ruin the whole community and drive it into poverty. In such cases trying to get beyond the average is neither necessary nor very promising. Cheerful contentment with one's inherited lot characterizes these occupations, until capital, at first in the form of usury capital, subjugates these occupations or those who practice them.

The success of concrete useful labor, at this stage of industrial development is limited by the powers of the individual; the success of trade has no limits. Trading profit has its limits set only by the quantity of money, of capital, that the trader owns, and this quantity may be expanded without limit. On the other hand this trade is exposed to much greater vicissitudes and dangers than the eternal monotony of peasant and handicraft production in simple commodity production. The merchant is always swinging between the extremes of great wealth and utter ruin. The passion for gain is stimulated to an extent unknown in the productive classes. Insatiable greed and merciless brutality toward competitors and the objects of exploitation—these are the marks of the merchant. This is still seen today in a way that revolts people who work for a living, and especially where the exploitation by capital does not meet with powerful resistance, as in the colonies.

This is not a way of thinking that makes disinterested scientific thought possible. Trade develops the requisite mental traits, but not their application in science. On the contrary, where it influences science its effect is to falsify and twist it to its own ends, a procedure of which bourgeois science today shows countless examples.

Scientific thought could only arise in a class that was influenced by all those traits, experiences and knowledge that trade brought with it, but at the same time was free from the need for earning money and so had time and opportunity for, and joy in unprejudiced research, in solving problems without considering their immediate, practical and personal results. Philosophy developed only in the great commercial centers, but only in those where there were elements outside of commerce who were assured of leisure and freedom by their property or their social position. In many Greek trading cities such elements were the great landowners, who were relieved of work by their slaves and did not live in the country, but in the city, so that they avoided falling into the boorishness of the country squire but felt all the influences of the city and its great commerce.

It would seem however that such a class of landholders, living in the city and philosophizing, appeared only in maritime cities whose land area was large enough to produce such a landed aristocracy, but not large enough to keep them from the city and tie their interests down to extending their land holdings. These conditions are to be seen above all in the Greek maritime cities. The lands of the Phoenician cities by the sea were too small to produce such landed property; everybody lived by trade.

In cities surrounded by extensive territories, the landholders seem to have remained more under the influence of country life, to have developed further toward the mentality of the country squire. In the great inland trading centers of Asia, the group who were most free from working for a living and least engaged in practical activities were the priests of certain shrines. Quite a few of these shrines won importance and wealth enough to maintain permanent priests, whose duties were light enough. The same social task that fell to the share of the aristocracy in the Greek seaside towns was incumbent on the priests of the temples in the great trade centers of the Oriental mainland, in particular Egypt and Babylon: that is, the development of scientific thought, of philosophy. This however set a limit to Oriental thinking from which Greek thought was free: constant connection with and regard for a religious cult. The cult gained what philosophy lost, and the priests gained too. In Greece the priests remained simple officials of the rites, guardians of the shrines and performers of the religious acts there; in the great commercial centres of the Orient they became preservers and administrators of all of knowledge, scientific as well as social, mathematics, astronomy and medicine as well as history and law. Their influence in the state and society was enormously increased by this. Religion itself however was able to attain a spiritual depth of which the Greek mythology was not capable, since Hellenic philosophy soon put this to one side, without trying to fill out its naive intuitions with deeper knowledge, and to reconcile the two.

It is the aloofness of philosophy from the priesthood, along with the flowering of the fine arts, that gives Greek religion its sensual, vivid, joyous, artistic quality. On the other hand, in a region with important international trade but without well-developed plastic arts, without a lay aristocracy with intellectual inclinations and needs, but with a strong priesthood and a religion that had not yet developed a polytheism with clear-cut individual deities, it must have been easier for that religion to take on an abstract, spiritualized character and for the deity to become an idea or a concept rather than a person.

TRADE AND NATIONALITY

Trade influences men's thinking in still another way. It greatly fosters national feeling. We have already mentioned the narrowness of the mental horizon of peasant and petty bourgeois as compared with the broad view of the merchant. He acquires that breadth in the course of his constant pressing forward, away from the place in which the accident of birth had set him. We see this most sharply in maritime nations, like the Phoenicians and Greeks in antiquity; the first ventured far beyond the Mediterranean into the Atlantic Ocean, and the latter opened up the Black Sea. Land commerce did not allow such wide sweeps. And trading by sea presupposed advanced technology, especially in shipbuilding; it was trade between higher and lower peoples, in which the latter could be easily subjugated and colonies founded by the commercial nation. Commerce on land was first and most easily carried on by nomads, who came to more highly developed peoples and there found surpluses of agricultural and industrial products all ready. There could be no question of the founding of colonies by single expeditions. Now and then a number of nomad tribes might get together to plunder or conquer a richer, more advanced country, but in that case too they did not come as colonists, bearing a higher civilization. Such unions of roving tribes occurred seldom, under exceptional circumstances, since the whole nature of nomadic cattle-raising isolates the tribes and clans, and even the single families, from each other and scatters them over vast areas. As a rule, the traders from these tribes could enter into the rich and powerful states with which they traded, only as tolerated refugees.

This applies as well to the traders of the small nations that had settled athwart the international route from Egypt to Syria. Like the Phoenicians and the Greeks they too founded settlements in the countries they traded with, but they were not colonies in the strict sense of the word: they were not powerful cities by means of which a civilized nation dominated and exploited barbarians, but weak communities of refugees within powerful and highly cultivated cities. That made it all the more necessary for the members of these communities to cohere most tightly against the foreigners in whose midst they lived, and gave urgency to their desire for the power and prestige of their nation, since it was on that that their own security and prestige abroad depended, and hence too the conditions under which they carried on their commerce.

As I have remarked in my book on Thomas More, the merchant is, down to the nineteenth century, at once the most international and the most national member of society. In merchants from small nations, exposed without defence to mistreatment in foreign parts, the need for national cohesion and national greatness must have grown especially strong, along with hatred toward the foreigner.

The Israelite traders were in such a position. The Israelites must have been carried off to Egypt early, while they were still wandering herdsmen, long before they became sedentary dwellers in Canaan. Canaanite migrations into Egypt are reported by testimony that may go as far back as the third millennium. Eduard Meyer says on this matter:

"A famous painting in the tomb of Chnemhotep in Benihassan shows us a Bedouin family of 37 people led by their head, Absha, came to Egypt in the sixth year of the reign of Usertesen III.[10] They are described as Amu, that is Canaanites, and their features clearly show them to be Semites. They wear the bright clothes that had been favored in Asia since ancient times, are armed with bow and spear and bring asses and goats with them; one of them is able to play the lyre. As valuables, they brought the eye-pigment meszemuth with them. Now they ask for admission and address themselves to the count of Menachufu, Chnemhotep, to whom the eastern mountain lands are subject. A royal scribe, Neserhotep, brings them before him for further orders and reports to the king. Scenes like the one here immortalized must have taken place often, and doubtless many Canaanite traders and craftsmen must have settled in the eastern cities of the delta in this way, and there we find them in later times. Conversely it is certain that Egyptian

10. A ruler of the XII dynasty, which lasted from 2100 to 1900 B.C., more or less.

traders often came to Syrian cities. Even though with many inter-
mediary links, Egyptian commerce by this time must have extended as far as Babylon."

Some hundreds of years later, perhaps around the year 1800 B.C.,
at a time when Egyptian society was in decline, North Egypt was
conquered by the Hyksos, undoubtedly Canaanite nomad tribes,
whom the weakness of the Egyptian government tempted, and enabled, to invade the rich Nile country, where they maintained
themselves for over two hundred years. "The significance of the
Hyksos' rule in world history is that by means of it there arose a
lively intercourse between Egypt and the Syrian regions which
was never interrupted thereafter. Canaanite merchants and artisans came in droves to Egypt; we find Canaanite personal names
and cults at every step in the new kingdom; Canaanite words begin to penetrate into Egyptian. How lively the communication
was is shown by the fact that a medical work written about the
year 1550 B.C. contains a prescription for the eyes prepared by a
certain Amu of Kepni, which is very probably the Phoenician city
of Byblos."[11]

We have no reason to assume that among the Amu, the Semitic
Bedouins and city folk east and northeast of Egypt, there were not
Hebrews too, although they are not specifically mentioned. On
the other hand it is hard to make out today what we should take
to be the historical core in the legends of Joseph, the stay of the
Hebrews in Egypt and their exodus under Moses. Equating them
to the Hyksos, as Josephus does, is untenable. This much does
seem to follow, that, if not all of Israel, at least single families and
caravans of Hebrews early came to Egypt, where they were treated
more or less well according to changing situations there, gladly received at some times and later harried and hunted as "burdensome" foreigners. That is the typical fate of such settlements of
foreign traders from weak nations in powerful empires.

The "Diaspora," the scattering of the Jews over the world, does
not in any case begin for the first time with the destruction of
Jerusalem by the Romans, nor even with the Babylonian exile,

11. Ed. Meyer, *Geschichte des alten Aegyptens,* 1887, p. 182, 210.

but much earlier; it is a natural consequence of trade, a phenomenon shared by the Jews in common with most commercial peoples. But of course agriculture remained the principal source of the livelihood of the Jews down to the time of the exile, as it did with most of these peoples. Previously commerce had been only a secondary occupation for the nomadic herdsmen. When they became sedentary and the division of labor appeared, the roving merchant and the peasant were differentiated; but the number of merchants was relatively small, and the peasant determined the character of the people. The number of Israelites living abroad was small in any case compared to the number of those who remained at home. In all this the Jews did not differ from other nations.

But they lived in conditions in which the hatred of foreigners and strong national feeling, even sensitiveness, which had arisen among the merchants, were transmitted to the mass of the people to a greater extent than was the case with the general run of peasant peoples.

CANAAN, ROAD OF THE NATIONS

We have seen the importance of Palestine for the commerce of Egypt, Babylonia and Syria. From time out of mind these states had endeavored to get the country into their hands.

In the struggle against the Hyksos (about 1800 to 1530 B.C.), a military spirit had arisen in Egypt; at the same time the Hyksos had greatly furthered communication between Egypt and Syria. After the expulsion of the Hyksos, the Egyptians turned to military expansion, above all in the direction of controlling the commercial route to Babylonia. They forced their way as far as the Euphrates, occupying Palestine and Syria. They were soon driven out of Syria by the Hittites; in Palestine they held out longer, from the fifteenth down to the twelfth century. There too they garrisoned a series of fortresses overawing the country, including Jerusalem.

Finally the military power of Egypt weakened, and from the

twelfth century on it could no longer hold Palestine; at the same time the Syrian Hittites were weakened because their southward pressure was brought to a halt by the incipient expansion of the Assyrians.

In this way the foreign domination of Palestine was broken. A group of Bedouin tribes, assembled under the name of Israelites, made use of the opportunity to break into the country and gradually conquer and occupy it. They had not yet finished the enterprise, and were still in fierce battle with the former inhabitants of the country, when new enemies arose in the shape of other Bedouin tribes pushing after them into the "promised land." At the same time they clashed head on with an opponent, the inhabitants of the plain between the highlands occupied by the Jews, and the sea. These were the Philistines. They must have felt themselves desperately menaced by the aggression of so warlike a people as the Israelites. On the other hand, the coastal plain must have been particularly attractive to the Israelites, for through it went the high road linking Egypt with the north. Whoever controlled it also had control of almost the entire external trade of Egypt with the north and the east. The sea-borne trade of Egypt on the Mediterranean was still very small at that time. If the inhabitants of the mountain ranges that ran along the plain were warlike and predatory clans, they would constitute a constant threat to commerce to and from Egypt, and to the riches derived from it. And they were warlike and predatory. We are often told of the formation of robber bands in Israel, by Jephtha for example, "and there were gathered vain men to Jephtha, and went out with him," (Judges 11, verse 3). Robber raids into the land of the Philistines are often spoken of. In the case of Samson, "the Spirit of the Lord came upon him, and he went down to Ashkelon, and slew thirty men of them, and took their spoil" to pay a lost bet (Judges 14, verse 19). David is shown beginning as the leader of a robber band, "and every one that was in distress, and every one that was in debt, and every one that was discontented, gathered themselves unto him; and he became a captain over them; and there were with him about four hundred men" (I Samuel 22, verse 2).

It is no wonder that there was an almost continuous feud between the Philistines and the Jews, and that the former did everything in their power to tame their troublesome neighbors. Hardpressed on one side by the Bedouins and on the other by the Philistines, Israel sank into dependence and distress. It succumbed to the Philistines the more easily because living in the hills favored cantonal spirit and split up the tribes, whereas living in the plain helped the various tribes and communities of the Philistines to unite for action. It was only after the strong warrior king David succeeded in welding the different tribes of Israel into a firm unity that this tribulation came to an end.

Now the Philistines were overthrown and the last strong cities in Canaan that had still resisted Israel were taken, including Jerusalem, an unusually strong and defensible place, that resisted the Israelites the longest and controlled the approaches into Palestine from the south. It became the capital of the kingdom and the seat of the fetish of the union, the ark of the covenant, in which the war god Jahveh dwelt.

David now won domination over the entire trade between Egypt and the north, and great gains came to him from it, which enabled him to increase his military power and extend the frontiers of his state to the north and the south. He overcame the plundering Bedouin tribes as far as the Red Sea, made the trade routes thither safe, and with the help of the Phoenicians, for the Israelites knew nothing of sea-faring, began to carry on, on the Red Sea the commerce that had previously gone by land north from Southern Arabia (Saba). This was Israel's golden age, and it achieved a dazzling fullness of power and wealth from its position dominating the most important trade routes of its time.

And yet it was precisely this position that was its ruin. Its commercial importance was not a secret to the great neighbor states. The more the country flourished under David and Solomon, the more it must have aroused the greed of its neighbors, whose military power was on the increase again just at this time; in Egypt, in particular, because of the replacement of the peasant militia by mercenaries, who were more easily made ready for wars of aggression. It is true the power of Egypt was no longer adequate to the task of permanently conquering Israel: that was so much the worse for Israel. Instead of becoming permanently tributary to a great state whose power would at least have brought it peace and protection from foreign enemies, it became the bone of contention between Egyptians and Syrians, and later of Assyrians as well; Palestine was the battlefield on which these powers clashed. To the devastations of the wars it had to wage in its own interests there were added the devastations of the great armies that now fought there for interests that were entirely alien to the inhabitants of the country. And the burdens of tribute and dependency that were imposed on the Israelites from time to time now were none the easier for the fact that it was not always the same master who imposed them, that their master changed with the fortunes of war, each one holding it as a precarious possession out of which he wanted to get as much as possible as quickly as possible.

Palestine was in a situation at that time much like that of Poland in the eighteenth century or Italy, especially Northern Italy, from the Middle Ages on down to the nineteenth century. Like Palestine then, Italy and Poland later found themselves unable to carry on a policy of their own, and constituted the theatre of war and the object of plunder for foreign great powers: Poland for Russia, Prussia and Austria; Italy for Spain and France, along with the master of the German Empire, later Austria. And as in Italy and Poland, a national splintering took place in Palestine too, and for similar reasons: In Palestine, as in Italy, the various sections of the country were influenced by their neighbors in different ways. The northern part of the region occupied by the Israelites was most threatened, and also dominated, by the Syrians and then by the Assyrians. The southern part, Jerusalem with its surroundings, essentially the district of the tribe of Judah, was more threatened by Egypt or dependent on it, according to circumstances. Israel proper therefore often seemed to require different policies than Judah did. This difference in foreign policies was the principal cause for Israel's splitting up into two kingdoms, in contrast with the prior situation, when foreign policy had constituted the reason for uniting the twelve tribes against the common enemy, the Philistines.

But the similar situation must have evoked similar effects in Palestine as in Italy and Poland in still another respect: here as well as there we meet with the same national chauvinism, the same national sensitiveness, the same xenophobia, going beyond the measure of what national enmities produced in the other peoples of the same era. And this chauvinism was bound to increase the longer this intolerable situation lasted, making the country constantly a football of fate and a battleground for the robber incursions of its great neighbors.

Given the importance that religion had in the Orient, for reasons to which we have referred, chauvinism had to appear in religion too. The vigorous trade relations with neighboring countries brought their religious ideas, cults and images into the land. Hatred of the foreigner had more and more to become hatred of his gods, not because their existence was questioned, but just because they were regarded as the most effective helpers of the enemy.

This does not distinguish the Hebrews from the other peoples of the Orient. The tribal god of the Hyksos in Egypt was Sutekh. When the Hyksos were driven out, their tribal god had to give way too; he was identified with the god of darkness, Seth or Sutekh, from whom the Egyptians turned with horror.

The patriots of Israel and their leaders, the prophets, must have turned against the strange gods with the same fury that the German patriots at the time of Napoleon turned against French fashions and French words in the German language.

CLASS STRUGGLES IN ISRAEL

The patriots however could not long be satisfied with xenophobia alone. They were moved to regenerate the state and give it greater strength. Social decomposition increased in the Israelite community in proportion to the external pressure. The growth of trade since David's time had brought great wealth into the land, but, as elsewhere in antiquity, agriculture remained the basis of society and landholding the surest and most honorable form of property. Just as elsewhere, elements that had become wealthy tried to own land or to increase their holdings if they were already landowners. Here too the tendency to form latifundia appeared. This was made easier by the fact that in Palestine, as elsewhere, the peasant was ruined under the new conditions. Previously the struggles of the Iraelites had been little local feuds for the most part, which did not take the peasant militiaman far from his soil or keep him away long; but it was no longer so once Israel was a more important state and was involved in the wars of the great powers. Military service now ruined the peasant and made him dependent on his moneyed and influential neighbor, who became a usurer, with the choice of driving him from his little farm or leaving him there, only as a debt slave obliged to work out his debt. The latter method must often have been preferred, for we do not hear much of purchased slaves of other nationalities in Palestine. If slaves by purchase are to be anything more than a costly luxury in the house, if they are to be a profitable investment in production, they presuppose constant successful wars which provide abundant cheap slave material. This was out of the question for the Israelites. For the most part they belonged to those unfortunate peoples that furnished slaves rather than acquired them. All this must have led the owners of the latifundia, who needed cheap and dependent labor forces, to prefer the debt slavery of their own countrymen, a system that has been preferred elsewhere, as for example in Russia after the abolition of serfdom, when the great landowners lack slaves or serfs.

As a result of this process, there was a serious reduction in the military power of Israel and its ability to stand up against external enemies, together with a reduction in the number of free peasants. The patriots and social reformers and friends of the people united to call a halt to this fatal development. They called the people and the kingdom to battle against the strange gods and the enemies of the peasant within the land. They prophesied the fall of the state

if it was not able to put an end to the oppression and impoverishment of the peasantry.

"Woe unto them," Isaiah cried, "that join house to house, that
lay field to field, till there be no place, that they may be placed
alone in the midst of the earth? In mine ears said the Lord of
hosts, Of a truth many houses shall be desolate, even great and
fair, without inhabitant" (5, verses 8 and 9).

And the prophet Amos predicted, "Hear this word, ye kine of
Bashan, that are in the mountain of Samaria, which oppress the
poor, which crush the needy, which say to their masters, 'Bring,
and let us drink.' The Lord God hath sworn by his holiness, that,
lo, the days shall come upon you, that he will take you away with
hooks, and your posterity with fishhooks" (4, verses 1 and 2).

"Hear this, O ye that swallow up the needy, even to make the
poor of the land to fail, saying, When will the new moon be gone,
that we may sell corn? and the sabbath, that we may set forth
wheat, making the ephah small, and the shekel great, and falsify-
ing the balances by deceit? That we may buy the poor for silver,
and the needy for a pair of shoes; yea, and sell the refuse of the
wheat? The Lord hath sworn by the excellency of Jacob, Surely I
will never forget any of their works. Shall not the land tremble for
this, and every one mourn that dwelleth therein?" (Amos 8, verses
4 to 8).

"It can be clearly seen from the continual complaints of the
prophets against existing law that the wealthy and mighty made
use of the government apparatus to give legal sanction to the new
order of things: 'Woe unto them that decree unrighteous decrees,'
says the eloquent Isaiah, ' . . . to turn away the needy from
judgment, and to take away the right from the poor of my people'
(10, verses 1 and 2). 'Zion shall be redeemed with judgment' (ibid.
1, verse 27). 'The pen of the scribes is in vain' (Jeremiah 8, verse
8). 'For ye have turned judgment into gall, and the fruit of righteousness into hemlock' (Amos 8, verse 12)."[12]

It was lucky for the prophets that they did not live in Prussia or

12. M. Beer, "Ein Beitrag zur Geschichte des Klassenkampfes in hebräischen
Altertum," Neue Zeit, XI, p. 447.

Saxony! They would never have escaped prosecution for sedition, libel and high treason.

But no matter how forceful their agitation was, or how urgent the needs from which it arose, they could not succeed, even though they might now and then obtain legislation for easing poverty or ironing out social contradictions. Their efforts could tend only to restore the past and dam up the stream of economic development. This was impossible, as were the similar efforts of the Gracchi in Rome. The fall of the peasantry and hence of the state was as irresistible in Israel as it was later in Rome. But the fall of the state was not such a slow death in Israel as it was in the world empire of Rome. Overwhelmingly powerful opponents put a sudden end to it long before its vitality was exhausted. These opponents were the Assyrians and the Babylonians.

THE DECLINE OF ISRAEL

From Tiglath-Pileser I on (about 1115-1050 B.C.), with occasional interruptions, the Assyrians begin their policy of conquest on the grand scale which brought them closer and closer to Canaan. These powerful conquerors introduced a new method in handling the vanquished which had a devastating effect on the Israelites.

During their nomad period, the whole people had an interest in a military adventure, for every member of the nation profited from it. The expedition ended either with the plunder of a rich country or with its conquest, in which case the victors settled there as aristocratic exploiters of the native masses.

On the sedentary agricultural stage the mass of the population, the peasants and craftsmen, no longer had any inteerst in a war of conquest, but increased interest in a successful defensive war, for in case of defeat they faced the loss of their freedom and that of their country. A forcible policy of outward expansion was desired by the masters of commerce, who needed protection of trade routes and foreign markets, something that usually could be assured only by military occupation of at least a few points. The landed aristocracy also pressed for territorial expansion, being always hungry for more land and new slaves, and the kings too were warlike in feeling, smelling increased tax yields.

So long however as there was no standing army, and no bureaucracy detached from the land and free to be installed anywhere, the permanent occupation and administration of a conquered land by a victor was hardly possible at this stage. What he usually did was, after a thoroughgoing plundering and weakening of the subdued nation, to exact an oath of loyalty and fix tribute payments, leaving the ruling classes of the country in their positions and changing nothing in its political constitution.

This had the disadvantage that the vanquished took the first opportunity to shake off the hated yoke, so that a new military expedition was necessary to overcome them again, accompanied of course with the most barbarous punishment of the "rebellion."

The Assyrians hit upon a system that promised greater permanence to their conquests: where they encountered stubborn resistance or experienced repeated rebellions, they crippled the nation by taking away its head, that is by stealing the ruling classes, by exiling the noblest, richest, most intelligent and warlike inhabitants, particularly of the capital, to a distant region, where the deportees were completely powerless without the lower stratum of ruled-over classes. The peasants and small handicraftsmen who were left behind now constituted a disconnected mass incapable of any armed resistance to the conquerors.

Shalmaneser II (859 to 825 B.C.) was the first Assyrian king to invade Syria proper (Aleppo, Hamath, Damascus), and also the first who gives us tidings of Israel. In a cuneiform report of the year 842 he mentions among other things a tribute of the Israelite king Jehu. This forwarding of tribute is illustrated; it is the oldest representation of Israelite figures that has come down to us. From that time on Israel came into ever closer contact with Assyria, paying tribute or rising up in rebellion, while the practice of transplanting the upper layer of the conquered, and especially of rebellious, peoples kept spreading. It was now but a question of time when at the hands of the unconquered and apparently unconquerable Assyrians the day of destruction would come for Israel too. No great gift of prophecy was required to foresee this end, which the Jewish prophets so vividly foretold.

For the northern kingdom the end came under King Hosea, who in 724 refused to pay the tribute to Assyria, relying on help from Egypt; but the help did not come. Shalmaneser IV marched on Israel, beat Hosea, took him prisoner and besieged his capital, Samaria, which was taken by Shalmaneser's successor Sargon in 722 after a three-year siege. The "flower of the population" (Wellhausen), 27,290 men by Assyrian accounts, were now removed to Assyrian and Median cities. In their stead the king of Assyria brought people from rebellious Babylonian cities "and placed them in the cities of Samaria instead of the children of Israel; and they possessed Samaria, and dwelt in the cities thereof" (II Kings 17, verse 24).

Thus, it was not the entire population of the northerly ten tribes of Israel that was carried off, but only the most noble from the cities, which were resettled by foreigners. But that was enough to begin the end of the nationality of these ten tribes. The peasant is not capable by himself of building up a community apart. The Israelite city-dwellers and aristocrats who were transplanted to Assyria disappeared into their new surroundings in the course of generations.

THE FIRST DESTRUCTION OF JERUSALEM

Of the people of Israel, only Jerusalem was left with its surrounding district, Judah. It seemed that this little residue would soon share the fate of the large mass and the name of Israel thus disappear from the face of the earth. But it was not to be the lot of the Assyrians to take and destroy Jerusalem.

It is true that the army of the Assyrian Sennacherib that was marching on Jerusalem (701) was compelled to return home by disorders in Babylon, and Jerusalem was saved; but that was only a reprieve. Judah remained an Assyrian vassal state, which could be snuffed out at any moment.

But from Sennacherib's time on the attention of the Assyrians was more and more drawn to the north, where warlike nomads were increasing their pressure, and more and more force was required to repel them: Cimmerians, Medes, Scythians. About 625 the last named broke into the Near East, plundering and devastating up to the borders of Egypt, but finally left again after 28 years without founding an empire of their own. They did not disappear, however, without leaving marked traces behind them. Their attack shook the Assyrian monarchy to its foundations. The Medes were now able to attack it with more success, Babylon broke away and liberated itself, while the Egyptians took advantage of the situation to bring Palestine under their sovereignty. Josiah, king of Judah, was defeated and killed by the Egyptians at Megiddo (609), after which Necho, the Egyptian king, set up Jehoiakim in Jerusalem as his vassal. Finally in 606 Nineveh was destroyed by the combined Babylonians and Medes. The empire of the Assyrians had come to an end.

That however did not save Judah by any means. Babylon now followed in the footsteps of Assyria and at once tried to get control of the road to Egypt. In the process the Babylonians under Nebuchadnezzar clashed with Necho, who had penetrated as far as Northern Syria. In the battle at Carchemish the Egyptians were defeated and soon thereafter Judah was made a Babylonian vassal state. We see how Judah was handed from one to another, having lost all independence. Goaded on by Egypt, it refused to pay its tribute to Babylonia in 597. The rebellion collapsed almost without a struggle. Jerusalem was besieged by Nebuchadnezzar and surrendered unconditionally.

"And Nebuchadnezzar came against the city, and his servants did besiege it. And Jehoiachin the king of Judah went out to the king of Babylon, he, and his mother, and his servants, and his princes, and his officers: and the king of Babylon took him in the eighth year of his reign. And he carried out thence all the treasures of the house of the Lord, and the treasures of the king's house, and cut in pieces all the vessels of gold which Solomon king of Israel had made in the temple of the Lord, as the Lord had said. And he carried away all Jerusalem, and all the princes, and all the mighty men of valour, even ten thousand captives, and all the craftsmen and smiths: none remained, save the poorest sort of people of the land. And he carried away Jehoiachin to Babylon, and the king's mother, and the king's wives, and his officers, and the mighty of the land, those carried he into captivity from Jerusalem to Babylon. And all the men of might, even seven thousand, and craftsmen and smiths a thousand, all that were strong and apt for war" (II Kings 24, verses 11 to 16).

Thus Babylon continued the old method of Assyria; but here too it was not the whole people that was deported, but only the royal court, the aristocrats, the military men and the propertied city dwellers, 10,000 men in all. The "poorest sort of people of the land," and of the cities as well, stayed behind, and along with them a part of the ruling classes too. Judah was not exterminated. A new king was assigned to it by the lords of Babylon. But now the old game was repeated once more, for the last time. The Egyptians instigated the new king, Zedekiah, to desert Babylon.

Thereupon Nebuchadnezzar laid siege to Jerusalem, took it and put an end (586) to the unruly city that was so disturbing because of its dominant position on the great route from Babylon to Egypt.

"And . . . came Nebuzar-adan, captain of the guard, a servant of the king of Babylon, unto Jerusalem; and he burnt the house of the Lord, and the king's house, and all the houses of Jerusalem, and every great man's house burnt he with fire. And all the army of the Chaldees, that were with the captain of the guard, brake down the walls of Jerusalem round about. Now the rest of the people that were left in the city, and the fugitives that fell away to the king of Babylon, with the remnant of the multitude, did Nebuzar-adan the captain of the guard carry away. But the captain of the guard left of the poor of the land to be vinedressers and husbandmen" (II Kings 25, verses 8 to 12).

Similarly in Jeremiah 39, verses 9 and 10: "Then Nebuzar-adan the captain of the guard carried away captive into Babylon the remnant of the people that remained in the city, and those that fell away, that fell to him, with the rest of the people that remained. But Nebuzar-adan the captain of the guard left of the poor of the people, which had nothing, in the land of Judah, and gave them vineyards and fields at the same time."

There were thus peasant elements remaining behind. It would have been senseless to leave the land uninhabited, without people to cultivate it, for then it could have paid no taxes. Obviously the Babylonians wanted to eliminate in one way or another that part of the population that could keep the nation together and give it leadership, and so menace the suzerainty of the Babylonians. The peasant by himself has rarely been able to shake off foreign domination.

What the 39th chapter of Jeremiah reports is quite understandable in the light of the formation of latifundia in Judah. No doubt the latifundia were broken up and given to the expropriated peasants, or else the debt slaves and tenants were transformed into free owners of the soil they cultivated. Their masters were the men who had led Judah in the war against Babylon.

According to the Assyrian report, the population of Judah under Sennacherib came to 200,000 men, not including Jerusalem, which may be reckoned at 25,000. The number of important landholders is set at 15,000. Nebuchadnezzar took 7,000 of these away after the first capture of Jerusalem, thus leaving 8,000.[13] Nevertheless II Kings 24, verse 14 relates that at that time only "the poorest sort of people of the land" were left. These 8,000 were now, at the second destruction, taken away. It must have been their vineyards and fields that were given to "the poor of the people, which had nothing."

At any rate, even now it was not the entire people that was taken away, although the entire population of Jerusalem was taken away. The rural population remained, in large part; but those who remained ceased to constitute a specifically Jewish community. All the national life of Jewry was now concentrated in the deported city-dwellers in exile.

This national life now took on a peculiar coloration, corres-

13. Cf. F. Buhl, *Die sozialen Verhältnisse der Israeliten*, p. 52 f.

ponding to the peculiar position of these city Jews. Though the Israelites had not differed markedly from the other peoples around them, what was left of it, what still continued a specific national life, now became a people unique of its kind. It is not only after the destruction of Jerusalem by the Romans, but already at the destruction by Nebuchadnezzar that the abnormal situation of the Jews begins, a situation which makes them a phenomenon unique in history.

BOOK THREE: THE JEWS

2

THE JEWS AFTER THE EXILE

THE EXILE

ON THE SURFACE, with the destruction of Jerusalem, Judah had met with the same fate as the ten tribes of Israel after the destruction of Samaria. But what made Israel disappear from history, raised Judah from obscurity to one of the most powerful factors in world history, because its greater distance from Assyria, the natural strength of Jerusalem and the incursions of the northern nomads caused Jerusalem to fall 135 years later than Samaria.

The Jews were subjected for four generations more than the ten tribes to those influences we have discussed, which stimulate national fanaticism to its extreme. That factor alone made the Jews go into exile with a national feeling far stronger than that of their northern brothers. Another circumstance working in the same direction was that Judah was recruited essentially from a single large city with its surrounding territory, whereas the northern kingdom was a conglomerate of ten tribes which had not grown very close together. Judah was a much more unified and coherent mass than Israel.

Nevertheless the Judeans too would have lost their nationality in exile if they had remained under foreign rule as long as the ten tribes. The exile abroad may long for his old country and not strike roots in his new dwelling-place. Exile may even deepen his national feeling. In children born in exile, and growing up in the new conditions, aware of the old conditions only through their fathers' tales, it is rare for that national feeling to be as intense, unless it is continually kept alive by absence of rights or mistreatment in the new country or the hope of speedy return to the homeland. The third generation hardly knows its nationality unless it is discriminated against and forcibly set apart from the rest of the population as a peculiar and inferior nation, and subject to oppression and mistreatment.

This does not seem to have been the case with the deportees to Assyria and Babylonia, and the Jews might well have lost their nationality and been taken up into the Babylonians if they had stayed among them longer than for three generations. But soon after the destruction of Jerusalem the victor's empire began to totter, and the exiles gained new hope of returning to the land of their fathers soon; and in the course of the second generation the hope was fulfilled, and the Jews were allowed to return to Jerusalem from Babylon. For the peoples pressing from the north against Mesopotamia that had put an end to Assyria were still unquiet. The most powerful among them proved to be the nomad people of the Persians, who wiped out the two heirs of the Assyrian predominance, the empires of the Medes and of the Babylonians; the Persians not only restored the Assyrian-Babylonian empire in new form, but enormously enlarged it by conquering Egypt and Asia Minor. They created a military organization and a civil administration that for the first time constituted a solid foundation for a world empire, held it together and kept a lasting peace within it.

The conquerors of Babylon had no reason for keeping from their homes the people that Babylon had conquered and taken into exile. In 538 Babylon was taken by the Persians without a blow being struck, a sign of how weak it felt itself to be; and within only a year Cyrus, the Persian king, permitted the Jews to return. Their exile had lasted not quite fifty years, and yet so many had already become accustomed to the new conditions that only a part took advantage of the permission, while many remained in Babylon, where they felt more at home. That would indicate how little chance there would have been of Judah's avoiding complete disappearance if Jerusalem had had the same fate as Samaria; if 180 years rather than fifty had elapsed between its destruction and the fall of Babylon.

Short as the Jewish exile was, it brought sweeping changes in Judaism, making possible the full development and reinforcement of a series of tendencies that had previously been produced by conditions in Judah and which now assumed most peculiar forms in virtue of the most peculiar situation in which Judaism was placed from this time on.

It persisted as a nation while in exile, but a nation without farmers, a nation with an exclusively urban population. That constitutes one of the most important characteristics of Judaism down to the present day, and is the basis of its most essential "racial" characteristics, which actually are nothing more than the qualities of the city-dweller, carried to an extreme point by long city life and the absence of fresh additions to the population from the peasantry. This is a point I referred to as far back as 1890.[14] The return from exile to Palestine had only a minor and superficial effect on this state of affairs, as we shall see.

The Jews were not merely a nation of city-dwellers, but also a nation of traders. Industry was not highly developed in Judah, as we have seen; it was just enough for simple household purposes. This was a disadvantage among the Babylonians with their advanced technology. Military service and administration were not open to the Jews because of the loss of their independence: what other livelihood was left open to the city-dwellers than trade?

It had always played a large part in the life of Palestine; in exile it must have been their chief way of earning a living.

With the growth of trade there must have come a growth in the sharpness of their intelligence, of mathematical sense, of the capacity for reflection and abstraction. At the same time the national misfortune gave this increased keenness nobler objects than personal profit. In exile the fellow-countrymen came still closer together; the feeling of belonging is stronger when contrasted with the foreigner, for the individual feels himself weaker

14. "Das Judentum," *Neue Zeit*, VIII, p. 23 f.

and more imperilled. Social feeling, ethical emotion became stronger and filled the Jewish acuteness with the most profound thought about the causes of the national misfortune and the means of raising the nation up again.

Another powerful stimulus to Jewish thought must have been the magnificence of the city of Babylon with its millions of inhabitants, its world-wide trade, its ancient culture, its science and philosophy. Just as in the first half of the last century a stay in the Babylon on the Seine elevated German thinkers and spurred them to their highest and best works, so must staying in the Babylon on the Euphrates in the sixth century B.C. have affected the Jews from Jerusalem and burst open their horizon.

In Babylon, however, as in all the Oriental commercial centers that were not situated on the Mediterranean coast but inland, science remained mixed up with religion and bound to it, for reasons we have pointed out. In Judaism too, all the new strong impressions came through in religious form. In fact religion necessarily came even more into the foreground for the Jews because after the loss of their national independence the common national cult was the only bond that still held any authority over the entire nation. The tribal organization seems to have received new strength in exile, after the national government had ceased to exist.[15] But clannishness and its separatism are not enough to hold a nation together. It was in religion that Judah now sought the conservation and salvation of its nation and the leadership of the nation now fell to the priesthood.

The priesthood of Judea borrowed the pretensions of the Babylonian hierarchy, and also adopted many of their religious notions. A whole series of legends in the Bible are of Babylonian origin: for example, the Creation of the world, Paradise, the Fall, the Tower of Babel, the Deluge. The strict observance of the Sabbath is equally Babylonian. It was stressed for the first time during the Exile.

"The emphasis that Ezekiel puts on the reverence for the Sab-

15. See Frank Buhl, *Die sozialen Verhältnisse der Israeliten*, p. 43.

bath is something quite new. No earlier prophet stresses it in this way; for Jeremiah 17, verses 19 f. is spurious."[16]

Even after the return from the Exile, in the fifth century, the enforcement of the Sabbath rest was a matter of the greatest difficulty, "since it went too strongly against the old customs."[17]

It may be safely assumed, although there is no direct evidence, that the Jewish priesthood learned not only popular legends and customs from the lofty Babylonian hierarchy, but also a higher, more spiritual conception of the divinity.

The notion the Israelites had of God was long a very crude one. No matter how much pains later collectors and editors and revisers of the old stories took to clear them of all traces of paganism, there are still some left in the version of these stories that has come down to us.

Let us take for example the stories about Jacob. Not only does his god help him in all sorts of dubious affairs, but he gets involved in a wrestling match with Jacob, in which the god is vanquished by the man:

"And there wrestled a man with him (Jacob) until the breaking of the day. And when he saw that he prevailed not against him, he touched the hollow of his thigh; and the hollow of Jacob's thigh was out of joint, as he wrestled with him. And he said, Let me go, for the day breaketh. And he said, I will not let thee go, except thou bless me. And he said unto him, What is thy name? And he said, Jacob. And he said, Thy name shall be called no more Jacob, but Israel: for as a prince hast thou power with God and with men, and hast prevailed. And Jacob asked him, and said, Tell me, I pray thee, thy name. And he said, Wherefore is it that thou dost ask after my name? And he blest him there. And Jacob called the name of the place Peniel: for I have seen God face to face, and my life is preserved." (Genesis 32, verses 24 to 30).

The Great Unknown with whom Jacob wrestled victoriously and from whom he extorted a blessing was thus a god, mastered by a man, just as gods and men fight in the *Iliad*. But when

16. B. Stade, *Geschichte des Volkes Israel*, II, p. 17.
17. *Ibid.*, p. 187.

Diomedes succeeds in wounding Ares, it is with the help of Pallas Athene. Jacob disposes of his god without the aid of any other god.

In contrast to the naive ideas of God among the Israelites, many of the priests among the civilized peoples that surrounded them had attained monotheism, at least in their secret teachings.

This once found drastic expression among the Egyptians. "We are not now in a position to give in detail and follow in chronological sequence all the vagaries of speculation and all the phases of the intellectual development of the Egyptians. The final conclusion is that for the secret doctrine even Horus and Re, the son and the father, are completely identical, that the god begets himself by his own mother, the goddess of Heaven, and she too in turn is by a creation of the one eternal god. This doctrine is first expressed clearly and unequivocally with all its consequences at the beginning of the New Empire (after the expulsion of the Hyksos, in the fifteenth century); but it had begun to spread after the end of the sixth dynasty (about the year 2500), and during the Middle Kingdom the fundamental concepts are already fixed. . . . The starting-point of the new doctrine is Anu, the city of the sun (Heliopolis)."[18]

This doctrine remained esoteric, but it came to practical application once. This happened before the Hebrews had entered into Canaan, under Amenhotep IV, in the fourteenth century. It seems that this ruler came into conflict with the priesthood, whose wealth and power threatened to overwhelm him. He knew no other way of protecting himself from them than taking their esoteric doctrine seriously, compelling the cult of the one god and bitterly persecuting all the other gods, which amounted in practice to confiscating the enormous wealth of their colleges of priests.

We do not have the details of this struggle between hierarchy and monarchy. It was long-drawn out, but a century after Amenhotep IV, the priesthood had won a complete victory and completely restored the old cults.

18. Ed. Meyer, *Geschichte des alten Aegypten*, p. 192 f.

The whole incident shows how far monotheistic ideas had developed in the secret priestly doctrines of the centers of civilization in the ancient Orient. We have no reason to presume that the priests of Babylon were more backward than those of Egypt, whom they matched in all the arts and sciences. Thus Jeremias too speaks of a "latent monotheism" in Babylon. Marduk, the creator of heaven and earth, was also the lord of gods, whom he "pastures like sheep," that is, the various gods were only particular forms in which the one god appeared. Thus a Babylonian text says of the various gods: "Ninib: Marduk of Strength. Nergal: Marduk of Battle. Bel: Marduk of Rule. Nabu: Marduk of Commerce. Sin: Marduk Illuminator of the Night. Samas: Marduk of Justice. Addu: Marduk of Rain."

Just at the time of the Jewish Exile, when a sort of monotheism was becoming predominant among the Persians, now in contact with Babylon, there are signs that "in Babylonia too the germ of a monotheism had been planted, which must have had a strong similarity to the Pharaonic sun-cult of Amenophis IV (Amenhotep). At any rate, in an inscription dating from just before the fall of Babylon, and quite in accordance with the importance of the moon cult in Babylon, the moon god appears in a role like that of the sun god for Amenophis IV."[19]

The colleges of priests in Babylon and Egypt had a vital interest in keeping their ultimate monotheistic views from the people, since their entire power and wealth rested on the traditional polytheistic cult; but it was a different matter with the priesthood of the fetish of the covenant at Jerusalem.

Even before the destruction of Jerusalem this fetish had gained greatly in significance, ever since Samaria had been destroyed and the northern kingdom of Israel overthrown. Jerusalem was now the only large city of the Israelitish nationality; the lands around it were relatively unimportant in comparison. The prestige of the fetish of the covenant which had long, even before David perhaps, been great in Israel and particularly in the tribe of Judah, must now have overshadowed and obscured all the other

19. H. Winckler, *Die Babylonische Geisteskultur*, 1907, p. 144.

shrines of the people, as Jerusalem overshadowed all the other towns of Judah. Likewise the priesthood of this fetish must have achieved a dominant position with respect to the other priests in the land. There was a struggle between the rural clergy and the priests of the capital which ended, perhaps even before the Exile, with the fetish of Jerusalem obtaining a monopoly. That at least is the meaning of the story of Deuteronomy, the "Book of the Doctrine," which a priest is said to have "discovered" in the Temple in 621. It contains the divine command to demolish all the shrines outside of Jerusalem, an order which King Josiah faithfully obeyed:

"And he put down the idolatrous priests, whom the kings of Judah had ordained to burn incense in the high places in the cities of Judah, and in the places round about Jerusalem; them also that burned incense unto Baal, to the sun, and to the moon, and to the planets and to all the host of heaven. . . . And he brought all the priests out of the cities of Judah, and defiled the high places where the priests had burned incense, from Geba to Beersheba. . . . Moreover the altar that was at Bethel, and the high place which Jeroboam the son of Nebat, who made Israel to sin, had made, both that altar and the high place he brake down and burned the high place, and stamped it small to powder. . ." II Kings 23, verses 5 f.)

Not only the shrines of strange gods but even those of Jahveh himself, the oldest of his altars, were thus profaned and annihilated.

Perhaps this whole story, like so many others in the Bible, is but a fiction made up after the Exile, an attempt to justify actions taken after the Exile by representing them as repetitions of earlier proceedings, by inventing precedents or at least grossly exaggerating them. It may be assumed, at any rate, that there were rivalries between the priests of the capital and those of the provinces even before the Exile, occasionally ending in the closing down of inconvenient competitive shrines. It was easy for the Jews in exile, among whom those from Jerusalem predominated, to accept the monopolistic position of the Temple at Jerusalem.

Under the influence of Babylonian philosophy and their own national catastrophe, and perhaps of the Persian religion, which developed in a similar direction at much the same time as the Jewish religion and came into contact with it, stimulating it and perhaps receiving stimulation from it as well—under all these influences the efforts of the priests to create a monopoly for their fetish took the form of an ethical monotheism in which Jahveh was no longer merely the particular tribal god of Israel but the only god in the world, the personification of the good, the sum and substance of all morality.

Thus, when the Jews returned to Jerusalem from captivity, their religion had developed so highly and become so spiritual that the crude religious ideas and practices of the Jewish peasants who had been left behind must have seemed to them no more than revolting heathen abominations. If it had not yet taken place, it was now possible for the priests and masters of Jerusalem to see to it that these competitive provincial cults were done away with and the monopoly of the Jerusalem hierarchy permanently established.

Thus Jewish monotheism arose. It was ethical in nature, like that of the Platonic philosophy, for example. But among the Jews the new concept of the deity did not arise outside of religion, as with the Greeks; it was not propounded by a class standing outside the priesthood. Thus the one God did not appear as a new god, standing above and outside of the old world of gods, but as a reduction of the old society of gods to a single most powerful god, standing closest to the inhabitants of Jerusalem, that is to the old warrior, ethical, tribal and local god, Jahveh.

This introduced a number of knotty contradictions into the Jewish religion. As an ethical god Jahveh is God of all mankind, since good and bad are concepts that are taken as absolute, as valid for all men alike. And as an ethical god, as personification of the moral idea, the one God is everywhere, as morality is considered to be universally valid. But for Babylonian Judaism religion and the Jahveh cult were also their strongest national link; and any possibility of reestablishing their national independence was inseparably linked to the reconstruction of Jerusalem. The erection of the Temple in Jerusalem, and then its preservation, became the watchword which brought the Jewish nation together. The priesthood of this temple had become the highest national authority of the Jews, the class that had every interest in maintaining the ritual monopoly of this temple. Thus there was a remarkable amalgam of the high philosophical abstraction of a single omnipresent God, who requires not sacrifices, but only for a pure heart and a life free from sin, with the old primitive fetishism which localized the god in a particular place, the only place where the deity could be successfully influenced by entreaties of all sorts. The Temple of Jerusalem remained the exclusive seat of Jahveh, to which every pious Jew had to turn in his longing.

There was another contradiction, just as bizarre, in the fact that God as the epitome of the moral requirements which are the same for all men now became the God of all men, and yet remained the Jewish tribal god. The attempt was made to solve the contradiction by saying that God was to be sure the God of all men, and that all men were bound to love and worship him, but that the Jews were the only people that he had chosen to bear witness to this love and worship, to whom he had revealed his majesty, leaving the Gentiles in blindness. It was precisely during the Exile, in the time of deepest humiliation and desperation, that this proud supremacy over the rest of mankind appeared. Formerly Israel had been a nation like other nations, and Jahveh a god like the other gods; perhaps stronger than the other gods, in the way that one gave one's own nation pre-eminence over other nations, but still not the only real God, and Israel not alone in possession of the truth.

"The God of Israel was not the Almighty, but only the most powerful among the gods. He was on the same plane with them and had to battle against them; Chemosh and Dagon and Hadad were in every way comparable with him, less powerful but no less real. 'Wilt not thou possess that which Chemosh thy god giveth thee to possess?' Jephtha warns the neighbors who have crossed

the border, 'So whomsoever the Lord our God shall drive out
from before us, them will we possess.' The domains of the gods
were separate like those of the peoples, and one god had no right
in the land of another."[20]

But now it is quite different. The author of Isaiah, chapters 40
ff., who wrote at the end of the Exile or shortly thereafter, has
Jahveh proclaim:

"I am the Lord [Jahveh]; that is my name: and my glory will I
not give to another, neither my praise to graven images. . . . Sing
unto the Lord a new song, and his praise from the end of the
earth, ye that go down to the sea, and all that is therein, the isles,
and the inhabitants thereof. Let the wilderness and the cities
thereof lift up their voice, the villages that Kedar doth inhabit:
let the inhabitants of the rock sing, let them shout from the top
of the mountains. Let them give glory unto the Lord, and declare
his praise in the islands."[21]

Here there is no limitation to Palestine or Jerusalem. But the
same author has Jahveh say:

"But thou, Israel, art my servant, Jacob whom I have chosen,
the seed of Abraham my friend. Thou whom I have taken from the
ends of the earth, and called thee from the chief men thereof, and
said unto thee, Thou art my servant; I have chosen thee, and not
cast thee away. Fear thou not; for I am with thee: be not dis-
mayed; for I am thy God. . . . They that war against thee shall
be as nothing, and as a thing of nought. For I the Lord thy God
will hold thy right hand. . . . The first [viz., the Lord] shall say
to Zion, Behold, behold them: and I will give to Jerusalem one
that bringeth good tidings."[22]

These are strange contradictions, but contradictions which
come out of life, out of the contradictory position of the Jews in
Babylon. There they had been placed within a new civilization
which revolutionized their whole way of thinking, while all the
conditions of their lives drove them to conserve their old tradi-

20. Wellhausen, *op. cit.,* p. 32.
21. Isaiah 42, verses 8 to 12.
22. Isaiah 41, verses 8 to 27.

tions as the only way to conserve their national existence, which had become so especially dear to them; for a difficult position lasting for centuries had developed their national feeling to an unusually marked degree.

The task of the thinkers of Judaism was to combine the new ethics with the old fetishism and to reconcile the narrow views of a little mountain people with the knowledge of the world and of life achieved by the broad civilisation centering around Babylon. And this reconciliation was to take place on the level of religion, that is of traditional beliefs. The task was hence to show that the new things were not new but old, that the new truth of the foreigners, to which one could not close his eyes, was neither new nor foreign, but an authentic Jewish possession, by recognizing and accepting which the Jews would not lose their nationality in the Babylonian melting-pot, but would emerge a stronger and firmer people.

This was a task well suited to sharpen the wits and develop the art of interpretation and hair-splitting, which from this point on reached such a high degree of perfection among the Jews. It also gave the historical literature of the Jews its specific character.

This process, one which has often occurred, was described by Marx in the *Introduction to the Critique of Political Economy,* in discussing the views of the eighteenth century on the state of nature in the following terms: "The individual and isolated hunter and fisher who forms the starting point with Smith and Ricardo, belongs to the insipid illusions of the Eighteenth Century. They are Robinsonades, which do not by any means represent, as students of the history of civilisation imagine, a reaction against over-refinement and a return to a misunderstood natural life. They are no more based on such a naturalism than is Rousseau's *Contrat Social,* which makes naturally independent individuals come in contact and have intercourse by contract. They are the fiction and only the aesthetic fiction of the small and great Robinsonades. They are, moreover, the anticipation of 'bourgeois society', which had been in course of development since the Sixteenth Century and made gigantic strides towards maturity

in the Eighteenth. In this society of free competition the individual appears free from the bonds of nature, etc., which in
former epochs of history made him a part of a definite, limited
human conglomeration. To the prophets of the Eighteenth Century, on whose shoulders Smith and Ricardo are still standing,
this Eighteenth Century individual, constituting the joint product
of the dissolution of the feudal form of society and of the new
forces of production which had developed since the Sixteenth
Century, appears as an ideal whose existence belongs to the past;
not as result of history, but as its starting point. Since that individual appeared to be in conformity with nature and corresponded to their conception of human nature, he was regarded
not as a product of history, but of nature. This illusion is characteristic of every new epoch."

This was the illusion of those thinkers too who during the
Exile and after it developed the notion of monotheism and
theocracy in Judaism. The idea did not seem to them to be one
which had arisen in the course of history, but as something laid
down from the beginning, not a "historical result," but the "initial point of history." History itself was now taken in the same
sense, and it was the more easily adapted to the new needs; the
more it was based on merely oral tradition, the less it was docu-
mented. The belief in the one God and the domination of Israel
by the priests of Jahveh was now transposed to the beginnings of
Israel's history; the polytheism and fetishism, which could not be
denied, were explained away as later apostasy from the faith of
the fathers, not as their original faith, which in fact it was.

And this view had another great advantage, that there was
something exceptionally consoling about it, as there was about
the self-proclamation of Israel as the chosen people of God. If
Jahveh were only the tribal god of Israel, the disasters of his
people would signify so many disasters to its god, since he would
have turned out to be the weaker in battle with other gods; and
in that case there would be every reason to despair of Jahveh and
his priests. It was something else again if there was no other god
but Jahveh, if he had chosen the Israelites above the other

peoples and they repaid him with ingratitude and apostasy. Now all the tribulations of Israel and Judah appeared merely as merited punishment for their sins and their disregard for the priests of Jahveh, as proofs not of the weakness but of the strength of God, who is not mocked with impunity. But in this there lay the basis for the conviction that God would once more have mercy on his people, rescue and deliver it, if it only would hold fast to the true faith in him and in his priests and prophets. If the life of the nation were not to disappear, such a faith was needed, given the hopelessness of the situation of the tiny people, the "worm Jacob" (Isaiah 41, verse 14) among the hostile and powerful communities.

Only by a supernatural, superhuman, divine power, a savior sent by God, only by the Messiah could Judah still be saved, freed and finally made ruler over the nations that now abused it. The belief in the Messiah arrives at the same time as monotheism and is closely connected with it. Precisely for this reason the Messiah is not thought of as God, but as a man sent by God. He was to establish an earthly kingdom, not a heavenly kingdom (for Jewish thought was not as abstract as all that), a Jewish kingdom. In fact Cyrus, who released the Jews from Babylonia and sent them back to Jerusalem, is already designated as the Lord's anointed, Messiah, Christ (Isaiah 45, verse 1).

This transformation in Jewish thinking could not have been carried out all at once nor peacefully; it started in the Exile but could not have ended there. We must suppose that there were violent polemics after the fashion of the prophets, profound doubts and searchings after the fashion of the book of Job, and historical accounts after the fashion of the various components of the Pentateuch, which were written at about that time.

It was only long after the Exile that this revolutionary period came to a close. Certain dogmatic, ritual, legal and historical views emerged victorious and were recognized as correct by the priesthood, which had become the rulers of the people, and by the mass of the people themselves. Certain writings, which agreed with these views, were now labeled as primordial and sacred, and handed down to posterity as such. In the process radical "revisions," eliminations and interpolations had to be made in order to bring some sort of unity into the various components of this contradictory body of literature in which the old and the new, things correctly understood and things misunderstood, the genuine and the spurious stood side by side in inextricable confusion. Despite all this "editorial work" there is still fortunately enough of the original material left in the end product, the "old Testament," for us to be able to distinguish, under the luxuriant undergrowth of forgeries, at least the general character of the old Hebrew community before the Exile, a community of which the new Judaism was not only the continuation but also the complete contradiction.

THE JEWISH DIASPORA

In the year 538 B.C., the Babylonian Jews received permission from Cyrus to return to Jerusalem. We have seen that by no means all of them took advantage of this privilege. How could they all make a living there? The city was in ruins, and some time was needed until it was made habitable and fortified, and the Temple of Jahveh restored. Even then it did not by any means give all the Jews the hope of a livelihood. Then as now the peasant often moved to the city, but the transition from city-dwelling to farming is hard and rare.

The Jews had probably not acquired industrial skill in Babylon; perhaps they were not there long enough. Judea achieved no political autonomy, remaining dependent on foreign conquerors, first the Persians, then Alexander the Great, the Greeks, and finally, after a brief interval of independence and various disastrous convulsions, the Romans. None of the conditions existed in Judea for a military monarchy gaining wealth by subjugating and plundering weaker neighbors.

If there was not much to be got by the Jews in farming, industry or military service on their return from the Exile, the majority of them had no other occupation open to them but trade, as in

Babylon. They took to it with a vigor arising out of the mental abilities and knowledge needed for trade that they had developed over the centuries.

However, since the Babylonian captivity there had been revolutionary changes in politics and commerce that were fateful for the commercial position of Palestine. Peasant farming and handicrafts are highly conservative occupations.

Technical advances in these occupations occur rarely, and are slow to be adopted so long as the stimulus of competition is lacking, as it is under primitive conditions, and so long as in the normal course of events, that is if there are no bad harvests, droughts, wars and such catastrophes, the worker who labors in the traditional way is sure of his bread, whereas the new and untried may lead to failures and losses.

As a rule technical advances in peasant agriculture and the handicrafts do not arise in those fields themselves, but in trade, which brings new products and procedures from abroad that arouse thought and in the end produce new profitable crops and methods.

Trade is much less conservative. Of necessity it rises above local and professional narrowness and is critical of home traditions, because it can compare them with what has been achieved in other places under different conditions. In addition, the merchant is subject to competition, sooner than the farmer or the artisan, because he encounters competitors from many nations in the great centers of commerce. He continually has to look for something new, and above all for improved means of communication and travel and for broader fields of trade connections. Until agriculture and industry become capitalistic and are put on a scientific footing, trade is the only revolutionary factor in the economy. This is especially true of sea-borne commerce. Navigation makes it possible to cover greater distances and bring more different peoples into contact with each other than commerce by land does. At first the sea separates peoples more, and makes their development more independent of others and more individualized. When navigation develops and the hitherto isolated peoples come into contact with each other, the contrasts and contradictions are often sharper than in the case of land trading. Navigation too requires higher technical development; sea-borne commerce comes much later than trade by land, for building a seaworthy ship calls for a much greater mastery of nature than say taming a camel or a donkey. On the other hand, the great profits of maritime commerce, which can only be obtained on the basis of a highly developed shipbuilding technique, are one of the strongest incentives to perfect this technique. There is perhaps no other field in which ancient technology developed so early and registered such triumphs as in shipbuilding.

Navigation however does not hamper commerce on land, but furthers it. If a city port is to prosper, it needs as a rule to be supported by a region furnishing the goods to be shipped and in turn absorbing the goods brought in by the ships. It must strive to develop land communications along with navigation; but the latter becomes more and more important until it is the decisive factor, and land commerce is subordinate to it. If the routes of navigation change, the land routes must change accordingly.

The first long-distance seafarers in the Mediterranean came from Phoenicia, which lay between the old civilized countries on the Nile and the Euphrates and participated in the intercourse between them. It was on the Mediterranean, as Egypt was; but the Egyptians were led to agriculture rather than to navigation by the very nature of their land, whose fertility is inexhaustible thanks to the annual inundations by the Nile. Moreover the Egyptians did not have the necessary timber, nor the pressure of need, which in the early stages is the only whip that could make men brave the dangers of the open sea. The river navigation of the Egyptians reached a high point of development, but on the sea they did not go beyond coastal shipping over short distances. They developed agriculture and industry, especially weaving, and their commerce flourished, but they did not go abroad as traders, but waited for the foreigners to come to them with their wares. The desert and the sea remained alien elements to them.

The Phoenicians on the other hand lived on a seacoast that

forced them to the sea; it was so close to the mountains and gave such meager plowlands that farming had to be eked out with fishing, while the mountain slopes supplied excellent timber for ships. These were conditions that led the Phoenicians to take to the sea. Their situation among industrially developed regions gave them the stimulus to prolong their fishing voyages into trading voyages at sea. In this way they became the transporters of Indian, Arabian, Babylonian and Egyptian products, especially textiles and spices, to the West, from which they brought products of different kinds, chiefly metals.

In time dangerous competitors arose in the Greeks, who inhabited islands and coasts whose fields were as barren as those of Phoenicia, so that they too were driven to fishing and seafaring. Their shipping kept increasing and became more and more dangerous to the Phoenicians. At first the Greeks tried to bypass the Phoenicians and win new ways to the Orient. They entered the Black Sea; from these ports commerce with India was established through Central Asia. At the same time they tried to make connections with Egypt and open it to sea-borne commerce. Shortly before the time of the Babylonian captivity of the Jews the Ionians and Carians succeeded in this undertaking. From the time of Psammetichus (663) they were firmly established in Egypt and their traders flooded into it. Under Amasis (569 to 525) they acquired a region on the Western branch of the Nile in order to found a port city of their own, Naukratis. This was to be the sole center of Greek commerce. Soon after, Egypt fell to the Persians (525), as had Babylonia. But the situation of the Greeks in Egypt did not suffer as a result. On the contrary, foreigners now had the right to trade freely in all of Egypt, and the lion's share of the profits went to the Greeks. As soon as the Persian regime grew feeble, as the military spirit of the former nomad nation softened in city life, the Egyptians rose and tried to win their independence once more, and succeeded for a while (from 404 to 342). This was possible only because of the aid of the Greeks, who had grown so strong meanwhile that they had beaten back the mighty Persians on land and at sea, and along with them pushed back their vassals, the Phoenicians. Under Alexander of Macedon Greece took the offensive (from 334 on) against the Persian Empire, annexed it and put a final end to the glory of the Phoenician cities, which had long been in decline.

Palestine's commerce had fallen off even earlier than Phoenicia's; world trade had turned from the Palestinian routes, the exports of India as well as those of Babylonia, Arabia, Ethiopia and Egypt. Palestine, as the borderland between Egypt and Syria, remained the theatre in which the wars between the masters of Syria and those of Egypt took place, but the trade between these regions now went by sea, bypassing the land. Palestine had lost all the advantages of its central position and kept all the disadvantages. At the same time that the mass of the Jews were driven more and more to trade as their only means of support, the chances of doing business in their own country kept shrinking.

Since business did not come to them, they were forced to go out after business abroad, among those nations which did not produce a commercial class of their own but had foreigners come to them as traders. There were not a few such nations. In countries where agriculture supported the mass of the people without needing to be supplemented by nomadic cattle-raising or by fishing, and the aristocracy satisfied their drive for expansion by piling up latifundia at home and making war abroad, people preferred to have traders come to them rather than go abroad themselves to fetch foreign goods. That was the attitude of the Egyptians and of the Romans, as we have seen. In both countries the traders were aliens, chiefly Greeks and Jews. They prospered most in such lands.

Now we have the Diaspora, the dispersion of the Jews outside of their own homeland, just after the Babylonian Exile, precisely when they were allowed to return home. This dispersion was not the result of an act of violence, like the fall of Jerusalem, but of an imperceptible revolution that began at that time, a change in trade routes.

Their largest groups accumulated where the flow of trade was strongest and where the greatest wealth came together, in Alexandria and later in Rome. There the Jews increased not only in number but in wealth and power. Their strong national feeling gave them a strong cohesion, too, that was all the more effective in times like those just preceding Christ, when society was falling apart more widely and more intensively, and the general bonds of society were dissolving. And since the Jews were to be found in all the commercial centers of the Hellenic and Roman civilized world of that time, their internal cohesion extended over all those regions, forming an internationale which gave powerful support to its members wherever they might happen to be. If we add to this the commercial abilities they had developed over so many centuries, and which after the Exile were necessarily sharpened, we can understand the growth of their power and wealth.

Mommsen says of Alexandria that it "was almost as much a city of Jews as of Greeks; the Jewish community there was at least the equal of that of Jerusalem in number, wealth, ability and organization. At the beginning of the Empire there were reckoned to be a million Jews among 8 million Egyptians, and their influence presumably was greater than in that proportion. . . . They and only they were allowed to form a community within the community, so to speak, and have a certain degree of self-rule while the other aliens were ruled by civil authorities."

" 'The Jews,' Strabo says, 'have a national chief of their own in Alexandria, who presides over the people and decides lawsuits and regulates contracts and arrangements as if he were the ruler of an independent community.' This took place because the Jews claimed that such a special jurisdiction was required by their nationality or, what amounts to the same thing, their religion. In addition, the general government ordinances took the national and religious feeling of the Jews into account on an extensive scale and where possible helped them by means of exemptions. Congregating helped in this respect too; in Alexandria, for example, two of the five districts of the city were chiefly inhabited by Jews."[23]

The Alexandrian Jews achieved not only wealth but also pres-

23. Mommsen, *Römische Geschichte,* V, p. 489-92.

tige and influence over the rulers of the world. For example, an important role was played by the tax farmer of the Arabian side of the Nile, the alabarch [or, arabarch] Alexander. Agrippa, who later became king of Judea, borrowed 200,000 drachmas from him in the days of Tiberius. Alexander gave him 5 talents in cash and a letter for payment of the rest in Dikaearchia.[24] This shows the close commercial relations between the Jews of Alexandria and those of Italy. There was a strong Jewish community in Dikaearchia, or Puteoli, near Naples. Josephus further reports of the same Alexandrian Jew: "He, the Emperor Claudius, released the alabarch Alexander Lysimachus, his old good friend, who had been guardian of his mother Antonia and imprisoned by Gaius in anger. This man's son Marcus later married Berenice, daughter of King Agrippa."[25]

What was true of Alexandria also applied to Antioch: "In the capital of Syria, as in that of Egypt, a certain communal independence and privileged position was granted the Jews, and their position as centers of the Jewish Diaspora is not the least important cause for the development of both cities."[26]

In Rome the presence of Jews may be traced back to the second century B.C. In 139 B.C. the Roman foreign praetor expelled Jews who had allowed Italian proselytes at their Sabbath. These Jews might have been members of an embassy sent by Simon Maccabee to gain the good-will of the Romans and who took advantage of the opportunity to make propaganda for their religion. We soon find Jews settled in Rome, however, and the Jewish community there was considerably reinforced when Pompey took Jerusalem in 63 B.C. He brought many Jewish prisoners to Rome, who then continued to live there as slaves or as freedmen. The community won considerable influence. About the year 60 Cicero complained that their power was felt even in the Forum. Their power increased under Caesar. Mommsen describes the situation as follows:

24. Josephus, *Jewish Antiquities*, 18, 6, 3.
25. *Ibid.*, 19, 5, 1.
26. Mommsen, *Römische Geschichte*, V, p. 456.

"How large the Jewish population was in Rome itself even before Caesar and what a close association of fellow-countrymen they formed, is shown by the remark of a writer of the time, that a governor should think twice before interfering with the Jews of his province, since he would surely have to pay for it by being booed on his return by the rabble of the capital. This Jewry, although not the most cheerful spot in the not at all cheerful picture of the amalgam of peoples of that time, was nevertheless an historical factor evolving in the natural course of events; the statesman could not deny its existence or combat it, and instead Caesar, like his forerunner Alexander of Macedon, understood it and gave it all possible aid. Alexander, the founder of Alexandrian Jewry did almost as much for their nation as did David when he built the Temple; Caesar aided the Jews in Alexandria and in Rome through special favors and privileges and in particular protected their cult against the local Greek and Roman priests. The two great men did not of course have any idea of putting the Jewish nation on the same level as the Hellenic or the Italo-Hellenic. But the Jew, who has not received the Pandora's gift of political organization, as the Occidental Westerner has, and is basically indifferent toward the state; who moreover is just as unwilling to give up the core of his national characteristics as he is ready to wrap that core in the trappings of any nationality and comply with the ways of the alien folk up to a certain point—just for these reasons the Jew was particularly suited to a state that was founded on the ruins of a hundred city-states and had to be fitted out with a rather abstract and decrepit nationality. Even in the ancient world Judaism was an active ferment of cosmopolitanism and national decomposition and to that extent preeminently entitled to membership in Caesar's state, whose city was really nothing more than world citizenship and whose nationality basically only humanity."[27]

Mommsen manages here to squeeze three kinds of professorial views of history into a couple of lines. First, the notion that monarchs make history, that a decree or two of Alexander the

27. Mommsen, *Römische Geschichte,* III, p. 549-551.

Great were what created the Jewish community of Alexandria, and not anything like the change of the trade routes, that had given rise to a large Jewish community in Egypt well before Alexander and developed and strengthened it after Alexander. Or shall we assume that the entire world-wide trade of Egypt lasting many centuries, was created by a passing idea of the Macedonian conqueror as he passed through that country?

Along with this superstitious belief in royal decrees marches race superstition: the peoples of the West have been given by nature, as a racial capacity, the "Pandora's gift" of political organisation, something presumably lacking in Jews from birth. Nature, that is, creates political capabilities out of its own viscera before there is any such thing as politics, and distributes them arbitrarily among the various "races," whatever that term may be supposed to signify. This mystical whim of nature seems all the more ridiculous in this context when we recall that until the Exile the Jews had and made use of just as large a share of the "Pandora's gift" of political organization as other nations of their degree of social evolution. It was only the pressure of external conditions that deprived them of their state and along with it of the materials for a political organization.

On top of the monarchistic and "scientific" concepts of history there comes a third ideology, which holds that military leaders and organizers of states act in accordance with trains of thought of the kind that German professors contrive in their studies. The unscrupulous swindler and adventurer Caesar is said to have desired to create an abstract nationality of world citizenship and humanity, and recognized the Jews as the most useful instrument to that end and hence favored them!

Even if Caesar had said things of the sort, they should not have been taken at once as representing his actual thoughts. No more so than, let us say, the phrases of Napoleon should be taken at face value. Liberal professors of the time in which Mommsen wrote his Roman history were easily captivated by Napoleonic phrase-making, but that was not the basis of their political strength. Caesar in fact never voiced anything at all like such ideas. Caesars always dealt exclusively in phrases that were fashionable and could be used for demagogy among credulous proletarians or credulous professors.

The fact that Caesar not only tolerated the Jews but favored them has a much simpler explanation, if not so noble a one, in his eternal debts and his eternal greed for money. Money had become the decisive power in the state. The reason that Caesar protected the Jews and gave them privileges was that they had money and hence were useful to him and could be still more useful in the future, and not that their racial characteristics could be applied to the creation of an "abstract decrepit" nationality.

They appreciated his favor, and deeply mourned his death. "At the great public funeral he was mourned by the foreign residents [of Rome], each nation in its own way, especially the Jews, who even came to view the bier several nights in a row."28

Augustus too appreciated the importance of the Jews. "Under Augustus, the communities of the Near East attempted to call up their Jewish fellow-citizens for military service on the same basis as the others and not to allow them the observance of the Sabbath any longer; Agrippa however decided against this and upheld the status quo in the Jews' favor, or rather perhaps now made legally binding for the first time what had previously been a privilege granted by individual governors or communities of Greek provinces, namely the exemption of the Jews from military service and the Sabbath privilege. Augustus further directed the governor of Asia not to apply to the Jews the strict imperial laws against societies and meetings. . . . Augustus showed himself kindly disposed toward the Jewish colony in the suburbs of Rome across the Tiber, and allowed those who had refrained from sharing in his donations because of the Sabbath to claim their part on another day."29

The Jews in Rome must have been extremely numerous at that time. In the year 3 B.C. a Jewish delegation to Augustus included

28. Suetonius, *Julius Caesar*, chap. 84.
29. Mommsen, *Römische Geschichte*, V, p. 497 f.

over 8000. Quite recently numerous Jewish burial places have been discovered in Rome.

Incidentally, although trade was their chief calling, not all Jews abroad were traders. Where many of them lived together, Jewish artisans too were busy. Jewish physicians are mentioned in inscriptions from Ephesus and Venosa.[30] Josephus tells us even of a Jewish court actor in Rome: "In Dikaearchia, or Puteoli as the Italians call it, I became the friend of the actor (*mimologos*) Aliturus, who was of Jewish origin and very well liked by Nero. Through him I became acquainted with the Empress Poppaea."[31]

THE JEWISH PROPAGANDA

Until the Exile the people of Israel had not increased in any exceptional degree. Not more than other peoples. After the Exile however it grew incredibly. Now the promise of Jahveh was fulfilled, which was said to have been imparted to Abraham:

"That in blessing I will bless thee, and in multiplying I will multiply thy seed as the stars of the heaven, and as the sand which is upon the sea shore; and thy seed shall possess the gate of his enemies; And in thy seed shall all the nations of the earth be blessed."[32]

This promise, like virtually all the prophecies in the Bible, was fabricated after the state of affairs it foresaw was already present—like the prophecies that some divinely favored heroes enunciate in modern historical dramas. What Jahveh set before Abraham could only have been written down after the Exile, for only then does the statement make sense. Then however it fits very well. Jewry did increase surprisingly, so that it was able to make itself at home in all the important cities of the Mediterranean world, "possess the gates of his enemies" and keep its trade going, "bless all nations of the earth."

30. Schürer, *Geschichte des jüdischen Volkes*, III, 90.
31. Josephus, *Autobiography*.
32. Genesis 22, verses 17 and 18.

The geographer Strabo, writing about the time of Christ's birth, said of the Jews: "This people is already in every city, and it is hard to find a place on the inhabited earth that has not received this nation and is not [financially] dominated by it."

This rapid increase of the Jewish population is in part to be attributed to the great fertility of the Jews. But this too is not a special characteristic of their *race*—or else it would always have been present—but a particular property of the *class* they now represented with distinction, the merchants.

Not only does every form of society have its law of population, but so does each class within a given society. For example, the modern wage proletariat increases rapidly thanks to the fact that proletarians, male and female alike, early become economically independent and have the opportunity of having their children employed early too; in addition, the proletarians have no inheritance to divide up which might induce them to limit the number of their children.

The law of increase for settled farmers is different. In places where they find free land, as is generally the case when they occupy a country heretofore inhabited by hunters or herdsmen, they increase rapidly, for the conditions under which they live are far more favorable to bringing up children than let us say those of nomad hunters with their uncertain food supplies and lack of any milk supply other than mothers' milk, so that mothers are compelled to give suck to their children for several years. The farmer produces adequate, regular food, and the cow he raises gives copious milk, more than the cow of the nomad herdsmen, which wastes so much energy in searching for fodder.

But cultivable land and fields are limited, and can be restricted by private property even more than they already are by nature. In addition the technical development of agriculture is usually extremely slow. Accordingly there comes sooner or later to a farming nation the time when there is no more new land on which to establish new homes and families. That forces the farmers, if their excess progeny does not find an outlet in another field, such as military service or city industry, artificially to limit the number of their children. Peasants in this situation are the Malthusian ideal.

But even mere private property in land can have the same effect even if not all the cultivable land has been put into use. Possessing land now gives power: the more land one owns, the more power and wealth in society one has at his disposal. The landowner's endeavor is now to increase his holdings, and since the land area is a fixed quantity and can not be enlarged, landed property can only be increased by putting together already existing properties. The law of inheritance may hinder or foster this accumulation: further it by marriages in which both parties inherit land, which they combine, or hinder it when a property is divided among several heirs. The point comes for large landowners, as for peasants, when they either limit their offspring as much as possible in order to keep their properties large, or disinherit all the offspring but one. When the sharing of the inheritance among the children remains the rule, private property in land leads sooner or later to limitation of offspring on the part of the landowners, and under some conditions to the constant shrinkage of the numbers of the class. This was one of the reasons for the depopulation of the Roman Empire, which was based essentially on agriculture.

The fertility of the Jewish families was a vivid contrast. The Jews were no longer a people among whom agriculture was predominant. The large majority were tradespeople, capitalists. Capital, however, can be increased, unlike land. If trade is prosperous, capital may grow faster than the tradespeople's offspring, so that although the number increases rapidly, each individual is richer. The centuries after the Exile up to the early years of the Empire were times in which trade expanded enormously. The exploitation of the workers engaged in agriculture—slaves, tenants, peasants—mounted rapidly, and the sphere of their exploitation expanded at the same time. The exploitation of the mines increased, at least until the supply of fresh slaves began to give out. In the end, as we have seen, that led to the decline of agriculture, the depopulation of the land, and finally to the exhaustion of the military power and hence of the supply of fresh slaves, which could only come from constant successful wars; and all this amounted to the decline of mining as well. But it was long before these results were felt, and until then the accumulation of wealth in a few hands went forward together with the ruin of the population as the luxury of the wealthy swelled. Trade however was at that time primarily trade in luxuries. Means of transport were ill-developed; cheap transportation in bulk was only in its infancy. The grain trade from Egypt to Italy had a certain importance, but in general luxury articles were the main items of commerce. Modern commerce is primarily devoted to the production and consumption of great masses; formerly commerce served the arrogance and extravagance of a small number of exploiters. Today it depends on the growth of mass consumption; formerly it depended on the growth of exploitation and wastefulness. It never found more favorable conditions for this than in the period from the founding of the Persian Empire to the first Caesars. The change in the routes of commerce hit Palestine hard, but gave new life to trade in general from the Euphrates and the Nile to the Danube and the Rhine, from India to Britain. Nations whose economic basis was agriculture might well decline and be depopulated in that era; but a people of merchants would profit and would not have to restrain its natural increase at all, especially if there were no external obstacles restraining it.

But no matter how high we set the natural fertility of the Jews, that by itself would not suffice to explain the swift increase in Jewry. It was supplemented by its propaganda power.

The fact that a nation should increase by religious propaganda is something as extraordinary as the historical position of Judaism itself.

Originally the Jews were held together by ties of blood, as were other peoples. The kingdom replaced the gentile organization by the territorial union, the state and its districts. This bond lapsed with the transplantation into exile, and the return to Jerusalem put it back into effect for only a small fraction of the nation. The larger and constantly increasing part of it lived outside of the Jewish national state, abroad, not only temporarily, like the

merchants of other nations, but permanently. As a result yet
another bond of nationality was lost, community of language.
The Jews living abroad had to speak the language of the land,
and after several generations had lived there the younger ones
spoke only the language of the land and forgot the language of
the homeland. Even in the third century B.C. the holy scriptures
of the Jews were translated into Greek, since few of the Alexandrian Jews understood Hebrew any longer. Perhaps too as a
means of propaganda among the Greeks. Greek became the language of current Jewish literature, and also the language of the
Jewish people, even in Italy. "The various Jewish communities
in Rome had to some extent common burial places, of which
five are known; up to now. The inscriptions are overwhelmingly
in Greek, although partially in a vernacular which is almost unintelligible; there are some in Latin too, but none in Hebrew."[33]
Not even the Jews in Palestine were able to maintain Hebrew; they
adopted the language of the surrounding population, Aramaic.

Centuries before the destruction of Jerusalem by the Romans,
Hebrew had already ceased to be a living language. It was no
longer of use as a means of communication among fellow-countrymen, but merely a way of access to the holy scriptures of olden
times—scriptures to be sure which were mistakenly thought to go
back many centuries and millennia, since actually they had been
fairly recently put together from old remnants and new inventions.

This religion, ostensibly revealed to the forefathers of Israel
and actually formed in the Exile and after, became, along with
commercial relations, the firmest bond of Judaism, the only feature distinguishing it from the other nations.

But the one God of this religion was no longer one among
many tribal gods; he was the only God of the world, a God for
all men, whose commandments held for all men. The Jews differed from the others only in that they had learned of Him,
while the others in their blindness knew nothing of Him. Knowledge of this God was now the mark of Judaism: anyone who knew

33. Friedländer, *Sittengeschichte Roms*, II, 519.

him and accepted his commandments belonged to the elect of God, and was a Jew.

This monotheism made it logically possible to broaden the sphere of Judaism by propaganda for it, but this possibility might have come to nothing if it had not coincided with the drive of Judaism to expand. The tininess of the Jewish people had led it to the deepest humiliation, but it had not gone under. It had weathered the heaviest storms and had solid ground under its feet once more, and now was beginning to acquire wealth and power in the most diverse regions. That gave them the proud assurance that they really were the chosen people, really called upon at some time to rule over the other peoples. But no matter how it might count on its God and the Messiah it expected from God, it had to admit to itself that its chances were hopeless so long as it was so tiny a folk among the millions of Gentiles, whose enormous superiority in numbers they realized even more clearly as the radius of their commercial relationships expanded. The stronger their desire for power and position, the more they had to try to increase the number of their fellow-countrymen by winning supporters among foreign peoples. Accordingly, Judaism developed a powerful tendency toward expansion during the last centuries before the destruction of Jerusalem.

For the inhabitants of the Jewish state the most direct way to this end was forcible conversion. Subjugation of a people was nothing uncommon. Where the Jews did it, they now tried to impose their religion as well. This took place in the era of the Maccabees and their successors, say from 165 to 63 B.C., when the fall of the Syrian Empire gave the Jewish people some elbow room for a while, which they used not only to shake off the Syrian yoke but to extend their own territories. Galilee was conquered in this period; previously it had not been Jewish, as Schürer has proved.[34] Idumea and the country east of the Jordan were subjugated, and a foothold was even gained on the coast, at Joffa. There was nothing exceptional about such a policy of conquest; what was unusual was that it became a policy of religious ex-

34. *Geschichte des jüdischen Volkes*, II, p. 5.

pansion. The inhabitants of the newly-conquered regions had to adopt as their own the god who was worshiped in the Temple at Jerusalem; they had to make pilgrimages to Jerusalem to worship Him, paying the Temple fee in the process, and were required to set themselves apart from the other nations by circumcision and the peculiar Jewish ritual prescriptions.

Such proceedings were totally unheard of in the ancient world, where as a rule the conqueror left the conquered complete freedom of religion and customs, merely exacting taxes to the limit of endurance.

This mode of extending Judaism was possible only temporarily, so long as the power of the Syrians was too weak and that of the Romans not yet near enough to contain Judah's military advances. Even before Pompey occupied Jerusalem the advance of the Jews in Palestine had come to a halt. Then the dominance of the Romans put a powerful curb on the forcible method of expanding the Jewish religious brotherhood.

From that point on the Jews threw themselves energetically into the alternative method of enlarging their religious community, the way of peaceful propaganda. At the time this too was an unprecedented phenomenon. Even before Christianity, Judaism manifested the same sort of zeal for instruction, with considerable success. It was thoroughly understandable, if not very logical, for the Christians to blame the Jews for this zeal, which they exercised so vigorously on behalf of their own religion:

"Woe unto you, scribes and Pharisees, hypocrites! for ye compass land and sea to make one proselyte, and when he is made, ye make him twofold more the child of hell than yourselves" (Matthew 23, verse 15).

It is competition that speaks in so Christian a manner.

Mere material interest alone would attract many an adherent to Judaism from the "heathen" world. There must have been not a few to whom it was very attractive to be a partner in such a widespread and flourishing trading company. Wherever a Jew came, he could count on being energetically supported and helped by his brothers in belief.

But there were still other considerations that lent Judaism its propagandistic power. We have seen how a state of mind favorable to ethical monotheism grows out of urban life once it reaches a certain extension. But the monotheism of the philosophers was in opposition to the traditional religion, or at the very least outside its domain. It called for independent thought. But the same social developments that favored monotheistic ideas led, as we have seen, to the decadence of state and society, to an increasing sense of insecurity on the part of the individual, to a growing need for stable authority; in the realm of world outlooks, this meant the need for religion, which is presented to the individual as a complete and fixed product of a super-human authority, instead of philosophy, which leaves the individual on his own resources.

Among the peoples of ancient civilization only two, the Persians and the Jews, because of special circumstances, arrived at monotheism not as a philosophy but as a religion. Both religions made considerable progress among the Hellenistic peoples and then in the Roman Empire. But Judaism was driven to greater zeal for conversion by its gloomy national situation, and in Alexandria it came into intimate contact with Greek philosophy.

Thus Judaism was best able to offer what was wanted to the minds of the declining ancient world, who doubted their traditional gods but lacked the strength to construct on their account a view of the world without gods or with but a single God; and all the more so because it tied belief in the one primeval ethical force to belief in a savior to come, for whom all the world was thirsting.

Among the many religions that came together in the Roman world empire the Jewish was the one best suited to the thoughts and needs of the time. It was not superior to the *philosophy* of the "heathen" but to their *religions*—no wonder that the Jews felt far superior to the Gentiles and that the number of their supporters grew rapidly. "Judaism wins over all men," says the Alexandrian Jew Philo, "and exhorts them to virtue; barbarians, Hellenes, men of the mainland and men of the islands, the nations of the East like those of the West, Europeans, Asiatics, the peoples of the world." He expected Judaism to become the religion of the world. This was at the time of Christ.[35]

We have pointed out above that as early as 139 B.C. in Rome itself Jews were expelled for making Italian proselytes. It was reported from Antioch that the larger part of the Jewish community there consisted of converted Jews (rather than born Jews). It must have been so in many other cities as well. This fact alone proves how preposterous it is to try to derive the characteristics of the Jews from their race.

Even kings went over to Judaism: Izates, king of the country of Adiabene in Assyria was led to Judaism by some female Jewish proselytes, as had his mother Helena. His zeal went so far that he had himself circumcised, although his Jewish teacher advised against it, lest he endanger his position. His brothers went over to Judaism too. All this took place in the time of Tiberius and Claudius.

Lovely Jewish women brought many another king to Judaism.

Thus King Aziz of Emesa adopted Judaism in order to marry Drusilia, sister of Agrippa II. She did not repay his devotion very well, for she gave up her royal husband for a Roman procurator, Felix. Her sister Berenice was no better. King Polemon had had himself circumcised for her sake; but the looseness of his wife disgusted him not only with her but with her religion. Madame Berenice was able to console herself. She was used to changing men. First she had married a certain Marcus, and after his death her uncle Herod. When he died too, she lived with her brother Agrippa until she married the Polemon mentioned above. Finally she attained to the position of mistress of the Emperor Titus.

Though this lady was untrue to her people, there were many others who embraced Judaism, among them Nero's wife Poppaea Sabina, of whom it is said that she became a zealous Jew, though her moral life was not affected thereby.

Josephus relates that the inhabitants of the city of Damascus had decided at the beginning of the Jewish uprising under Nero to wipe out the Jews living in the city. "They were only afraid of

35. Cf. the Book of Tobit 14, verses 6 and 7.

their wives, who were almost all devoted to the Jewish religion. Accordingly the men kept their design secret. The plot succeeded. They killed ten thousand Jews in one hour."[36]

The forms of adherence to Judaism differed widely. The most zealous of the new converts adopted it in toto. Their acceptance involved three procedures: circumcision, then baptismal immersion to cleanse them of heathen sinfulness, and last a sacrificial victim.

But not all the converts could make up their minds to follow all the precepts of Judaism without exception. We have seen how contradictory a thing it was, how it combined a highly enlightened international monotheism with a very narrow tribal monotheism, a pure ethics with a frightened grip on traditional rites; along with ideas that seemed very modern and magnificent to men of that time there were conceptions that seemed very peculiar, even repugnant, to a Hellene or a Roman, and that made social intercourse with non-Jews very difficult for members of the Jewish community. Among these latter were the dietary laws, circumcision and the strict observance of the Sabbath, which often assumed the most extreme forms.

We learn from Juvenal that the fireless cooker, which is touted today as the latest discovery in housekeeping, was known to the ancient Jews. On the eve of the Sabbath they put their victuals in baskets stuffed with hay, to keep them warm. It is said that there was no Jewish household without such a basket. This already indicates the difficulties involved in strict observance of the Sabbath. But it was carried so far on occasions that it was ruinous to the Jews. In wartime, pious Jews who were attacked on a Sabbath neither defended themselves nor fled, but let themselves be cut down in order not to violate God's commandment.

There were not many who were capable of such a degree of fanaticism and faith in God. But even a less thorough-going compliance with the Jewish law was too much for many people. There were, along with those who entered into the Jewish community and assumed all the obligations of the Jewish law, many who

36. *Jewish War*, II, 20, 2.

shared the Jewish worship of God and frequented the synagogues, but did not observe the rites and prescriptions. Among the Jews outside of Palestine there were many who did not attach much value to these precepts. Often they let it go at the worship of the true God and faith in the Messiah to come, got along without circumcision and were content if the new-won friend cleansed himself of sin by immersion.

These "pious" (*sebomenoi*) associates of the Jews constituted the majority of the heathen who turned to Judaism. They were at first the most important area for recruiting the Christian communities, as soon as these communities spread beyond Jerusalem.

ANTI-SEMITISM

Great though the propagandist power of Judaism was, it clearly did not affect all classes in the same way. Many must have been repelled by it. This was particularly true of the landholders, whose conservatism and narrow parochialism is most opposed to the restlessness and internationalism of the merchant. Moreover, a part of the merchant's profits was made at their expense; the merchant tried to reduce the prices of what he bought from them and drive up the price of those things they bought from him. The large landowners always got along very well with usury capital; we have seen that they early derived great strength from usury. As a rule however they were hostile to trade.

But the industrialists who produced for export were likewise hostile to the merchants, as home craftsmen today are against the contractors.

This hostility to trade was turned primarily against the Jews, who held so fast to their nationality, and who, while not differing from their neighbors in speech, clung tenaciously to their traditional national customs, which were now fused with the religion which was their one national tie and which was so astonishing to the mass of the population outside of Palestine. Like anything exotic, these peculiarities would only have aroused the ridicule of the mob except that they were the marks of a class that like all merchants lives by exploitation and held tightly together in close international association against the rest of the population, growing in wealth and privileges while the rest grew poorer and more devoid of rights: under these circumstances they aroused enmity.

We can see from Tacitus the effect that Judaism had on the other nations. He says: "Moses introduced new customs contrary to those of the rest of mankind. There everything is profane that is sacred for us; and what is repugnant to us is permitted among them." Among such customs he mentions abstinence from pork, frequent fasting, and the Sabbath.

"Whatever may have been the origin of these religious customs, they defend them on the grounds of their great antiquity. Other disgusting and horrible institutions received support from their depravity: for they got to the point where the worst people were untrue to their ancestral religion and brought them contributions and offerings: in this way the wealth of the Jews increased; and also because they practice the strictest honesty and helpfulness toward each other, but bitter enmity toward everyone else. They go apart from the others at their meals and will not sleep with women of other faiths, while among themselves there is nothing that is not permitted. They introduced circumcision to make a difference between themselves and other men. Those who go over to them undergo circumcision too, and the first thing they are indoctrinated with is contempt for the gods, renunciation of the fatherland, neglect of their parents, children and brothers. Their object in this is to increase their numbers, and doing away with offspring seems to them a crime. The souls of those who die in battle or on the scaffold for their religion are believed by them to be immortal: hence their urge to beget children and their contempt of death."

Tacitus then speaks of their rejection of all worship of images and concludes: "The customs of the Jews are absurd and squalid."[37]

37. *Histories*, V, 5.

The satirists were fond of scoffing at the Jews; jokes directed at them always had a receptive audience.

In his fourteenth satire Juvenal shows how the example of the parents affects the children. A bad example is set by a father with inclinations toward Judaism:

"You find people to whom fate has given fathers that observe the Sabbath. Such people pray only to the clouds and the divinity of heaven. They believe that pork is no different from human flesh, because their father abstains from pork. Soon they dispose of their fore-skin and contemn the laws of the Romans. Instead they learn, follow and honor Jewish law, everything that Moses hands down in his mysterious scroll. They will not show the way to anybody who asks them unless he is of the same faith; when people are thirsty, they will lead only the circumcised to the spring. That is the effect of the father for whom every seventh day was one for idling, on which he abstained from any sign of life."[38]

As social discontent rose, anti-Semitism increased. Even then it was already the handiest and safest means of showing exasperation over the decline of state and society. It was too dangerous to attack the aristocrats and owners of latifundia, the usurers and the generals, let alone the despots on the throne; but the Jews, despite their privileges, were ill-protected by the government.

At the beginnings of the Empire, when the pauperization of the peasantry was well on its way and large masses of the lumpenproletariat assembled in the large cities, eager for loot, there were regular pogroms from time to time.

Mommsen gives us a vivid picture of one of these Jew-baitings, which occurred under the emperor Gaius Caligula (37-41 A.D.), more or less at the time at which the death of Christ is said to have taken place:

"A grandson of Herod I and the fair Mariamne, named Agrippa after the protector and friend of his grandfather Herod, perhaps the pettiest and most degenerate of the many princelings living in Rome, but yet, or perhaps therefore, the favorite and child-hood friend of the new emperor; a man hitherto known only for

38. *Satires,* XIV, 96 to 105.

his dissoluteness and his debts, had got from his protector, to whom he was the first to bring the news of the death of Tiberius, the gift of one of the little Jewish principalities that was vacant, and with it the title of king. In the year 38 on his way to his new dominions he arrived at the city of Alexandria, where a few months previously he had tried, as an absconding debtor, to get a loan from Jewish bankers. When he appeared in royal robes with a troop of gaudily-uniformed guards, it was natural that the non-Jewish inhabitants of the scandal- and ridicule-loving city, who had no particular fondness for the Jews anyway, should start a parody; and it went further than that, to a fearful pogrom. The Jewish houses which were singly located and not in groups were robbed and burned, the Jewish ships in the harbor were plundered, and the Jews found in non-Jewish districts were manhandled and beaten up. But the Jew-baiters did not venture to attack the Jewish districts by force. Their leaders hit upon the idea of making the synagogues, which were the principal object of attack, or at least those that still were standing, into temples of the new ruler, and to set up statues of him in all of them, with a statue on a quadriga for the chief synagogue. The emperor Gaius believed himself to be a genuine god in the flesh, in so far as his crazy mind was able to function; this was known to everyone, including the Jews and the governor. His name was Avilius Flaccus, a brave man and an excellent administrator under Tiberius, but now crippled by the disfavor of the new emperor and in constant fear of recall and prosecution; he therefore was not above making use of the occasion to reestablish himself. He not only did not issue a decree to prevent the installation of the statues in the synagogues, but took part in the Jew-baiting himself. He ordered the Sabbath done away with. He declared further in his proclamation that these tolerated aliens had without permission taken possession of the best parts of the city; they were confined to a single one of the five districts and all the other Jewish houses were handed over to the mob, while the ejected tenants were put on the streets without a roof over their heads. No protest was even listened to; thirty-eight members of the council

of elders, which at that time headed the Jews instead of the
ethnarch, were publicly flogged in the circus in view of the entire
population. Four hundred houses lay in ruins; trade and exchange
stopped; the factories were still. The only recourse was to the
emperor. Two delegations from Alexandria came to him. The
Jewish group was headed by Philo, a scholar of the neo-Judaic
school and rather timid than bold, although he stood up stoutly
for his kind in this emergency; the anti-Semites were headed by
Apion, also an Alexandrian scholar and author, the 'world-bell',
as the emperor Tiberius called him, full of big words and bigger
lies, of loudest omniscience and unconditional self-confidence,
knowing men, or if not men at least their worthlessness, a veteran
master of oratory and betrayal, quick-witted, clever, shameless and
implicitly loyal. It was clear from the beginning how the affair
would turn out; the emperor admitted the parties as he was in-
specting the gardens, but instead of hearing the suppliants, he
asked them derisive questions; the anti-Semites, violating all
etiquette, laughed out loud; and the emperor, being in a good
mood, went no further than to regret that these otherwise good
people were so unfortunately constituted as not to be able to
understand his innate divine nature; in this he was undoubtedly
in earnest. So Apion won and wherever the anti-Semites wanted
to they turned the synagogues into temples of Gaius."[39]

In Rome itself the military forces at hand were too strong, and
the emperors too much opposed to any sort of popular commo-
tion, for any such scenes to take place there. But as soon as the
imperial power was consolidated and the Caesars no longer needed
the Jews, they felt a distaste for them. Given their suspicion of
any union, even the most harmless, this international religious
organization must have grated on their nerves.

Persecutions of the Jews, already under way in the reign of
Tiberius, are explained by Josephus as follows: "There was a
Jew in Rome, a thoroughly godless man, who had been guilty of
many misdeeds in his own country and had fled in fear of punishment. He pretended to be a teacher of the Mosaic law, got to-

39. Mommsen, *Römische Geschichte*, V, p. 515 f.

gether with three accomplices and convinced Fulvia, a noble lady
who had adopted the Jewish faith and was taking instruction from
him, that she should send a gift of gold and purple to the Temple
at Jerusalem. When they got it from the lady, they used it for
themselves, as had been their intention. Saturninus, Fulvia's husband, complained at her request to the emperor Tiberius, his
friend, and the emperor ordered all Jews out of Rome at once.
Four thousand of them were made soldiers and sent to Sardinia."[40]

The account is interesting as showing the inclination of noble
ladies in Roman society towards Judaism. If the incident was
really the occasion for such severe measures against all the Roman
Jewry, it was certainly not the whole cause. It would have been
enough to punish the guilty, if there had not been a feeling of
hostility against all Judaism. Gaius Caligula, we have seen, was
equally hostile. Under Claudius (41 to 54 A.D.) the Jews were
banished from Rome once more, because, as Suetonius says
(*Claudius,* chap. 25) they were causing unrest under the leadership
of a certain Chrestos. This Chrestos was not a Jew by birth, but
a converted Greek. Here too evidences of anti-Semitism go along
with evidences of the propaganda power of Judaism.

JERUSALEM

With the attitude of both ruling classes and the masses of the
people thus set against them, it is clear that the Jews, despite
all the great progress they were making abroad and the increasing
impossibility of thriving in the home-land, would always look
back with longing to Jerusalem and its surrounding country, the
only corner on earth where they were masters in their own house,
at least to a certain extent, where all the inhabitants were Jews:
the only corner on earth from which the promised great Jewish
kingdom could start and on which the expected Messiah could
found the dominion of Judaism.

Jerusalem remained the center and capital of Judaism; they
grew together. It became a rich city once more, a big city with
perhaps 200,000 inhabitants; but, unlike the days of David and

40. *Antiquities,* XVIII, 3, 5.

Solomon, it no longer derived its greatness and wealth from military might or the trade of the peoples of Palestine, but only from the temple of Jehovah. Every Jew, wherever he might live, had to contribute to its upkeep and pay a double drachma every year as temple tax, which was sent to Jerusalem.

Many additional and exceptional gifts flowed in toward the shrine. Not all of them were intercepted, like the precious offering of which the four Jewish embezzlers swindled Fulvia, in Josephus' story. But in addition every pious Jew had the obligation of making the pilgrimage at least once in his life to the place where his God lived and where alone He would accept offerings. The synagogues of the Jews in the various cities outside of Jerusalem were only places of assembly and prayer, and schools, but not temples in which sacrifices were offered to Jehovah.

The temple taxes and the pilgrims must have brought quantities of money into Jerusalem and given employment to many men. Directly or indirectly the Jehovah cult in Jerusalem supported not only the priests of the temple and the scribes, but also the shopkeepers and money-changers, the craftsmen, the peasants, farmers, herdsmen and fishermen of Judea and Galilee, who found an excellent market in Jerusalem for their wheat and their honey, their lambs and kids, and for the fish they caught in the coastal waters or on the Sea of Chinnereth in Galilee, and brought to Jerusalem dried or salted. If Jesus found buyers and sellers in the Temple, money-changers and those that sold doves, this was thoroughly in keeping with the function of the Temple in the life of Jerusalem.

What was inserted into the Jewish literature as the condition of their ancestors was actually the case in the days in which this literature came into being: now all Jewry literally lived on the worship of Jahveh, and ruin menaced them if this worship fell off, or even took on different forms. There were attempts to set up other shrines of Jahveh outside of Jerusalem.

A certain Onias, the son of a Jewish High Priest, built a temple of Jahveh in Egypt under Ptolemy Philopator (173-146 B.C.), with the support of the king, who hoped that the Egyptian Jews would be more loyal subjects if they had a temple of their own in his country.

But the new temple never amounted to much, precisely because it aimed at affirming the loyalty of the Jews of Egypt. In Egypt they were and remained aliens, a tolerated minority: how could a Messiah arise there to bring their people independence and national greatness? And belief in the Messiah was one of the strongest factors in the Jahveh cult.

There was much more unpleasantness over a rival temple not far from Jerusalem on Mt. Gerizim near Shechem, built by the sect of Samaritans in the time of Alexander the Great according to Josephus, a century earlier according to Schürer; there the Samaritans practiced their Jahveh cult. It is no wonder that there was the bitterest enmity between the two competitors. But the older enterprise was too rich and reputable for the newcomer to do it serious damage. Despite all the propaganda of the Samaritans they did not grow as fast as the Jews who looked to the seat of their god in Jerusalem.

The menace to the monopoly of Jerusalem made its inhabitants watch even more zealously over the "purity" of its cult and oppose even more fanatically any attempt to change anything in it. Hence the religious fanaticism and intolerance of the Jews of Jerusalem, so unlike the religious broad-mindedness of the other peoples at that time. For the others their gods were a means of explaining mysterious events, a source of comfort and help in situations in which human powers seemed to fail. For the Palestinian Jews their God was the means from which they derived their existence. He was for the whole people what other gods were only for their priests. Priestly fanaticism became in Palestine the fanaticism of the whole population.

But although they were like one man in defending the Jahveh cult, in opposing anyone who dared to infringe it, it was nevertheless subjected to class contradictions from which even Jerusalem was not spared. Every class sought to please Jahveh and protect His Temple in its own way. Each regarded the coming Messiah in a different way.

THE SADDUCEES

In the eighth chapter of the second book of his history of the Jewish war, Josephus reported that there were three trends of thought among the Jews: the Pharisees, the Sadducees and the Essenes. Of the first two he says:

"As for the other two sects, the Pharisees are thought to construe the Law most strictly. They were the first to form a sect. They believe that everything is determined by fate and God. In their opinion it does depend on man whether he does good or evil, but fate has an influence on it too. As to the human soul they believe it to be immortal, the souls of the good entering into new bodies while those of the wicked are tortured with eternal torments.

"The other sect is the Sadducees. These deny any efficacy to fate and say that God is not responsible for anyone's doing good or evil; that is entirely up to man, who can in accordance with his free will do the one and refrain from the other. They deny also that souls are immortal and that there is punishment or reward after death.

"The Pharisees are helpful and try to live in unison with the mass of the people. The Sadducees are severe even to each other, and hard toward their countrymen as well as toward foreigners."

In this passage the sects appear as representatives of different religious views. But although up to now Jewish history has been studied almost exclusively by theologians, for whom religion is everything and class antagonisms nothing, even they have found that the contradiction between Sadducees and Pharisees was basically not a religious one, but a class contradiction, one that may be compared with the contradiction between the nobility and the Third Estate before the French Revolution.

The Sadducees represented the priestly nobility that had got hold of the power in the Jewish state and exercise it first under Persian domination and then under the successors of Alexander the Great. This group had unrestricted sway in the Temple and hence in Jerusalem and over all of Judaism. They received all the taxes that came to the Temple, which were not small. Up to the

Exile the revenues of the priesthood were modest and irregular; after it, they grew mightily. We have mentioned the tax of the double drachma (or half-shekel, about 40 cents) that every male Jew, rich or poor, over the age of two had to send to the Temple. Then there were the presents coming in. How much money came to them can be seen from the fact that Mithridates once confiscated on the island of Cos 800 talents destined for the Temple.[41]

Cicero says in the speech (59 B.C.) in defence of Flaccus, who had been governor of the province of Asia two years previously: "Since the money of the Jews is exported year after year from Italy and all the provinces to Jerusalem, Flaccus decreed that no money might be exported [to Jerusalem] from the province of Asia [Western Asia Minor]." Cicero goes on to relate how Flaccus confiscated money collected for the temple in various places in Asia Minor, a hundred pounds of gold in Apamea alone.

In addition there were the sacrifices. Formerly those who offered up victims had eaten them themselves in a joyous feast, and the priests were merely partakers. After the Exile the share of those making the offerings became smaller and smaller, and the share of the priests larger and larger. What had been a gift to a festival of joy, which the giver himself consumed in merry company, pleasing not only God but himself as well, now became a tax in kind, which God claimed for himself, that is, his priests.

These taxes yielded more and more. In addition to the sacrifices in beasts and other edibles, which came more and more to be the sole appanage of the priests, there were the tithes, the tax of a tenth part of all crops as well as every first-born animal. The first-born of "clean" animals, cattle, sheep, goats, that is, those that were eaten, were delivered in natura in the house of God. "Unclean" animals, horses, asses, camels, were to be redeemed for money. So were the first male birth of human beings; these cost five shekels.

We find a clear summary of what the Jewish priesthood took from the people—and this increased later on; thus the third part

41. Josephus, *Antiquities,* XIV, 7. 1 Talent = $1200.

of a shekel was soon raised to half a shekel—in the book of Nehemiah 10, verse 32 f.:

"Also we made ordinances for us, to charge ourselves yearly with the third part of a shekel for the service of the house of our God. . . . And we cast the lots among the priests, the Levites, and the people, for the wood offering, to bring it into the house of our God, after the houses of our fathers, at times appointed year by year, to burn upon the altar of the Lord our God, as it is written in the law; and to bring the first fruits of our ground, and the first fruits of all fruit of all trees, year by year, unto the house of the Lord; Also the firstborn of our sons, and of our cattle, as it is written in the law, and the firstlings of our herds and of our flocks, to bring to the house of our God, unto the priests that minister in the house of our God; And that we should bring the first fruits of our dough, and our offerings, and the fruit of all manner of trees, of wine and of oil, unto the priests, to the chambers of the house of our God; and the tithes of our ground unto the Levites, that the same Levites might have the tithes in all the cities of our tillage. And the priest the son of Aaron shall be with the Levites, when the Levites take tithes: and the Levites shall bring up the tithe of the tithes unto the house of our God, to the chambers, into the treasure house. For the children of Israel and the children of Levi shall bring the offering of the corn, of the new wine, and the oil, unto the chambers, where are the vessels of the sanctuary, and the priests that minister, and the porters, and the singers: and we will not forsake the house of our God."

We see that this temple was not the same sort of thing as a church, let us say. It had huge warehouses in which huge quantities of goods in bulk were stored up, as well as gold and silver. Accordingly it was strongly fortified and well guarded. Like the pagan temples it was a place where money and property were especially safe; and like them it was used by the public as a place to deposit valuables. This function of a safe-deposit vault, we may be sure, was not performed gratis by Jahveh.

It is certain that the wealth of the priesthood of Jerusalem grew enormously.

Marcus Crassus, the fellow-conspirator of Caesar, took advantage of this fact when he went on his robber expedition against the Parthians. On the way he took with him the treasures of the Jewish Temple.

"When Crassus was preparing to move against the Parthians, he came to Judea and took all the money from the Temple that Pompey had left, 2000 talents, together with all the uncoined gold, to the amount of 8000 talents. Finally he stole a bar of gold weighing three hundred minae; among us a mina weighs two and a half pounds."[42]

All that amounts to something like twelve million dollars. Nevertheless, the Temple was soon full of gold once more.

The priesthood was determined by birth; it constituted a hereditary aristocracy. According to Josephus (*Against Apion*, I, 22), who bases himself on Hecataeus, there were "1500 Jewish priests, who received the tithes and governed the community."

Even among them there grew up a division into a lower and a higher aristocracy. Certain families succeeded in getting the entire power of government permanently into their own hands, in order to increase their wealth, and that in turn increased their influence. They formed a closely-knit clique which always named the high priests from among its ranks. They reinforced their rule by using mercenary soldiers and defended it against the other priests, whom they managed to dominate.

Thus Josephus tells us: "about this time King Agrippa gave the high priesthood to Ismael, who was a son of Phadi. However, the high priests came into conflict with the priests and leaders of the people in Jerusalem. Each of them got together a crowd of the most desperate and turbulent people, and was their leader. Occasionally they would come to words, revile each other and throw stones. Nobody restrained them; violence was committed as if there were no laws in the city. Finally the high priests became so insolent that they even ventured to send servants into the granaries and have the tithes due the priests removed, so that some priests even died of starvation."[43]

42. Josephus, *Antiquities*, XIV, 7.   43. *Jewish Antiquities*, XX, 8, 8; cf. 9, 2.

To be sure, things reached this stage only when the Jewish community was already approaching its end. From the very beginning, however, the priestly aristocracy set itself above the mass of the people, and adopted views and tendencies that were opposed to those of the people, especially to those of the Jewish population of Palestine. That is particularly clear in the field of foreign policy.

We have seen that Palestine, because of its geographical position, was always under foreign rule or at least under the menace of it. There were two ways to ward it off or mitigate it: diplomacy or armed rebellion.

So long as the Persian empire lasted, neither of these alternatives was very promising, but the situation changed after Alexander had destroyed that empire. The new state which he set up in its place fell apart after his death, and a Syrian-Babylonian kingdom fought as before against an Egyptian kingdom for the mastery of Israel. Now both were ruled by Greek dynasties, the Seleucids and the Ptolemies, and both increasingly Greek in spirit.

It was not possible to defeat either of these powers by military means. But there was the possibility of winning by shrewd diplomacy, by joining the stronger and getting a privileged position as part of its empire. That however could not be achieved by xenophobia and aversion to the superior Hellenic civilization and its ways. On the contrary, it was imperative to adopt this civilization. The aristocracy of Jerusalem was led to this step by its greater knowledge of external affairs, an advantage it had over the rest of the population by virtue of its social position and official functions. The plastic arts and the arts of the enjoyment of life were not advanced in Palestine, while the Greeks had brought them to a level which no other people at that time or for many centuries thereafter could equal. The rulers of all nations, even those of victorious Rome, borrowed the forms of splendor and pleasure from Greece; the Greek way became the way of life of all exploiters, as the French way was to do in the eighteenth century in Europe.

The more intense the exploitation of Jewry by its aristocracy became and the more wealth the aristocrats obtained, the more eager they were for Hellenic culture.

The first book of the Maccabees complains with respect to the period of Antiochus Epiphanes (175-164 B.C.): "In those days there arose worthless men in Israel; they convinced many, saying: let us then unite like brothers with the nations about us! For since we have separated from them much woe has come upon us! Such talk pleased them, and some of the people said they would go to the king; he gave them permission to introduce the ways of the heathen. So they built a Gymnasium in Jerusalem—(a school for athletics, where the athletes exercised naked), after the fashion of the Gentiles, replaced the foreskin and were unfaithful to the holy covenant, but rather allied themselves with the heathen and sold themselves to them, to do evil."

So mad were these evil men, that put on artificial foreskins, that they also renounced their Jewish names and replaced them by Greek ones. A high priest Jesus called himself Jason, another high priest Jakim became Alcimos, a Manesseh became Menelaus.

The masses of the people of Judah resented this encouragement of Hellenic ways. We have several times pointed out how undeveloped industry and art were in Judea. The penetration of the Hellenic influence meant that foreign products drove out the native. The Hellene too always came as oppressor and exploiter, even if he now came as Syrian or Egyptian king. Judah, already pumped dry by its own aristocracy, was bitter about the tribute it had to pay to the alien monarchs and their officials. The aristocrats managed now and then to get out of it themselves by having themselves appointed as representatives and tax-collectors for the foreign masters. Usury at the expense of those oppressed by taxes would add to their own riches. The people had to bear the entire weight of foreign rule.

Even under the Persians similar things had occurred, as is shown by a vivid description made by the Jew Nehemiah, whom the King Artaxerxes appointed his governor in Judea (445 B.C.). He reports his own activity in glowing terms, "in relieving the distress caused among the poor by exactions of the aristocracy and on his own unselfishness as governor."

Self-praise of this sort is not uncommon in ancient documents, especially of the Orient. We can not take it for granted that the official in question really rendered such services to the people as he boasts of. One thing however is proved by such statements: the way in which governors and nobles as a rule bled and oppressed the people. Nehemiah would not have boasted of his actions if they had not been an exception. Nobody will go about proclaiming he has not stolen any silver spoons except in a society in which such thefts were the rule.

Under the Syrian and Egyptian kings the taxes of Palestine were farmed. As a rule the high priest was the tax farmer, but now and then he had rivals among his colleagues, causing discord among the estimable body of priests.

The mass of the people in Judea thus had much better reason to oppose alien domination than the aristocracy, which profited by it. Their rage against the foreigners was intensified by their ignorance as to the power relationships that existed. The mass of the Jews in Palestine was not aware of the overwhelming might of their opponents. For all these reasons they held diplomacy in contempt and called for forcible action to gain freedom from the foreign yoke. But only this, not the yoke of the aristocracy as well. The aristocracy lay just as heavy on the people; but did not the people get their whole livelihood in Jerusalem and its surroundings from the Temple, from the importance of its cultus and its priesthood? Therefore, their indignation over their poverty had to concentrate entirely on the foreign oppressors. Democracy turned into chauvinism.

A fortunate combination of circumstances made it possible that for once an uprising of the little nation against its powerful masters was crowned with success. This occurred at a time, as we have shown, when the kingdom of the Seleucids was shaken to its foundations by civil wars and was in complete decline, as was that of the Ptolemies, and both of them at continual odds with each other, with the subjection of both to the Romans, the new masters of East and West, close at hand.

Like every declining regime, that of the Seleucids increased its pressure, which naturally produced counter-pressure. Jewish patriotism became more and more rebellious, finding its nucleus and leadership in the organization of the Assideans.

This group also produced the book of Daniel (between 167 and 164 B.C.), an agitational work which predicted to the oppressed that Israel would soon rise and free itself. It would be its own savior, its own Messiah. This was the first of a series of Messianic propaganda works announcing the defeat of the alien domination and the victory of Judaism, its salvation and its rule over the nations of the earth.

In the book of Daniel this thought still finds democratic expression. The Messiah in it is still the people itself. The Messiah is "the people of the saints of the most High." "And the kingdom and dominion, and the greatness of the kingdom under the whole heaven, shall be given to the people of the saints of the most High, whose kingdom is an everlasting kingdom, and all dominions shall serve and obey him."

This Messianic prophecy soon seemed to be brilliantly fulfilled. The guerrilla warfare against the oppressor kept increasing in scale, until successful partisan leaders of the house of the Asmoneans, with Judas Maccabaeus the first among them, were able to stand up successfully in the opean field to Syrian troops, and finally to win Jerusalem which was under Syrian occupation. Judea became free and even extended its frontiers. After Judas Maccabaeus had fallen (160 B.C.), his brother Simon did what many generals of the democracy have done before and since after winning freedom for their people in war: he made use of the victory to put the crown on his own head. Or rather, he allowed the people to put it on his head. A great assembly of priests and people decided he should be high priest, commander-in-chief and prince (*archierus, strategos,* and *ethnarchos*) (141 B.C.). Thus Simon became the founder of the Asmonean dynasty.

He knew how insecure the newly-won independence was, for

he hurried to look for external support. In the year 139 we see an embassy from him at Rome to ask the Romans to guarantee the territory of the Jews. This was the embassy of which we recounted that several members were expelled from Rome for making proselytes.

The embassy however achieved its purpose. Simon did not suspect that it would not be long before Judea's new friends would be their most dangerous enemies, and put an end to the Jewish state for good. As long as the civil wars raged among the rulers of Rome, the fate of Judea fluctuated up and down. Pompey conquered Jerusalem in 63 B.C., took many prisoners of war, whom he sent to Rome as slaves, restricted the Jewish domain to Judea, Galilee and Peraea, and imposed a tax on the Jews. Crassus looted the Temple in 54. After his defeat the Jews rose against the Romans in Galilee and were put down, many of the prisoners being sold as slaves. Caesar treated the Jews better, and was even friendly with them. The civil wars after his death laid Judea waste along with other regions and put heavy burdens on it. When Augustus finally emerged victorious, he was as favorable to the Jews as Caesar had been, but Judea remained subject to the Romans, occupied by Roman troops; it was under the supervision and finally under the direct administration of Roman officials; and we have seen how these rascals acted in the provinces and bled them white. Hatred for the Romans grew fiercer and fiercer, especially in the mass of the population. The puppet kings and priestly aristocracy tried to ingratiate themselves with the new Roman masters as they had with the Greeks before the Maccabean uprising, no matter how bitterly many of them may have hated the aliens in their hearts. But their party, the Sadducees, had less and less power compared to the democratic party of the patriots, the Pharisees.

As early as the year 100 B.C. Josephus writes in his *Antiquities:* "The rich were on the side of the Sadducees, the mass of the people supported the Pharisees" (XIII, 10, 6).

And of the time of Herod (also the time of Christ) he reports:

"The sect of the Sadducees was supported by only a few, although they are the noblest in the land. However, the affairs of the state are not conducted as they wish. As soon as they come to public office, they must, willy-nilly, act according to the views of the Pharisees, otherwise the common people would not tolerate them" (*Ibid.*, XVIII, 1, 4).

The Pharisees became more and more the spiritual rulers of the Jewish people, in the place of the clerical aristocracy.

THE PHARISEES

We learned above, during the Maccabean wars, of the "pious", the Assideans. Some decades later, under John Hyrcanus (135 to 104 B.C.), this doctrine is represented by the Pharisees, and the opposing doctrine by the Sadducees.

It is not certain where the latter got their name; perhaps from the Priest Zadok, after whom the priesthood was called the clan of Zadokites. The Pharisees (*Perushim*), that is, those set apart, called themselves "comrades" (*khaberim*) or colleagues.

On one occasion Josephus specifies that they were six thousand strong, a considerable political organization for so small a country. He reports, dealing with the time of Herod (37 to 4 B.C.):

"At that time there were men among the Jews who were proud that they strictly observed the law of their fathers, and believed that God loved them especially. The women in particular supported this group. These people were called Pharisees. They were very powerful and were the first to oppose the king, but were shrewd and cautious and bided their time, when they wanted to make an insurrection. When the whole Jewish people promised under oath to be loyal to the emperor [Augustus] and obey the king [Herod], these men refused to take the oath, and they were more than six thousand."[44]

Herod, the cruel tyrant, who ordinarily was very free with executions did not dare to punish this refusal of the oath of allegiance severely; a sign of how powerful he thought the influence of the Pharisees on the masses of the people.

The Pharisees became the spiritual directors of the masses;

44. *Antiquities*, XVII, 2, 4.

and among them the dominant group was the "scribes", or men learned in the scriptures, who are always coupled with them in the New Testament, the rabbis (rabbi—my lord, *monsieur*).

Originally the class of intellectuals was among the Jews, as everywhere in the Orient, the caste of priests. But the story of the Jewish aristocracy was the same as that of any aristocracy: the richer they became, the more they neglected the functions that were the basis of their privileged position. They barely went through the most obvious external rites to which they were obligated. They neglected scientific, literary, legislative and judicial labor more and more, with the result that these functions were almost entirely performed by educated elements from the people.

The law-giving and judicial activity was especially important. The states of the ancient Orient had no legislative assemblies. All law was customary law, primordial law. It is true that social evolution continues, bringing with it new relationships and new problems which require new legal norms; but the feeling that the law is eternally the same, stemming from God, is so deeply rooted in the minds of the people that the new law gains recognition more quickly if it takes the form of customary law, traditional law, which has existed from times immemorial and is only reappearing, because it had been forgotten and neglected.

The simplest way for the ruling classes to make new law count as old law in this manner is to forge documents.

The priesthood of Judah made copious use of this expedient, as we have seen. That was fairly easy to do so long as the masses of the people were confronted with a single ruling class as experts and guardians of the religious heritage, something which in the Orient embraced all knowledge beyond the rudimentary. However, when a new class with literary education arose alongside the old priesthood, both of them found it more difficult to present an innovation as something that Moses or some other ancient authority had created. The rival class now was keeping close watch.

In the last two centuries before the destruction of Jerusalem there is a continuous series of attempts by the rabbis to break the rigid canon of the holy scriptures set up by the priesthood and to enlarge it by new literary productions which would count as ancient and be as highly considered as the former ones. They did not succeed, however.

Josephus examines the credibility of the Jewish scriptures in his book against Apion (I, 7 and 8): "For it is not everybody that has the right to write as he pleases, but that belongs to the prophets alone, who have reliably set down the things of the past, by God's inspiration, as well as a true account of the circumstances of their times. Hence we do not have thousands of books, which contradict and conflict with each other, but only twenty-two books, which recount what has taken place since the beginning of the world, and are justly held to be divine"; namely, the five books of Moses, thirteen books of the prophets, who cover the time from the death of Moses to Artaxerxes, and four books of Psalms and sayings.

"From Artaxerxes down to our time everything has been described and set down, but it is not so trustworthy. . . . How highly we value our scriptures can be seen from the fact that over so long a period no one ventured to add or take away anything, or make any changes."

In Josephus' time this was undoubtedly true. The more difficult it became to alter the existing law, which was fixed in this body of literature, the more the innovators were compelled to make the law fit the new needs by the process of exegesis. The holy scriptures of the Jews were especially suited to this treatment, since they were not all of a piece, but literary precipitates from the most diverse epochs and social conditions. They contained legends of the earliest Bedouin era together with the highly cultivated urban sagacity of Babylon, all put together in a post-Babylonian priestly version, often a very clumsy and obtuse one in which the crudest contradictions lie side by side. Anything could be proved from a "law" of this sort if a man had a keen enough mind and a good enough memory to learn all the passages of the law by heart and have them at his fingertips. This was precisely the extent of rabbinical wisdom. They did not undertake to study life, but to drive into their students' heads an exact knowledge of the sacred writings and to bring their disputatiousness and subtlety in exegesis to its highest point. Without being aware of it, they were of course influenced by the life around them, but the longer the rabbinical wisdom of the schools developed the more it ceased to be a means of understanding life and hence mastering it, and became on the one hand the art of outwitting everybody, even the Lord God himself, by amazing legalistic pettifogging and chicanery, and on the other of consoling and edifying oneself in any situation by a pious quotation. This learning contributed nothing to knowledge of the world, and became more and more ignorant of the world. This became obvious in the wars that ended with the destruction of Jerusalem.

The shrewd, worldly-wise Sadducees were perfectly well aware of the power relationships of their time. They knew it was impossible to ward off the Romans. The Pharisees however strove all the harder to shake the Roman yoke off by force as it lay heavier on Judea and was driving the people to desperation. The Maccabean insurrection had furnished a brilliant example of how a people can and should defend its freedom against a tyrant.

The expectation of the Messiah had been a strong support for that insurrection, and the success of the insurrection had reinforced the expectation, which grew with the intensity of the desire to shake off the Roman yoke. The Romans were, it is true, more dangerous opponents than the decadent kingdom of the Syrians, and confidence in the self-activity of the peoples had lost ground all over the ancient world since the time of the Maccabees. What were called the Roman civil wars were actually nothing but the competition of individual successful generals for world domination. Likewise, the concept of the Messiah was no longer identified with the Jewish people in its struggle for self-liberation; it now took the form of a mighty war hero, sent by God to save and deliver the tormented people of the chosen saints from trial and tribulation.

Without such a miraculous leader even the most fanatical

Pharisees considered it impossible to get rid of the oppressors. But they did not count on him alone. They proudly calculated how the number of their supporters was growing in the Empire, especially among the neighboring nations, and how strong they were in Alexandria, in Babylon, Damascus, Antioch. Would not they come to the aid of the hard-pressed homeland when it rose? And if a single city like Rome could succeed in winning world mastery, why should it necessarily be impossible for the great and proud Jerusalem?

The basis of the Revelation of John is a Jewish agitational pamphlet in the manner of the book of Daniel. It was probably composed during the period when Vespasian and then Titus were besieging Jerusalem. It prophesies a duel between Rome and Jerusalem. Rome is the woman that sitteth on seven mountains, "Babylon, the mother of harlots and abominations," with whom "the kings of the earth have committed fornication," and through the abundance of whose delicacies "the merchants of the earth are waxed rich" (chapters 17 and 18). This city will fall, judgment will be passed on her, "the merchants of the earth shall weep and mourn over her: for no man buyeth their merchandise any more;" the holy city of Jerusalem will take her place, "and the nations of them which are saved shall walk in the light of it: and the kings of the earth do bring their glory and honor to it" (chap. 21, verse 24).

To naive minds, ignorant of the power of Rome, Jerusalem might well have seemed to be a dangerous rival.

Josephus reports that under Nero the priests once counted the throng of people in Jerusalem at the Passover feast. "The priests counted 256,500 Passover paschal lambs. Now at least ten sat at a table per lamb. Sometimes those at table came to twenty per lamb. If only ten persons are counted to each lamb we come to about 2,700,000 persons," not counting the impure and the unbelievers, who were not allowed to partake of the Passover feast.[45]

Although Josephus refers to an enumeration here, the figure he gives seems incredible, even if we assume that among the two

45. *Jewish War*, VI, 9, 3.

and a half million men there were many countrymen from around Jerusalem who did not require food or lodging in Jerusalem. Transport of foodstuffs in bulk from any considerable distance was possible only by water in those days. The large cities were all on navigable rivers or by the sea. In the case of Jerusalem there could be no question of water transport. The sea and the Jordan were far distant, and the Jordan is not navigable. Such a mass of humanity could not even have found enough water to drink in Jerusalem. The city depended partly on rain water that was caught in cisterns.

What Josephus says in the same place to the effect that 1,100,000 Jews died in Jerusalem during the siege leading up to its destruction, is equally incredible.

The figure Tacitus gives is considerably smaller.[46] The besieged, of all ages and sexes, are said to have amounted to 600,000. Since many were shut up in the city who did not usually live there, half this number may be taken perhaps as the average population in the last decades before its destruction; even if we took only a third, that was quite a respectable population for a city of those times. Josephus' figures show, however, how this throng was magnified in the imagination of the Jewish people.

At any rate, no matter how large and strong Jerusalem may have been, it had no chance of victory without outside help. The Jews counted on such help. But they forgot that the Jewish population outside of Palestine was purely urban, in fact metropolitan, and everywhere a minority. At that time, however, even more than later, it was only the peasant who was capable of prolonged military service. The urban masses of shopkeepers, home craftsmen and proletarians could not make up any army that could stand up to trained troops in the open field. There were indeed cases of Jewish unrest outside of Palestine during the last great insurrection in Palestine, but they never amounted to an action in aid of Jerusalem.

Unless a Messiah worked wonders, any Jewish uprising was hopeless. The more rebellious the situation became in Judea,

46. *Histories*, V, 13.

the more ardently the expectation of the Messiah was cultivated among the Pharisees. The Sadducees took quite a skeptical attitude toward the expectation of the Messiah, and toward the doctrine of the resurrection that was closely linked with it.

As with the rest of their mythology, the ideas of the Israelites as to the condition of man after death contained nothing that distinguished them from other peoples on the same level of civilization. The fact that the dead appear in dreams led to the assumption that the dead person still leads a personal existence, though one which is shadowy and without a body. And it must have been the placing of the deceased in a dark grave that gave the idea that his shadowy existence was connected with a dark subterranean place. The joy and pleasure of life could not conceive that the end of life could mean anything but the end of all pleasure and joy, or that the shadow life of the dead could be anything but joyless and gloomy.

We find these conceptions originally among the Israelites as among the ancient Greeks. The Greek Hades corresponded to the Israelite Sheol, a place deep in the earth, of blackest night, well-guarded to keep the deceased who have descended there from ever returning. The shade of Achilles in Homer complains that a living laborer is better off than a dead prince, and the preacher Solomon in *Ecclesiastes* (a book written during the time of the Maccabees) continues: "A living dog is better than a dead lion," "The dead know not anything, neither have they any more a reward; for the memory of them is forgotten. Also their love, and their hatred, and their envy, is now perished; neither have they any more a portion in anything that is done under the sun."

So the dead have no reward. Whether they were godless or just, the same fate comes to them all in the lower world. Joy and pleasure are only to be had during life.

"Go thy way, eat thy bread with joy, and drink thy wine with a merry heart; for God now accepteth thy works. Let thy garments be always white; and let thy head lack no ointment. Live joyfully with the wife whom thou lovest all the days of the life of thy vanity, which he hath given thee under the sun, all the days of thy vanity: for that is thy portion in this life, and in thy labor which thou takest under the sun. Whatsoever thy hand findeth to do, do it with thy might; for there is no work, nor device, nor knowledge, nor wisdom, in the grave, whither thou goest." (Ecclesiastes 9, verses 7 to 10.)

In this there speaks a quite "Hellenic" joy in life, but also a quite "pagan" view of death. These were the old Jewish conceptions, preserved by the Sadducees. However, conceptions of an opposite sort were already arising at the time of Ecclesiastes the Preacher.

The love of life corresponded to popular feeling in a period when the peasantry was healthy and flourishing. After the decline of the peasantry, the aristocracy could still feel joy in reality, in life, and even intensify them into a quest for pleasure; but such feelings were lost to the lower classes in their tortured existence. Still, they had not yet reached the point of despairing of the possibility of improving their conditions. The more wretched these became, the more desperately they clung to the hope of the revolution that would bring them a better life and with it joy in life. The Messiah was that revolution, which increasingly had to rely on superhuman forces and miracles as the relations of real forces turned against the exploited and tormented masses.

The growth of the belief in miracles and confidence in the miraculous power of the coming Messiah was paralleled by a similar increase in the mass of sufferings and sacrifices, of the martyrs who succumbed in the struggle. Were they all to have hoped and persevered in vain? Were the most devoted and boldest champions of the Messiah to be excluded from the splendid life that his victory would bring to the chosen? Were those who, for the sake of the saints and the chosen, had given up all enjoyment of life, and even life itself, to have no reward? Were they to lead a shadowy existence of sorrow in Sheol while their victorious comrades in Jerusalem ruled the world and enjoyed its pleasures?

If the Messiah was credited with the power to conquer Rome,

he could be trusted to dispose of death too. For the dead to arise was not then looked upon as something impossible.

The idea thus arose that the champions of Judaism who had fallen in the struggle would arise from their graves in the fullness of the flesh after the victory, and begin a new life of joy and pleasure. It was not a question of the immortality of the soul, but a resuscitation of the body to very real delights in triumphant Jerusalem. Abundant wine-drinking figured largely in these expectations; and the joys of love were not forgotten. Josephus tells of a eunuch of Herod who was won over by the Pharisees because they promised that the Messiah would give him the power of copulating and begetting children.[47]

If the Messiah was credited with such powers to reward his faithful, he would naturally be given the power of punishment as well. The thought that the martyrs should go unrewarded must have been intolerable; and equally so the notion that all their persecutors, dying happily, should escape their vengence and lead the same unfeeling existence in the lower world as the shades of the just. Their bodies too had to be resurrected by the Messiah and given over to horrible tortures.

This did not originally imply by any means the resuscitation of all the dead. The resurrection would signify the close of the struggle for Jerusalem's independence and world dominion. It would only involve those of the dead who had fought on one side or the other. Thus the book of Daniel says about the victory of Judaism: "And many of them that sleep in the dust of the earth shall awake, some to everlasting life, and some to shame and everlasting contempt" (12, verse 2).

The so-called Revelation of St. John comes from the same intellectual milieu, as we have seen. In the Christian revision that has come down to us there are two resurrections. The first is not at all that of all men, but only of the martyrs (the Christian martyrs, of course, in the traditional version), who are awaked to a life of a thousand years on this earth: ". . . the souls of them

47. *Antiquities*, XVII, 2, 4.

that were beheaded for the witness of Jesus, and for the word of God, and which had not worshipped the beast, neither his image, neither had received his mark upon their foreheads, or in their hands; and they lived and reigned with Christ a thousand years. But the rest of the dead lived not again until the thousand years were finished" (20, verses 4 and 5).

The belief in resurrection was a battle slogan. Born of the fanaticism of a long and furious struggle with an enemy of superior power, and only to be explained in this way, it had the power of sustaining and reinforcing that fanaticism.

The counterpart of this belief in the non-Jewish world was a desire for immortality on the part of men, a desire that had nothing in common with the needs of the struggle, but came instead from tired resignation. This was the source of the wide propagation of the philosophical ideas of immortality in Platonism and Pythagoreanism. But a much more concrete and vital effect was produced by the Pharisees' hope of resurrection on the credulous masses of that era, untrained as they were in abstract thinking. They gladly shared in a hope which they translated from the Jewish terms into terms which suited their own particular conditions.

The doctrine of resurrection was one of the chief sources of the propaganda successes of Judaism up to the destruction of Jerusalem. That destruction however killed off the majority of those who had confidently expected the Messiah to arrive soon, and it shook the belief in his speedy coming among the other Jews. Messianic expectation was no longer a factor in practical politics in Judaism; it became a pious wish, a doleful longing. Simultaneously the Pharisees' belief in resurrection lost its roots in Jewish thought. It was preserved, along with the belief in the Messiah, only in the Christian community, which thus took over from the Pharisees a part of their best propaganda.

However, the Christian community won even more strength from the proletarian elements in Jewry than from the bourgeois democrats, if we may use the term.

THE ZEALOTS

The Pharisees represented the mass of the people as opposed to the clerical aristocracy. But this mass, more or less like the Third Estate in France before the great revolution, was made up of very disparate elements with very different interests, different degrees of willingness and ability to fight.

That was true also for the Jews outside of Palestine. They were an exclusively urban population, that got its living principally from trade and banking operations, tax-farming and so forth; but it would be a great mistake to think it consisted exclusively of rich merchants and bankers. We have already pointed out how much more capricious trade is than farming or craftsmanship. That was even more applicable then than now; navigation was more primitive and piracy rife. And how many livelihoods were ruined by the civil wars!

But although there must have been many Jews who had been rich and became poor, there must have been many more who never managed to get rich. Trade may have been the field in which they had the best opportunities, under the given circumstances; that did not mean that everybody had the capital for large-scale commerce. The trade of most of them must have been small shopkeeping or peddling.

They could also engage in such crafts as did not require great artistic ability or taste. Where Jews congregated in numbers, the special nature of their manners and customs must have created the need for many craftsmen of their own faith. When we read that a million out of the eight million inhabitants of Egypt were Jews, they could not all have made a living in trade. Actually, Jewish industries in Alexandria are mentioned as well. Jewish artisans are reported in other cities too.

In many cities, especially in Rome, there must have been a good number of Jewish slaves and hence freedmen. Their continual unsuccessful wars and insurrection kept furnishing new prisoners, who were sold into slavery.

Out of these groups grew a layer of lumpenproletarians who must have been very numerous in some regions. For example the

Jewish beggars were a notable part of the proletarians of Rome.
At one point Martial describes the street life of the capital.
Among the artisans working out in the street, the procession of
priests, the jugglers and peddlers, he mentions also the Jewish
boy sent out to beg by his mother. Juvenal speaks in his third
satire of the grove of Egeria, which "is leased to the Jews now,
whose entire household effects consist of a basket and a bundle
of hay; for every tree must bring us profit now. The beggars have
the woods, the Muses are driven out."[48]

This is testimony stemming from the era after the destruction
of Jerusalem, from the reign of Domitian, who had driven the
Jews out of Rome and allowed them to stay in the grove on
payment of a poll tax. It proves at least the presence of a great
number of Jewish beggars in Rome.

The principal goal of the wandering of the Jewish beggars
must certainly have been Jerusalem. There they felt at home and
need not fear being ridiculed or mistreated by a hostile or un-
comprehending populace. There too were assembled prosperous
pilgrims from all the corners of the earth, in great numbers and
with their religious feelings and charitableness at their height.

There was no great city in Christ's time that did not have a
numerous lumpenproletariat. After Rome, Jerusalem must have
had the largest number of such proletarians, at least relatively;
for both these cities drew on the whole Empire. The artisans
were very close to this proletariat, as we have seen; they were as
a rule nothing more than home workers, and these people even
today count as proletarians. They easily came to make common
cause with beggars and porters.

Where such propertyless strata of the people come together in
large numbers, they turn out to be especially combative. They
have nothing to lose; their social position is unendurable and they
have nothing to gain by being patient. Awareness of their great
numbers makes them bold. In addition, it was hard for the army
to make its superiority count in the narrow, tortuous streets of
that time. The city proletarians were not worth much in military

48. Juvenal, *Satires*, III, 13-16.

service in open battle, but were excellent in street-fighting. This was shown by events in Alexandria and in Jerusalem.

In Jerusalem this proletariat had a lust for battle that was lacking in the propertied people and intellectuals who went to make up the ranks of the Pharisees. In normal times, it is true, the proletarians let themselves be led by the Pharisees; but as the opposition between Jerusalem and Rome came to a head and the time of decision came closer, the Pharisees became increasingly cautious and timid, and increasingly in conflict with the proletariat which was pushing forward.

The latter got powerful support from the peasant population of Galilee, where the peasants with their tiny holdings and the herdsmen had been bled white by taxes and usury, and driven into debt slavery or expropriated, as throughout the Roman Empire. Some of them must have come to Jerusalem, increasing the city's proletariat. But the most energetic of the desperate expropriated peasants must have taken to insurrection and banditry, as elsewhere in the empire. The proximity of the deserts, that kept Bedouin habits alive, made their fight easier, furnishing many hiding-places that nobody but a native would know. Galilee, with its broken terrain, full of caves, was itself an aid in the trade of banditry. The flag under which the bandits fought was the expectation of the Messiah. Robber chiefs declared themselves to be the Messiah, or at least his forerunners, and fanatics who felt themselves called to be prophets or the Messiah became robber chiefs.

The robbers of Galilee and the proletarians of Jerusalem were in close contact and gave each other mutual support, and finally formed a party in common against the Pharisees, the party of the Zealots. The opposition between the two groups resembles in many ways the contrast between Girondins and Jacobins.

The link between the proletarians of Jerusalem and the armed bands of Galilee comes to the fore in the days of Christ.

During Herod's last illness (4 B.C.) the people of Jerusalem rose in revolt against his innovations; above all the indignation was directed against a golden eagle that Herod had had put up over the Temple. The riot was put down by arms. But after Herod's death the people rose again, at Passover, so violently that the troops of Archelaus, Herod's son, had to spill much blood before the insurrection was quelled. Three thousand Jews were slain. Even that did not quiet the belligerency of the people of Jerusalem. When Archelaus went to Rome to be confirmed there as King, the people rose again. Now the Romans intervened. Varus, the same man who later fell fighting against the Cherusci in Germany, was governor of Syria at the time. He hurried to Jerusalem, suppressed the insurrection, and then returned to Antioch leaving a legion in Jerusalem under the procurator Sabinus. Sabinus had such full confidence in his military power that he pushed the Jews to the wall, plundering and robbing at will. That put the fat in the fire. At Pentecost many people assembled in Jerusalem, especially Galileans. They were strong enough to encircle and besiege the Roman legion together with the mercenaries that Herod had recruited and left as a heritage to his son. The Romans vainly made sorties in which they killed many Jews; the besiegers did not weaken. They succeeded in getting a part of Herod's troops over to their side.

At the same time the insurrection spread to the country. The brigands of Galilee now got strong detachments of recruits, and made up whole armies. Their leaders had themselves called Kings of the Jews, that is Messiah. Especially prominent among them was Judas, whose father Hezekiah had been a famous bandit and executed as such (47 B.C.). In Peraea Simon, a former slave of Herod, got together a band; a third force was commanded by the shepherd Athronges.

The Romans suppressed the revolt with great difficulty, after Varus had come to the relief of the legion besieged in Jerusalem with two legions and many auxiliaries. There was an unspeakable slaughter and pillage; two thousand of the prisoners were crucified and many others sold into slavery.

This was about the time in which the birth of Christ is set.

There was quiet for several years, but not for long. In the year 6 A.D. Judea came under direct Roman rule. The first measure taken by the Romans was a census for tax-collecting purposes. In answer, there was a new attempt at insurrection by Judas the

Galilean, the same who had been so prominent in the uprising ten years earlier. He got together with the Pharisee Sadduk, who was to incite the people of Jerusalem. The attempt failed, but it led to the break between masses of the common people and the rebellious Galileans on the one hand, and the Pharisees on the other. They had been together in the rebellion of 4 B.C. Now the Pharisees had had enough, and the party of the Zealots arose in opposition to them. From that time to the destruction of Jerusalem, the fires of insurrection were never completely extinguished in Galilee and Judea.

Josephus, from his Pharisaical standpoint, reports on this: "Thereafter Judas, a Gaulanite from the city of Gamala, with the aid of Sadduk, a Pharisee, incited the people to rebellion. They convinced the people they would be slaves if they submitted to having their property appraised, and they should protect their freedom. They pointed out that in this way they not only would keep their property, but achieve still greater happiness, for they would win great honor and fame by their boldness. God would not help them unless they took vigorous decisions and spared no pains to carry them into execution. The people willingly listened to this and were all heartened to bold deeds.

"One can hardly express how much evil these two men did among the people. There was no wickedness they did not cause. They aroused one war after another. Constant violence ruled among them; anyone who spoke up against them paid for it with his life. Bandits ran riot in the land. The noblest people were done away with on the pretext of saving freedom; actually the motive was greed and the desire to appropriate their property. There followed repeated disorders and general bloodshed; in part the people of the country raged against each other, and one party tried to put the other down; in part external enemies slaughtered them. Finally famine was added to everything else, breaking all bonds and driving the cities to the extreme of ruin, until finally the Temple of God was reduced to ashes by enemies. So the innovations and changes of old customs brought the mutineers themselves to ruin. In this way Judas and Sadduk, who introduced a fourth doctrine and won many supporters for themselves, not only disturbed the state in their own time, but also left the way open for all the subsequent evil by means of this new doctrine, which had been unknown up to that time. . . . The younger people who supported them brought us to destruction" (*Antiquities*, XVIII, 1,1).

At the end of the same chapter, however, Josephus speaks with far more respect of the same Zealots whom he despises so at its beginning: "The fourth of these doctrines [along with those of the Pharisees, Sadducees and Essenes] was introduced by Judas the Galilean. His supporters were with the Pharisees in everything except that they showed a stubborn love of liberty and declared that God alone should be recognized as lord and prince. They will much rather suffer the greatest tortures and let their friends and relations be tortured than call a man their lord. I will not go into details on this subject, since it is sufficiently well known how stubborn they have proved to be in these matters. I am not afraid that I will not be believed, but rather that I will not be able to find words enough to describe with what heroism and what firmness they suffer the greatest tortures. This madness attacked the whole people like an epidemic when the procurator Gessius Florus (64 to 66 A.D.) abused his power so against them that he drove them to desperation and revolt against the Romans."

As the Roman yoke became more oppressive and the desperation of the Jewish masses more intense, the more they abandoned the Pharisees and took to Zealotism. At the same time the latter manifested strange by-products.

One of these was ecstatic enthusiasm. Knowledge was not a characteristic of the ancient proletariat, nor was the thirst for knowledge. Subject, more than any other class of people, to social forces they did not understand and which appeared to them as sinister; more than any other class desperate, in a situation in which men grasp at any straw; they were especially given to belief in miracles. Deeply affected by Messianic prophecies, they were more inclined than any other groups to complete misunderstanding of real conditions and to the expectation of the impossible.

Every fanatic who proclaimed himself a Messiah and promised to free the people by his miracles found supporters. One such was the prophet Theudas under the procurator Fadus (from 44 A.D. on), who led a throng of people to the River Jordan, where they were dispersed by the cavalry of Fadus. Theudas was captured and beheaded.

Under the procurator Felix (52 to 60 A.D.) fanaticism went still further: "There was a band of rascals who did not indeed murder people but had godless ideas and kept the city [Jerusalem] restless and unsafe. For they were seductive deceivers who preached all sorts of innovations as divine revelations and moved the people to riot. They led the people out into the desert and pretended that God would let them see a sign of freedom. Since Felix assumed that this was the beginning of the uprising, he sent soldiers against them, cavalry as well as infantry, and a great number were killed.

"Still greater misfortune was brought upon the Jews by a false prophet from Egypt [that means an Egyptian Jew.—K.]. He was a sorcerer and by his magic managed to get himself considered a prophet. He led astray some 30,000 people who supported him. He led them out of the desert to the so-called Mount of Olives in order to break into Jerusalem from there, overcome the Roman garrison and establish dominion over the people. As soon as Felix got wind of his project, he went against him with the Roman soldiers and all of the people who were willing to take steps for the common good, and gave battle to him. The Egyptian escaped with only a few of his mob. Most were taken, the rest hiding in the country.

"Hardly had this unrest been stilled than a new plague broke out, just as in a sick and infected body. Some sorcerers and murderers got together and won a great following. They called on everyone to demand freedom and threatened those with death who would be obedient subjects to the Roman authority from that time on, saying: Those must be freed against their will who voluntarily bow under the yoke of slavery.

"They went all through the Jewish land, plundered the houses of the rich, burned the villages, and behaved so abominably that because of them the whole Jewish people was oppressed. And from day to day this ruinous disease spread."[49]

Within Jerusalem itself open rebellion against the Roman army was not easy, and the most embittered enemies of the established order took to assassination. Under the procurator Felix, under whom the bandits and fanatics teemed, there also was organised a sect of terrorists. Explosives were unknown, and the favorite weapon of the terrorists was a curved dagger hidden under the cloak; they were called *sicarii* after this dagger (*sica*).

The desperate frenzy of all these champions of the popular cause was only the inevitable answer to the shameless brutality of the oppressors of the people. This is how Josephus, who witnessed all these events, describes the actions of the last two procurators who ruled Judea before the destruction of Jerusalem:

"Festus obtained the office of procurator (60 to 62 A.D.). He seriously combated the bandits who infested the Jewish land, and captured and killed many of them. His successor Albinus (62 to 64 A.D.) did not follow his example, unfortunately. There was no crime and no sin too great for him not to have done and practiced it. He not only embezzled public monies in the administration, but laid hold of the private property of the subjects and took it by force for himself. He loaded the people with huge and unjust taxes. For money he set free the robbers that the city authorities or his own predecessors in office had put in prison, and only those remained prisoners who could not pay. This increased the boldness of the revolutionaries in Jerusalem. The rich got so far with presents and gifts to Albinus that he winked at their having a suite following them. The masses, however, who do not love quiet, began to attach themselves to such people, because Albinus favored them. Accordingly every rascal surrounded himself with a band and let his mercenaries plunder and rob all the good citizens. Those who were robbed kept quiet, and those who had not been robbed yet flattered the rowdies for fear the like would happen to them. No one could complain, for the pres-

49. Josephus, *Jewish War*, II, 13, 4 to 6.

sure was too great. Thus the seed of the destruction of our city was planted.

"Although Albinus acted so disgracefully and wickedly, his successor Gessius Florus (64-66) went far beyond him, so that in a comparison of the two Albinus would still seem the better. For Albinus committed his misdeeds in secret and was able to put a good face on everything. The other one did everything openly, as if he sought his glory in mistreating our people. He robbed, he plundered, he punished and conducted himself as if he had not been sent as procurator but as executioner, to torture the Jews. Where he should have used mercy, he used terror. He was shameless and false into the bargain, and there was nobody who could have found more ruses for deceiving people than he did. He was not satisfied with bleeding private individuals white and profiting by their ruin. He plundered whole cities and ruined the entire people. All that was lacking was for him to proclaim publicly: robbery and theft are allowed at will, so long as he gets his share. Thus it came about that the whole land was devastated, and many left their fatherland and went abroad."[50]

Under Florus the situation finally led to the great uprising in which the whole people rose with all its might against its tormentors. When Florus went so far as to try to rob the Temple, in May 66, Jerusalem went wild, or rather, the lower classes in Jerusalem went wild. The majority of those who owned property, Pharisees as well as Sadducees, feared the uprising and desired peace. With the rebellion against the Romans civil war began as well. The war party won. The peace party was defeated in street-fighting, but the Roman garrison in Jerusalem was forced to withdraw and was cut down on the way.

The combat morale of the insurgents was so great that they succeeded in routing a relief column of 30,000 men led by the Syrian legate Cestius Gallus.

The Jews all over Palestine rose in insurrection, and those outside of Palestine as well. The mutiny of the Jews in Alexandria

50. *Jewish War*, II, 14, 1, 2.

required the dispatch of all the military forces of the Romans in Egypt.

There was of course no possibility that Rome could be overthrown by the Jews whose forces were too weak and too exclusively urban. It might however have compelled Rome to spare Judea a little longer, if the rebels had gone at once vigorously on the offensive, following up the successes they had won. Circumstances soon came to their aid. In the second year of the Jewish War the soldiers in the Western part of the Empire rose against Nero, and the battles of the legions against each other continued after his death (June 9, 68 A.D.); Vespasian, commander-in-chief of the army that was engaged in subduing Judea, gave more attention to the events in the West, where the throne was at stake, than to the little local war.

The one small chance the rebels had was passed by. It was to be sure the lower classes that had declared war on the Romans and put down the Jewish peace party, but the wealthy and educated still had enough influence to get the conduct of the war against the Romans into their hands. That meant that it was waged only with a faint heart, not with the purpose of wiping out the enemy but only to stand up to him. The rebels finally saw how lukewarm their leaders were in the fight, and the Zealots were then able to get the leadership into their own hands.

"In the fanatical popular party the unsuccessful course of events was ascribed—not without reason—to the lack of energy in the conduct of the war thus far. The men of the people bent all their efforts to getting control of the situation themselves and supplanting the previous leaders. Since the latter did not give up their control willingly, a fearfully bloody civil war resulted in Jerusalem in the winter of 67/68 A.D., with scenes of horror that are to be seen nowhere else except in the first French Revolution."[51]

The comparison with the French Revolution will strike every observer of these events. However, for France the Reign of Terror was a means of saving the revolution and making it capable of advancing victoriously against all of Europe; for Jerusalem

51. Schürer, *Geschichte des jüdischen Volkes*, I, 617.

any such outcome was impossible in the very nature of the situation. The reign of terror of the lower classes came too late in fact even to win a short reprieve for the Jewish state, whose days were numbered; it would only prolong the battle, increase the suffering, make the rage of the eventual victor more atrocious. But it could also give the world a monument of fortitude, heroism and devotion that stands out all the more impressively against the filth of the general cowardice and self-seeking of that era.

It was not all the Jews of Jerusalem who continued the hopeless struggle against the overpowering enemy for another three years, until September 70 A.D. in the stoutest, most resolute and resourceful of defenses, covering every inch of ground with corpses before giving up, and finally, weakened by hunger and disease, finding their graves in the burning ruins. The priests, the scribes, the merchant princes had for the most part fled to places of safety at the beginning of the siege. It was the small artisans and shopkeepers and proletarians of Jerusalem that became the heroes of their nation, in conjunction with the proletarianized peasants of Galilee who had forced their way into Jerusalem.

Such was the atmosphere in which the Christian community came into being. It does not by any means offer the smiling picture of Christ's surroundings drawn by Renan in his *Life of Jesus;* Renan based his conception, not on the social conditions of the time, but on the picturesque impressions the modern tourist in Galilee receives. Hence Renan is able to assure us in his romance about Jesus that in Jesus' time this fair land "abounded in plenty, joy and well-being," so that "every history of the origin of Christianity becomes a charming idyll."

As charming as the lovely month of May 1871 in Paris.

THE ESSENES

It must however be conceded that in the midst of the spectacle of woe and blood that constitutes the history of Judea in the epoch of Christ, there is one phenomenon which gives the impression of a peaceful idyll. This is the order of the Essenes or

Essaeans, which arose about the year 150 B.C., according to Josephus and lasted until the destruction of Jerusalem.[52] From that point on the order disappears from history.

Like the Zealots, it was obviously of proletarian origin; but its nature was quite different. The Zealots did not develop any social structure of their own. They differed from the Pharisees not in the goal, but in the means, the harshness and violence with which they sought to reach it. If the goal had been attained and Jerusalem enthroned as mistress of the world in the place of Rome, with all the riches of the Roman people going to the Jews, then there would be an end to all sorts of hardship for all classes. In this way nationalism seemed to make socialism unnecessary, even for the proletarians. What was characteristically proletarian in the Zealots was the energy and fanaticism of their patriotism.

But not all the proletarians were willing to wait until the Messiah should inaugurate the new, world-ruling Jerusalem. Many sought to improve their position at once, and since politics did not seem to promise any speedy assistance, they took to economic organization.

This must have been the sort of thinking that led to the foundation of Essenianism. We have no evidence on the point.

The nature of the organisation clearly indicates that it was an outspoken communism. They lived in common dwellings, 4000 strong in the time of Josephus, in various villages and rural cities of Judea.

"They live there together," Philo says of them, "organized by corporations and clubs for friendship and dining (*kata thasous, hetairias kai syssitia poioumenoi*), and regularly occupied in labors for the community.

"None of them desires to have property of his own, neither a house nor a slave nor a piece of land nor herds nor whatever else constitutes wealth. But they put everything together indiscriminately, and all of them use it in common.

52. Josephus writes "Essenes," Philo "Essaeans." The word is a Hellenized form of the Syrian *chase* (Hebrew, *chasid*), pious. The plural of the word has two forms, *chasen* and *chasuja*.

"The money they earn by their labor in various ways they hand over to an elected administrator. Out of it he buys what is needed, and gives them ample food and whatever else is needed for life."

It might be inferred from this that each man produced for himself or worked for wages.

Josephus describes their life as follows:

"After this [the morning prayer] they are dismissed by their chiefs and each goes to the work he has learned, and when they have diligently labored until the fifth hour [counting from sunrise, about eleven o'clock] they come together at a stated place, gird themselves with white cloths and wash their bodies in cold water. After this purification they go into the refectory, into which no one has entry who is not a member of their sect. When they have sat down in silence, the baker puts bread before each man and the cook sets a dish before each with one kind of food. Then a priest blesses the food; and it is not permitted to taste anything before prayer. At the end of the midday meal they give thanks again, and thus before and after eating they praise God, the giver of all food. Then they put off their mantles like sacred clothing and go to work again until evening. Supper is taken in the same way as dinner, and when guests come [members of the order from elsewhere, since strangers were not allowed in the refectory.—K.], they too sit at table with them. Neither outcries nor disorder sully the house, and when they converse, one speaks after the other, not all at once, so that people who are not of their order feel the quiet in the house as mysteriously impressive. The cause of their quiet life is their constant moderation, for they eat and drink no more than is required for maintaining their life.

"In general they do no work except on the instructions of their chiefs, with the exception that they may be free in showing sympathy and helpfulness. Whenever an emergency requires it, any one of them may assist those who need and deserve help, or bring food to the poor. But they may not contribute anything to their friends or relatives without the consent of their chief."

Their communism was carried to an extreme. It extended to their clothing. Philo says:

"Not only food, but clothing as well is in common with them. For there are heavy cloaks prepared for the winter, and light outer garments for summer, so that every man may make use of them as he will. For what one has counts as the property of all, and what all of them have counts as everyman's."

They rejected slavery. Farming was their chief occupation, but they also engaged in crafts. Only the manufacture of luxury articles and weapons of war was forbidden, along with trade.

The basis of their whole communistic system was community of consumption, not social production. There is some talk of the latter too, but it is only a question of work that brings in money for individuals either for wages or for goods sold, in either case the work is done outside the social organization. All the members of the order however have their lodging and meals in common. That is what holds them together, above all. It is communism of common housekeeping. This requires giving up separate house-keeping, separate families and separate marriages.

Actually we find, in every organization which rests on the basis of a communism of consumption and community housekeeping that separate marriage causes difficulties and an effort is made to eliminate it. This may be done in two ways that apparently are mutually exclusive, the sharpest extremes of sexual relationships, greatest chastity and greatest "looseness." And yet both ways are equally likely to be followed by communistic organizations of the sort in question. From the Essenes down through all the Christian communistic sects to the colonies of the communistic sects in the United States in our times, we can see that all of them are against marriage, but are just as likely to incline to community of women as to celibacy.

This would be unthinkable if it were merely ideological considerations that had brought people to this communism and its superstructure of ideas. It is easily explainable on the basis of its economic conditions.

Most of the Essenes rejected all contact with women.

"They reject marriage, but adopt strange children while they are still young and teachable, consider them as their own children

and instruct them in their ways and customs. It is not that they
would do away with or forbid marriage or the reproduction of the
species. But they say that the unchastity of women must be
guarded against, since none of them is satisfied with one man
alone."

That is what Josephus says in the eighth chapter of the second
book of his history of the Jewish War, from which these quota-
tions on the Essenes have been taken. But in the eighteenth book
of his Jewish Antiquities, chapter one, he says on the same
question:

"They do not take wives and hold no slaves. They hold that the
latter is unjust, and the first would give rise to disputes."

In both places it is only practical considerations, not asceticism,
that is the basis of opposition to marriage. Josephus knew the
Essenes from his own observations. He had been successively with
the Sadducees, Essenes and Pharisees until he stayed finally with
the latter.

Thus Josephus is in an excellent position to tell us the basis of
the Essenes' hostility to marriage. That is not to say that what he
says constitutes the ultimate cause; for we must constantly distinguish between the arguments someone adduces to justify his
actions and the psychological motives that actually cause those
actions. Very few men are clearly aware of these motives. It is a
favorite procedure of our historians however to take the arguments that are handed down to them as the actual motives of the
historical events and relations. They reject investigation into the
actual motives as arbitrary "constructions," that is they demand
that our knowledge of history should never reach a higher point
of view than it had at the time from which our sources come. All
of the enormous body of facts that has been accumulated since
then, which enables us to separate what is essential and typical
in the most diverse historical phenomena from what is unessential
and accidental, and to discover the actual motives of men behind
what they profess—all this, they would say, is to be ignored.

Anyone who knows the history of communism will realize at
once that it was not the nature of women, but the nature of com-

munistic housekeeping that poisoned marriage for the Essenes. When many males and females lived together in a common household, the temptation to infidelity and jealous quarrels was too near at hand. If this sort of housekeeping was not to be abandoned either men would have to stop living with women or monogamy would have to be eliminated.

Not all the Essenes took the first way. Josephus reports in the previously cited eighth chapter of the second book on the Jewish War:

"There is still another sort of Essenes, who are in thorough accord with the previous ones in their way of living, their manners and rules, but differ from them in the matter of marriage. For they say, that those who refrain from marital relations would deprive life of its most important function (*meros*), reproduction would constantly decrease and the human race would soon die out, if everyone thought as they did. These people have the custom of trying (*dokimazontes*) wives for three years. If they have shown after three purifications that they are fit to bear children, they marry them. As soon as one is pregnant, her husband no longer sleeps with her. That is to show that they enter into marriage not for the sake of sensual pleasure, but only for the sake of producing children."

The passage is not quite clear; but it says at least that these marriages of the Essenes were very different from the customary ones. The "trying" of wives does not seem conceivable except on the presumption of a sort of community of wives.

Out of the ideological superstructure that was built on these social foundations, one thought should be particularly stressed, namely, the Essenes' assertion of the unfreedom of the will, in opposition to the Sadducees, who taught the freedom of the will, and to the Pharisees, who took an intermediate position.

"When the Pharisees say that everything happens in accordance with fate, they do not do away with the free will of man, but say that it pleased God to bring to pass a mixture as it were between the decree of fate and that of men, who will to do good or evil."[53]

53. Josephus, *Antiquities*, XVIII, 1, 3.

"The Essenes on the other hand ascribe everything to fate. They hold that nothing can happen to man that is not decreed by fate. The Sadducees will have none of fate. They say there is no such thing, and it does not determine the lot of men. They ascribe everything to the free will of man, so that he has himself to thank if something good happens to him; while unhappy experiences are to be considered as results of his own folly."[54]

These divergent views would seem to arise out of pure thought. We already know, however, that each of these tendencies represents a different class. And when we understand history, we find that very often ruling classes incline to assume the freedom of the will, and still more often the oppressed classes uphold the idea of its unfreedom.

This is not difficult to understand. The ruling classes feel themselves free to do what they please, or to refrain from action. That comes not merely from their powerful position but also from the small number of their members. Regularity appears only in the mass, where the different deviations from the norm cancel each other out. The smaller the number of individuals observed, the greater the weight of the personal and fortuitous as compared with the general and typical. In the case of a monarch the latter seems to be entirely abolished.

The rulers thus easily come to consider themselves as raised above social influences, which appear to men, so long as they are not understood, as an occult power, as fate. The ruling classes feel themselves driven however to attribute freedom of the will not only to themselves but to those who are ruled. The misery of the exploited appears to them as the fault of the exploited themselves, every offence that they commit as a wanton misdeed, that arises from mere personal joy in evil and calls for rigorous punishment.

Assuming freedom of the will makes it easier for the ruling classes to carry out their function of judging and holding down the oppressed classes while feeling moral superiority and in-

54. *Antiquities*, XIII, 5, 9.

dignation, a factor which undoubtedly makes them more energetic in their task.

The mass of the poor and the harried, however, find that at every step they are the slaves of circumstances, of fate; its decrees are incomprehensible to them, but at any rate it is more powerful than they. It comes bitterly home to them what a mockery it is when the prosperous tell them to be the artisans of their own fortune. They try in vain to escape from the conditions that oppress them. And they realize that this happens not merely to isolated individuals among them, but that each of them drags the same chain after him. They see very clearly that not only their actions and the success of those actions, but their feelings and thoughts and hence their will are dependent on their circumstances.

It may seem queer that the Pharisees, in view of their intermediate social position, should accept freedom of the will and natural necessity at one and the same time. But almost two thousand years after them the great philosopher Kant did the same thing.

We need not here examine the rest of the ideological superstructure which arose on the basis of the Essenian social structure, although this is precisely what historians in the main are concerned with. For that gives them the opportunity to make profound explanations of the derivation of Essenianism from Parseeism or Buddhism or Pythagoreanism or some other ism.

That does not answer the question of the actual roots of Essenianism. Social tendencies within a people always arise out of actual needs within that people, and not through mere imitation of foreign models. It is possible to learn from other countries or other times, certainly, but people take from these sources only what they can use, what corresponds to a need. For example, the only reason why Roman law found such acceptance in Germany after the Renaissance was that it fitted in so well with the needs of strong rising classes, the absolute monarchy and the merchants. Naturally one does not go to the trouble of inventing a new tool when an existing one is ready to hand. The fact that a tool comes from abroad does not answer the question of why it finds application; that can only be explained by actual needs in the people themselves.

All the influences from Parseeism, Buddhism or Pythagoreanism that may have had an effect on Essenianism are dubious at best; there is no proof that any of them affected it directly. The similarities may very well arise from the fact that all of them arose under fairly similar conditions, which led to similar attempts at salvation in each case.

One would be most tempted to infer a connection between the Pythagoreans and the Essenes. Josephus says in fact (*Antiquities*, XV, 10, 4) that the Essenes lived in a way that was very similar to that of the Pythagoreans. But one might raise the question whether the Essenes learned from the Pythagoreans or vice versa. Josephus says to be sure (*Against Apion*, I, 22) that Pythagoras himself adopted Jewish conceptions and put them out as his own, but that is mere bragging to glorify Judaism, and is probably based on some forgery or other. Actually we know almost nothing certain about Pythagoras. It is only long after his death that information about him begins to be more abundant; and there are more bits, and in more detail, and more incredible, the further we go from the time in which he lived. We pointed out at the beginning that Pythagoras was treated like Jesus. He became an ideal figure, credited with everything expected of an ethical model, as well as a miracle-maker and prophet who showed his divine mission by the most astonishing feats. It was precisely because nothing definite was known of him that it was possible to attribute to him and put into his mouth anything that was desired.

Even the way of life said to have been introduced by Pythagoras, much like that of the Essenes, with community of property, is probably of relatively recent origin, perhaps no older than that of the Essenes.

This Pythagoreanism probably originated in Alexandria.[55]

55. On this question and the Pythagoreans in general, cf. Zeller, *Philosophie der Griechen*, volumes I and III.

There a link with Judaism was quite likely, and the transmission of Pythagorean conceptions to Palestine not at all out of the question. The reverse too was possible. Finally, it may be that both drew on a common source: Egyptian practice. In Egypt the advanced social development had already led, relatively early, to cloister-like institutions.

Its old civilization had long been declining, and as a result revulsion against private property and the pleasures of life together with flight from the world had set in earlier than in the other parts of the Roman Empire; nowhere was such a course of action easier to put into execution than in Egypt, where the desert reaches up to the edge of civilization. Elsewhere anyone fleeing from the great city found private property in the country too, and in its most oppressive form, private property in land. He either had to withdraw into wildernesses many miles away from civilization, which only the most strenuous efforts could make habitable, a labor that the city-dweller is least of all capable of.

In the Egyptian desert, as in any desert, there was no private property in land. It was not hard to live there: the climate did not require any great outlay on buildings, clothing and heating to protect one from the weather. Moreover, it was so close to the city that the hermit could easily get the necessities of life from friends, or even fetch himself by walking a few hours.

Accordingly Egypt had begun early to produce a monk-like group of hermits. Then neo-Pythagoreanism arose in Alexandria, and finally in the fourth century of our era Christian monasticism got its start there. But Alexandrian Judaism as well had its own peculiar monastic order, the Therapeutae.

The treatise *On the Contemplative Life* in which Philo reports on them has been said to be spurious, but in this case the suspicion is groundless.

Like the sage, he says, they renounce their property, which they divide among their relatives and friends; they leave their brothers, children, wives, parents, friends and native city, and find their true home in union with others of like mind. These associations are to be found in many parts of Egypt, especially near Alexandria. Here each lives by himself in a simple cell, near to those of the others, where he spends the time in pious contemplation. Their food is very simple, bread, salt and water. On the Sabbath they come together for pious lectures and singing, men and women in a common hall, but the sexes separated by a partition. They reject meat-eating, wine and slavery. There is nothing said, however, about work on their part. They must have lived by alms from friends and admirers.

It is quite possible that Alexandrian Jews brought the notions of the Therapeutae to Palestine and thereby influenced Essenianism. And yet the two are fundamentally different. The Therapeutae live in contemplative idleness on others' labor, the Essenes work diligently and earn so much that they not only support themselves but have a surplus to share with the needy. Both reject private property, but the Therapeutae have nothing at all to do with the goods of the world. They hate work as much as pleasure, they renounce means of production as they do means of consumption, and hence distribute their property among friends and relatives. The Essenes labor, and for that they need means of production; accordingly their members do not distribute what they own among friends, but collect them in a fund for common use.

Since they worked, they had to be able-bodied and eat well. Rigid asceticism is impossible for men who have work to do.

The difference between the Therapeutae and still more the neo-Pythagoreans, who for the most part merely prated about asceticism, withdrawal from the world, and giving up property, on the one hand, and the Essenes on the other points up the contrast between the Jewry of Palestine and of the rest of the civilized world of the Roman Empire at the time in which Christianity arose. In Essenianism we see the same vigor that we observe in the Zealots and that raises the Judaism of that era so far above the cowardly dejection of the other civilized nations, who fled from pleasure and temptation because they were afraid of struggle. Even the communistic tendencies among them had a cowardly and ascetic character.

What made Essenianism possible was the vigor of Judaism, but not that alone. There are other factors which brought it about that it was precisely Judaism that produced this unique phenomenon.

In general, we find in the last century before Christ that along with mass poverty there also increases the effort of the proletarians and their friends to relieve the misery by organized effort. Meals in common, the last remnant of primitive communism, are at the same time the initial point of the new communism.

Under Judaism the need for cohesion and mutual aid was especially strong. Fellow-countrymen abroad clung together more closely than at home, and no one was more homeless and was more constantly in foreign parts than the Jew outside of Judea. Thus the Jews were marked by a mutual helpfulness that was as striking as their segregation from the non-Jews. In a single phrase Tacitus emphasizes both their hostile hatred against all others and their constant gentleness toward one another.[56]

They also seem to have clung with especial stubbornness to their associations with meals in common. There is no other explanation for the fact that Caesar, who forbade all associations that had not come down from antiquity, permitted the Jewish ones.

"Although in all other cases he required the permission of the Senate for the formation of independent corporate bodies with their own funds, he immediately permitted the formation all over the Empire of Jewish associations with common meals and corporate property. In view of the desire, widespread at that time, for belonging to societies, which the state so feared and persecuted, this toleration of Jewish religious societies led many pagans to apply for membership in the Jewish associations as so-called Godfearing men, a request that was easily granted."[57]

Such an association of proletarians would be very likely to take on a purely communistic character. But it was not easy for it to go much beyond meals in common out of a common fund, under

56. *Histories*, V, 5.
57. O. Holtzmann, *Das Ende des jüdischen Staatswesens und die Entstehung des Christentums*, 1888, p. 460.

urban conditions. Nor was there much incentive to go further. At that time, in the southern countries, clothing did not play an important part in the budget of proletarians; it served more for display than as protection against the weather. For sleeping quarters the proletarian of the city looked for some nook or corner. Finally, earning a living scattered them to the farthest ends of the city whether they begged or stole or peddled or were porters, or however it was they got by.

The common meal of the society, to which each brought his share and in which every member shared, whether he had been in a position to contribute something or not, was the strongest link that held the society together, and the most effective way of insuring the individual against the vicissitudes of life, which can so easily destroy the destitute.

In the country, household and occupation are inseparable. Meals in common presuppose a common dwelling and a common economy. Large agricultural estates were not rare at that time: operated by slaves to some extent, but also enlarged communistic families and lodging associations are found at this stage of development.

Palestine was by now the only region where Judaism still had a peasantry, and this we have seen to have been in constant and close connection with the metropolis of Jerusalem and its proletariat. It was easy for communistic tendencies, which were nearer to the heart of the Jewish proletariat than to any other proletariat of that time, to extend to the open country and there take the form that marks the Essenian doctrine.

The economic basis of the organization of the Essenes was peasant agriculture. "They are all engaged in farming," says Josephus, with some exaggeration (*Antiquities*, XVIII, 1,5).

Such an organization on the land could last only as long as it was tolerated by the state. There was no way in which a productive commune could exist as a secret society, especially in the country.

Essenianism was therefore linked up with the preservation of Jewish freedom. When that was lost, it too had to go under. It was not suited to an existence in great cities outside of Palestine, as an illicit society.

Nevertheless the great city of Jerusalem was to develop a form of organization that proved to be more adaptable than any other to the needs of the urbən proletariat all over the Empire, and in the end better adapted than any other to the needs of the Empire itself.

This organization started in Judaism and spread over all the Empire, and incorporated all the elements of the new way of feeling and thinking that had arisen out of the social transformation and decay of that time.

We now go on to consider this organization: the Christian community.

BOOK FOUR: THE BEGINNINGS
OF CHRISTIANITY

1

THE PRIMITIVE CHRISTIAN
COMMUNITY

THE PROLETARIAN CHARACTER OF THE COMMUNITY

WE HAVE SEEN that the purely national democratic movement of the Zealots did not satisfy many proletarian elements of Jerusalem. However, escape from the city to the country, as the Essenes did, was not to everyone's taste either. At that time, as today, escape from the country was very easy, escape from the city very difficult. The proletarian, accustomed to urban life, was not at home in the country. The rich man might well see his country villa as an agreeable change from the turmoil of the city; for the proletarian, return to the land meant hard work in the fields, work that he did not understand and was not fitted for.

The mass of proletarians must therefore have preferred to stay in the cities, in Jerusalem as elsewhere. Essenianism did not give them what they needed, least of all those who were mere lumpenproletarians and had got into the habit of living as parasites on society.

A third proletarian tendency therefore necessarily arose, along with the Zealots and Essenes, and in fact combining the two. This found expression in the Messianic community.

It is generally recognized that the Christian community originally contained proletarian elements exclusively, and was a proletarian organization. This remained true long after the first beginnings.

Paul stresses, in his first letter to the Corinthians, that neither education nor wealth are represented in the community:

"For ye see your calling, brethren, how that not many wise men after the flesh, not many mighty, not many noble, are called: But God hath chosen the foolish things of the world to confound the wise; and God hath chosen the weak things of the world to confound the mighty; And base things of the world, and things which are despised, hath God chosen." (chap. 1, verses 26 f.)

Friedländer gives a good description of the proletarian nature of the primitive Christian community in his *Sittengeschichte Roms:*

"No matter how many factors contributed to the dissemination of the Gospel, it obviously had found only isolated supporters among the upper classes up to the middle or the end of the second century. Their philosophical tendencies, and the rest of their education, so intimately intertwined with polytheism, was strongly opposed to Christianity; then, acceptance of Christianity led to the most perilous conflicts with the established social order; and finally, giving up all worldly interests was most difficult for those who had honor, power and wealth. The poor and lowly, says Lactantius, are more ready to have faith than the rich; among the latter there must often undoubtedly have been a hostile attitude toward the socialistic tendencies in Christianity. In the lower classes, however, the spread of Christianity, which was extraordinarily favored by the dispersion of the Jews, must have been very rapid, especially in Rome proper; in the year 64 the number of Christians there was already considerable."

Nevertheless, this spread for a long time was confined to single places.

"The data we have, which have been preserved by mere chance, show that up to the year 98 there are some 42 places in which it can be shown that there were Christian communities; by the year 180, the figure is 74, and by 325, more than 550.

"The Christians however were not merely a small minority in the Roman Empire up to the third century, but this minority, at least at the outset, was made up exclusively of the lowest groups in society. The heathen scoffed that the Christians were only able to convert simpletons and slaves, women and children, that they were uneducated, crude and peasant-like men, and that their communities consisted chiefly of little people, artisans and old women. Nor did the Christians deny this. It was not from the Lyceum and the Academy that the community of Christ was assembled, says Jerome, but from the lowest (*de vili plebecula*) in society. Christian writers expressly state that the new faith had only isolated adherents among the upper classes until the middle of the third century. Eusebius says that the peace the church enjoyed under Commodus (180 to 192) had helped a great deal to extend it, 'so that even many men in Rome prominent in wealth and birth turned to salvation with their whole household and clan.' Under Alexander Severus (222 to 235) Origen said that now the rich too, and even haughty and nobly-born ladies accepted the Christian message of the Word: successes therefore that Christianity could not claim previously. . . . From the time of Commodus on therefore the spread of Christianity in the upper orders is confirmed just as expressly and often as such testimony is lacking for the earlier period. . . . The only people of high rank in the period before Commodus whose conversion to Christianity is conceded as being very probable are Flavius Clemens, consul, executed in 95, and Flavia Domitilla, his wife or sister, banished to Pontia.''[1]

This proletarian character is one of the principal reasons for our being so ill-informed about the beginnings of Christianity. Its first champions may have been eloquent orators, but they were not expert in reading and writing. Those were arts that were even further removed from the masses of the people than they are today. For generations the Christian doctrine and the history of its communities were confined to oral traditions, traditions handed down by people who were feverishly excited and incredibly credulous, traditions dealing with events in which only a small group were involved, in so far as they took place at all; and hence traditions that could not be tested by the mass of the people, and especially by its critical, impartial elements. The putting down of

1. *Sittengeschichte Roms*, II, pp. 540-43.

these traditions in writing began only as better educated elements, of higher social standing began to turn toward Christianity, and then this recording had a polemical not a historical purpose; it aimed at supporting definite views and demands.

It requires a great deal of boldness, as well as of bias, in addition to total ignorance of the conditions of historical trustworthiness, to use documents that came into existence in this way and teem with impossibilities and crass contradictions, to narrate the lives of individuals and even their speeches, in detail. We showed at the outset that it is impossible to make any concrete statement about the alleged founder of the Christian community. On the basis of what has been said thus far, we can add that there is no need to know anything concrete about him. All the systems of ideas that are usually indicated as characterizing Christianity, whether in praise or in blame, have been seen to be products of the Greco-Roman or the Judaic development. There is not a single Christian thought that would make it necessary to refer to some sublime prophet and superman, no thought that can not be traced in the "heathen" or Jewish literature.

But although it is of no significance for our historical insight to be instructed as to the personalities of Jesus and his disciples, it is of the utmost importance to be clear about the character of the primitive Christian community.

Fortunately, this is not at all impossible. The speeches and actions of the persons whom Christians honor as their champions and teachers may have been fantastically adorned or made up out of the whole cloth; at any rate, the first Christian authors wrote in the spirit of the Christian communities in which and for which they lived. They repeated traditions handed down from an earlier period, which they might alter in details, but whose general character was so clearly established that any attempt to alter them noticeably would have met with violent opposition. People might have tried to water down or reinterpret the spirit that prevailed in the beginnings of the Christian community, but they could not completely falsify it. We still can trace such attempts at watering down, and they become bolder as the Christian community loses its originally proletarian character and takes in educated, prosperous and reputable people. But it is precisely from these attempts that the original character can be clearly inferred.

The insight won in this way is confirmed by the evolution of the later Christian sects, whose history is known to us from the beginning and repeats, in its later development, the patterns of the Christian community from the second century on. We may therefore consider this development to be a regular one, and that the known beginnings of the later sects are analogous to those of Christianity. Such an inference by analogy is not of course in itself a proof, but it can very well serve to substantiate a conception otherwise arrived at.

Both sorts of evidence, the analogy with later sects and the remains of the earliest traditions of primitive Christian life, exhibit tendencies that were to be expected as a result of the proletarian character of the community.

CLASS HATRED

The first thing we encounter is a fierce class hatred against the rich.

It appears clearly in the Gospel according to St. Luke, a composition of the beginning of the second century, especially in the story of Lazarus, which is found only in this gospel (16, verses 19 f.). The rich man goes to hell and the poor man to Abraham's bosom, and not because the rich man was a sinner and the poor man just: nothing is said about that. The rich man is damned just because he was rich. Abraham says to him: "Remember that thou in thy lifetime receivedst thy good things, and likewise Lazarus evil things: but now he is comforted, and thou art tormented." The thirst of the oppressed for vengeance is gloating here. The same gospel has Jesus say: "How hardly shall they that have riches enter into the kingdom of God! For it is easier for a camel to go through a needle's eye, than for a rich man to enter into the kingdom of God" (18, verses 24 f.). Here too the rich man is damned for his wealth, not for his sinfulness.

Likewise in the Sermon on the Mount (6, verses 20 f.):

"Blessed be ye poor: for yours is the kingdom of God. Blessed are ye that hunger now: for ye shall be filled. Blessed are ye that weep now: for ye shall laugh. . . . But woe unto you that are rich! for ye have received your consolation. Woe unto you that are full! for ye shall hunger. Woe unto you that laugh now! for ye shall mourn and weep."

As we see, being rich and enjoying wealth is a crime that merits the most bitter atonement.

The same spirit breathes through the epistle of James "to the twelve tribes which are scattered abroad," dating from the middle of the second century:

"Go to now, ye rich men, weep and howl for your miseries that shall come upon you. Your riches are corrupted, and your garments are motheaten. Your gold and silver is cankered: and the rust of them shall be a witness against you, and shall eat your flesh as it were fire. Ye have heaped treasure together for the last days. Behold, the hire of the labourers who have reaped down your fields, which is of you kept back by fraud, crieth: and the cries of them which have reaped are entered into the ears of the Lord of sabaoth. Ye have lived in pleasure on the earth, and been wanton; ye have nourished your hearts, as in a day of slaughter. Ye have condemned and killed the just; and he doth not resist you. Be patient therefore, brethren, unto the coming of the Lord" (5, verse 1 f.).

He even thunders against the rich in the ranks of the faithful:

"Let the brother of low degree rejoice in that he is exalted; But the rich, in that he is made low: because as the flower of the grass he shall pass away. For the sun is no sooner risen with a burning heat, but it withereth the grass, and the flower thereof falleth, and the grace of the fashion of it perisheth: so also shall the rich man fade away in his ways. . . . Hearken, my beloved brethren, Hath not God chosen the poor of this world rich in faith, and heirs of the kingdom which he hath promised to them that love him? But ye have despised the poor. Do not rich men oppress you, and draw you before the judgment seats? Do not they blaspheme that worthy name by the which ye are called?" (James 1, verses 9 to 11; 2, verses 5 to 7).

The class hatred of the modern proletariat has hardly reached such fanatical forms as did that of the Christian. In the brief moments in which the proletariat of our days has come to power hitherto, it has never taken vengeance on the rich. It is true that it feels stronger today than the proletariat of budding Christianity did; and one who knows he is strong is always more magnanimous than the weak man. It is an indication of how weak the bourgeoisie feels today that it always takes such frightful vengeance on the proletariat in rebellion.

The Gospel according to St. Matthew is some decades later than that of Luke. In the interval prosperous and educated people had begun to come close to Christianity. Many Christian propagandists felt the need of giving the Christian doctrine a form which would be more attractive to these people. The uncompromising tradition of primitive Christianity became inconvenient. Since however it had struck too deep roots to be simply put aside, an effort was made at least to revise the original composition in an opportunistic way. By virtue of this revisionism the Gospel according to St. Matthew has become the "Gospel of Contradictions,"[2] and the "favorite gospel of the church." Here the church found "the unruly and revolutionary elements of enthusiasm and socialism in primitive Christianity so moderated to the golden mean of a clerical opportunism that it no longer seemed to endanger the existence of an organized church making its peace with human society."

Naturally, the various authors who successively worked on the gospel according to St. Matthew left out all the inconvenient things they could, such as the story of Lazarus and the rejection of the inheritance dispute, which too gives rise to an attack on the rich (Luke 12, verse 13 f.). But the Sermon on the Mount was already too popular and well-known to be treated in the same way. It was patched up: in Matthew, Jesus is made to say:

2. Pfleiderer, *Das Urchristentum*, I, p. 613.

"Blessed are the poor in spirit: for theirs is the kingdom of heaven. . . . Blessed are they, which do hunger and thirst after righteousness: for they shall be filled" (chap. 5).

Of course all the traces of class hatred have been washed away in this adroit revisionism. Now it is the poor in spirit that are blessed. It is not certain what sort of folk these are, whether idiots or people who were paupers only in an imaginary sense; who continued to have possessions, but assert their heart is not in them. Apparently the latter are meant; but in any case the condemnation of wealth which was contained in the blessing of the poor is gone.

It is really amusing to find the hungry transformed into those that hunger after righteousness, who are assured that they shall be filled; the Greek word used here (*chorazein*—have their fill) is used of beasts for the most part, and applied to men humorously or in contempt. Having the word used in the Sermon on the Mount is another indication of the proletarian origin of Christianity. The expression was current in the circles from which it sprang, to indicate the complete quenching of their bodily hunger. It is ludicrous to apply it to quenching the hunger for righteousness.

The counterpart to these blessings, the cursing of the rich, has disappeared in Matthew. Here even the shrewdest manipulation could not find a formulation acceptable to the prosperous groups whose conversion was being aimed at. The curses had to go.

But although influential groups of the Christian community, turning opportunistic, strove to efface its proletarian character, the proletariat and its class hatred were not eliminated, and there were always individual thinkers who expressed it. The little book of Paul Pflüger, *Der Sozialismus der Kirchenväter*, gives a good collection of passages from the writings of Saint Clement, Bishop Asterius, Lactantius, Basil the Great, Saint Gregory of Nyssa, Saint Ambrose, Saint John Chrysostom, Saint Jerome, Augustine, etc., almost all figures of the fourth century, in which Christianity was already the official state religion. They all contain bitter attacks on the rich, whom they equate with robbers and thieves.

COMMUNISM

In view of the strong proletarian imprint on the community, it was likely that it should strive toward a communistic form of organization. This is testified to expressly. The Acts of the Apostles says:

"And they continued steadfastly in the apostles' doctrine and fellowship [communism, *koinonia*], and in breaking of bread, and in prayers. . . . And all that believed were together, and had all things common; And sold their possessions and goods, and parted them to all men, as every man had need" (2, verses 42 f.). "And the multitude of them that believed were of one heart and of one soul: neither said any of them that ought of the things which he possessed was his own; but they had all things common. . . . Neither was there any among them that lacked: for as many as were possessors of lands or houses sold them, and brought the prices of the things that were sold, And laid them down at the apostles' feet, and distribution was made unto every man according as he had need" (4, verse 32 f.).

We all know that Ananias and Sapphira, who withheld some of their money from the community were immediately punished by death, by a divine visitation.

Saint John, called Chrysostom (Golden Mouth) because of his fiery eloquence, a fearless critic of his time (347 to 407), attached to the above description of primitive Christian communism a discussion of its advantages which sounds very realistically economic and not at all ecstatic and ascetic. This is in his eleventh homily (sermon) on the Acts of the Apostles. There he said:

"Grace was among them, since nobody suffered want, that is, since they gave so willingly that no one remained poor. For they did not give a part, keeping another part for themselves; they gave everything in their possession. They did away with inequality and lived in great abundance; and this they did in the most praiseworthy fashion. They did not dare to put their offering into the hands of the needy, nor give it with lofty condescension, but they laid it at the feet of the apostles and made them the masters and distributors of the gifts. What a man needed was then taken from the treasure of the community, not from the private property of individuals. Thereby the givers did not become arrogant.

"Should we do as much today, we should all live much more happily, rich as well as poor; and the poor would not be more the gainers than the rich . . . for those who gave did not thereby become poor, but made the poor also rich.

"Let us imagine things as happening in this way: All give all that they have into a common fund. No one would have to concern himself about it, neither the rich nor the poor. How much money do you think would be collected? I infer—for it cannot be said with certainty—that if every individual contributed all his money, his lands, his estates, his houses (I will not speak of slaves, for the first Christians had none, probably giving them their freedom), then a million pounds of gold would be obtained, and most likely two or three times that amount. Then tell me how many people our city [Constantinople] contains? How many Christians? Will it not come to a hundred thousand? And how many pagans and Jews! How many thousands of pounds of gold would be gathered in! And how many of the poor do we have? I doubt that there are more than fifty thousand. How much would be required to feed them daily? If they all ate at a common table, the cost could not be very great. What could we not undertake with our huge treasure! Do you believe it could ever be exhausted? And will not the blessing of God pour down on us a thousand-fold richer? Will we not make a heaven on earth? If this turned out so brilliantly for three or five thousand [the first Christians] and none of them was in want, how much more would this be so with such a great quantity? Will not each newcomer add something more?

"The dispersion of property is the cause of greater expenditure and so of poverty. Consider a household with man and wife and ten children. She does weaving and he goes to the market to make a living; will they need more if they live in a single house or when they live separately? Clearly, when they live separately. If the ten sons each go his own way, they need ten houses, ten tables, ten servants and everything else in proportion. And how of the mass of slaves? Are these not fed at a single table, in order to save money? Dispersion regularly leads to waste, bringing together leads to economy. That is how people now live in monasteries and how the faithful once lived. Who died of hunger then? Who was not fully satisfied? And yet men are more afraid of this way of life than of a leap into the endless sea. If only we made the attempt and took bold hold of the situation! How great a blessing there would be as a result! For if at that time, when there were so few faithful, only three to five thousand, if at that time, when the whole world was hostile to us and there was no comfort anywhere, our predecessors were so resolute in this, how much more confidence should we have today, when by God's grace the faithful are everywhere! Who would still remain a heathen? Nobody, I believe. Every one would come to us and be friendly."[3]

The first Christians were not capable of going into such clear and calm details. But their brief remarks, appeals, demands, wishes, all point to the same communistic character of the beginning of the Christian community.

In the Gospel according to St. John (dating, it is true, only from the middle of the second century) the communistic life of Jesus and the apostles is taken for granted. They had only one purse among them, kept by Judas Iscariot. John, who here as elsewhere tries to outdo his predecessors, deepens the revulsion felt at Judas' treason by branding him as a thief from the common fund. He describes how Mary anointed the feet of Jesus with costly ointment.

"Then saith one of his disciples, Judas Iscariot, Simon's son, which should betray him, Why was not this ointment sold for three hundred pence, and given to the poor? This he said, not that he cared for the poor; but because he was a thief, and had the bag, and bare what was put therein" (chap. 12, verses 4 f.).

At the Last Supper Jesus says to Judas: "That thou doest, do quickly. Now no man at the table knew for what intent he spake this unto him. For some of them thought, because Judas had the

3. *S.P.N. Joanni Chrysostomi opera omnia quae exstant.* Paris 1859, ed. Migne, IX, 96-98.

bag, that Jesus had said unto him, Buy those things that we have need of against the feast; or, that he should give something to the poor" (chap. 13, verses 27-29).

Over and over again in the gospels Jesus requires of his disciples that each give everything that he owns.

". . . whosoever he be of you that forsaketh not all that he hath, he cannot be my disciple" (Luke 14, verse 33).

"Sell that ye have, and give alms" (Luke 12, verse 33).

"And a certain ruler asked him [Jesus], saying, Good Master, what shall I do to inherit eternal life? And Jesus said unto him, Why callest thou me good? none is good, save one, that is, God. Thou knowest the commandments, Do not commit adultery,. Do not kill, Do not steal, Do not bear false witness, Honour thy father and thy mother. And he said, All these have I kept from my youth up. Now when Jesus heard these things, he said unto him, Yet lackest thou one thing: sell all that thou hast, and distribute unto the poor, and thou shalt have treasure in heaven: and come, follow me. And when he heard this, he was very sorrowful: for he was very rich" (Luke 18, verses 18-23).

This leads Jesus to the image of the camel who goes more easily through the eye of a needle than a rich man into the kingdom of God. Only those can share in that kingdom who share their goods with the poor.

The gospel attributed to Mark describes the matter in the same way.

The revisionist Matthew however weakens the original vigor here too. The requirement is put as a condition. Matthew has Jesus say to the rich youth: "If thou wilt be perfect, go and sell that thou hast, and give to the poor" (19, verse 21).

What Jesus was originally supposed to have required of each of his supporters, every member of his community, was reduced in time to a requirement only of those who professed perfection.

This development is quite natural in the case of an organization that was originally purely proletarian and later admitted more and more wealthy elements.

There are however many theologians who deny the communistic character of early Christianity, on the grounds that the report of it in the Acts of the Apostles is of later origin, and allege that, as so often happened in antiquity, the ideal condition that one dreamed of was represented as having been actual in the past. In all this it is forgotten that for the official church of later centuries, going out to meet the rich half-way, the communistic character of primitive Christianity was most inconvenient. If the account of it were based on a later invention, the champions of the opportunistic tendency would have protested against it at once and seen to it that the writings containing such accounts were stricken from the canon of the books recognized by the church. The church has tolerated only those forgeries which are in its interest. This, however, would not apply to communism. If it was officially recognized as the original requirement of the primitive community, this surely took place only because no other course was possible, because the tradition on this point had too deep roots and was too generally accepted.

OBJECTIONS TO THE EXISTENCE OF COMMUNISM

The objections of those who contest the communism of the primitive community are not very efficacious. They are all to be found assembled by a critic who opposes the account I gave of primitive Christianity in *Forerunners of Socialism*.

The critic A. K., a doctor of theology, published his objections in an article in *Neue Zeit* on "So-called Primitive Christian Communism" (Vol. XXVI, No. 2, p. 482).

First of all, it is objected that "the preaching of the Nazarene did not aim at economic revolution." How does A. K. know that? The Acts of the Apostles seem to him an unreliable source for descriptions of organizations whose origin is set in the period after the supposed death of Christ; but the Gospels, he thinks, which are in part later than Acts, are to give us a sure idea of the character of Christ's words!

The same can be said for the Gospels as for Acts: what we can learn from them is the character of those who wrote them. In addition they may give reminiscences; and memories of organizations last longer than memories of words, and can not be distorted as easily.

Moreover we have seen that is is possible to find in the words attributed to Christ a character corresponding to the communism of the primitive community.

The particular doctrines of Jesus, of which we know virtually nothing definite, can not serve therefore to prove anything against the reality of communism.

Next A. K. tries very hard to have us believe that the practical communism of the Essenes, which the proletarians of Jerusalem had before their eyes, had no effect on them, but that the communistic theories of the Greek philosophers and thinkers had the deepest of influences on the uneducated proletarians of the Christian communities outside of Jerusalem and inculcated these communistic ideals, whose actuality they transposed into the past (as was the custom in that period), namely into the primitive community in Jerusalem.

Thus we are to believe that the educated imbued the proletarians with communism at a later time, when the practical image of communism had previously left them unmoved. It would require the very strongest of proofs to make this conception plausible; but what proofs there are, tend to the contrary. The more influence the educated have on Christianity, the further it gets from communism, as Matthew tells us and as we will later see in discussing the development of the community.

A. K. has entirely false notions of the Essenes. He says of the communistic Christian community of Jerusalem:

"It arouses our suspicions that this solitary communistic experiment was made precisely in a society consisting of Jews. Jews never made social experiments of this nature down to the beginning of our era; up to that time there was never a Jewish communism. Among the Greeks, however, theoretical and practical communism was nothing new."

Our critic does not let it be known where he finds the practical communism of the Hellenes at the time of Christ. But it is downright incredible that he should find less communism among the

Jews than among the Hellenes, when actually the Jews' communism with its practical realization rises far above the communistic dreams of the Greeks. And it is obvious that A. K. has no suspicion of the fact that the Essenes were already mentioned a century and a half before Christ; he seems to believe that they first arose in Christ's time!

Now these same Essenes, who are supposed to have had no influence on the practices of the Jerusalem community, are to have produced the communistic legend that found its way into the Acts of the Apostles in the second century after Christ. The Essenes, who disappear from view after the destruction of Jerusalem, probably because they were carried off in the fall of the Jewish commonwealth, are to have transmitted legends about the origin of the Christian community to the Hellenic proletarians and to have suggested a communist past to them, at a time when the opposition between Judaism and Christianity was already inflamed; and yet at the time when the Jewish proletarians in Jerusalem were founding an organization that must have had many personal and operational points of contact with Essenianism, they are not to have been influenced by it in the slightest!

It is quite possible that Essenian legends and conceptions too are woven into the beginnings of Christian literature; but it is much more probable that in the early stages of the Christian community, when it was not producing any literature, their organization was influenced by Essenian models. This can only have been an influence in the direction of putting a genuine communism into effect, not in the sense of the representation of a supposed communistic past that did not correspond to anything actually existing.

All this artificial construction, introduced by modern theologians and accepted by A. K., which denies the influence of the Essenes for a period when it existed, in order to claim for it a decisive role at a time when it had ceased to exist, shows only how inventive many a theological brain can be when it is a question of taking the "evil odor" of communism from the primitive church.

All this is not however what is decisive for A. K. He knows of a "main point," that has hitherto "never been noticed: The opponents of the Christians threw everything possible into their teeth, but not their communism. And yet they would not have overlooked this point of their indictment, if it had had a foundation." I am afraid that the world will not take this "main point" either into consideration. A. K. can not deny that the communistic character of Christianity is sharply stressed in many statements, both of the Acts of the Apostles and the Gospels. He merely asserts that these statements are purely legendary. But they were there, at any rate, and corresponded to actual Christian tendencies. Now if despite this the enemies of Christianity did not raise the objection of its communism, the reason can not be that they found no basis for such an accusation: for, they reproached the Christians for things like child murder and incest for which there was not the slightest justification in Christian literature. And they would refrain from accusations which they could confirm from the Christian writings from the earliest Christian literature!

That cause lies in the fact that ideas about communism were quite different at that time from what they are now.

Today communism in the primitive Christian sense, that is sharing, is irreconcilable with the progress of production, with the existence of society. Today, economic conditions definitely require the opposite of sharing, the concentration of wealth in a small number of places, whether in private hands, as today, or in the hands of society, the state, the communities, perhaps in cooperatives, as in the socialist system.

At the time of Christ matters were different. Apart from mining, what industry there was was on a petty scale. There was extensive production on a large scale in agriculture, but being worked by slaves it was not technically superior to the small farms and could sustain itself only in those cases where merciless predatory exploitation was possible, based on the labor power of hordes of cheap slaves. The large enterprise was not the basis of the whole mode of production as it is today.

Hence the concentration of wealth in a few hands did not by any means signify increased productivity of labor, let alone a basis for the productive process and so for social existence. Instead of constituting a development of the productive forces, it meant nothing more than accumulation of the means of pleasure in such quantity that the individual was simply unable to consume them all himself, and had no alternative to sharing them with others.

The wealthy did this on a large scale, in part willingly. Generosity was considered to be one of the principal virtues in the Roman Empire. It was a means of winning supporters and friends, and thus of increasing one's power.

"The emancipation [of slaves] was probably often accompanied by a more or less liberal gift. Martial mentions one of ten million sesterces, apparently on this sort of occasion. The Roman magnates extended their generosity and their protection to the families of their supporters and clients as well. Thus, a freedman of Cotta Messalinus, a friend of the Emperor Tiberius, says proudly in his epitaph, found on the Appian Way, that his patron had several times given him sums equal to the census of a knight [400,000 sesterces, or $20,000], had taken care of the education of his children, provided for his sons as a father would, helped his son Cottanus, who was serving in the army, to the position of military tribune, and had set up this gravestone for him himself."[4]

Many such cases occur. But in addition to voluntary generosity there was involuntary generosity, where democracy ruled. Anyone who sought public office had to purchase it by rich gifts to the people; in addition the people laid high taxes on the rich, and lived on the proceeds by using the public revenues for paying citizens for attending popular assemblies, and even public spectacles, or providing common meals or distributions of foodstuffs.

The idea that it was the function of the rich to share was not one which alarmed the mass of people or went against common notions. On the contrary, it attracted the masses rather than alienated them. The enemies of Christianity would have been fools to stress this side of it. We need only look at the respect with which writers as conservative as Josephus and Philo speak of the

4. Friedländer, *Sittengeschichte Roms,* I, p. 111.

Essenes' communism. It does not seem to them to be either unnatural or preposterous, but very noble.

The "main objection" of A.K. against primitive Christian communism, namely that it was not assailed by its enemies, proves merely that he looks at the past with the eyes of modern capitalist society, not with the eyes of the past.

Along with these objections, which are not supported by any evidence, but are mere "constructions," A.K. makes a number of other reservations which are based on facts related in the Acts of the Apostles. It is remarkable that our critic, who is so skeptical with respect to descriptions of persistent conditions in primitive Christian literature, takes every account of an isolated event at face value. It is almost as though he wanted to explain the descriptions of social conditions of the Heroic Age in the Odyssey as fabrications, but accept Polyphemus and Circe as historical personages, who really did what is related of them.

But in any case these single facts prove nothing against the communism of the primitive community.

The first point A.K. makes is that the community in Jerusalem is supposed to have been 5000 strong. How could such a throng, including women and children, make up a single family?

But who says that they made a single family, eating at a single table? And who would take his oath that the primitive community really was five thousand strong, as the Acts of the Apostles says (IV, 4). Statistics were not the strong point of ancient literature, least of all in the Orient; exaggeration for the sake of an effect was a favorite procedure.

The exact figure of five thousand is often given when it is desired to indicate a great throng. Thus the gospels know with precision that there were five thousand men, "beside women and children" (Matthew 14, verse 21), that Jesus fed with five loaves. Is my critic willing to swear in this case too that the figures are exact?

Actually, we have every reason to consider the number of five thousand members of the primitive community as exaggerated. Soon after Jesus' death Peter, according to Acts, makes a fiery agitational speech, and three thousand have themselves baptised on the spot (2, 41). Further exhortation makes many more believe, and now the number is five thousand (4, 4,). How large then was the community when Jesus died? Immediately after his death there was a gathering and "the number of names together were about an hundred and twenty." (1, verse 15).

This indicates that the community was very small at the beginning, despite the most intense propaganda by Jesus and his apostles. And now after his death are we to say that the community suddenly grew from something over a hundred to five thousand, because of a couple of speeches? If we have to take any definite number, the first would be much more likely than the second.

Five thousand organized members would have been something very striking in Jerusalem, and Josephus would certainly have taken notice of something so powerful. The community must have been quite insignificant as a matter of fact for all its contemporaries to have let it pass unnoticed.

A.K. makes a further objection: After describing the communism of the community, Acts continues: "And Joses, who by the apostles was surnamed Barnabas, (which is, being interpreted, The son of consolation), a Levite, and of the country of Cyprus, having land, sold it, and brought the money, and laid it at the apostles' feet. But a certain man named Ananias, with Sapphira his wife, sold a possession, and kept back part of the price, his wife also being privy to it, and laid it at the apostles' feet" (chapters 4 to 5).

This is supposed to be testimony against communism, for, A. K. holds, Barnabas would not have been picked out for mention if all the members had sold their goods and brought the money to the apostles.

A. K. forgets that Barnabas is contrasted with Ananias here, an example of how to act. This brings out the communistic requirement even more clearly. Should the Acts of the Apostles name every one who sold his property? We do not know why Barnabas is singled out, but that emphasizing him means to say that he was the only one that practiced communism—that is really having too low an opinion of the authors of Acts. The example of Barnabas comes directly after the account of how all that owned anything sold it. If Barnabas is named particularly, that may be because he was a favorite figure of the authors, who often mention him later. Perhaps also because only his name was handed down along with that of Ananias. After all, these two may have been the only members of the primitive community who had something to sell, the others being all proletarians.

The third objection rests on the fact that in Acts 6, verses 1 f., it is said: "And in those days, when the number of the disciples was multiplied, there arose a murmuring of the Grecians against the Hebrews, because their widows were neglected in the daily ministrations."

"Is this possible in a thorough-going communism?" asks A. K. indignantly.

But who says that in putting communism into operation there were no difficulties, or even that there could be no difficulties? The account goes on, not to say that communism was abandoned, but that the organization was improved by introducing the division of labor. From then on the Apostles were concerned only with propaganda, and a committee of seven was chosen for the economic functions of the community.

The whole account is in excellent accord with the assumption of communism, but is meaningless if we accept the view of our critic, which he borrows from Holtzmann, that the primitive Christians did not differ from their Jewish fellow citizens in their social organization, but only in their faith in the "recently executed Nazarene."

What was the point of the complaints about the division, if there was no sharing?

Again: "In chapter 12 [of Acts] it is said, in strict contradiction to the report of communism, that a certain Mary, a member of the group, lived in a house of her own."

That is correct, but how does A. K. know that she had the right to sell the house? May not her husband have been alive, and not a member of the community? And anyway, even if she was allowed to sell the house, the community might not have been helped thereby. This house was the place where the comrades assembled. Mary had put it at the disposition of the community, and they used it, even though it may have belonged to Mary in the legal sense. It is not evidence against the existence of communism that the community used places of assembly, that it was not a juristic person that could acquire such premises, that hence individual members formally owned them. We can not ascribe such a senseless spirit of routine to primitive Christian communism as to require that the community should have put those houses of its members up for sale, and divided up the proceeds, when they were needed for use.

Finally, and as the last objection, there is the point that communism is reported as applied only with respect to the Jerusalem community, and that nothing is said about the other Christian communities. We shall have more to say on this when we come to the further development of the Christian communities. We shall see whether, and how far, and for how long, communism was practiced. That is a separate question. It has already been suggested that the large city created difficulties which did not exist in agricultural communities such as the Essenes, for instance.

Here we are dealing only with the original, communistic tendencies of Christianity; and there is not the slightest reason for doubting them. They are attested to by the testimony of the New Testament, by the proletarian nature of the community, by the strong communistic element in the proletarian part of Judaism in the last two centries before the destruction of Jerusalem, so strongly expressed in Essianism.

What is alleged against it are misunderstandings, subterfuges and empty constructions without any support in reality.

CONTEMPT FOR LABOR

The communism to which primitive Christianity aspired, in accord with the conditions of its period, was a communism of the means of consumption, a communism of sharing them and eating them in common. Applied to agriculture, this communism could have led to a communism of production, planned work in com-

mon. In the metropolis under the conditions of production at that
time, the proletarians were kept apart by their occupations,
whether those were handicrafts or begging. Urban communism
could not aim any higher than intensifying the process of bleeding the rich by the poor, which the proletariat had developed to
such a pitch of perfection in the cities where it had achieved political power, as in Athens and Rome. The communalism it aimed
at could not go beyond common consumption of the victuals thus
obtained, a communism of housekeeping, a family community. As
we have seen, Chrysostom discusses it from this point of view
solely. He does not care who is to produce the wealth that is to
be consumed in common. The same attitude is to be found in
primitive Christianity. The Gospels have Jesus discuss everything
under the sun, but not work. Or rather, when he does speak of it,
it is in the most disdainful manner. Thus he says, in Luke (12,
verses 22 f.):

"Take no thought for your life, what ye shall eat; neither for
the body, what ye shall put on. The life is more than meat, and
the body is more than raiment. Consider the ravens: for they
neither sow nor reap; which neither have storehouse nor barn;
and God feedeth them: how much more are ye better than the
fowls? And which of you with taking thought can add to his
stature one cubit? If ye then be not able to do that thing which is
least, why take ye thought for the rest? Consider the lilies how
they grow: they toil not, they spin not; and yet I say unto you,
that Solomon in all his glory was not arrayed like one of these. If
then God so clothe the grass, which is today in the field, and
tomorrow is cast into the oven; how much more will he clothe
you, O ye of little faith! And seek not what ye shall eat, or what
ye shall drink, neither be ye of doubtful mind. For all these things
do the nations of the world seek after: and your Father knoweth
that ye have need of these things. But rather seek ye the kingdom
of God; and all these things shall be added unto you. Fear not,
little flock; for it is your Father's good pleasure to give you the
kingdom. Sell that ye have, and give alms."

Here the theme is not that the Christians should not worry

about eating and drinking on ascetic grounds, because he should care only for the weal of his soul. No, the Christians should seek the kingdom of God, that is their own kingdom, and then everything they need will come to them. We shall see how earthy was their conception of the "kingdom of God."

DESTRUCTION OF THE FAMILY

If communism does not rest on community of production, but of consumption, it tries to convert its community into a new family, for the presence of the traditional family tie is felt as a disturbing influence. We have seen this in the case of the Essenes, and it is repeated in Christianity, which often voices its hostility to the family in harsh terms.

Thus the gospel attributed to Mark says (3, verses 31 f.): "There came then his [Jesus'] brethren and his mother, and, standing without, sent unto him, calling him. And the multitude sat about him, and they said unto him, Behold, thy mother and thy brethren without seek for thee. And he answered them, saying, Who is my mother, or my brethren? And he looked round about on them which sat around him, and said, Behold my mother and my brethren! For whosoever shall do the will of God, the same is my brother, and my sister, and mother."

Luke is particularly harsh in this point too. He says (9, verses 59 f.): "And he [Jesus] said unto another, Follow me. But he said, Lord, suffer me first to go and bury my father. Jesus said unto him, Let the dead bury their dead; but go thou and preach the kingdom of God. And another also said, Lord, I will follow thee; but let me first go bid them farewell, which are at home at my house. And Jesus said unto him, No man, having put his hand to the plough, and looking back, is fit for the kingdom of God."

This demands extreme disregard for the family, but the following passage from Luke breathes direct hatred of the family (14, verse 26): "If any man come to me, and hate not his father, and mother, and wife, and children, and brethren, and sisters, yea, and his own life also, he cannot be my disciple."

Here too Matthew shows himself an opportunistic revisionist. He gives the foregoing sentence the following form (10, verse 37: "He that loveth father or mother more than me is not worthy of me: and he that loveth son or daughter more than me is not worthy of me." The hatred of the family is toned down here.

A closely related theme is the aversion to marriage, which primitive Christianity required as did the Essenians. The resemblance goes so far that it seems to have developed both forms of being unmarried: celibacy, abstinence from all marital practices, and unbridled extra-marital sexual intercourse, which is also described as community of women.

There is a noteworthy passage in Campanella's *City of the Sun*. A critic says: "St. Clement of Rome says that by apostolic institutions wives too should be in common, and praises Plato and Socrates for having also said that this must be done. But the commentary takes this to mean community of obedience towards all, not the community of the couch. And Tertullian confirms the gloss, and says that the first Christians had everything in common, excepting the women, who were in common only in obedience." This community "in obedience" reminds one strongly of the blessedness of the poor "in spirit."

Peculiar sexual relations are indicated by a passage in the *Doctrine of the Twelve Apostles* or *Didache,* one of the oldest books of Christianity, from which we can see its organization in the second century. It says (XII, 11):

"But every prophet, tried and true, who acts with a view to the earthly secret of the church, yet does not preach that all should do as he does, shall not be judged by you, for he has his judgment in God; for just so did the old [Christian] prophets act."

Harnack comments on these obscure words that the "earthly secret of the church" is marriage. The aim is to counteract the mistrust of the communities towards such prophets, who practiced strange sorts of marriage. Harnack conjectures that these lived in marriage like eunuchs or treated their wives as sisters. It is hard to conceive that such restraint would have aroused scandal. It would be different if these prophets did not merely preach sexual intercourse without marriage but practiced it "like the old prophets," that is, the first teachers of Christianity.

Harnack himself cites as a "good illustration of acting with a view to the earthly secret of the church" the following passage from the letter on virginity, falsely attributed to Clement (I, 10): "Many shameless people live together with virgins under the pretense of piety and so fall into danger, or they go out alone with them on paths and in solitary places, in ways that are full of dangers and scandals, snares and pitfalls. . . . Others again eat and drink with them, reclining at table, with virgins and consecrated women (sacratis), in the midst of pride and ease and much shamefulness; yet such things should not be among believers, and least of all among those who have chosen the virgin state for themselves."

In the first letter of Paul to the Corinthians the apostles, who are pledged to remain unmarried, claim the right to roam freely through the world with ladies. Paul cries out: "Am I not free? . . . Have we not power to lead about a sister, a wife, as well as other apostles, and as the brethren of the Lord, and Cephas [Peter]?" (I Corinthians 9, verses 1 and 5).

This comes immediately after Paul has advised against marriage.

This going about of the apostles with young ladies plays a great role in the *Acts of Paul*, a romance which according to Tertullian was written by a presbyter in Asia Minor, during the second century, as he himself confessed. None the less, "these Acts were for a long time a favorite book of edification,"[5] a sign that the facts related in it did not scandalize many pious Christians, but seemed highly edifying to them. The most remarkable thing in it is the "pretty legend of Thecla . . . which gives an excellent picture of feeling in the Christian world of the second century."

This legend tells how Thecla, the betrothed of a noble youth in Icarium, heard Paul speak and immediately became an admirer of his. In the course of the tale we get a description of the apostle: small stature, bald head, crooked legs, projecting knees,

5. Pfleiderer, *Urchristentum,* II, p. 171 f.

big eyes, eyebrows grown together, longish nose, full of charm, looking sometimes like a man and sometimes like an angel. Unfortunately we are not told which of these features is classified as angelic.

In any case, the magic power of his words makes a deep impression on the beautiful Thecla and she leaves her betrothed, who accuses Paul before the governor as a man who induces women and youths to withdraw from marriage; Paul is thrown into prison, but Thecla gets to see him and is found in prison with him. The governor sentences Paul to be banished from the city and Thecla to be burned. A miracle saves her; the burning pyre is extinguished by a rainstorm, which also drives away the spectators.

Thecla is free and goes after Paul, finding him on the road. He takes her by the hand and goes with her to Antioch. There they encounter a nobleman who falls in love with Thecla at once and seeks to take her from Paul, offering a large sum as compensation. Paul answers that she is not his and he does not know her, a timid answer indeed for so proud a confessor. Thecla however defends herself vigorously against the dissolute aristocrat, who tries to obtain her by force. She is therefore cast to the wild beasts in the circus, who will not harm her, and so once more she goes free. She now puts on men's clothing, cuts off her hair and wanders off again after Paul, who directs her to preach the word of God, and probably gives her the right to baptize, to judge by a comment of Tertullian's.

Obviously the original form of this tale contained much that scandalized the later church; "but since these acts were found edifying and instructive in other respects, they made it do by means of a clerical revision that excised the most objectionable parts without however eliminating all traces of its original character" (Pfleiderer, *op. cit.*, p. 179). But although much of the data may have been lost, the hints that have come through suffice to attest very peculiar sexual relations, quite at variance with traditional rules, that caused great scandal and hence needed to be energetically defended by the Apostles: relations that the later church, turned responsible, sought to palliate so far as it could.

How easy it is for celibacy to go over into extra-marital sexual intercourse, except in the case of fanatical ascetics, needs no elaboration.

The Christians expected marriage to come to an end in their future state, which would be inaugurated at the resurrection; this is shown by the passage in which Jesus has to answer the ticklish question as to who will be a woman's husband after the resurrection if she has had seven on earth, one after the other:

"And Jesus answering said unto them, the children of this world marry, and are given in marriage: But they which shall be accounted worthy to obtain that world, and the resurrection from the dead, neither marry, nor are given in marriage: Neither can they die any more: for they are equal unto the angels; and are the children of God, being the children of the resurrection" (Luke 20, verses 34 to 36).

This should not be taken to mean that in the future state of the primitive Christians men would be pure spirits without bodily needs. Their corporeality and their delight in material pleasures is particularly stressed, as we shall see. At any rate, Jesus says here that in the future state all existing marriages will be dissolved, so that the question as to which of the seven husbands is the right one becomes academic.

It is not to be taken as a proof of hostility to marriage that the Roman bishop Callixtus (217-222) permitted maidens and widows of senatorial rank to have extra-marital intercourse even with slaves. This permission was not the product of a communism whose hostility to the family was carried to an extreme, but mere opportunistic revisionism, which by way of exception, in order to win rich and powerful supporters, makes concessions to their tastes.

Communistic tendencies constantly kept arising in the Christian church in opposition to this sort of revisionism, and they were often linked up with rejection of marriage, either in the form of celibacy or what is called community of women, as often among

Manichaeans and Gnostics. The most energetic of these were the Carpocratians.

"The divine justice, taught Epiphanes, the son of Carpocrates, gave everything to his creatures for equal possession and enjoyment. Human laws first brought thine and mine into the world, and along with them theft and adultery and all the other sins; as the apostle says, 'By the law is the knowledge of sin' (Romans 3, verse 20; 7, verse 7). Since God himself implanted the powerful sex drive in men for the conservation of the species, it would be ridiculous to prohibit sexual desire, and doubly ridiculous to prohibit coveting your neighbor's wife, which would make what is common into private property. According to these Gnostics, then, monogamy is just as much a violation of the community of women required by divine justice as the private ownership of property is a violation of the community of goods. . . . Clement concludes his description of these libertine Gnostics (Carpocratians and Nicholaites, a branch of the Simonians) with the remark that all these heresies may be divided into two tendencies: they either preach moral indifferentism or an overwrought sanctimonious abstention."[6]

Those were as a matter of fact the two alternatives of thorough-going housekeeping communism. We have already pointed out that the two extremes meet, that they rise from the same economic root, however discordant they may be in thought.

With the dissolution, or at least the loosening, of the traditional family ties a change in the position of woman must have taken place. If she ceased to be tied down to the narrow family housekeeping, she would get a feeling for and an interest in, other ideas outside the family. Depending on her temperament, talents and social position, she might now, along with family ties, get rid of all ethical thinking, all respect for social prohibitions, all discipline and shame. This was largely the case with the noble ladies of Imperial Rome, who were relieved of all family work by the size of their fortunes and artificial childlessness.

Conversely, the elimination of the family by housekeeping com-

6. Pfleiderer, *Urchristentum*, II, p. 113 f.

munism produced a marked rise of ethical feeling in the proletarian women which was now carried over from the narrow family
circle to the much broader sphere of the Christian community,
and rose from the selfless care for the daily needs of husband and
child, a concern for the freeing of the human race from all misery.

Thus at the beginning we find not only prophets but also
prophetesses active in the Christian community. For example, the
Acts of the Apostles tells us of Philip the "Evangelist," who "had
four daughters, virgins, which did prophesy" (21, verse 9).

The story of Thecla, whom Paul entrusts with preaching and
even baptism, probably, also indicates that the existence of female
teachers of the divine word was not at all unheard-of in the Christian community.

In the first Epistle to the Corinthians (chapter 11), Paul expressly conceded the right of women to appear as prophetesses.
He requires of them only that they keep their heads covered,—in
order not to excite the lust of the angels. The fourteenth chapter
it is true says (verses 34 f.): "Let your women keep silence in the
churches; for it is not permitted unto them to speak; but they are
commanded to be under obedience, as also saith the law. And if
they will learn any thing, let them ask their husbands at home:
for it is a shame for women to speak in the church."

But this passage is considered by modern textual critics to be
a later forgery. Likewise, the entire first letter of Paul to Timothy (together with the second one and the letter to Titus) is a
forgery of the second century. Here the woman is vigorously
forced back into the narrow realm of the family: "She shall be
saved in childbearing" (I Timothy 2, verse 15).

That was not at all the position of the primitive Christian community. Its notions of marriage, the family and the position of
women are in complete correspondence with what followed logically from the forms of communism that were possible at that
time, and are one proof more that this communism dominated
the thinking of early Christianity.

BOOK FOUR: THE BEGINNINGS
OF CHRISTIANITY

2

THE CHRISTIAN IDEA OF THE MESSIAH

THE COMING OF THE KINGDOM OF GOD

THE TITLE OF this chapter is redundant. We know that Christus is nothing more than the Greek word for Messiah. From the point of view of philology the Christian Idea of the Messiah is nothing but the messianic idea of the Messiah.

Considered historically, however, Christianity does not embrace all the believers in a Messiah, but only one variety among them, whose messianic expectations were at the beginning not very different from those of the rest of Judaism.

Above all, the community of Christians in Jerusalem, like the rest of the Jews, expected the coming of the Messiah in a foreseeable, though not precisely predictable, time. Although the gospels that have come down to us date from a period in which the majority of Christians were no longer so sanguine, when it was clear in fact that the expectation of Christ's contemporaries had gone completely astray, they still conserve some remnants of this expectation which they had taken over from the oral or written sources on which they drew.

According to Mark (1, verse 14) "Now after that John was put in prison, Jesus came into Galilee, preaching the gospel of the kingdom of God, And saying, The time is fulfilled, and the kingdom of God is at hand."

The disciples ask Jesus for the signs that will show that the

Messiah is coming. He cites them all, earthquakes, pestilence, the evils of war, eclipses of the sun, and so forth, and tells how the Son of man will come with power and great glory to save his faithful, and adds: "Verily I say unto you, This generation shall not pass away, till all shall be fulfilled" (Luke 21, verse 32).

Mark says the same (13, verse 30). In the ninth chapter of the same gospel Jesus is made to say: "But I tell you of a truth, there be some standing here, which shall not taste of death, till they see the kingdom of God."

Finally, in Matthew Jesus promises his disciples: "He that endureth to the end shall be saved. But when they persecute you in this city, flee ye into another: for verily I say unto you, Ye shall not have gone over the cities of Israel, till the Son of man be come" (10, verses 22 f.).

Paul speaks similarly in his first Epistle to the Thessalonians (4, verses 13 f.): "But I would not have you to be ignorant, brethren, concerning them which are asleep, that ye sorrow not, even as others which have no hope. For if we believe that Jesus died and rose again, even so them also which sleep in Jesus will God bring with him. For this we say unto you by the word of the Lord, that we which are alive and remain unto the coming of the Lord shall not prevent them which are asleep. For the Lord himself shall descend from Heaven with a shout, with the voice of the archangel, and with the trump of God: and the dead in Christ shall rise first: Then we which are alive and remain shall be caught up together with them in the clouds, to meet the Lord in the air: and so shall we ever be with the Lord."

Thus it was not at all necessary to have died in order to enter into the kingdom of God. The living could count on seeing its coming. And it was thought of as a kingdom in which both those who lived through it and those who arose from the dead would rejoice in full-bodied existence. There are still traces of it in the gospels, although the later conception of the church dropped the earthly state of the future and replaced it by a heavenly one.

So Jesus says in Matthew (19, verses 28 f.):

"Verily I say unto you, That ye which have followed me, in the regeneration when the Son of man shall sit in the throne of his glory, ye also shall sit upon twelve thrones, judging the twelve tribes of Israel. And every one that hath forsaken houses, or brethren, or sisters, or father, or mother, or wife, or children, or lands, for my name's sake, shall receive an hundredfold, and shall inherit everlasting life."

And so they are to be richly rewarded with earthly pleasures in the future state for having broken up their families and given up their property. These pleasures are thought of especially as those of the table.

Jesus threatens those that will not follow him with exclusion from the society on the day after the great catastrophe: "There shall be weeping and gnashing of teeth, when ye shall see Abraham, and Isaac, and Jacob, and all the prophets, in the kingdom of God, and you yourselves thrust out. And they shall come from the east, and from the west, and from the north, and from the south, and shall sit down [at table] in the kingdom of God" (Luke 13, verses 28 f.; cf. also Matthew 8, verses 11 f.).

But he promises the apostles: "And I appoint unto you a kingdom, as my Father hath appointed unto me; That ye may eat and drink at my table in my kingdom, and sit on thrones judging the twelve tribes of Israel." (Luke 22, verses 29 f.).

There are even disputes among the apostles over the order of precedence in the future state. James and John claim the places at the right and left of the master, and the others are displeased (Mark 10, verses 35 f.).

Jesus tells a Pharisee in whose house he is eating that he should not invite his friends nor kinsmen to table, but the poor, the maimed, the lame, the blind: "And thou shalt be blessed: for they cannot recompense thee: for thou shalt be recompensed at the resurrection of the just." We find out at once what this blessedness is: "And when one of them that sat at meat with him heard these things, he said unto him, Blessed is he that shall eat bread in the kingdom of God" (Luke 14, verse 15).

Drinking is done there too. At the Last Supper Jesus announces: "But I say unto you, I will not drink henceforth of this fruit of the vine, until that day when I drink it new with you in my Father's kingdom" (Matthew 26, verse 29).

The resurrection of Jesus is the model for the resurrection of his disciples. The gospels expressly stress Jesus' corporeality after the resurrection.

He meets two of his disciples then near the village of Emmaus. He sups with them and vanishes. "And they rose up the same hour, and returned to Jerusalem, and found the eleven gathered together, and them that were with them, Saying, The Lord is risen indeed, and hath appeared to Simon. And they told what things were done in the way, and how he was known of them in breaking of bread. And as they thus spake, Jesus himself stood in the midst of them, and saith unto them, Peace be unto you. But they were terrified and affrighted, and supposed that they had seen a spirit. And he said unto them, Why are ye troubled? and why do thoughts arise in your hearts? Behold my hands and my feet, that it is I myself: handle me and see; for a spirit hath not flesh and bones; as ye see me have. And when he had thus spoken, he showed them his hands and his feet. And while they yet believed not for joy, and wondered, he said unto them, Have ye here any meat? And they gave him a piece of a broiled fish, and of an honeycomb. And he took it, and did eat before them" (Luke 24, verses 33 f.).

In the Gospel according to St. John too Jesus shows not only corporeality after his resurrection, but a healthy appetite as well. John describes how Jesus appeared to the disciples, the doors being shut, and is touched by doubting Thomas, and then goes on:

"After these things Jesus showed himself again to the disciples at the sea of Tiberias; and on this wise showed he himself. There were together Simon Peter, and Thomas called Didymus, and Nathaniel of Cana in Galilee, and the sons of Zebedee, and two other of his disciples. Simon Peter saith unto them, I go a fishing. They say unto him, We also go with thee. They went forth, and entered into a ship immediately; and that night they caught nothing. But when the morning was now come, Jesus stood on the shore: but the disciples knew not that it was Jesus. Then Jesus saith unto them, Children, have ye any meat? They answered him, No. And he said unto them, Cast the net on the right side of the ship, and ye shall find. They cast therefore, and now they were not able to draw it for the multitude of fishes. Therefore that disciple whom Jesus loved saith unto Peter, it is the Lord. . . . As soon then as they were come to land, they saw a fire of coals there, and fish laid thereon, and bread. . . . Jesus saith unto them, Come and dine. . . . This is now the third time that Jesus showed himself to his disciples, after that he was risen from the dead" (John 21).

The third and last time. Perhaps it was after the refreshment of the fish breakfast that Jesus went to heaven in the fancy of the evangelist, thence to return as the Messiah.

Although the Christians held that the resurrected would arise in the flesh, they must have said to themselves those bodies must be of a different nature than the former ones, if only for the sake of the eternity of life. In an era that was as ignorant and credulous as that of the early Christians, it is no wonder that the most fantastic ideas came into Christian heads, just as they did into those of Jews.

Thus the first letter of Paul to the Corinthians develops the idea that those of his fellows who live until the future state, together with those who will be waked from the dead, will have a new and higher form of body:

"Behold, I show you a mystery: We shall not all sleep, but we shall all be changed, In a moment, in the twinkling of an eye, at the last trump: for the trumpet shall sound, and the dead shall be raised incorruptible, and we shall be changed" (15, verses 51 f.).

The Revelation of John even has two resurrections. The first takes place after the overthrow of Rome:

"And I saw thrones, and they sat upon them, and judgment was given unto them: and I saw the souls of them that were beheaded for the witness of Jesus, and for the word of God, . . . and they lived and reigned with Christ a thousand years. But the rest of the dead lived not again until the thousand years were finished.

This is the first resurrection. Blessed and holy is he that hath part in the first resurrection: on such the second death hath no power, but they shall be priests of God and of Christ, and shall reign with him a thousand years" (chap. 20).

Then however there is a rebellion of the peoples of the earth against these saints. The rebels are cast into a lake of fire and brimstone, and the dead, who now all arise, are judged; the unjust are cast into the lake of fire, the just will not know death any more but rejoice in their life in the new Jerusalem, to which the nations of the earth shall bring their glory and honor.

Here Jewish nationalism appears in a most naive form. As a matter of fact, as we have pointed out, the picture of John's Christian revelation is of Jewish origin, and arose at the time of the siege of Jerusalem.

After the fall of Jerusalem there were Jewish apocalypses with similar Messianic expectations, for example Baruch and the fourth book of Ezra.

Baruch announces that the Messiah will assemble the peoples and confer life on those that submit to the descendants of Jacob, and wipe out the others, who have oppressed Israel. Then he will ascend the throne, and eternal joy will reign, and nature will offer everything in profusion, especially wine. The dead will arise, and men will be differently organized. The just will no longer grow weary when they labor, their bodies will be changed into gleams of light, while the unjust will be even uglier than before, and given over to be tortured.

The author of the fourth book of Ezra expands on similar themes. The Messiah will come and live four hundred years, and then die with all of mankind. Then follows a general resurrection and judgment, the just shall have rest and sevenfold joy.

We see how little the Messianic expectations of the first Christians differed from the general Jewish hopes. The fourth book of Ezra also gained prestige in the Christian church, after numerous additions, and was included in many a Protestant translation of the Bible.

THE LINEAGE OF JESUS

The original Christian idea of the Messiah is so completely in accord with the Judaism of its time that the Gospels attach the greatest value to showing Jesus as a descendant of David. For, according to the Jewish notion, the Messiah should be of royal lineage. Over and over again he is spoken of as the "Son of David" or "Son of God," which in the Jewish system amounted to the same thing. Thus the second book of Samuel represents God as saying to David: "I will be his [your descendants'] father, and he shall be my son" (II Samuel 7, verse 14).

And in the second Psalm the king says: "The Lord hath said unto me, Thou art my Son: this day have I begotten thee."

This is why it was necessary to show that Jesus' father, Joseph, had a long pedigree going back to David, and to have Jesus the Nazarene born in Bethlehem, the city of David. The strangest statements are introduced to make this plausible. Early in the book we referred to the story in Luke (2, verse 1 f.):

"And it came to pass in those days, that there went out a decree from Caesar Augustus, that all the world should be taxed. (And this taxing was first made when Cyrenius was governor of Syria.) And all went to be taxed, every one into his own city. And Joseph also went up from Galilee, out of the city of Nazareth, into Judaea, unto the city of David; (because he was of the house and lineage of David:) To be taxed with Mary his espoused wife, being great with child."

The author or authors of Luke had heard an echo of something, and in their ignorance made complete nonsense of it.

Augustus never ordered a general census of the empire. What is referred to is obviously the census that Quirinius had taken in Judaea in the year 7 A.D., Judaea being then a Roman province. This was the first census of the sort there.

But this confusion is the least of it. What are we to say of the idea that in a general imperial census, or even in a provincial census everyone must go to his birthplace to be recorded. Even today, in the age of railroads, such a decree would lead to the most frightful confusion, only to be surpassed by its uselessness. As a

matter of fact every one registered in his dwelling-place in a
Roman census also, and only men had to do so in person.

But it would not have suited the pious purpose, if the worthy
Joseph had gone by himself to the city of David. And so, after
inventing the census, they have to invent the regulation that every
head of a household must go to his native place with his whole
tribe, so that Joseph would be forced to drag his wife along despite
her advanced state of pregnancy.

The whole labor of love was in vain, however, and actually
caused serious embarrassment for Christian thought as the community outgrew the Jewish framework. For the pagan world
David was a matter of complete indifference, and it was no particular recommendation to be a descendant of David. Hellenistic
and Roman thinking however was quite inclined to take seriously
the fatherhood of God, which to the Jews was merely a symbol of
royal descent. As we have seen, it was nothing unusual for Greeks
and Romans to regard a great man as the son of Apollo or some
other god.

Yet Christian thought encountered a slight difficulty in its effort
thus to raise the Messiah in the eyes of the heathen, namely, the
monotheism it had taken over from Judaism. The fact that a god
begets a son presents no difficulty to polytheism: there is just one
more god. But that God begets a god and there is still but one
God, that is something not easy to conceive. The question is not
made simpler by going on to separate the generating power that
emanated from the Deity as a separate Holy Ghost. All that was
needed was to get three persons under one hat. On this task the
most sweeping fantasy and acute hair-splitting were wrecked. The
Trinity became one of those mysteries that can be only believed,
not understood; one that had to be believed precisely because it
was absurd.

There is no religion without contradictions. None of them
arose in a single mind by a purely logical process; each one is the
product of manifold social influences, often going back centuries
and reflecting very diverse historical situations. But there is
hardly another religion so rich in contradictions and absurdities

as the Christian religion, since there was hardly another that grew out of such harsh contradictions: Christianity evolved from Judaism to Romanism, from proletarianism to world domination, from the organization of communism to organizing the exploitation of all classes.

Meanwhile the union of Father and Son in a single person was not the only difficulty for Christian thinking that arose out of the picture of the Messiah as soon as it came under the influence of the non-Jewish environment.

What was to be done about Joseph's fatherhood? Mary could now no longer have conceived Jesus by her husband. And since God had mated with her not as a man but as spirit, she must have remained a virgin. That was the end of Jesus' descent from David. Yet so great is the power of tradition in religion that despite everything the beautifully constructed pedigree of Joseph and Jesus' designation as Son of David continued to be handed down faithfully. Poor Joseph now had the thankless role of living with the Virgin without touching that virginity, and without being in the least disturbed by her pregnancy.

JESUS AS A REBEL

If the Christians in later times could not resign themselves to abandoning the royal descent of their Messiah, despite his divine origin, they were all the more eager to erase another mark of his Jewish birth: his rebelliousness.

From the second century on Christianity was more and more dominated by patient obedience. The Judaism of the previous century had been something quite different. We have seen how rebellious those strata of Jews were who were expecting the Messiah at that time, especially the proletarians of Jerusalem and the bands of Galilee, the same elements from which Christianity arose. The obvious assumption is that Christianity was violent in its beginnings. This assumption becomes a certainty when we see that the gospels still have traces of it despite the fact that their later revisers tried most desperately to eliminate everything from them that might give offense to the powerful.

Although Jesus usually appears as gentle and submissive, occasionally he says something of a quite different nature which suggests that whether he really existed or is only an imaginary, ideal figure, he lived as a rebel in the original tradition, one who was crucified for his unsuccessful uprising.

He occasionally speaks of legality in a striking manner: "I came not to call the righteous, but the sinners" (Mark 2, verse 17). The Authorized Version translates: "I came not to call the righteous, but sinners to repentance," and their manuscripts may have read so. The Christians early felt how dangerous it was for them to concede that Jesus called to himself just those groups that were against legality. Luke therefore added to the word "call" the phrase "to repentance" (*eis metanoian*), an addition which is also found in many manuscripts of Mark as well. But this addition leaves the sentence without any meaning. Who would ever think of calling the "just" (*dikaious*) to repentance? Moreover this contradicts the context, for Jesus uses the expression because he is reproached for eating and associating with men who were despised; he is not pictured as exhorting them to change their way of life. No one would have held "calling sinners to repentance" against him.

Bruno Bauer is correct in his interpretation of this passage:

"The saying in its original form simply ignores the question of whether the sinners actually do penance, hear the call and merit Heaven by obeying the preacher of repentance—instead, as sinners they are privileged as against legality—as sinners they are called to holiness, absolutely favored—the kingdom of Heaven is made for sinners, and the call that goes out to them merely puts them in possession of the rights they have as sinners."[7]

This passage signifies contempt of traditional law; but the words in which Jesus announces the coming of the Messiah point to violence: The existing Roman Empire will go down in fearful slaughter; and the saints should by no means play a passive role in it.

Jesus declares:

7. *Kritik der Evangelien und Geschichte ihres Ursprungs*, 1851, p. 248.

"I am come to send fire on the earth; and what will I, if it be already kindled? But I have a baptism to be baptized with; and how am I straitened till it be accomplished! Suppose ye that I am come to give peace on earth? I tell you, Nay; but rather division: For from henceforth there shall be five in one house divided, three against two, and two against three" (Luke 12, verses 49 f.).

In Matthew it runs directly:

"Think not that I am come to send peace on earth: I came not to send peace, but a sword" (10, verse 34).

Arriving in Jerusalem at Eastertide, he drives the money-changers out of the temple, something that is inconceivable without the forcible action of a large mob excited by him.

Shortly thereafter, at the Last Supper, just before the catastrophe, Jesus says to his disciples:

"But now, he that hath a purse, let him take it, and likewise his scrip; and he that hath no sword, let him sell his garment, and buy one. For I say unto you, that this that is written must yet be accomplished in me, And he was reckoned among the transgressors (anomōn): for the things concerning me have an end. And they said, Lord, behold, here are two swords. And he said unto them, It is enough" (Luke 22, verses 35 f.).

Immediately after this, they come up against the armed power of the state on the Mount of Olives. Jesus is about to be arrested.

"When they which were about him saw what would follow, they said unto him, Lord, shall we smite with the sword? And one of them smote the servant of the high priest, and cut off his right ear" (Luke 22, verses 49 f.).

However, Jesus, according to the Gospel story, is against all bloodshed, lets himself be fettered and executed without resistance, while his comrades are not molested at all.

In the form just given this is a very strange story, full of contradictions, and originally it must have run quite differently.

Jesus calls for swords, as though the hour of action had come; his faithful followers go out armed with swords—and when they meet the enemy and draw their swords, Jesus suddenly declares that he is against any use of force, on principle—naturally, most sharply in Matthew:

"Put up again thy sword into his place: for all they that take the sword shall perish with the sword. Thinkest thou that I cannot now pray to my Father, and he shall presently give me more than twelve legions of angels? But how then shall the scriptures be fulfilled . . . ?" (26, verses 52 f.)

Now if Jesus had been against all violence altogether, why should he have called for swords? Why did he direct his friends to go along with him carrying arms?

This contradiction becomes intelligible only if we assume that the Christian tradition originally told of a planned *coup de main* in the course of which Jesus was taken prisoner, a bold stroke for which the time seemed to be ripe after the driving of the money-changers from the temple had been successful. The later editors did not dare simply to do away with this story, whose roots went deep; instead, they blunted its point, reducing the use of force to an act attempted by the apostles against Jesus' will.

It may not be without significance that the clash took place on the Mount of Olives. That was the best place from which to make an attempt on Jerusalem.

We may remember the account of Josephus about the plot of an Egyptian Jew under the procurator Felix (52 to 60 A.D.).

This man came out of the desert with a force of 30,000 and went up the Mount of Olives in order to fall on the city of Jerusalem, expel the Roman garrison and become ruler. Felix engaged the Egyptian in battle and dispersed his followers. The leader himself succeeded in escaping.

The history of Josephus is full of similar occurrences. They show the state of mind of the Jewish population at the time of Christ. An attempted putsch by the Galilean prophet Jesus would be fully in accord with it.

If we think of his undertaking as such an attempt, the treason of Judas becomes understandable as well, intertwined as it is with this questionable account.

In the version that has come down to us, Judas betrays Jesus by his kiss, which points him out to the police as the man to arrest. Now that is a senseless way to act. According to the Gospels, Jesus was well known in Jerusalem; he preached in public day in and day out, and was received by the masses with jubilation; and now he is to have been so unknown that he had to be pointed out by Judas to be distinguished from the crowd of his supporters! That would be a good deal like having the Berlin police pay an informer to indicate the person called Bebel.[8]

It would be an entirely different matter if it was a question of a plotted coup d'etat. In that case there would be something to betray, a secret worth paying for. If the plot and the coup d'etat were eliminated from the story, the account of Judas' treason would be to no purpose. Since the betrayal was obviously too well known among the comrades and the bitterness against the traitor too strong, it would not do for the evangelist to pass over this circumstance. He had to construct a new betrayal out of his imagination, however, and did not succeed very well.

The capture of Jesus is just as unhappy an invention as the present version of the betrayal by Judas. The man who is arrested is precisely the one who preaches the peaceful way, while the apostles, who drew their swords and smote, are not molested in the least. Indeed Peter, who cut off the ear of Malchus, follows the constables and calmly sits down among them in the courtyard of the high priest and chats with them. Imagine a man who resists the arrest of a comrade with force, fires a revolver and wounds a policeman and then peacefully accompanies the forces of the law to the station-house to get warm and drink a glass of beer with them!

It would be hard to invent anything more absurd. But it is this absurdity that shows there was something here to be covered up at any cost, and so a likely and easily understandable action, an encounter that ended in defeat and the capture of its leader, through the treason of Judas, became an incomprehensible and

8. Note: this is a reference to August Bebel, a leading socialist in Germany during the period in which this book was written.

senseless event that takes place only in order that "the scriptures
be fulfilled."

The execution of Jesus, which is easy to understand if he was
a rebel, is an unintelligible act of sheer malice, which gets its
way even against the will of the Roman governor, who wants to
release Jesus. That is an accumulation of inconsistencies that
can only be explained by the need of the later revisers not to let
the actual events be known.

That was a period in which even the peaceful Essenes, who were
against any struggle, were carried away by the general patriotism.
We find Essenes among the Jewish generals in the last great war
against the Romans. Thus for example Josephus tells of the beginning of the war:

"The Jews had chosen three mighty generals, who were not
only gifted with bodily strength and courage, but also endowed
with understanding and wisdom, Niger from Peraea, Sylas from
Babylon and John the Essene."[9]

The conjecture that the execution of Jesus was brought about
by his rebellion is therefore not merely the only assumption that
makes the allusions in the Gospels intelligible, but it is also
completely in accordance with the nature of the time and the
place. From the time in which the death of Jesus is set down to
the destruction of Jerusalem, disorders never ceased there. Street
fighting was something quite usual, and so was the execution of
individual insurgents. Such a street fight on the part of a small
group of proletarians, and the consequent crucifixion of their
ringleader, who came from eternally rebellious Galilee, could
very well have made a deep impression on the survivors who had
taken part in it, without obliging historians to take notice of such
an everyday occurrence.

Given the mutinous excitement that was sweeping throughout
all Jewry in that era, the sect that arose out of this attempted
revolt would gain a propaganda advantage by emphasizing it, so
that it would become fixed in tradition and in the process particularly exaggerate and ornament the person of Jesus, its hero.

9. *Jewish War*, III, 2, 1.

The situation changed however once Jerusalem was destroyed. With the Jewish community the last trace of democratic opposition disappeared in the Roman Empire. At about the same time the civil wars among the Romans ended as well.

In the two centuries from the Maccabees to the destruction of Jerusalem by Titus the Eastern Mediterranean basin had been in a state of constant unrest. One regime after another fell; one nation after another lost its independence or its dominant position. The power that directly or indirectly brought about all these revolutions, the Roman commonwealth, was torn by the stormiest inner disorders during this period, from the Gracchi to Vespasian, disorders which more and more emanated from the armies and their generals.

This was a period in which the expectation of a Messiah developed and solidified; during it no political organization seemed permanent; all of them seemed merely provisional, while political revolution was the inevitable, always to be expected. All that ended with Vespasian. Under him the military monarchy finally got the financial system the Emperor needed in order to make any competition impossible, that is, any purchase of the soldiers' favor by a competitor; and with this the source of the military rebellions was dried up for a long time.

Thus began the "golden age" of the Empire, a general state of internal peace that lasted over a hundred years, from Vespasian (69) to Commodus (180). Unrest had been the rule for the previous two hundred years; in this century quiet was the rule. Political changes, which had been the normal thing, now became abnormal. Submission to the imperial power, patient obedience, now seemed not merely a counsel of prudence for cowards, but struck deep root as a moral obligation.

This naturally had its effect on the Christian community. They could have no more use for the Messiah of rebellion, since he had suited Jewish thinking. Their very moral thinking rose up against that. Yet since they had become accustomed to worship Jesus as their God, the epitome of all the virtues, the change did not take place by dropping the person of the rebellious Jesus and replacing it by the ideal picture of a different personality better suited to the new condition; instead, the Christian community kept removing everything rebellious from the picture of the god Jesus and changed the rebellious Jesus into a suffering one who was put to death not because of an uprising but only because of his infinite goodness and holiness, by means of the wickedness of the insidious and invidious.

Fortunately this retouching was done so clumsily that traces of the original colors can still be seen, and from them the whole picture can be inferred. It is because these remains do not fit in with the later revisions that it is safe to assume that they are part of an earlier, genuine account.

In this connection, as in others we have so far studied, the picture of the Messiah in the early Christian community was in full conformity with the original Jewish idea. It was only the later Christian community that began to depart from it. There are however two points in which the Messiah picture of the Christian community diverged sharply from the Jewish Messiah from the very beginning.

THE RESURRECTION OF THE CRUCIFIED

There was no shortage of Messiahs at the time of Christ, especially not in Galilee, where prophets and leaders of bands were constantly springing up, proclaiming themselves to be saviors and anointed of the Lord. But if one of them was defeated by the power of the Romans, was taken, crucified or slain, that put an end to his role as the Messiah, for in that case he was regarded as a false prophet and false Messiah. The real one was still to come.

The Christian community clung to its champion. For it too, it is true, the Messiah was still to come in his glory, but the Messiah to come was no other than the one who had come, the crucified one who had arisen three days after his death and ascended into Heaven after revealing himself to his following.

This conception was peculiar to the Christian community. Whence had it come?

In the primitive Christian view it was the miracle of Jesus' resurrection on the third day after his crucifixion that proved his divine nature and justified the expectation of his return from Heaven. That is as far as the theologians have got even today. Of course the "freethinkers" among them no longer take the resurrection literally. According to them, Jesus did not actually arise, but his disciples believed they had seen him in ecstatic raptures after his death, and inferred from that his divine nature:

"Just as Paul saw the heavenly vision of Christ on the road to Damascus in a momentary ecstatic vision, we must think of the appearance of Christ, first revealed to Peter, in the same light—a spiritual experience that is not to be thought of as an unintelligible miracle, but as something that is to be explained psychologically in accordance with many analogies from all eras. . . . But from various analogies we find it quite understandable that this experience of inspired intuition did not remain confined to Peter alone, but was soon repeated in other disciples, and even in whole assemblies of the faithful. . . . Thus we find the historical basis of the disciples' belief in the resurrection in the ecstatic and visionary experiences undergone by individuals at first and then gaining conviction among all, experiences in which they believed they saw their crucified master living and elevated in heavenly majesty. Fancy, at home in the world of wonders, wove the fabric and the soul filled it out and moved it. The motive force of this resurrection of Jesus in their faith was at bottom nothing but the ineradicable impression his personality had made on them: their love and confidence in him was stronger than death. This miracle of love, and not a miracle of omnipotence, was the basis of the faith in resurrection of the primitive community's faith in resurrection. However, it went beyond passing feelings of excitement, and the newly-awakened inspired faith went on to action; the disciples saw it as their calling to bring the tidings to their countrymen that the Jesus of Nazareth whom they had delivered into the hands of the enemy had been the Messiah, now first made so by God through his resurrection and ascension to Heaven, from whence he would soon return to inaugurate his Messianic glory on earth."[10]

According to this, we should attribute the spread of the Messiah belief of the primitive Christian community, and hence all the enormous historical phenomenon of Christianity to the accidental hallucination of a single little man.

It is by no means impossible that one of the apostles had a vision of the crucified one. It is possible too that this vision found believers, since the period was an exceptionally credulous one and Judaism was deeply permeated by the belief in resurrection. Wakings from the dead were not considered as something incomprehensible; we may add examples to those we have previously given.

In Matthew, Jesus prescribes activities for the apostles: "Heal the sick, cleanse the lepers, raise the dead, cast out devils" (10, verse 8). Raising the dead is quite prosaically presented as the daily occupation of the apostles, along with healing the sick. The warning is added that they should not take money for their services. Jesus, or rather the author of the gospel, therefore considers it possible to engage in raising the dead for pay, as an occupation.

The description of the resurrection is characteristic. The grave of Jesus is guarded by soldiers so that the disciples should not steal the corpse and spread the tale that he had risen again. But in the midst of lightnings and earthquakes the stone is rolled from the grave and Jesus arises.

"Some of the watch came into the city, and showed unto the chief priests all the things that were done. And when they were assembled with the elders, and had taken counsel, they gave large money unto the soldiers, Saying, Say ye, His disciples came by night, and stole him away while we slept. And if this come to the governor's ears, we will persuade him, and secure you. So they took the money, and did as they were taught: and this saying is commonly reported among the Jews until this day" (28, verses 11 f.)

10. O. Pfleiderer, *Die Entstehung des Christentums*, 1907, p. 112 f.

These Christians thus had the idea that the resurrection of a man who had been dead and buried for three days could make so slight an impression on the eyewitnesses that a good gratuity would be enough, not merely to keep their mouths closed forever, but to get them to spread the opposite of the truth. It may be taken for granted that the authors of such views as are expressed in the Gospels believed in the tale of the resurrection without questioning it.

But that is not the end of the story. This credulousness and confidence in the possibility of resurrection was not peculiar to the Christian communities. It was something they had in common with all the Jewry of the time, to the extent that Judaism expected the Messiah. Why was it the Christians alone who had the vision of the resurrection of their Messiah? Why did it not come to any supporter of one of the other Messiahs that suffered the death of the martyr in that period?

Our theologians will rejoin that the fact is to be attributed to the especially deep impression made by the personality of Jesus, an impression produced by none of the other Messiahs. Against this there is the circumstance that Jesus' activity, which by all accounts lasted only a short time, passed unnoticed by the masses, so that no contemporary took note of it. Other Messiahs, on the contrary, fought the Romans a long time and occasionally won great victories against them, which were recorded in history. Would these Messiahs have made less of an impression? But let us assume that Jesus could not attract the masses, but that the force of his personality left ineradicable memories among his few adherents. That would explain at most why the belief in Jesus lived on in his personal friends, but not why it had propaganda power among people who had not known him and on whom his personality could not have any effect. If it had been only the personal impression made by Jesus that produced the faith in his resurrection and his divine mission, this faith would have had to grow weaker as personal memories of him faded and the ranks of those who had known him personally became thinner.

Posterity, we know, weaves no garlands for the mime; but in

this as in other points the player and the parson have much in common. What is true for the actor can be said of the preacher as well, if he limits himself to preaching and works only through his personality and leaves no works behind him which outlast his person. No matter how moving or elevating his sermons may be, they cannot have the same effect on people that do not hear them and know of them only by hearsay. His person will leave them cold; it will not touch their fancy.

No one leaves the memory of his personality beyond the circle of those who knew him personally, unless he leaves some creation that is impressive apart from his personality, an art work like a building, a picture, a piece of music, or a poem; or a scientific achievement, an ordered collection of materials, a theory, an invention or discovery; or a political or social institution or organization of some kind that he called into being or in whose creation and erection he had a prominent part.

So long as such a work lasts and operates, interest in the personality of its creator will last. Indeed, if such a creation goes unnoticed in his lifetime, and grows in significance after his death, as is often the case for discoveries, inventions and organizations, it is possible for the interest in the creator of the work to begin only after his death and keep growing. The less attention was paid to him during his life, the less that is known of his personality, the more the imagination is aroused; and if his work is a powerful one, the greater the crown of anecdotes and legends that will be spun around it. Man's need for causes, which seeks in every social event—and originally in every natural event— for an active person who brought it about, is so great that it tends to make men invent an originator for any production of great importance, or to connect it with some traditional name if the real originator is forgotten or if, as often happens, the discovery is the product of the united powers of so many men, no one standing out beyond the others, that it would have been utterly impossible to name one definite orginator.

The reason why the Messianic career of Jesus did not end in the same way as those of the Judases and Theudases and other

Messiahs of the period is not his personality, but in the handiwork that is linked with his name. Fanatical confidence in the personality of the prophet, thirst for miracles, ecstasy, belief in the resurrection—all these are to be found among the adherents of the other Messiahs as well as among those of Jesus. The reason for singling out one of them can not lie in what they all have in common. Theologians, even the most freethinking of them, are never very far from the assumption that even if we have to give up all the miracles that are related of Jesus, he himself still remains a miracle, a superman whose like the world has not seen; but we cannot accept this miracle. In that case however the only difference that remains between Jesus and the other Messiahs is that the others did not leave anything behind in which their personalities lived on, while Jesus bequeathed an organisation with institutions excellently adapted to holding his adherents together and attracting new ones.

The other Messiahs merely gathered bands together for an uprising; if defeated the bands scattered. If Jesus had not done anything more than that, his name would have disappeared without leaving a trace after he had been nailed to the cross. But Jesus was not merely a rebel; he was also the representative and champion, and perhaps the founder, of an organization that survived him and kept growing stronger and more powerful.

The traditional assumption has been that the community of Christ was not organized by the apostles until after his death. But nothing compels us to make this improbable assumption, no less an assumption than that immediately after the death of Jesus his adherents introduced something entirely new into his doctrine, something he had not considered and willed; and that people who had hitherto been unorganized entered into an organization he had never intended, and that right at the moment of a defeat that was capable of breaking up a solid organization. Judging by the analogy of similar organizations whose beginnings are better known, it would be closer to the truth to assume that communistic mutual aid societies of the proletarians of Jerusalem with Messianic overtones had existed before Jesus, and that a bold agitator and rebel of this name from Galilee was only their most outstanding champion and martyr.

According to John the twelve apostles had a common purse even in Jesus' lifetime. But Jesus requires that every other disciple as well contribute all his property.

The Acts of the Apostles nowhere states that the apostles first organized the community after the death of Jesus; we find it already organized at that time, holding meetings of its members and performing its functions. The first mention of communism in the Acts of the Apostles runs as follows: "And they continued steadfastly in the apostles' doctrine and fellowship, and in breaking of bread, and in prayers" (2, verse 42). That is, they continued their previous common meals and other communistic practices. If this had been newly introduced after the death of Jesus, the version would have to be quite different.

The communal organization was the link that kept Jesus' following together even after his death and preserved the memory of their crucified champion, who had proclaimed himself to be the Messiah, according to the tradition. The more the organization grew, and the more powerful it became, the more its martyrs must have occupied the imagination of the members, and the more they must have revolted at considering the crucified Messiah as false; the more too must they have felt themselves impelled to regard him as the genuine one, despite his death, as the Messiah that would come again in all his glory; the more they inclined to believe in his resurrection, and the more did faith in the Messianic nature of the crucified one and in his resurrection become the mark of the organization, setting it apart from the believers in other Messiahs. If the belief in the resurrection of the crucified Messiah had grown out of personal impression, it must have grown weaker and weaker with the passing of time, and tended to be replaced by other impressions, and finally disappeared with those who had known Jesus personally. But if the belief in the resurrection of him who was crucified stemmed from the effect that his organization produced, that belief would become stronger and more luxuriant as the organization grew; and the less positive information there was about the person of Jesus, the less the imagination of his worshippers would be hampered by definite facts.

It was not belief in the resurrection of him who was crucified that created the Christian community and lent it strength, but the converse: the vitality of the community created the belief in the continued life of their Messiah.

The doctrine of the crucified and resurrected Messiah did not contain anything that was irreconcilable with Jewish thought. We have seen how it was full of resurrectionary beliefs at that time; but in addition the notion that future glory was to be purchased only by the suffering and death of the just ran all through Jewish Messianic literature, and was a natural consequence of the sorry plight of the Jews.

Belief in the crucified Messiah thus need have been only one more variation of the manifold Messianic expectations of the Judaism of that period, if the basis on which it was erected had not been one which had to develop a contradiction to Judaism. This basis, the vitality of the communistic organization of the proletariat, was closely linked with the special form of the Messianic expectations of the communistic proletarians in Jerusalem.

THE INTERNATIONAL SAVIOR

The Messianic hopes of the rest of Jewry were exclusively national, including those of the Zealots. Subjection of the rest of the nations under Jewish world domination, which was to replace that of the Romans; revenge on the nations that were oppressing and mistreating Jewry: this was the content of these hopes. The Messianic expectations of the Christian community were different. They too were Jewish patriots and enemies of the Romans, and throwing off the alien domination was the precondition of any liberation, but the adherents of the Christian community wanted more than that. It was not only the yoke of the foreign rulers but the yoke of all rulers, including the native ones, that was to be thrown off. They called only the weary and heavily-laden to them; the day of judgment would be a day of vengeance on all the rich and powerful.

Their most inflamed passion was not race hatred but class hatred. This contained the seeds of severance from the rest of Judaism with its national unity.

At the same time it held the seeds of a rapprochement with the non-Jewish world, which naturally rejected the Jewish idea of the Messiah with its implied subjection of themselves. Class hatred against the rich, and proletarian solidarity, were ideas that were acceptable to other than only Jewish proletarians. A Messianic hope that extended to the salvation of the poor must have been listened to eagerly by the poor of all nations. The social Messiah could go beyond the limits of Judaism, where a national Messiah could not; only he could come victoriously through the fearful catastrophe of the Jewish commonwealth that culminated in the destruction of Jerusalem.

On the other hand, the only place in the Roman Empire in which a communist organization could maintain itself would be where it was reinforced by faith in the Messiah to come and his deliverance of all the oppressed and mistreated. In practice, these communistic organizations, as we shall see, did not come to more than mutual aid societies. There had been a general need for such societies in the Roman Empire since the first century of our era, a need felt more intensely as the general poverty increased and the last remnants of traditional primitive communism disappeared. But the suspicious despotism put an end to all societies; we have seen how Trajan was afraid even of volunteer fire companies. Caesar had spared the Jewish organizations, but later these too lost their privileged position.

The only way in which the mutual aid societies could continue to exist was as secret leagues. But who would risk his life for the chance of getting mere subsistence, or from a feeling of solidarity in a period when public spirit had all but died out? What public spirit and devotion to the common weal was left did not meet with a large and lofty idea except in that of the renovation of the world, that is of society, by a Messiah. Meanwhile, the more self-seeking among the proletarians, who looked to the mutual aid societies for the sake of their personal gain, were reassured as to the danger to their persons by the idea of personal resurrection accompanied by ample rewards. This was an idea that would not have been needed to encourage the persecuted in periods when conditions powerfully stimulated the social instincts and feelings, so that the individual felt himself irresistibly impelled to follow them, even at the risk of harm, or even death. The idea of a personal resurrection became indispensable for the conduct of a dangerous struggle against powerful governments in an age in which all the social instincts and feelings had been attenuated to the utmost by the galloping social decomposition, and not merely in the ruling classes but in the oppressed and exploited as well.

The notion of the Messiah could take root outside of Judaism only in the communistic form of the Christian community, of the crucified Messiah. It was only by faith in the Messiah and the resurrection that the communistic organization could establish itself and grow as a secret league in the Roman Empire. United, these two ideas—communism and belief in a Messiah—became irresistible. What Judaism had vainly hoped for from its Messiah of royal lineage was achieved by the crucified Messiah from the proletariat: he subjugated Rome, made the Caesars kneel and conquered the world. But he did not conquer it for the proletariat. In the course of its victorious campaign the proletarian, communistic mutual aid organisation was transformed into the world's most powerful machine for mastery and exploitation. This dialectical process is not unprecedented. The crucified Messiah was neither the first not the last conqueror who ended by turning the armies, with which he had conquered, against his own people, subjugating and enslaving them.

Caesar and Napoleon also emerged from democratic victories.

BOOK FOUR: THE BEGINNINGS
OF CHRISTIANITY

3

JEWISH CHRISTIANS AND GENTILE CHRISTIANS

AGITATION AMONG THE PAGANS

THERE IS NO REASON whatever to doubt the statement in the Acts of the Apostles that the first communistic Messiah community was formed in Jerusalem. However, communities soon came into existence in other cities with a Jewish proletariat. There was heavy travel between Jerusalem and the other parts of the Empire, especially its eastern half, if only because of the many hundreds of thousands, perhaps millions of pilgrims that came there year after year. And many penniless vagabonds roamed from place to place, staying in any one locality as long as charity lasted. The rules that Jesus gave to his apostles must be seen in the light of this state of affairs.

"Carry neither purse, nor scrip, nor shoes: and salute no man by the way. And into whatsoever house ye enter, first say, Peace be to this house. And if the son of peace be there, your peace shall rest upon it: if not, it shall turn to you again. And in the same house remain, eating and drinking such things as they give: for the laborer [!] is worthy of his hire. Go not from house to house. And into whatsoever city ye enter, and they receive you, eat such things as are set before you: And heal the sick that are therein, and say unto them, The kingdom of God is come nigh unto you. But into whatsoever city ye enter, and they receive you not, go your ways out into the streets of the same, and say, Even the very dust of your city, which cleaveth on us, we do wipe off against you: notwithstanding be ye sure of this, that the kingdom of God is come nigh unto you. But I say unto you, that it shall be more tolerable in that day for Sodom, than for that city" (Luke 10, verses 4 to 12).

The final threat that the evangelist puts in Jesus' mouth is typical of the revengefulness of the beggar disappointed in his hopes of alms: he would like to see the whole city go up in flames; but the Messiah will take care of that for him.

All the roving penniless agitators of the new organization ranked as apostles, not merely the twelve whose names were handed down as Jesus' appointed preachers of his word. The already mentioned *Didache (Doctrine of the Twelve Apostles)* still speaks, in the middle of the second century, of apostles active in the communities.

It was roving "beggars and conspirators" like these, feeling themselves full of the Holy Ghost, that brought the "good tidings," the Evangel[11] from Jerusalem first to the neighboring Jewish communities and then further and further until they reached Rome. But as soon as the Evangel left the soil of Palestine, it entered an entirely different social milieu and acquired a different character.

There the apostles found along with the members of the Jewish community and in closest relationship with them the "God-fearing" Gentiles (*sebomenoi*), who worshipped the Jewish God and went to the synagogue, but could not make up their minds to conform to all the Jewish practices. At most they might undergo baptism; but they would not have anything to do with circumcision nor dietary laws, the Sabbath and other externalities, which would have detached them completely from their "pagan" surroundings.

The social content of the Gospel must have found a willing reception in the proletarian groups of such "God-fearing Gentiles." They in turn carried it on to other non-Jewish proletarian circles, which were fertile soil for the doctrine of the crucified

11. From *eu*, well, bringing good luck, and *angellō*, announce, report.

Messiah in so far as that doctrine looked forward to a social over-turn and immediate organization of mutual aid institutions. But as for anything specifically Jewish, these groups had an attitude of complete lack of sympathy, even aversion or mockery.

The further the new doctrine spread in the Jewish communities outside of Palestine, the clearer it must have been that it would gain tremendously in propaganda power if it abandoned its Jewish peculiarities, ceased to be national and became exclusively social.

The name of Saul is given as that of the man who first recognized this and took vigorous measures in that direction. He was a Jew who was not of Palestinian origin, according to tradition, but from the Jewish community of a Greek city, Tarsus in Cilicia. An ardent spirit, he flung himself first wholeheartedly into Phariseeism, and as a Pharisee fought the Christian community, which was so close to Zealotism, until finally, the story runs, a vision undeceived him in a flash and sent him to the opposite extreme. He joined the Christian community, but in it he was a subverter of the traditional conception, by insisting on propagandizing the new doctrine among non-Jews and abandoning their conversion to Judaism.

It is characteristic for his tendency that he changed his Hebraic name Saul to the Latin Paul. Such changes of name were frequent among Jews who wanted to advance in non-Jewish circles. If a Manasseh could call himself Menalaus, why not Saul Paul?

We can hardly say what there is in the tale of Paul that has any historical foundation. Here as in every other case that deals with personal occurrences, the New Testament is an unreliable source, full of contradictions and impossible miracle stories. But the personal actions of Paul are a secondary matter. What is decisive is the active opposition to the previous conception of Christianity that he personifies. This contradiction arose from the very nature of the situation; it was unavoidable, and no matter how unreliable the Acts of the Apostles may be as to any single happening, the fact of the struggle between the two tendencies can be seen plainly in it. In fact, it is a book written with a definite purpose in mind, that of making propaganda for the Pauline tendency while still seeking to cover up and palliate the contradiction between the two camps.

At first, no doubt, the new tendency must have been modest, demanding nothing but tolerance in some points, which the mother community might indulgently overlook. So at least it would seem from the account in Acts, which it is true painted in bright colors and under the banner of peace something that actually took place in the course of a bitter struggle.[12]

Thus it relates, of the period of Paul's agitation in Syria:

"And certain men which came down from Judaea taught the brethren, and said, Except ye be circumcised after the manner of Moses, ye cannot be saved. When therefore Paul and Barnabas had no small dissension and disputation with them, they determined that Paul and Barnabas, and certain other of them, should go up to Jerusalem unto the apostles and elders about this question. And being brought on their way by the church, they passed through Phenice and Samaria, declaring the conversion of the Gentiles; and they caused great joy unto all the brethren. And when they were come to Jerusalem, they were received of the church, and of the apostles and elders, and they declared all things that God had done with them. But there rose up certain of the sect of Pharisees which believed, saying, That it was needful to circumcise them, and to command them to keep the law of Moses." (Acts 15, verses 1 to 5).

Now the apostles and elders come together, the party leaders as it were. Peter and James make conciliatory speeches, and finally it is decided to send Judas Barsabas and Silas, likewise "chief men among the brethren," to Syria to tell the brethren there: "It seemed good to the Holy Ghost and to us, to lay upon you no greater burden than these necessary things; That ye abstain from meats offered to idols, and from blood, and from things strangled, and from fornication." The leaders gave up the circumcision of

12. Cf. Bruno Bauer, *Die Apostelgeschichte, eine Ausgleichung des Paulinismus und des Judentums innerhalb der christlicher Kirche,* 1850.

Gentile proselytes. Charitable work however must not be neglected: "Only they would that we should remember the poor; the same which I also was forward to do," is how Paul tells it in his Epistle to the Galatians (2, verse 10).

Charity and mutual aid appealed equally to Jewish and Gentile Christians; that was not a moot point. For that reason it is little mentioned in their literature, which is almost exclusively polemical. It is incorrect to conclude from the rarity of these references that it played no part in primitive Christianity; it simply played no part in Christianity's internal divisions. These continued despite all attempts at conciliation.

Paul's Epistle to the Galatians, previously cited, accuses the defenders of circumcision of being opportunists:

"As many as desire to make a fair show in the flesh, they constrain you to be circumcised; only lest they should suffer persecution for the cross of Christ" (6, verse 12).

After the congress of Jerusalem which we have just mentioned, the Acts have Paul make a propaganda trip through Greece, still preaching to the Gentiles. On his return to Jerusalem, he reports to his comrades on the success of his agitation.

"And when they heard it, they glorified the Lord, and said unto him, Thou seest, brother, how many thousands of Jews there are which believe; and they are all zealous of the law: And they are informed of thee, that thou teachest all the Jews which are among the Gentiles to forsake Moses, saying that they ought not to circumcise their children, neither to walk after the customs" (Acts 21, verses 20 f.).

He is now asked to clear himself of the charge and show that he was still a pious Jew. He is willing to do this, but is prevented by an uprising of the Jews against him; they want to kill him as a traitor to their nation. The Roman government takes him into a sort of protective custody and finally sends him to Rome; there he can carry on his agitation unmolested, not as in Jerusalem: "Preaching the kingdom of God, and teaching those things which concern the Lord Jesus Christ, with all confidence. no man forbidding him" (Acts 28, verse 31).

THE OPPOSITION BETWEEN JEWS AND CHRISTIANS

It was inevitable that the Gentile Christians upheld their view more strongly as the number increased, and that thus the opposition should increase in intensity.

The longer the opposition lasted and the more points of friction there were, the more hostile the two trends must have been toward each other. This was made still worse by the intensification of the contrast between Judaism and the peoples it lived among during the last decades before the destruction of Jerusalem. The proletarian elements in Judaism, especially those of Jerusalem, had a more and more fanatical hatred for the non-Jewish peoples, above all the Romans. The Roman was the worst enemy, the most cruel oppressor and exploiter. The Hellene was his ally. Everything that distinguished the Jew from them was stressed now more than ever before. Those who laid the main emphasis on propaganda within Judaism would be impelled merely by the needs of their agitation to accent the characteristically Jewish and retain all the Jewish precepts, a course to which they already inclined under the influence of their surroundings.

The growth of the Jews' fanatical hatred for the nations of their oppressors was matched by the growth of aversion and contempt for the Jews among the masses of those nations. This in turn led the Gentile Christians and those who were carrying on agitation among them not merely to demand freedom from the Jewish law for themselves, but to criticize these precepts more and more sharply. The opposition between Jewish and Gentile Christians became, among the latter, more and more an opposition to Judaism itself. However the belief in the Messiah, including the belief in the crucified Messiah, was too organically linked to Judaism for the Gentile Christians simply to reject it out of hand. They took over from the Jews all the Messianic predictions and other supports of the hope for the Messiah, and at the same time became more and more hostile to that very Judaism, adding one more contradiction to the many we have already seen in Christianity.

We have seen the value that the Gospels set on Jesus' descent from David and what fantastic assumptions they introduced in order to have the Galilean born in Bethlehem. They keep citing passages from the holy books of the Jews to attest the Messianic mission of Jesus. On the other hand they have Jesus protest that he has no intention of doing away with the Jewish law:

"Think not that I am come to destroy the law, or the prophets: I am not come to destroy, but to fulfil. For verily I say unto you, Till heaven and earth pass, one jot or one tittle shall in no wise pass from the law, till all be fulfilled" (Matthew 5, verses 17 f. Cf. Luke 16, verse 16).

Jesus bids his disciples: "Go not into the way of the Gentiles, and into any city of the Samaritans enter ye not: But go rather to the lost sheep of the house of Israel" (Matthew 10, verses 5 f.).

Here is a direct prohibition against propaganda outside of Judaism. Jesus expresses himself similarly, in Matthew, although somewhat more mildly, to a Phoenician woman (in Mark a Greek woman, a Syro-Phoenician by birth). She cried to him:

"Have mercy on me, O Lord, thou Son of David; my daughter is grievously vexed with a devil. But he answered her not a word. And his disciples came and besought him, saying, Send her away; for she crieth after us. But he answered and said, I am not sent but unto the lost sheep of the house of Israel. Then came she and worshipped him, saying, Lord, help me. But he answered and said, It is not meet to take the children's bread, and to cast it to dogs. And she said, Truth, Lord: yet the dogs eat of the crumbs which fall from their masters' table. Then Jesus answered and said unto her, O woman, great is thy faith: be it unto thee even as thou wilt. And her daughter was made whole from that very hour" (Matthew 15, 22 f. cf. Mark 7, 25 ff.).

Here Jesus lets himself be persuaded; but at first he is most ungracious toward the Greek woman, merely because she is not a Jew, even though she calls on him as the son of David, in the sense of the Jewish Messiah cult.

Finally, it is a thoroughly Jewish way of thinking when Jesus promises his apostles that in his future state they shall sit on twelve thrones and judge the twelve tribes of Israel. This prospect would not seem over-attractive to anyone but a Jew, and indeed a Jew in Judea; it would be worthless for propaganda among the Gentiles.

Although the Gospels preserved such strong remnants of the Jewish Messiah cult, they simultaneously show outcroppings of the aversion to Judaism that inspired their authors and revisers. Jesus is continually warring against all the things that are dear to the pious Jew: the fasts, the dietary laws, the Sabbath. He exalts the Gentiles above the Jews:

"Therefore say I unto you, The Kingdom of God shall be taken from you, and given to a nation bringing forth the fruits thereof" (Matthew 21, verse 42).

Jesus even goes so far as to curse the Jews:

"Then began he to upbraid the cities wherein most of his mighty works were done, because they repented not: Woe unto thee, Chorazin! woe unto thee, Bethsaida! for if the mighty works, which were done in you, had been done in Tyre and Sidon, they would have repented long ago in sackcloth and ashes. But I say unto you, it shall be more tolerable for Tyre and Sidon at the day of judgment, than for you. And thou, Capernaum, which art exalted unto heaven, shall be brought down to hell: for if the mighty works, which have been done in thee, had been done in Sodom, it would have remained until this day. But I say unto you, that it shall be more tolerable for the land of Sodom in the day of judgment, than for thee" (Matthew 15, verses 20 f.).

These words show direct hatred of the Jews. It is no longer a sect within Judaism speaking against other sects of the same nation. Here the Jewish nation as such is branded as morally inferior, as particularly perverse and obdurate.

This appears too in the prophecies as to the destruction of Jerusalem which are put into the mouth of Jesus, but which of course were fabricated after the event.

The Jewish War showed the enemies of Judaism how strong and dangerous it was. This outbreak of fierce desperation brought the opposition between Judaism and the Gentiles to its height; it had something of the effect of the June massacres of 1848 and the Paris Commune on the class hatred between proletariat and bourgeoisie in the nineteenth century. It also deepened the rift between Jewish Christianity and Gentile Christianity, but always tended to cut the ground away from under the feet of the former. The destruction of Jerusalem meant that there was no longer any basis for an independent class movement of the Jewish proletariat. Any such movement presupposes the independence of the nation. After the destruction of Jerusalem Jews existed only in foreign countries, among enemies who hated and persecuted them all, rich and poor alike, and against whom all the Jews had to stand fast together. The charity of the wealthy toward his poor countrymen therefore reached a high point in Judaism; the feeling of national solidarity far outweighed class opposition. Thus Jewish Christianity gradually lost its propaganda power. Afterwards, Christianity became more and more exclusively Gentile Christianity, changing from a party in Judaism to a party outside of Judaism, indeed in opposition to Judaism. More and more, Christian feeling and anti-Jewish feeling tended to become identical concepts.

With the fall of the Jewish commonwealth, the Jewish-national hopes for the Messiah lost their basis. They could still persist a few decades, still produce some death-twitches, but as an effective factor in the political and social development, the annihilation of the Jewish capital had been their death-blow.

This was not the case for the Messianic hopes of the Gentile Christians. The idea of the Messiah kept its vitality only in the form of the crucified Messiah, only in the form of the extra-Jewish Messiah, the Messiah translated into Greek, the Christ.

In fact the Christians were able to transform the gruesome event that signified the utter destruction of the Jewish expectation of the Messiah into a triumph of their Christ. Jerusalem now appeared as the enemy of Christ, and Jerusalem's destruction as Christ's vengeance on Judaism, as a fearful proof of his victorious might.

Luke says of Jesus' entry into Jerusalem:

"And when he was come near, he beheld the city, and wept over it, Saying, if thou hadst known, even thou, at least in this thy day, the things that belong unto thy peace! but now they are hid from thine eyes. For the days shall come upon thee, that thine enemies shall cast a trench about thee, and compass thee round, and keep thee in on every side, And shall lay thee even with the ground, and thy children within thee; and they shall not leave in thee one stone upon another; because thou knewest not the time of thy visitation" (Luke 19, 41 f.).

Thereafter Jesus declares that the days of the crushing of Jerusalem, that will bring destruction even to "them that are with child, and to them that give suck," are "days of vengeance" (Luke 21, 22).

The September slaughters of the French Revolution, which were not revenge on suckling babies, but protection against a cruel enemy, are pleasant things compared to this verdict of the good shepherd.

The destruction of Jerusalem had still other consequences for Christian thought. We have already pointed out how Christianity, which had hitherto been violent, now took on a peaceful character. The only place where there had been a strong democracy at the beginning of the Empire had been among the Jews. The other nations of the Empire no longer had any fight left in them, and even their proletarians were cowardly. The destruction of Jerusalem stifled the last popular force in the Empire; any rebellion was hopeless from that point on. Christianity became more and more exclusively Gentile Christianity, becoming subservient and even servile in the process.

The Romans ruled in the Empire, and the primary task was to show oneself obsequious to them. The first Christians had been Jewish patriots and enemies of all alien rule and exploitation; the Gentile Christians added to their anti-Semitism devotion to Rome and the imperial throne. This can be seen in the Gospels as well. There is the well-known story of the agents provocateurs sent to Christ by the "chief priests and the scribes," to trick him into a treasonable utterance:

"And they watched him, and sent forth spies, which should feign themselves just men [that is, comrades of Jesus], that they might take hold of his words, that so they might deliver him unto the power and authority of the governor. And they asked him, saying, Master, we know that thou sayest and teachest rightly, neither acceptest thou the person of any, but teachest the way of God truly: Is it lawful for us to give tribute unto Caesar, or no? But he perceived their craftiness, and said unto them, Why tempt ye me? Show me a penny. Whose image and superscription hath it? They answered and said, Caesar's. And he said unto them, Render therefore unto Caesar the things which be Caesar's, and unto God the things which be God's" (Luke 20, verses 20 f.).

Jesus here elaborates a splendid theory of money and taxes. The coin belongs to the man whose image and superscription it bears. Paying taxes is only giving the emperor his own money back.

The same spirit pervades the writings of the champions of the Gentile Christian propaganda, as in Paul's Epistle to the Romans (13, verse 1 f.):

"Let every soul be subject unto the higher powers. For there is no power but of God: the powers that be are ordained of God. Whosoever therefore resisteth the power, resisteth the ordinance of God: and they that resist shall receive to themselves damnation . . . for he [the ruler] beareth not the sword in vain: for he is the minister of God, a revenger to execute wrath upon him that doeth evil. Wherefore ye must needs be subject, not only for wrath, but also for conscience sake. For this cause pay ye tribute also: for they are God's ministers, attending continually upon this very thing. Render therefore to all their dues: tribute to whom tribute is due; custom to whom custom; fear to whom fear; honour to whom honour."

How far this is already from that Jesus who bids his disciples buy swords, and preached the hatred of the rich and powerful; how far from that Christianity that in the Revelation of John bitterly curses Rome and the kings bound up with it: "Babylon the great is fallen, and is become the habitation of devils, and the hold of every foul spirit, and a cage of every unclean and hateful bird. For all nations have drunk of the wine of the wrath of her fornication, and the kings of the earth have committed fornication with her, and the merchants of the earth are waxed rich through the abundance of her delicacies. . . . And the kings of the earth, who have committed fornication and lived deliciously with her, shall bewail her, and lament for her, when they shall see the smoke of her burning" (18, verses 2 f.).

The basic theme of Acts is emphasis on the hostility of Judaism to the doctrine of the crucified Messiah, and on an alleged receptiveness to this doctrine on the part of the Romans. Something that Christianity either desired or imagined after the fall of Jerusalem is represented as a fact in Acts. According to this book, Christian propaganda in Jerusalem was more and more suppressed by the Jews; the Jews persecute and stone the Christians wherever they can, while the Roman authorities protect them. We have seen Paul telling that he was gravely menaced in Jerusalem, but could speak freely in Rome without hindrance. Freedom in Rome, forcible suppression in Jerusalem!

Anti-Semitism and flattery of the Romans are most apparent in the story of the Passion, the story of the suffering and death of Christ. In it we can clearly trace how the original content of the tale was changed into its contrary under the influence of the new tendencies.

Since the story of the Passion is the most important part of the Gospel story, the only part with respect to which we can pretend to speak in historical terms, and since it is such a clear embodiment of the way in which the first Christians wrote history, we shall now go into it intensively.

BOOK FOUR: THE BEGINNINGS

OF CHRISTIANITY

4

THE STORY OF CHRIST'S PASSION

THE GOSPELS give us uncommonly little that we can establish with any probability as actual facts in the life of Jesus: his birth and his death; two facts that could prove at least, if they can be verified, that Jesus really lived and was not a mere mythological figure, but that do not cast any light on the most important thing about a historical personage: the activity in which he engaged in between his birth and his death. The farrago of moral maxims and miracles supplied by the Gospels by way of an account of his activity contains so much that is impossible and demonstrably fabricated, and so little that is confirmed by any other evidence, that it can not be considered a factual source.

Matters are not much better with respect to the evidence on Jesus' birth and death. We do however have some reason here for holding that these accounts have a kernel of fact hidden under a tangle of concoctions. Some of these enable us to draw the conclusion that the stories contain data that were very inconvenient for Christianity, but that were obviously too well known and accepted among its supporters for the writers of the Gospels to dare to replace them by fabrications of their own, as they so often did without any compunction.

One of these facts is Jesus' Galilean origin. This was highly inconvenient for his Davidian-Messianic pretensions. The Messiah had at least to come from David's city. We have seen what strange subterfuges were resorted to in order to assign this birth-

338

place to the Galilean. If Jesus had been nothing more than the product of the imagination of a community bemused by the Messiah belief, they would never have thought of making a Galilean of him. His Galilean origin and hence his existence may therefore be taken as at least highly probable. His death on the cross, too. We have seen that passages may still be found in the Gospels that suggest the belief that he had planned an armed uprising and had been crucified for it. This too was so embarrassing a fact that it could hardly have been invented. It was too strongly in contradiction to the spirit that prevailed in Christianity at the time when it began to reflect upon itself and write the history of its origin, though not for historical purposes to be sure, but for polemical and propaganda purposes.

The crucifixion of the Messiah was an idea so alien to Jewish thought, which could only imagine the Messiah in all the glory of a conquering hero, that it would require an actual occurrence, the martyrdom of a champion of the good cause, who had made an indelible impression on his supporters, to make the idea of the crucified Messiah at all acceptable.

When the Gentile Christians took over the tradition of this death on the cross, they soon found a fly in the ointment: the tradition said that Jesus had been crucified by the Romans as a Jewish Messiah, as king of the Jews, that is, as a defender of Jewish independence and a traitor to Roman authority. After the fall of Jerusalem this tradition became doubly awkward. Christianity had come into complete opposition to Judaism, and in addition wanted to be on good terms with the Roman power. The trick was now to give the tradition such a twist that the guilt of Christ's crucifixion should be shifted on to the Jews and Christ himself cleared not merely of any violence, but of any feelings of Jewish patriotism or enmity to Rome.

However, since the evangelists were almost as ignorant as the masses of ignorant folk in that period, their recoloring of the original picture produced the strangest mixtures.

Nowhere perhaps in the Gospels do we find more contradictions and absurdities than in the part that for almost two thousand years has always made the greatest impression on the Christian world and most inspired its imagination. There is hardly another subject that has been so frequently painted as the Passion and death of Christ. And yet this story will not stand any serious examination and is a heap of crude inartistic effects.

It was only the power of habit that made even the greatest minds of Christendom insensible to the incredible additions of the authors of the Gospels, so that despite all this farrago the original tragedy that lies in the crucifixion of Jesus as in every martyrdom for a great cause still produced its effect and lent a higher glory even to things that were ridiculous and nonsensical.

The story of the Passion begins with the entry of Jesus into Jerusalem. It is the triumphal procession of a king.[13] The populace comes to meet him, some spread their garments in the road before him, others cut branches from the trees to strew his way, and all exult to him:

"Hosanna [help us]; Blessed is he that cometh in the name of the Lord: Blessed be the kingdom of our father David, that cometh in the name of the Lord" (Mark II, verse 9 f.).

This was how kings were received among the Jews (compare Jehu in II Kings 9, verse 13).

All the common people follow Jesus; only the aristocracy and bourgeoisie, the "chief priests and scribes," are hostile to him. Jesus behaves like a dictator. He is strong enough to drive the sellers and moneychangers from the temple without meeting with any resistance. In this citadel of Judaism he rules supreme.

Of course this is just tall talk on the part of the evangelists. If Jesus had ever had such power, it would not have gone unnoticed.

13. As a curiosity we may point to the literary miracle that Matthew accomplishes by having Jesus make his entry riding on two animals at once" (Bruno Bauer, *Kritik der Evangelien*, III, p. 114). The traditional translations mask this miracle. Thus the Authorized Version runs (Matthew 21, verse 7), "And brought the ass, and the colt, and put on them their clothes, and they set him thereon." The original says, however: "And they brought the ass, and the colt, and put their clothes on them *(ep' auton)* and set him on them *(epano auton)*."
And for all the liberties taken in falsification, this was transcribed over the centuries by one copyist after another, a proof of the thoughtlessness and emptiness of the compilers of the Gospels.

An author like Josephus, who recounts the most insignificant details, would have had to mention it. Moreover, the proletarian elements in Jerusalem, like the Zealots, were never strong enough to rule the city uncontested. They kept meeting with resistance. If Jesus intended to enter Jerusalem in opposition to the Sadducees and the Pharisees, and clean out the temple, he would first have to win in a street battle. Street fighting among the various factions in Judaism were every day occurrences in Jerusalem at that time.

A noteworthy aspect of the account of his entrance is that the story has the populace greet Jesus as bringer of the "kingdom of our father David," that is, as the restorer of the independence of the Jewish kingdom. That shows Jesus not merely as an opponent of the ruling classes in Judaism, but as opposing the Romans as well. In this opposition there is obviously not Christian imagination, but Jewish reality.

The gospels now relate those events we have already dealt with: the call to the disciples to arm themselves, Judas' betrayal, the armed conflict on the Mount of Olives. We have already seen that these are remnants of the old tradition, that were not acceptable later and refurbished to give an air of peaceable submission.

Jesus is taken, led to the palace of the high priest and tried there:

"And the chief priests and all the council sought for witness against Jesus to put him to death; and found none. For many bare false witness against him, but their witness agreed not together. . . . And the high priest stood up in the midst, and asked Jesus, saying, Answerest thou nothing? what is it which these witness against thee? But he held his peace, and answered nothing. Again the high priest asked him, and said unto him, Art thou the Christ, the Son of the Blessed? And Jesus said, I am: and ye shall see the Son of man sitting on the right hand of power, and coming in the clouds of heaven. Then the high priest rent his clothes, and saith, What need we any further witnesses? Ye have heard the blasphemy: what think ye? And they all condemned him to be guilty of death" (Mark 14, verses 55 f.).

A strange sort of trial procedure, indeed! The court convenes immediately after the arrest of the prisoner, in the night time, and not in the court building, which apparently was on the Temple hill,[14] but in the palace of the high priest! Imagine the trust-worthiness of a report of a trial for high treason in Germany that has the court sitting in the royal palace in Berlin! Now false witnesses testify against Jesus, but although nobody cross-examines them, and Jesus is silent at their charges, they produce no evidence that incriminates him. Jesus is the first to incriminate himself by acknowledging that he is the Messiah. Now what is the purpose of all the apparatus of the false witnesses if this admission is enough to condemn Jesus? Their only purpose is to show the wickedness of the Jews. The death sentence is immediately pronounced. This is a violation of the prescribed forms to which the Jews of that time adhered most scrupulously. The court was allowed to bring in only a verdict of acquittal at once; a verdict of guilty had to wait until the day after the trial.

Was the Sanhedrin still allowed to pronounce death sentences at that time? The Talmud says: "Forty years before the destruction of the Temple the power of life and death was taken from Israel."

A confirmation of this is to be found in the fact that the Sanhedrin does not inflict the punishment of Jesus, but after finishing his trial turns him over to Pilate for a new trial, this time on the charge of high treason towards the Romans, the charge that he had tried to make himself king of the Jews, that is, free Judea from the Roman rule. A fine accusation on the part of a court of Jewish patriots!

It is possible that the Sanhedrin did have the right to pass sentence of death, but that such sentences needed the sanction of the procurator.

Now what happens before the Roman governor?

"And Pilate asked him, Art thou the King of the Jews? And he answering said unto him, Thou sayest it. And the chief priests accused him of many things: but he answered nothing. And Pilate

14. Schürer, *Geschichte des jüdischen Volkes,* II, p. 211.

asked him again, saying, Answerest thou nothing? behold how many things they witness against thee. But Jesus yet answered nothing; so that Pilate marvelled. Now at that feast he released unto them one prisoner, whomsoever they desired. And there was one named Barabbas, which lay bound with them that had made insurrection with him, who had committed murder in the insurrection. And the multitude crying aloud began to desire him to do as he had ever done unto them. But Pilate answered them, saying, Will ye that I release unto you the King of the Jews? For he knew that the chief priests had delivered him for envy. But the chief priests moved the people, that he should rather release Barabbas unto them. And Pilate answered and said again unto them, What will ye then that I shall do unto him whom ye call the King of the Jews? And they cried out again, Crucify him. Then Pilate said unto them, Why, what evil hath he done? And they cried out the more exceedingly, Crucify him. And so Pilate, willing to content the people, released Barabbas unto them, and delivered Jesus, when he had scourged him, to be crucified." (Mark 15, 2 f.).

In Matthew Pilate goes so far as to wash his hands before the multitude and declare, "I am innocent of the blood of this just person: see ye to it." And all the people declare, "His blood be on us, and on our children."

Luke says nothing to the effect that the Sanhedrin sentences Jesus; they appear merely as complainants before Pilate.

"And the whole multitude of them arose, and led him unto Pilate. And they began to accuse him, saying, We found this fellow perverting the nation, and forbidding to give tribute to Caesar, saying that he himself is Christ a King. And Pilate asked him, saying, Art thou the King of the Jews? And he answered him and said, Thou sayest it. Then said Pilate to the chief priests and to the people, I find no fault in this man. And they were the more fierce, saying, He stirreth up the people, teaching throughout all Jewry, beginning from Galilee to this place" (Luke 23, verse 1 f.).

Luke must come closest to the truth. Here Jesus is directly accused of high treason before Pilate, and with proud courage does not deny his guilt. Asked by Pilate whether he is the king of the Jews, that is, their leader in their fight for independence, Jesus declares, "Thou sayest it." The Gospel according to St. John feels how embarrassing this remnant of Jewish patriotism is, and therefore makes Jesus answer, "My kingdom is not of this world: if my kingdom were of this world, then would my servants fight." Now John is the latest gospel; and so it took a fairly long time for the Christian writers to make up their minds to commit this falsification of the original facts.

The matter before Pilate was obviously a very simple one. In having the rebel Jesus executed he was merely doing his duty as representative of Roman authority.

The masses of Jews, on the contrary, had not the slightest reason to be angry at a man who wanted none of the Roman rule and called for refusing to pay taxes to the Emperor. If Jesus really did that, he was acting entirely in accord with the Zealots, the dominating trend among the population of Jerusalem at that time.

If we take the accusation given in the Gospels as authentic, the natural thing to expect would be that the Jews should be sympathetic to Jesus and that Pilate should condemn him.

What do the Gospels tell us? Pilate does not find the slightest guilt in Jesus, although Jesus admits it himself. The governor keeps repeating that the accused is innocent, and asking what evil he has committed?

This is strange enough. But still stranger, although Pilate does not admit the guilt of Jesus, he still does not set him free.

Now it happened now and then that a procurator found a political case too complicated to decide by himself. But it is unheard of that an official of the Roman Emperor should try to get out of his uncertainty by asking the mass of the people what should be done with the accused. If he did not himself want to condemn a traitor, he would have to send him to the Emperor in Rome. For instance, this was done by the procurator Antonius Felix (52 to 60). He enticed the head of the Zealots of Jerusalem, the guerilla chief Eleazar who had kept the land unsafe for twenty years, by a promise of safe-conduct, took him prisoner and sent him to Rome. He had many of his followers crucified, however.

Pilate too could have sent Jesus to Rome; but the role that Matthew has him playing is simply ridiculous: a Roman judge, a representative of the Emperor Tiberius, with power of life and death, begging an assembly of the people to Jerusalem to allow him to set the accused man free and answering their shouts of refusal by saying, "Well, put him to death, I am innocent in the matter!"

This was not the way the historical Pilate acted. Agrippa I, in a letter to Philo, calls Pilate "an inflexible and ruthless character," and reproaches him for "bribetaking, acts of violence, robberies, misdeeds, offences, constant executions without trials, endless and intolerable brutalities."

His harshness and ruthlessness created such intolerable conditions that it became too much even for the central government in Rome and he was recalled (36 A.D.).

And this was the man who is supposed to have shown the proletarian traitor Jesus such extreme love of justice and mercy, exceeded only, unfortunately for the defendant, by his idiotic weakness toward the people.

The evangelists were too ignorant to be amazed at that, and yet they might have had an inkling that they were assigning too strange a role to the Roman governor. They looked for something to make it look more credible; they report that the Jews were accustomed to having Pilate release a prisoner to them at Easter, and when he now offered them the release of Jesus, they answered, "No, we should rather have the murderer Barabbas."

It is strange that nothing is known of such a custom anywhere but in the Gospels. It is contrary to Roman institutions, which did not give governors any right to pardon. And it is contrary to any orderly law to give the right to pardon not to some responsible body but to a crowd that has happened to come together. Legal conditions of this kind can be taken at face value only by theologians.

But even if we are willing to let that pass and accept the singular pardoning power of the Jewish crowd as it chances to congregate around the procurator's lodgings, the question still arises, what does this power to pardon have to do with the case in question?

For Jesus has not yet been legally sentenced. Pontius Pilate is faced with the question: Is Jesus guilty of high treason or no? He answers with the question: Do you want to use your power to pardon in his favor, or no?

Pilate has to give sentence, and instead of doing so appeals to the pardoning power! Does he not have the power to set Jesus free if he considers him innocent?

Now a new monstrosity appears. The Jews allegedly have the right to pardon; and how do they exercise it? Are they content with asking the release of Barabbas? No, they demand the crucifixion of Jesus! The evangelists evidently imagine that the right to pardon one gives rise as well to the right to condemn the other.

This mad kind of administration of justice is matched by an equally mad sort of politics.

The evangelists show us a mob that hates Jesus to such a degree that it pardons a murderer rather than him; precisely a murderer —this mob found no worthier object to pardon—; and it is not quiet until Jesus is led to be crucified.

Now consider that this is the same mob that a few days earlier had greeted him with hosannas as a king, strewing his path with garments and hailing him with one voice, without any contradiction. It was just this devotion on the part of the multitude that according to the Gospels was the reason why the aristocrats had designs on Jesus' life but dared not arrest him by day, choosing the night time instead. And now this same mob is inspired just as unanimously with the wildest, most fanatical hatred against him —against the man who was accused of a crime that in the eyes of every Jewish patriot made him worthy of the greatest honor: an attempt to free the Jewish commonwealth from foreign rule.

What has happened to produce this astonishing change of attitude? The most powerful kind of motives would be required to make it plausible. The evangelists however stammer out a few ridiculous phrases, insofar as they say anything at all on the subject. Luke and John do not furnish any motivation. Mark says: "The chief priests moved the people" against Jesus, and Matthew, that they "persuaded the multitude."

All that these phrases prove is how badly the last shred of political feeling and political knowledge had been lost to the Christian writers.

Now no matter how much a mass of people may be lacking in character, it will not be led into fanatical hatred without some basis. The basis may be foolish or vile, but there must be some basis. In the evangelists' account the Jewish multitude outdoes the most infamous and idiotic stage villain in idiotic infamy, for without the slightest foundation, the least motive, it rages for the blood of the same man it was worshipping only the day before.

The matter becomes even more idiotic when we take the political conditions of the time into consideration. The Jewish commonwealth, unlike practically every other part of the Roman Empire, had an uncommonly vigorous political life, with all its social and political contrasts carried to their extreme. The political parties were well organized, and disciplined. Zealotism had completely won over the lower classes of Jerusalem, and they were constantly in bitter opposition to the Sadducees and Pharisees, and full of the fiercest hatred toward Rome. Their best allies were the rebellious Galileans.

Even if the Sadducees and Pharisees had succeeded in "moving" some elements of the people against Jesus, they could never have managed to get a unanimous demonstration, but at best a bitter street battle. There could hardly be a more fantastic idea than that of Zealots throwing themselves with wild screams, not on Romans and aristocrats, but on the accused rebel, whose execution they extort with fanatical rage from the Roman commander.

A more childish monstrosity has never been dreamed up.

After the evangelists have succeeded in this brilliant way in presenting the bloody Pilate as an innocent lamb, and the innate depravity of Judaism as the real cause of the crucifixion of the harmless and peaceful Messiah, they are exhausted. Their vein of invention gives out for the moment and the old account comes into its own temporarily. Jesus is mocked at and mistreated after his condemnation, but not by the Jews, but by the soldiers of that very Pilate who had just declared him guiltless. Now he has his soldiers not only crucify him but first scourge him and mock him for his Jewish kingdom: a crown of thorns is put on his head, a purple cloak set on him, and then they strike him in the face and spit at him. Finally they fasten to his cross the inscription: Jesus, King of the Jews.

In this the original character of the catastrophe appears clearly once more. Here the Romans are the bitter enemies of Jesus, and the basis of their hatred as of their mockery is his high treason, his aspiring to the Jewish throne, his effort to shake off the alien domination of the Romans.

Unfortunately this glimmering of the simple truth does not last long.

Jesus dies, and the task is now to prove by a series of stage effects that a god had died:

"Jesus, when he had cried again with a loud voice, yielded up the ghost. And, behold, the veil of the temple was rent in twain from the top to the bottom; and the earth did quake, and the rocks rent; And the graves were opened; and many bodies of the saints which slept arose, And came out of the graves after his resurrection, and went into the holy city, and appeared unto many" (Matthew 27, verses 50 f.).

The evangelists do not report what the resurrected "saints" did during and after their group excursion to Jerusalem, whether they remained alive or decently lay down again in their graves. In any case it would be expected that such an extraordinary event would have an overpowering effect on all who witnessed it and convince everybody of the divinity of Jesus. But the Jews remain obdurate even now. It is still only the Romans who bow down before the deity.

"Now when the centurion, and they that were with him, watching Jesus, saw the earthquake, and those things that were done, they feared greatly, saying, Truly this was the Son of God" (Matthew 27, verse 54).

The chief priests and Pharisees however, declare Jesus a deceiver, despite everything (Matthew 27, verse 63), and when he rises from the dead, that has no effect beyond the bribe we spoke of before, given to the Roman eyewitnesses to make them brand the miracle as a deception.

Thus at the end of the Passion story we still have Jewish corruption turning the honest Roman soldiers into tools of Jewish trickery and baseness, which opposes devilish rage to the noblest divine forgiveness.

All through this story the trend to servility toward the Romans and hatred toward the Jews is laid on so thick and described with such a mass of nonsense that one should think it would not have the slightest influence on thinking men. And yet we know that it was only too successful in accomplishing its ends. This tale, illuminated by the glorious light of divinity, ennobled by the martyrdom of the proud confessor of a high mission, was for many centuries one of the most effective means of arousing hatred and contempt for Jews even among very kindly spirits in Christendom. This story served to brand Jews as the scum of mankind, as a race naturally wicked and obdurate, which must be kept away from all human association and kept down with an iron hand.

But it would have been impossible for this conception of Judaism ever to have gained currency if it had not arisen in a period of general hatred and persecution of the Jews.

Born of the outlawry of the Jews, it infinitely reinforced, prolonged and extended that outlawry.

What was presented as the story of the Passion of the Lord Jesus Christ is nothing more than evidence of the suffering of the Jewish people.

BOOK FOUR: THE BEGINNINGS
OF CHRISTIANITY

5

THE DEVELOPMENT OF THE CHRISTIAN COMMUNITY

PROLETARIANS AND SLAVES

WE HAVE SEEN that some elements of Christianity, such as monotheism, Messianism, belief in resurrection and Essenian communism arose within Judaism, and that a part of the lower classes of that nation saw their longings and wishes best expressed in the combination of those elements. We saw further that all through the social organism of the Roman world empire conditions prevailed which tended to make it more receptive, particularly in its proletarian parts, to the new trends stemming from Judaism, but that these currents not only broke away from Judaism as soon as they came under the influence of the non-Jewish milieu, but were even directly hostile to it. They now merged with currents in the dying Greco-Roman world which changed the spirit of strong national democracy that prevailed in Judaism up to the destruction of Jerusalem into its complete opposite, replacing it with spineless submission, servility and longing for death.

As the current of thought was thus changing, the organization of the Christian community too was undergoing a deep transformation.

At first the community had been permeated by an energetic though vague communism, an aversion to all private property, a drive toward a new and better social order, in which all class differences should be smoothed out by division of possessions.

The Christian community was indeed originally a fighting organization, if our hypothesis is correct that the various violent passages of the Gospels, which are otherwise inexplicable, are remnants of the original tradition. That would also be in complete accord with the historical situation of the Jewish commonwealth of that time.

It would be quite incredible that a proletarian sect should be unaffected by the general revolutionary state of mind.

Hope for the revolution, for the coming of the Messiah, for social change permeated all the first Christian organizations in Judaism at any rate. Care for the present, that is practical work on a small scale, was far in the background.

This state of affairs changed after the destruction of Jerusalem. The elements that had given the Messianic community a rebellious character had lost, and the Messianic community became more and more an anti-Jewish community within the non-Jewish proletariat, which neither could nor wanted to fight. The longer the community lasted, the clearer it became that they could no longer count on the fulfillment of the prophecy, still to be found in the Gospels, that the contemporaries of Jesus would live to see the revolution. Confidence in the coming of the "Kingdom of God" here below faded; the Kingdom of God, that was to have descended from heaven to earth, was transferred more and more to heaven; the resurrection of the body was transformed into immortality of the soul, for which the bliss of heaven or the tortures of hell were reserved.

The more the Messianic expectation of the future took on these celestial forms, becoming politically conservative or indifferent, the more practical care for the present came to the fore.

And the practice of communism changed in the same degree in which revolutionary enthusiasm waned.

That practice had risen originally from an energetic though vague drive toward the abolition of all private property, a drive to relieve the poverty of the comrades by making all property common.

However, it has already been pointed out that the Christian

communities, unlike Essenianism, were originally urban, in fact chiefly metropolitan, and that this hindered them from making their communism something complete and lasting.

Among Essenes as among Christians communism started as a communism of the means of enjoyment, as consumers' communism. Now in agriculture even today consumption and production are closely linked, and then even more so. Production was production for one's own consumption not for the market; planting, cattle-raising and housekeeping were intertwined. Moreover large farms were quite possible, and even at that time superior to small-scale farming to the extent that they could have greater division of labor and make better use of buildings and equipment. It is true that these advantages were more than overbalanced by the drawbacks of slave labor. However, although cultivation by slaves was then by far the most common form of large-scale agriculture, it was not the only one possible. Large farms of extended peasant families already occur at the beginning of agricultural development. And it would seem that the Essenes too instituted large scale agriculture by comradely families in places where they formed great monastery-like settlements in the rural solitude, like the one on the Dead Sea, of which Pliny tells us (*Natural History*, Book 5) that they "lived in the society of the palm trees."

However, the mode of production is in the last analysis always the decisive factor in any social formation. Only those formations that are based on the mode of production are strong and endure.

Although social or comradely agriculture was possible at the time of the origin of Christianity, the conditions for comradely city industry were absent. The workers in urban industry were either slaves or free workers at home. Large enterprises with free workers, like the extended peasant family, were virtually unknown in the cities. Slaves, workers at home, porters, and then peddlers, small shopkeepers, lumpenproletarians—such were the lower classes of the urban population of that time that might be the soil in which communistic tendencies might grow. In all these there was no factor at work that was capable of extending community of goods into a community of production. It was limited from the outset to a community of consumption, and essentially only a community of meals. Clothing and shelter did not play a large role in the birthplace of Christianity, or in Southern and Central Italy. Even so far-reaching a communism as that of the Essenes had only hints of a community of clothing; private property can not be eliminated in this domain. Common dwellings were hard to manage in the metropolis, since the workrooms of the individual comrades might be far apart and there was so much speculation in housing, making large sums of money necessary for the purchase of a house in the days of early Christianity. The lack of means of communication forced the inhabitants of large cities together into confined spaces and made the owners of this land absolute masters of the tenants, who were thoroughly fleeced. The houses were built as high as the technology of the time allowed, seven stories high in Rome or even more, and rents were forced up to incredible heights. This made housing usury a favorite form of investment for the capitalists of the time. Crassus, one of the triumvirate that bought up the Roman republic, had become rich primarily through speculation in housing.

The proletarians of the metropolis could not compete in this field. This alone made it impossible for them to institute a dwelling community. In addition, the Christian community could only exist as a secret league under the suspicious imperial government, and common dwellings would have made them easier to discover.

Thus, Christian communism could only appear in the form of common meals, as a lasting general institution for all the comrades.

The Gospels hardly mention anything beyond meals in common in speaking of the "kingdom of God," that is the future state. It is the only blessedness that is looked forward to; obviously, it was the one closest to the hearts of the early Christians.

This sort of practical communism was important for the free proletarians, but meant little to the slaves who as a rule belonged in the houses of their masters and were fed there, often poorly enough. Few slaves lived outside the master's household, for example those who kept shops in the city to sell the products of their masters' estates.

The most attractive feature for the slaves must have been the hope of the Messiah, the prospect of a kingdom of universal happiness, much more so than the practice of a communism that was possible only in forms that had little significance for them so long as they remained slaves.

We do not know what the first Christians thought of slavery. The Essenes condemned it, as we have seen. Philo tells us: "Nobody is a slave among them, but all are free, one working for the other. They hold that owning slaves is not only unjust and impious, but godless as well, a violation of the order of nature, which produced all equal . . . as brothers."

It is likely that the proletarians of the Messiah community in Jerusalem thought likewise.

But with the destruction of Jerusalem the prospects of a social revolution disappeared. The spokesmen for the Christian communities, so anxiously concerned with avoiding any suspicion of opposition to the powers that were, must also have tried to calm down any rebellious slaves there might have been in their ranks.

Thus the author of Paul's Epistle to the Colossians (as we have it, a "revision" or forgery of the second century) says to the slaves: "Servants, obey in all things your masters according to the flesh; not with eyeservice, as menpleasers; but in singleness of heart, fearing God" (3, verse 22).

Even stronger language is used by the writer of the first Epistle of Peter (apparently composed in the reign of Trajan): "Servants, be subject to your masters with all fear; not only to the good and gentle, but also to the forward.[15] For this is thankworthy, if a man for conscience toward God endure grief, suffering wrongfully. For what glory is it, if, when ye be buffeted for your faults, ye shall take it patiently? but if, when ye do well, and suffer for it, ye take it patiently, this is acceptable with God" (2, verses 18 f.).

In fact, the budding Christian opportunism of the second century could reconcile itself to the fact that Christian masters should

15. The word is *skoliois*, combining injustice, dishonesty and guile.

own brothers of the community as slaves, as Paul's first letter to Timothy proves: "Let as many servants as are under the yoke count their own masters worthy of all honour, that the name of God and his doctrine be not blasphemed. And they that have believing masters, let them not despise them, because they are brethren; but rather do them service, because they are faithful and beloved, partakers of the benefit"[16] (6, verse 1 f.).

Nothing is more erroneous than the notion that Christianity did away with slavery; rather, it gave it fresh support. Antiquity kept slaves obedient only through fear. Christianity was the first to raise the spineless obedience of the slave to a moral duty, something to be performed with gladness.

Christianity, at least after it had ceased to be revolutionary, no longer held out the prospect of emancipation to the slave. Moreover, its practical communism seldom offered the slave any real advantages. The only thing that still might attract him was equality "before God," that is within the community, where every comrade was to be of equal value, where the slave could come to sit at the common love-feast alongside his master, if the latter also belonged to the community.

Callixtus, Christian slave of a Christian freedman, even became bishop of Rome (217-222).

But this kind of equality too no longer had much meaning. We need only recall how close the free proletariat had come to the status of the slaves, from whom it was often recruited; and now on the other hand the slaves of the imperial household could climb to high office in the state and often be fawned on even by aristocrats.

The fact that Christianity, for all its communism and all its proletarian feeling, could not do away with slavery even within its own ranks shows how deep its roots were in "pagan" antiquity, and how much ethics stands under the influence of the mode of production. Just as the human rights of the American Declaration of Independence made their peace with slavery, so did the all embracing brotherhood and love of neighbor, and equality of all

16. Actually, "partakers in the common meals" (agapētoi).

before God of the Messianic community. Christianity from the outset was primarily a religion of the free proletariat; and despite all the convergence of the two there always remained in antiquity some difference of interests between them and the slaves.

From the beginning the free proletarians predominated in the Christian community, so that the interests of the slaves were not always fully considered. That in turn must have helped to make the attraction of the community less for slaves than for the free proletariat, and strengthened the relative weight of the latter still more.

Economic developments worked in the same direction. Just at the time that gave the death-blow to the revolutionary tendencies within the Christian community, that is from the fall of Jerusalem on, a new era began for the Roman Empire, an era of universal peace—internal peace, and still more of external peace, for the expansive power of Roman power was gone. But war, civil war as well as wars of conquest, had been the means by which cheap slaves were supplied; that came to an end now. Slaves became rare and expensive; slave economy was no longer profitable, being replaced by the colonate in agriculture and by the labor of free workers in urban industry. The slave became less and less an instrument of the production of necessities and more and more an instrument of luxury. Personal services to the noble and the rich now became the chief function of slaves. The spirit of the slave became more and more identical with the spirit of the lackey. The days of Spartacus were over.

The opposition between slave and free proletarian must have been more acute on this account; and at the same time the number of slaves decreased while the number of free proletarians in the large cities grew. Both trends must have tended to reduce the influence of the slave element in the Christian community still further. No wonder that in the end Christianity had nothing left for the slaves.

This development is thoroughly understandable if we see in Christianity the precipitate of special class interests; it is inexplicable if we see it as a purely ideal formation. For the logical development of its basic ideas would have had to lead to the abolition of slavery; but all through history logic has always been brought up short by class interests.

THE DECLINE OF COMMUNISM

Acceptance of slavery, along with increasing restriction of the community of property to common meals, were not the only limitations the Christian community encountered in its effort to put its communistic tendencies into effect.

These tendencies required that every member of the community sell all he possessed and put the money at the disposal of the community for distribution to the comrades.

It is clear from the very beginning that any such procedure could not have been carried out on a large scale. It presupposed that at least half of society should remain unbelieving, for otherwise there would have been no one to buy the belongings of the faithful, nor any one from whom to buy the foodstuffs the faithful needed.

If the faithful wished to live by distributing rather than producing, there would always have to be enough unbelievers left to produce for the faithful. But even in this case the glory was in danger of a sorry end as soon as the faithful had sold, distributed and eaten up all their possessions. It is true that by that time the Messiah should have come down from the clouds and helped them over all the difficulties of "the flesh."

This never came to the test, however.

The number of the comrades that owned anything that would have been worth selling and distributing, was very small at the beginnings of the community. They could not live on that. The only way they could get a steady income was for each member to turn in his daily earnings to the community. Insofar as the comrades were not mere beggars or porters, they needed some property, however, in order to earn anything, property in means of production as weavers or potters or smiths, or in stocks of goods to sell as shopkeepers or peddlers.

Since, under the existing conditions, the community could not do like the Essenes and set up common workshops to produce what they required for themselves, since, that is, they could not emerge from the domain of commodity production and individual production, their communism had to adjust to private property in means of production and trading stocks.

Acceptance of the individual enterprise necessarily entailed acceptance of the separate household connected with it, the separate family and marriage, despite their common meals.

Here we come once more to meals in common as the practical upshot of their communistic tendencies.

It was not the only result. The proletarians had got together to face their poverty with united forces. If difficulties arose that prevented them from realizing complete communism, they felt all the more impelled to build up the mutual aid system to bring help to the individual in cases of unusual necessity.

The Christian communities were connected with each other. If a comrade came in from some other point, the community got him work, if he wanted to stay, or gave him travelling expenses, if he wanted to push on.

If a comrade fell sick, the community took care of him. If he died, they buried him at their expense and looked after his widow and children; if he got into jail, as was often enough the case, it was once more the community that gave him comfort and help.

The Christian proletarian organization thus made a set of functions for itself more or less corresponding to the insurance aspects of a modern trade union. In the Gospels, the practice of this mutual insurance association is what gives one a claim to eternal life. When the Messiah comes, he will divide men up into those that will have a share in the glory of the future state and eternal life, and those that will be condemned to eternal damnation. To the first, the sheep, the King will say:

"Come, ye blessed of my Father, inherit the kingdom prepared for you from the foundation of the world: For I was an hungered, and ye gave me meat: I was thirsty, and ye gave me drink: I was a stranger, and ye took me in: Naked, and ye clothed me: I was sick, and ye visited me: I was in prison, and ye came unto me."

The righteous will then answer that they had never done any such things for the King. "And the King shall answer and say unto them, Verily I say unto you, Inasmuch as you have done it unto one of the least of these my brethren, ye have done it unto me" (Matthew 25, verses 34 f.).

The common meals and mutual aid organization at any rate were the solid bond of the Christian community to hold its masses permanently together.

Yet it was precisely out of the performance of these mutual aids that a motive would arise that weakened and broke up the original communistic drive.

As the expectation of the Messiah lessened, it seemed more and more important to the community to obtain the means to operate the mutual aid machinery, the more the proletarian character of the Christian propaganda was undermined and the more the attempt was made to attract prosperous comrades, whose money could be put to good use.

The more money the community needed, the more strenuously its agitators exerted themselves to show rich sympathizers how vain treasures of gold and silver were, how worthless compared to the bliss of eternal life, which the rich could gain only by disposing of their possessions. And their preaching was not to go without success in that period of general moral depression, especially among the wealthy classes. How many there were who were disgusted with all enjoyment after a dissipated and profligate youth! After they had run through all the sensations that money could buy, there was only sensation left, that of being without money.

Down into the middle ages we keep coming from time to time upon rich people who give all their possessions to the poor and lead the life of a beggar—for the most part, after having tasted lavishly of all the world's delights.

Nevertheless, the appearance of such people was a stroke of good luck that did not occur as often as the community needed it. As

poverty increased in the Empire and the number of lumpenproletarians grew larger, the greater was the need to attract rich people
to meet the needs of the community.

It was an easier task to persuade a rich man to leave his whole
fortune to the community for charitable purposes after his death,
than getting him to give it away during his lifetime. Childlessness was widespread at that time, and family ties very weak; the
urge to leave one's inheritance to relatives was often small indeed.
Again, interest in one's own personality, individualism, had
reached a high point; desire for continued life of the personality
after death, and happy life at that, was highly developed.

Christian doctrine came more than halfway to meet this desire;
a convenient method of assuring eternal blissful life without stint-
ing oneself in the earthly life was open to the rich man, if he gave
his property away when he did not need it any more, after his
death. With his inheritance, which he did not know what to do
with in any case, he could now purchase eternal bliss.

While the Christian agitators impressed the young and pas-
sionate rich men through the revulsion they felt for the life they
had led, they impressed the old and tired rich through their fear
of death and the torments of Hell facing them. From that time
down to the present inheritance-hunting has been a favored means
of Christian agitators to bring new fodder to the good stomach
of the church.

In the first centuries of the community, however, the supply of
rich inheritances was meager, and the more so in that the community, being a secret league, was not a juristic person and thus
could not inherit directly.

The effort was accordingly made to get the rich to support the
community even during their lifetimes, even if they would not
consent to carry out strictly the command of the Lord to distribute among the poor everything they possessed. We have seen
that at that time generosity was very common among the rich,
since accumulation of capital did not yet play any role in the
mode of production. The community could profit by the generosity and derive a steady income from it, if it could only succeed

in arousing the interest and sympathy of the rich for the community. As the community ceased to be a fighting organization and charities came more and more to the fore within it, the stronger were its tendencies to temper its original proletarian hatred against the rich and to make staying in the community attractive to the rich, even if they stayed rich and held on to their money.

The world view of the community—abandonment of the old gods, monotheism, belief in resurrection, expectation of a savior— these were all things, we have seen, that corresponded to the general desires of the time and must have made the Christian doctrine welcome even in high circles.

Moreover, in view of the growing distress of the masses, the rich looked for ways of checking it, as the foundations of orphanages prove; for this distress menaced all of society. This too must have made them more sympathetic to the Christian organizations.

Finally, popularity-seeking was also an element in getting support for the Christian communities, at least wherever those communities had got influence over an important fraction of the population.

This lent the Christian community an attraction even for those rich people who had not come to escape from the world or from desperation, and were driven to promise their heritages out of fear of death and terror of the torments of Hell.

However, if rich people were to feel at home in the community, it would have to change its character completely, and give up its class hatred against the rich.

How painful this effort to attract the rich and make concessions to them was to proletarian fighters in the community is seen by the previously mentioned letter of James to the twelve tribes in the Diaspora in the middle of the second century. He warns the comrades:

"For if there come unto your assembly a man with a gold ring, in goodly apparel, and there come in also a poor man in vile raiment; And ye have respect to him that weareth the gay clothing, and say unto him, Sit thou here in a good place; and say to the poor, Stand thou there, or sit here under my footstool: Are ye not then partial in yourselves, and are become judges of evil thoughts? . . . ye have despised the poor . . . if ye have respect to persons, ye commit sin" (2, verses 2 to 9).

Then he turns against the tendency to require the rich only to accept the creed in theory and not give up their money:

"What does it profit, my brethren, though a man say he have faith, and have not works? can faith save him? If a brother or sister be naked, and destitute of daily food, And one of you say unto them, Depart in peace, be ye warmed and filled; nowithstanding ye give them not those things which are needful to the body; what doth it profit? Even so faith, if it hath not works, is dead, being alone" (2, verses 14 to 17).

The foundation of the organization was to be sure not changed by respect of the rich. It remained the same in theory and in practice. But the duty to contribute everything one owned to the community was replaced by a voluntary contribution, often of only a small part.

The *Apologeticus* of Tertullian is somewhat later than the Epistle of James; it dates from the end of the second century. In it too the organization of the community is depicted:

"If we too have a sort of fund, it is not built up by any kind of admission fee, which would be a sort of sale of religion, but each makes a reasonable gift on a fixed day of the month or when and as much as he can and will; for nobody is forced, but each man gives willingly. These are also the pence of charity; for none of it goes to feasting and drinking or useless gluttony, but to support and bury the poor, to help destitute orphan boys and girls, as well as house-ridden old people and the shipwrecked, or people who are in the mines, the islands or in prison only for belonging to the fellowship of God—these are entitled to be cared for because of their beliefs."

He continues: "We, knowing ourselves joined together in heart and soul, have no reservations as to community of goods: everything is in common with us, except the women; for community stops with us in the only place that others practice it."[17]

In theory, therefore, communism was maintained, only seeming to lose some of its rigor in practice. But as the wealthy were taken more and more into consideration, the entire nature of the community changed imperceptibly; for formerly it had been based exclusively on proletarian conditions. Not only must those elements that favored winning rich members have worked against class hatred in the community, but the inner procedures of the community must often have taken a different form now.

Despite all the qualifications that communism had undergone, the common meal had remained the firm bond that kept all the fellows together. The arrangements for support applied only to isolated cases of distress, which to be sure might strike anyone. The common meal satisfied the daily need of all. At it the whole community gathered together; it was the center around which the whole community revolved.

The common meal, however, as a meal, had no point for the prosperous comrades. They ate and drank better and more conveniently at home. The simple, often coarse fare must have repelled jaded palates. If they took part in it, they came only to share in the community life, not to eat their fill. What for the others was the satisfaction of a bodily need was for them only the satisfaction of a spiritual need, partaking of bread and wine was a purely symbolic action. The more wealthy people there were in the community, the greater the number of those elements at the common meals who came only for the assembly and its symbols, not for meat and drink. So in the second century the actual common meals for the poorer members were separated from the merely symbolical meals for the whole community, and in the fourth century, after the church had become the dominant power in the state, the first kind of meals were crowded out of the assembly houses of the community, the churches. The common

17. Cited in Harnack, *Die Mission und Ausbreitung des Christentums in den ersten drei Jahrhunderten*, 1906, I, p. 132. Cf. Pfleiderer, *Urchristentum*, II, p. 672 f.

meals decayed further and in the next century were abolished completely. With that the most prominent feature of practical communism disappeared from the Christian community, and was replaced by charity, care for the poor and the sick, which has come down to our time, in a stunted form to be sure.

There was now nothing left in the community that could displease the rich. It was no longer a proletarian institution. The rich, who originally, if they failed to share their property with the poor, had been completely excluded from the "kingdom of God," were now able to play the same role in that realm as in the "world of the devil," and they made full use of the possibility.

But not only were the old class oppositions duplicated in the Christian community: a new ruling class grew up in it, a new bureaucracy and a new chief, the bishop, whom we shall soon meet.

It was the Christian community, not Christian communism, to which the Roman emperors finally bowed. The victory of Christianity did not denote the dictatorship of the proletariat, but the dictatorship of the gentlemen who had grown big in their community.

The champions and martyrs of the early communities, who had devoted their possessions, their labor, their lives for the salvation of the poor and miserable, had only laid the groundwork for a new kind of subjection and exploitation.

APOSTLES, PROPHETS AND TEACHERS

Originally there were no officers in the community and no distinctions among the comrades. Every man and even every woman could come forward as teacher and agitator upon feeling the capacity to do so. Each one spoke as he thought, from the heart, or as they said then, as the spirit moved him. Most of the members of course continued to practice their trades, but those who won especial prestige gave away what they had and devoted themselves entirely to agitation as apostles or prophets. Out of this arose a new class difference.

Two classes took form now within the Christian community: the ordinary members, whose practical communism extended only to the common meals and charitable institutions that the community carried on: finding jobs, support of widows and orphans and prisoners, sickness insurance, burial fund. But there were also the "saints" or "perfect ones," who carried communism out radically, renouncing all possessions and individual marriage, and giving all they possessed to the community.

That made a fine impression and, as their mere titles show, these radical elements won a high position in the community. They felt themselves elevated above the ordinary comrades and acted like a select leadership.

Thus it was radical communism itself that give birth to a new aristocracy.

Like any aristocracy it did not limit itself to taking command over the rest of the community; it also tried to exploit it.

After all, what were the "saints" to live on if they had given away all the means of production and stocks of goods they possessed? They had nothing left but occasional employment as porters or messengers and so forth—or begging.

The first thing to come to mind would be to get a living by begging from the comrades and the community itself, who could not let a man or woman of merit go hungry, especially when the meritorious member possessed propagandistic gifts, gifts which at that time to be sure did not require any hard-learned knowledge, but only temperament, ingenuity and combativeness.

Paul was already quarreling with the Corinthians over the duty of the community to relieve him and the other apostles of manual labor and to support him:

"Am I not an apostle? am I not free? have I not seen Jesus Christ our Lord? are not ye my work in the Lord? . . . Have we not power to lead about a sister, a wife, as well as other apostles, and as the brethren of the Lord, and Cephas? Or I only and Barnabas, have not we power to forbear working? . . . who feedeth a flock, and eateth not of the milk of the flock? . . . For it is written in the law of Moses, Thou shalt not muzzle the mouth of the ox that treadeth out the corn. Doth God take care for oxen? Or saith he it altogether for our sakes?" By the ox that treadeth out the corn God means us, Paul explains. Naturally, it is not a case of oxen that are threshing empty straw. The apostle continues: "If we have sown unto you spiritual thing, is it a great thing if we shall reap your carnal things? If others be partakers of this power over you, are not we rather?" (I Corinthians 9, verses 1 to 12).

The last sentence, it may be noted in passing, hints at the communistic nature of the first Christian communities.

After this brief for taking good care of the apostles, Paul remarks that he is not speaking for himself, but for others; he asks nothing of the Corinthians. He lets himself be kept by other communities: "I robbed other churches, taking wages of them, to do you service . . . that which was lacking to me the brethren which came from Macedonia supplied" (II Corinthians 11, verses 8 f.).

This of course does not alter the fact that Paul stressed the obligation of the community to care for its "saints," who recognized no obligation to work.

The impression this sort of Christian communism made on the unbelievers is shown by the story of Peregrinus Proteus, written by Lucian in 165. The satirist is not an impartial witness, of course; he retails highly improbable malicious gossip, as when he claims that Peregrinus left his native city of Parium on the Hellespont because he had killed his father. Since no prosecution ensued, the event is doubtful to say the least.

But making all necessary reservations, there is still enough left in Lucian's report to be worth attention, for it not only shows how the Christian community appeared to the Gentiles, but also gives glimpses of their actual life.

After Lucian has said a number of unpleasant things about Peregrinus, he relates how the latter exiled himself after the murder of his father and roamed the world as a vagabond:

"At this time he also became acquainted with the remarkable wisdom of the Christians by associating with their priests and scribes in Palestine. Compared to him they soon turned out to be like little children, and he became their prophet, presided at their love-feasts (*thasiarchēs*), president of the synagogue [Lucian lumps Jews and Christians together.—K.], all in one; he explained and commented some writings to them; others he made up; in a word, they considered him a god, made him their lawgiver and named him their president. They still to be sure worship that great man, the one crucified in Palestine, because he introduced this new religion into the world.[18] For this reason Peregrinus was arrested then thrown into prison, which gave him a great reputation for the rest of his life, his cunning and ambition, which were his dominant passions.

"As he lay in jail, the Christians, who thought it a catastrophe, moved heaven and earth to help him escape. When they gave that up as impossible, they showered him with every conceivable attention and care. From early morning on old women, widows and orphans could be seen sitting outside the prison, while their leaders bribed the guards and passed the night with him. All sorts of dishes were brought in to him, they related their holy legends to each other, and Peregrinus the Good, as he was now called, was a new Socrates to them. Delegates even came from Christian communities in the cities of Asia to give him support, stand by him in court and comfort him. In cases such as this, which concerned their community, they show an incredible zeal, sparing nothing. Peregrinus also got much money from them on account of his imprisonment, and profited greatly thereby.

"For the poor fools live in the conviction that they will be quite immortal and live for ever, and on that account despise death and often seek it out of their own will. Moreover, their first legislator convinced them that they would all be brothers, once they had abjured the Greek gods, prayed to that crucified teacher (*sophistes*) of theirs and lived according to his laws; hence

18. This sentence interrupts the thought, and is not free from objections in other respects. In particular the word "to be sure" (*goun*) arouses suspicion. In addition, Suidas, a tenth century lexicographer, expressly notes that Lucian "slandered Christ himself" in his biography of Peregrinus. No such passage is to be found in extant texts. One is tempted to look for it in the sentence in question, and to assume that here Lucian had mocked Jesus, that pious souls had been scandalized at that and been led to change the text to have an opposite sense when they were copying it. As a matter of fact, various scholars believe the sentence to be a Christian forgery in its present form.

they thought equally little of all things and considered them as held in common, with no good reason for this outlook. Now if a shrewd scoundrel comes to them, one who knows how to take advantage of this situation, in a little while he will become very rich among them, because he will be able to lead the simple folk around by the nose."

This is of course not to be accepted literally. It is on a level with the myths about the riches that the agitators of social democracy pile up out of the workers' pennies. The Christian community would have to become richer than it was then for anyone to be able to get rich out of it. But it is quite probable that they looked carefully after their agitators and organizers, and that unscrupulous sharpers could take advantage of the system. A notable feature is the testimony to the communism of the community.

Lucian continues, saying that the governor of Syria releases Peregrinus as insignificant. Peregrinus then went back to his native city, where he found his father's inheritance well shrunk. There was still a considerable sum left, which seemed enormous to his supporters, and that even Lucian, who wishes him no good, sets at fifteen talents ($18,000). He gave this to the population of his city, Lucian says, to buy his way out of the accusation of parricide.

"He got up to speak in the popular assembly of the Parians. He already had long hair, wore a dirty cloak, had a scrip hanging from his shoulder and a staff in his hand, and in general was theatrically got up. In this costume he appeared before them and said that all the property that his blessed father had left was the property of the people. When the people heard this, poor devils whose mouth was watering for the division, they shouted that he was the only friend of wisdom and his country, the only follower of Diogenes and Crates. His enemies were muzzled, and if anyone had dared to recall the murder, he would have been struck down on the spot.

"He now set out as a vagabond for the second time, abundantly provided with travelling expenses by the Christians, who followed him everywhere and saw to it that he wanted for nothing. In this way he got by for a time."[19]

Finally however he was expelled from the community, allegedly for having eaten forbidden foods. This deprived him of his livelihood, and he now tried, but in vain, to get his property back. He now went through Egypt, Italy and Greece as an ascetic Cynic philosopher, and finally at the Olympic games put an end to his life in a theatrical manner, before an audience invited to witness the act, by jumping into a funeral pyre at midnight by the light of the moon.

We see that the period in which Christianity arose produced queer creatures. However, it would be unjust to men like Peregrinus to think of them only as swindlers. His voluntary death is against that. To use suicide as a means of advertisement requires infinite vanity and sensation-seeking, and a little contempt for the world and weariness of life, or insanity.

The Peregrinus Proteus that Lucian paints may not have been a genuine portrait but a caricature; still, it is a work of genius.

The essence of caricature is not mere distortion of the subject, but one-sided emphasis and exaggeration of its characteristic and decisive features. The true caricaturist can not be a mere grotesque buffoon; he has to see into things and recognize what is essential and significant about them.

Lucian too has brought out those aspects of Peregrinus that were to be of importance for the whole class of "holy and perfect" men that Peregrinus represented. They may have been impelled by the most diverse motives, partly sublime, partly insane, and may have thought of themselves as extremely unselfish, and yet their relationship to the community contained the germs of the exploitation that Lucian saw. The enrichment of the penniless "saints" by the community communism may still have been an exaggeration in those days, but it soon became a reality, and finally such a reality that it went far beyond the satirist's crudest exaggerations.

19. Lucian, *On the Death of Peregrinus*, 11 to 16.

Lucian stresses the "wealth" that the prophets obtained; another pagan, a contemporary of Lucian, derided their folly.

Celsus described "how prophecy is done in Phoenicia and Palestine":

"There are many who, although they are men without name or reputation, act freely and on the slightest provocation as if they had prophetic ecstasies, both in sacred matters and elsewhere; others wander about as beggars in cities and camps, presenting the same spectacle. On the lips of each one of them the words come freely, 'I am God,' or 'God's Son,' or 'God's Spirit.' 'I have come, for the end of the world is in sight, and you men are going to destruction for your injustices. But I will save you, and you will soon see me come again with celestial power! Blessed is he that honors me now! I will give all the rest to the eternal fire, cities as well as countries and men. Those who now refuse to recognize the judgment that awaits them will then be of a different mind, and sigh, but in vain! But those that believed in me, those will I keep forever!' They intersperse these high-sounding threats with strange, half-crazy and absolutely incomprehensible words, so obscure and meaningless that no one can make sense of them, no matter how ingenious he is; but any fathead or loafer can interpret them as he pleases. . . . These pretended prophets, whom I have heard with my own ears more than once, I have argued with, and they have confessed their weaknesses and admitted that they invented their unintelligible words themselves."[20]

Here again we have the agreeable mixture of swindler and prophet; but here too we should be going too far if we saw the whole thing merely as a swindle. All it proves is a general state of mind among the people that gave swindlers a fertile field to operate in, but that must also have aroused genuine enthusiasm and ecstasy in excitable minds.

Apostles and prophets must have been alike in this respect. There was one essential difference between them: the apostles had no fixed residence but moved around constantly (hence their

20. Cited in Harnack's edition of the *Lehre der zwölf Apostel,* p. 130 f.

name, *apostolos,* messenger, traveller, seafarer); the prophets were the local worthies.

The apostolate must have been the first to develop. So long as a community was small, it could not maintain a permanent agitator. As soon as they had exhausted their available resources, he had to go further. And so long as the number of communities was small, the most important objective was to establish new communities in cities that as yet had none. Extending the organization to new areas which it had not yet reached, and maintaining connections between them, were the chief tasks of these wandering agitators, the apostles. It is to them above all that the Christian organization owes its international nature, which contributed so much to keeping it alive. A local organization might be wiped out if it stood by itself; but the government hardly had means at that time to enable it to persecute all the Christian communities from one end of the Empire to the other. There always were some left to give material help to the persecuted and serve as places of refuge for them.

This was the work primarily of the roving apostles, who must have been fairly numerous at times.

Local agitators, devoting themselves exclusively to agitation, could only appear when some communities had become so large that their means allowed them to support such agitators.

As there came to be more and more cities with Christian communities, and the communities grew larger, the prophets flourished and the field of the apostles' activity dwindled, since they had operated chiefly in cities in which the communities were small or non-existent. The prestige of the apostles had to decline.

There must also have arisen a certain opposition between them them and the prophets. For, the communities had limited means. The more the apostles got, the less there was for the prophets. The latter must therefore have tried to lower the already declining prestige of the apostles, to limit the gifts made to them and on the other hand to raise their own prestige and establish fixed claims to the gifts of the believers.

These efforts come to light very well in the *Doctrine of the*

Twelve Apostles (Didache), which we have often cited, a work composed between 135 and 170. It says:

"Every apostle that comes to you shall be received like the Lord. But he will stay no longer than one day, or a second day if necessary. If he stays three days, however, he is a false prophet. When the apostle leaves, he shall receive no more than enough bread to get him to his next sleeping place. If he asks for money, he is a false prophet.

"Every prophet who speaks with the spirit is not to be examined or tested; for any sin can be forgiven, but this sin is not forgiven. But not everyone who speaks with the spirit is a prophet, but only if he acts like the Lord; the prophet and the false prophet can therefore be told apart by their actions. And no prophet who, driven by the Holy Ghost, makes a feast (for the poor.—Harnack) eats of it; such a one is a false prophet. Any prophet who teaches the truth, if he does not do as he teaches, is a false prophet. But every prophet, tried and true, who acts with a view to the earthly secret of the church, yet does not preach that all should do as he does, shall not be judged by you; for he has his judgment in God; just so did the old [Christian] prophets act."

We have already seen that this passage probably refers to the free love that should be permitted the prophets, if they do not call on the community to imitate their example.

The book goes on:

"But he who says in the name of the spirit: give me money or something else, hear him not; but if he asks gifts for other needy persons, no one shall condemn him.

"Let everyone who comes in the name of the Lord [i.e., every comrade.—K.] be received; but then you shall test him and distinguish the true from the false, for you must have insight. If the newcomer is a traveler, help him; but he should not stay more than two or three days with you, if it is necessary. If he wants to settle among you, let him work and eat, if he is a craftsman. If he has no trade, see to it with care that no Christian lives among you as an idler. If he will not be governed in that

THE BEGINNINGS OF CHRISTIANITY   373

sense, he is one who wants to gain by Christ. Keep far from such a one."

Thus it already seemed necessary to take precautions against having the community overrun and exploited by itinerant beggars. This was only to apply to ordinary beggars, however:

"But every true prophet that will settle down with you is worth his keep. A true teacher is worth his keep like every worker. Thou shalt take all the first fruit of wine-press and threshing-floor, of cattle and sheep, and give them to the prophets, for they are your high priests. But if you have no prophet, give them to the poor. When you prepare dough, take the first of it and give it to the prophets. Likewise, when you open a cask of oil or wine, give the first of it to the prophets. Take the first fruits of money and clothing and all kinds of belongings according to your measure and give it according to the commandment."

The apostles come off badly in these regulations. They could not yet be suppressed out of hand. But the community in which they appear is to pack them off as soon as possible. The ordinary roving comrade has a right to be supported for two or three days by the community, but the apostle, poor devil, only for one or two days. And of money he must take none at all.

The prophet however is "worth his keep"! He must be supported from the community purse. In addition the faithful are obliged to give him all the first fruits of wine and bread and meat, of oil and clothing, even of money income.

That fits well with the picture Lucian gives of the comfortable life of Peregrinus, who gave himself out to be a prophet, just at the time the *Didache* was being written.

While the prophets were thus getting the better of the apostles, new competition for them arose in the form of the teachers, who may not have had any great significance at the time the *Didache* was written, for they are hardly mentioned in it.

Along with these three there were other elements active in the the community who are not named in the *Didache*. Paul mentions all of them in the first Epistle to the Corinthians (12, verse 28): "And God hath set some in the church, first apostles, secondarily prophets, thirdly teachers, after that miracles, then gifts of healings, helps, governments, diversities of tongues."

Among these the gifts of helps and governments became very important, but not those of quackery and charlatanism which did not take on any forms within the community that would have distinguished them from the forms commonly known at that time. The rise of the teachers is connected with the entry of prosperous and educated elements into the community. The apostles and prophets were ignorant men, who spoke out without any previous study. The educated would turn their noses up at them. Soon some of these educated men, impressed by the charitable activities of the community organization or by its might, or perhaps attracted by the general character of the Christian doctrine, tried to raise that doctrine to the level of what counted as science at that time, which was no longer very much. These became the teachers. They first tried to fill Christianity with the spirit of a Seneca or a Philo, something of which there had not been much up to then.

Still they were regarded with mistrust and envy by the mass of the community as well as by the majority of the apostles and prophets; it may have been a relation analogous to that between "the workmen's horny hands" and the "intellectuals." Yet as the prosperous and educated elements in the community grew, the teachers gained in prestige and would finally have put an end to prophets and apostles.

But before things went so far, all three categories were absorbed by a power that became stronger than all of them, but is mentioned only incidentally in the *Didache,* namely the Bishop.

THE BISHOP

The beginnings of the Christian communities were like any new establishment of a proletarian society. Its founders, the apostles, had to do all the work in the community, propaganda, organization and administration. But as the community persists and grows, the need for a division of labor is felt, the necessity of assigning particular functions to definite men.

The administration of the income and expenditure of the community was the first definite community office.

Propaganda could be carried on by every member as he pleased. Even those who devoted themselves exclusively to it, were still not charged with it by the community even in the second century, as we have seen. Apostles and prophets named themselves to their calling, or, as it appeared to them, it was only God's voice that they were following. The prestige of the individual propagandist in the community, whether apostle or prophet, and therefore his income too, depended on the impression he made, on his personality.

In addition, the maintenance of party discipline, if we may use the term, was something the community itself took care of so long as it was small and all the members knew each other well. It decided for itself on the admission of new members; who performed the ceremony of admission, the baptism, was immaterial. They were the tribunal before which all the complaints of comrades against comrades were to be brought. The Christians distrusted the official courts as much as the Social Democrats do today. In addition, their social views were in sharp opposition to those of the official judge. A Christian would have considered it a sin to go before such a man to seek his rights, especially when the dispute was with a fellow Christian. This planted the seed of that special judicial power that the church has always claimed over its believers in the face of the civil courts. Later, of course, the original nature of the decisions here changed into their direct contrary, for at first they meant doing away with any class justice, the judgment of the accused by his fellows.

In Paul's first Epistle to the Corinthians (6, verses 1 f.), we find:

"Dare any of you, having a matter against another, go to law before the unjust, and not before the saints? Do ye not know that the saints shall judge the world? and if the world shall be judged by you, are ye unworthy to judge the smallest matters? Know ye not that we shall judge angels? how much more things that pertain to this life? If then ye have judgments of things pertaining to this life, set them to judge who are least esteemed in the church."

Maintenance of discipline and peace in the community was at first just as formless as was propaganda, and bound to no definite office or authority.

The economic factor however early required regulation, especially since the community was not merely a propaganda society, but was a mutual aid society from the very beginning.

According to the Acts of the Apostles the need was early felt in the community of Jerusalem of having special members take care of the collection and distribution of the members' contributions, especially with serving the food at table. *Diakoneō* means to serve, and particularly to serve at table. This was obviously the first function of the "deacons," as the common meal was the most important activity of primitive Christian communism.

Acts relates: "And in those days, when the number of the disciples was multiplied, there arose a murmuring of the Greeks against the Hebrews, because their widows were neglected in the daily ministration [viz. meals, *diakonia*]. Then the twelve [apostles; actually there were only eleven, if we take all the Gospel stories at face value] called the multitude of the disciples unto them, and said, It is not reason that we should leave the word of God, and serve tables. Wherefore, brethren, look ye out among you seven men of honest report, full of the Holy Ghost and wisdom, whom we may appoint over to this business" (6, verses 1 to 3).

That is how it happened according to the account, and that is pretty much as it must have happened, by the nature of the case.

The apostles were therefore relieved from acting as waiters in the people's house, something they must previously have done along with the propaganda work, and that became onerous as the community grew. But a division of labor must soon have been needed among the newly-introduced waiters, the deacons. Serving at table, cleaning up and other work of that sort was entirely different from the job of collecting and administering the members' contributions. The latter meant a confidential position of great importance, especially as the community grew and had larger income. This position required considerable eloquence, business experience and kindness combined with firmness.

An administrator was therefore set over the deacons.

The appointment of such an official was an obvious necessity. Any society that has property or income must have one. In the societies and unions of Asia Minor their administrative and financial officers bore the title of *epimeletes* or *episcopos* (observer, overseer). The same name was also used for certain civil functionaries. Hatch, who has studied this development in detail and described it in a book to which we owe much of our knowledge of the subject,[21] cites a Roman jurist, Charisius, who says: "*Episcopi* [bishops] are those who superintend the bread and the other things to be bought, that serve the people of the city as daily food."

The city bishop was therefore a superintendent who in the main saw to the right feeding of the population. It was a natural step to give the same title to the superintendent of the Christian "house of the people."

We have already read of the common purse of the community, of which Tertullian speaks. We learn from the first apology of Justin Martyr (born about 100 A.D.) that it was in charge of a special trustee: "Those who can and will give something of their property at their discretion, which is collected and presented to the overseer, who with it supports the orphans and widows, those who are in need on account of sickness or some other cause, the prisoners and visitors from foreign parts and in general is concerned with anyone in need."

Thus much work, much responsibility, and also much power was put into the hands of the bishops.

At the beginning of the community the office of bishop was an honorary post like that of his assistants and all the functionaries of the community, and was carried on gratis along with working for a living.

21. Edwin Hatch, *Die Gesellschaftsverfassung der christlichen Kirchen im Altertum*. Translated and with notes by A. Harnack, Giessen, 1883.

"The bishops and presbyters of that time ran banks, practiced as physicians, worked as silversmiths, herded sheep and sold their products in the open market. . . . The most important decisions of the old provincial synods that have come down to us with relation to them are that the bishops should not peddle their wares from market to market and should not use their position to buy cheaper and sell dearer than others."[22]

As a community grew, however, it became impossible to look after its many financial functions as a second job. The bishop was made an employee of the community, which paid him for his work.

With this his position became a permanent one. The community of course could discharge him at any time, if he did not suit them, but obviously they would not lightly put a man out on the streets after having taken him away from his occupation. Moreover, taking care of the business of the community required a good deal of ability and acquaintance with conditions in the community that could be obtained only by long service in the job. It was therefore in the interests of the smooth development of the community's affairs to avoid any unnecessary changing of bishops.

But the longer the bishop stayed in his position, the more his prestige and power must have increased, if he was big enough for the job.

He was not the only permanent employee of the community. The post of the deacons too could not be filled forever as a supplementary employment. Like the bishops they began to be paid out of the community funds, but were his subordinates. The bishop had to deal with them, and so in choosing them he was consulted first. Being able to fill offices in the community raised his influence still further.

As the community expanded, it became impossible for it to take care of its discipline by itself. It was not only that the number of members grew, but they included a greater variety of elements. If at first all formed a single family, in which every one knew all the other comrades, all were completely in accord in feeling and

22. Hatch, *op. cit.*, p. 152 f.

thinking and constituted a chosen band of enthusiasts glad to make sacrifices, this gradually ceased to be the case as the community became larger. All sorts of people came into it, from all sorts of classes and localities, often alien to each other and without mutual understanding, and sometimes even hostile to each other, such as slaves and slave-owners; in addition, there were elements who were not moved by enthusiasm but coolly reckoned on taking advantage of the credulity and self-sacrificing spirit of the comrades. Add to that differences in outlook and philosophy, and all this must have led to all sorts of disputes, often disputes that could not be settled off hand by discussion in the assembly but required long investigations into the facts of the case.

A committee of elders or presbyters was therefore entrusted with keeping the discipline of the community and smoothing out disputes within it, to report to the community on the expulsion of unworthy members and the admission of new ones, whose baptism they performed.

The bishop, who had the most exact knowledge of the relationships within the community, was the natural chairman of this committee. This also gave him influence over the moral supervision and legal functions of the community. As the presbyters (from which the word "priest" is derived) became regular paid officers of the community as a result of its growth, they came, along with the deacons, under the authority of the administrator of the community finances, the bishop.

In a large city the community could easily become so large that a single building would not be enough for their assembly. It was divided into districts. In every district group there was a deacon to serve the comrades and a presbyter was assigned by the bishop to conduct the group and to represent the bishop. Similar measures were taken with respect to the suburbs and villages. Where they were on the edges of a community like that of Rome or Alexandria, the influence of the great city was overwhelming, and the neighboring community came of their own accord under the influence of the city and its bishop, who sent them deacons and presbyters.

In this way there gradually was formed a community bureaucracy headed by the bishop, and it became increasingly independent and powerful. A man had to have the maximum of prestige in the community to be chosen for a post that was so much sought after. Once it was won, it carried with it so much power that given a little shrewdness and courage the will of the bishop, whose tendencies coincided with those of the majority of his community to begin with, would more and more be decisive, particularly in personal questions. As a result, his authority came to extend not only to persons engaged in the administration of the community, but also to those who were engaged with propaganda and theory.

As we have seen, the apostles were pushed into the background by the prophets in the second century. Both however, apostles as well as prophets, could often clash with the bishop, who would not hesitate to make his financial and moral power felt. It would not be hard for him to make life in the community miserable for apostles and prophets, and teachers too, if any of them manifested tendencies he did not care for. And that would happen frequently enough, especially with apostles and prophets.

Bishops, that is men who dealt with money, would not be chosen from among unworldly enthusiasts, but rather sober, business-like practical men. These men knew how to appreciate the value of money and of prosperous moneyed members of the community. It would be they who would represent opportunistic revisionism in the Christian community and work to mitigate hatred against the rich within it, to tone down the doctrines of the community in a way that would make it pleasanter for wealthy people to remain within it.

The rich of that period were also the educated.

Making the community fit the needs of the rich and educated meant weakening the influence of apostles and prophets and reducing their tendencies *ad absurdum,* as well as the tendencies of those who hated riches out of mere boorishness and of those unselfish elements who combatted riches out of their convictions, and the more so if they had once been rich and given their entire fortune to the community to help realize its lofty communistic ideal.

In the struggle between rigorism and opportunism it was the latter that won; that is, the bishops won over the apostles and the prophets, who had fewer and fewer opportunities for action, or even for existence, in the community. Their place was more and more taken by officers of the community. Since every comrade had originally had the right to speak in the assembly and engage in propaganda, officers could do so too, and they must have done so to a great extent. It is clear that comrades that stood out from the anonymous mass as well-known orators would be more likely to be elected to office than unknowns. In addition propaganda activity might be required of the successful candidates over and above their administrative and judicial work. Many administrators laid more stress on propaganda work than on their primary official duties, when the growth of the community created new organs that took some of the load off the others. Often the deacons could devote themselve more to propaganda, since their functions were performed in large communities by special hospitals, orphanages, asylums for the poor and hostels for visiting comrades.

At the same time the growth of the community and its economic functions made it necessary to provide the officers with some training in their duties. It would have been too expensive and dangerous now to let every man gain his skill by experience in practice. The new crop of officers of the community was brought to the house of the bishop and made acquainted there with the obligations of their positions in the church. If they had to carry on propaganda in addition to their official duties, it was natural to train them for that purpose too in the bishop's house, instructing them in the community's doctrines.

Thus the bishop became the center both of the economic and propaganda work of the community; in this case too ideology had to give way to economics.

There now grew up an official doctrine, recognized and propagated by the bureaucracy of the community; views that differed from it were put down by all the means at their disposal.

The tendencies the bishops opposed were those of the original proletarian communism with its hostility to state and property. In keeping with the ignorance of the lower strata of the population, their credulity, the incompatability of their hopes with actuality, it was just these tendencies that were linked up with a particular faith in miracles and spiritual exaltations. Although the official church could do very well in this domain, the sects which it persecuted in the first centuries were far ahead of it in weird exaggerations.

Sympathy with the oppressed and aversion to all oppression should not mislead us into regarding any opposition to the official church or every heresy as equivalent to a higher conception.

The formulation of an official church doctrine was aided by other circumstances too.

We do not know very much about the doctrines of the first Christian communities. To judge by various indications, they were not very comprehensive and were very simple. In any case we can not presume that they already contained everything that the Gospels later added as the doctrine of Jesus.

We may grant, if we have to, the probability that Jesus lived and was crucified, probably because of an attempted rebellion; but that is all that can be said of him. What is said about his teaching is so devoid of evidence, so contradictory and so unoriginal, such a collection of general moral commonplaces that were on everyone's lips at that time, that no part of it can be traced back to any genuine doctrine of Jesus'.

We are justified in imagining the beginnings of the Christian communities as more or less on the pattern of the beginnings of the socialistic societies, with which they have so many other resemblances. If we look at these beginnings, we never find an overpowering personality, whose theory sets the tone for the further course of the movement, but a chaotic fermentation, an uncertain instinctive search and groping by numerous proletarians, none of them standing out much beyond his fellows, all motivated by more or less the same tendencies while often falling into extreme peculiarities. For example, some such picture as this is presented by the beginnings of the proletarian-socialistic movement in the 1830's and 40's. The League of the Just, the later Communist League, already had a considerable history behind it before Marx and Engels gave it a definite theoretical basis in the form of the *Communist Manifesto*. And this league itself was but the continuation of earlier proletarian currents in France and England. Without Marx and Engels its doctrine would still have remained for a long time in the stage of fermentation. Nevertheless, the two fathers of the *Communist Manifesto* were able to attain their outstanding and decisive position only because they had mastered the science that their time provided.

There is nothing to prove, on the contrary it is quite out of the question, that a personality with a deep scientific training presided over the cradle of Christianity. It is expressly said of Jesus that he was no better educated than his comrades, the simplest of proletarians. Paul does not point to his outstanding knowledge, but to his martyr death and resurrection. It was this death that made the deepest impression on the Christians.

The kind of teaching that was done in the first century of Christianity bears this out.

The apostles and prophets do not reproduce a definite doctrine that they have received from others; they speak as the spirit listeth. The most diverse views were voiced; dispute and conflict filled the first communities.

Paul writes to the Corinthians (I Corinthians 11, verses 17 f.):

"Now in this that I declare unto you I praise you not, that ye come together not for the better, but for the worse. For first of all, when ye come together in the church, I hear that there be divisions among you; and I partly believe it. For there must be also heresies among you, that they which are approved may be made manifest among you."

The later official church did not at all see this need for different currents within the community, heresies (Paul uses the word *haireseis*).

In the second century the uncertain seeking and groping comes to an end. The community has a history. In the course of this history fixed articles of faith have won out and been accepted by the large mass of the members. But now educated people enter the community. On the one hand they write down the history of the movement and its articles of faith, as they get them orally, thereby preserving them from further alteration; secondly, they raise the naive doctrine that they find to the rather low level of the knowledge of the time, fill it out with their philosophy, with the purpose of making it attractive to educated people as well and arming it against the objections of pagan critics.

Anyone who now wished to be a teacher in the Christian community would have to possess a certain amount of knowledge. The apostles and prophets could no longer maintain the pace simply by continuing to thunder against the sinfulness of the world and to predict its early end.

The unfortunate apostles and prophets were restricted and harried on all sides. Their small-scale enterprises had in the end to succumb to the enormous apparatus of the Christian bureaucracy. They disappeared. The teachers were deprived of their freedom and subordinated to the bishop. Soon nobody dared to speak in the community assembly, the church,[23] without previous permission from the bishop; that is, nobody outside of the community bureaucracy directed by the bishop, the clergy,[24] which set itself more and more apart from the mass of the fellows, the laity[25] and above them. The image of shepherd and flock takes root; and by the flock is meant the patient kind of sheep that lets itself be herded and shorn. The chief shepherd is the bishop.

The international nature of the movement contributed still further toward increasing the power of the bishop. Formerly it had been the apostles who, by their constant roving, maintained the international links between the communities. As the apostolate faded, it became necessary to find other means of holding together and coordinating the communities. If disputes arose or a

23. *Ecclesia* means originally the assembly of the people.
24. *Kleros*, the inheritance, the property of God, the people of God, God's elect.
25. From *laos*, the people.

common action or a common rule was needed on any occasion, congresses of delegates of the communities came together, provincial and even imperial congresses, from the second century on.

At first these conventions served merely for discussion and consultation. They could not make binding decisions. Each individual community felt itself to be sovereign. Cyprian, in the first half of the third century, still proclaimed the absolute independence of each community. But it is clear that the majority must have had the moral advantage on its side. This advantage became more and more binding; the decisions of the majority came to be obligatory for all of the communities represented; and the latter fused into a single compact body. The total gained in power what the single community lost in freedom of movement.

Thus the Catholic church was forged.[26] Communities that refused to submit to the decisions of the congresses (synods, councils) had to leave the Catholic union of churches, were excluded from the community. The individual that was expelled from his community was no longer welcomed in other communities; he was excluded from all communities.

And the effects of this exclusion, or excommunication, became much more serious when the church changed into an organization covering the entire state, in fact all European society, of which the states formed only single parts. Exclusion from the church was now equivalent to being excluded from human society, and could amount to a death sentence.

From the democratic standpoint there is no objection to be made against the church's excommunications, so long as the church forms only one among several parties. Anyone who does not believe the church's articles of faith or will not obey its regulations does not belong in it. Democracy has no reason to demand tolerance of the church, so long as the church is content to be one party along with others, so long as the state does not act for it or even identify itself with it. This is where a democratic church

26. *Catholic* from *holos* (whole, complete), and the preposition *kata*, meaning down, concerning, belonging to. *Katholikos* means concerning the whole, and the Catholic Church is the whole church, or universal church.

policy comes into play, not in demanding tolerance for unbelievers in the church, which would be a feeble and shallow policy.

Although the church's right to excommunicate is unobjection-
able in and of itself from the democratic point of view, so long as
it was not a state church, there are many objections to be made
even at this time with respect to the way in which this right was
used. For it was no longer the mass of comrades but the bureaucracy that did the excommunicating. The more harm the individual could suffer in the process, the greater was the power of the
clerical bureaucracy and its head, the bishop.

An additional factor was that he was the delegate of his community at the church congresses. The bishops' power rose along
with the councils, which were from the beginning assemblies of
bishops.

The bishop had prestige and great power as a result of having
in his hands the administration of the community's property and
the appointment and conduct of the entire administrative, judicial and propaganda-scholarly apparatus of the community
bureaucracy. Now there was added the superior power of the
totality, the Catholic Church, as over against the part, the community. The bishop stood to the community as representative of
the entire church. The more rigid the organization of the entire
church became, the feebler the community compared to the
bishop, at least when he represented the trends of the majority
of his colleagues. "This bishops' cartel stripped the laity of all
power."[27]

The bishops were not entirely wrong in deriving their authority
from the apostles, whose successors they held themselves to be.
Both formed the international, cohesive element among the communities with relation to each individual community, and that
was the source of their immense influence and power.

The community soon lost the last remnant of its original democ-

27. Harnack, *Mission und Ausbreitung des Christentums*, I, 370. Harnack
cites Bishop Trophimus as an example of the great power the bishops had
over their communities. When the bishop went over to paganism during a
persecution, most of his community followed him. "When he returned and did
penance, the others followed him again; all would not have come back to the
church if Trophimus had not led them."

racy, the right to choose its officials. As the bishop and his men gained independence and greater power in the community, it became easier for him to get the community to choose men acceptable to him. He became the man who in fact filled the offices. In choosing the bishop himself the power of the clergy in the community always insured the election of their own candidates. It finally reached the point where the clergy alone chose the bishop, and the mass of comrades in the community had only the right to confirm or reject the choice; but this too turned into an increasingly empty formality. The community finally sank to the level of an applauding mob to whom the clergy presented the bishop that had been chosen for them, so that they could shout hurrah for him.

This constituted the final annihilation of the democratic organization of the community, and put the final seal on the clergy's absolutism; the clergy had been transformed from a humble "servant of God's servants" into their absolute master.

It goes without saying that the property of the community now became in fact the property of their administrators, though not their personal property, but that of the bureaucracy as a corporation. The church property no longer was the common property of the comrades, but the property of the clergy.

This transformation was mightily supported and hastened by the official recognition of Christianity at the beginning of the fourth century. On the other hand, this recognition of the Catholic Church by the emperors was but a consequence of the fact that the bureaucracy and episcopal absolutism had already absolute power.

So long as the church was a democratic organization, it was completely opposed to the essence of the imperial despotism in the Roman Empire; but the episcopal bureaucracy, absolutely ruling and exploiting the people, was quite useful for imperial despotism. It could not be ignored; the emperor had to come to terms with it, because otherwise it threatened to grow too strong for him.

The clergy had become a force which every ruler of the empire had to reckon with. In the civil wars at the beginning of the third century the victor was Constantine, the candidate to the throne who had allied himself with the clergy.

The bishops were now the lords who along with the emperors ruled the Empire. The emperors often presided at the councils of the bishops, but also put the power of the government at the disposal of the bishops to carry out the decisions of the councils and excommunications.

Now too the church achieved the rights of a juridical person capable of acquiring and inheriting property. This increased its excellent appetite, and the property of the church increased enormously, and along with it the exploitation practiced by the church.

The organization of a proletarian, rebellious communism thus became the staunchest support of despotism and exploitation, a source of new despotism and new exploitation.

The victorious Christian community was in every respect the exact opposite of that community that had been founded three centuries before by poor fishermen and peasants of Galilee and proletarians of Jerusalem. The crucified Messiah became the firmest support of that decadent and infamous society which the Messianic community had expected him to destroy down to the ground.

MONASTICISM

The Catholic Church, especially after it had achieved government recognition, transformed the principles of the original Messianic community into their exact opposite. However, this was by no means a peaceful process without opposition and strife. For the social conditions that had created the original democratic communism of Christianity continued to exist, and even became more aggravated as the Empire decayed.

We have seen how movements of protest against the new trend appeared from the outset. After it had become the dominant and official trend of the church, and no other was permitted within the community, new democratic and communistic sects kept arising alongside of the Catholic Church. In North Africa, for instance, at the time of the Church's recognition by Constantine, the sect of Circumcelliones was widespread. Fanatical beggars who carried to an extreme the struggle of the Donatist sect against the official church and the state, preached war against all the noble and rich. As in Galilee at the time of Christ, the peasant population of the fourth century in North Africa rose in desperation against their oppressors, and their protest took the form of banditry. As the Zealots had done before them, and probably the first adherents of Jesus as well, the Circumcelliones now gave these bands a goal, emancipation from all subjection. They boldly stood up in battle to the imperial troops who, hand in hand with the Catholic priests, sought to suppress the uprising, which lasted for decades.

This attempt to revive communism within the church failed, and so did every other, whether peaceful or violent. They all failed for the same reasons that had finally changed the first attempt into its opposite, and continued to operate, just as the need for such attempts persisted. This need was reinforced by the increasing distress; but it must not be forgotten that the church also was increasingly able to keep a large part of the proletariat from the worst distress by means of its charitable institutions, and also to make it dependent on the clergy, to corrupt it, to smother all enthusiasm and all higher thoughts in it.

When the Church became the State Church, an instrument of despotism and exploitation, on a scale of wealth and power that history had never yet known, the end of all its communistic tendencies seemed to have arrived. And yet these tendencies were to gain new strength precisely out of the state religion.

Up to the time of its official recognition, the expansion of the Christian community life had been confined essentially to the large cities. That was the only place it could maintain itself during the persecutions. In the country, where the individual is easily observed, secret organizations could exist only if they were supported by the entire population, like the Irish secret societies of the nineteenth century. Any minority movement of social opposition encounters tremendous difficulties in the country; and this was true for Christianity as well during the first three centuries.

There were no obstacles to Christianity's expansion in rural districts once it had ceased to be an opposition movement and been recognised by the state. For three hundred years Christianity, like Judaism, had been almost exclusively a religion of the cities. Now it began to be a religion of peasants too.

Christianity brought with it to the country its communistic tendencies. Here however these tendencies had much more favorable conditions than in town, as we have seen in discussing the Essenes. Essenianism awoke at once to a new life in Christian form, once it was possible to form open communistic organizations on the land; and this indicates how great the need for it was. Just at the time when Christianity was accepted by the government, at the beginning of the fourth century, the first monasteries came into existence in Egypt, soon to be followed by others in all parts of the Empire.

The clerical and secular powers not only raise no obstacles to this kind of communism, but even favor it, just as the communist experiments in America early in the nineteenth century were not repugnant to the rulers of France and England. It was an advantage for them to have the restless agitators of the large cities leave the world and go out into wildernesses and there quietly raise cabbages.

Unlike the communist experiments of the Owenites, the Fourierists and Cabetists in America, the experiments of the Egyptian peasant Anthony and his disciples succeeded most brilliantly, like the closely-related communist colonies set up in the United States during the eighteenth and nineteenth centuries. A favorite explanation of this fact is that they were imbued with religious enthusiasm, which is lacking in the adherents of modern utopianism. No religion, no communism. But the same religious enthusiasm that inspired the monks was alive in the Christians of the great cities in the first centuries, and yet their communistic experiments were neither thorough-going nor of long duration.

The cause of the failures on the one hand, and of the successes on the other, is not in religion, but in the material conditions.

Compared to the communistic experiments of primitive Christianity in the great cities, the monasteries or communistic colonies in the wilderness had the great advantage that agriculture requires the combination of the farm and the family, and that agriculture on a large scale, combined with industries, was already a possibility, and in fact had already reached a high point of development in the latifundia of the large landholders. The basis of this large-scale production was slavery, which set limits not only to its productivity but to its very existence. When the supply of slaves dwindled, the latifundia had to disappear. The monasteries picked up this large-scale production and developed it further, since free brothers replaced slaves in the work. Because of the general decline of society, the monasteries ended up by being the only places in the Empire where some remnants of ancient technology persisted and were preserved through the tempests of the great migrations, and even perfected in many points.

With the exception of the influence of the Orient, especially the Arabs, it was the monasteries in which the rise of culture in Europe had its source.

The comradely monastic mode of production was eminently suited to rural conditions of production in dying antiquity and the early Middle Ages. Hence their success. In the cities however the conditions of production worked against labor in association; communism could come into being only as mere communism of consumption; but it is the mode of production, not the mode of distribution or consumption that in the last analysis determines the nature of social relationships. It was only in the country, in the monasteries, that the community of means of consumption which Christianity had originally aimed at found a permanent basis in community of production. On such a basis the associations of the Essenes had flourished for a century, and had faded not from internal causes but because of the violent destruction of the Jewish commonwealth. On this foundation now arose the mighty structure of Christian monasticism, which has lasted until today.

But why did the colonies of modern utopian communism fail? They were constructed on a basis similar to that of the monasteries, but the mode of production had completely changed in the meantime. Instead of the scattered isolated enterprises of antiquity, which developed individualistic work and hindered the comradely cooperation of the city workers, giving him an anarchistic attitude towards work, today we find great giant factories in city industry, in which each worker is but one cog working together with numberless others. The habits of working together, discipline at labor, the subordination of the individual to the needs of the community, replace the anarchistic ideas of the individual labor.

But only in production; not in consumption.

Conditions of life were previously so simple and uniform for the mass of the population, that a uniformity of consumption anu needs resulted, making a constant community of consumption quite tolerable.

The modern mode of production, which shuffles all classes and nations together and brings the products of the entire world to the centres of commerce, constantly creates new things, constantly produces new methods for satisfying needs as well as producing new needs; this leads, even in the mass of the population, to a diversity of personal inclinations and needs, an "individualism," such as was formerly to be found only among the rich and noble classes. The coarsest, most material means of consumption—food, drink, clothing—are often uniform in the modern mode of production. But it is in the nature of this mode of production not to restrict the consumption even of the masses to such means, but to evoke, even in the working masses, a growing need for means of culture—scientific, artistic, sporting and so forth; this need becomes diversified and varies from individual to individual. Individualism in consumption, hitherto a privlege of the wealthy and educated, now spreads to the working classes too, first in the large cities and then to the rest of the population. Although the modern worker submits to discipline in working together with his comrades, since he recognizes its necessity, he revolts against any regimentation of his consumption, his enjoyment. In this field he becomes more and more of an individualist, an anarchist if you will.

It can now be seen how the modern city proletarian must feel in a little communistic community in the wilderness, which is basically nothing but a large-scale farm with subsidiary industrial enterprises. As has been said several times, labor and housekeeping had hitherto been very closely linked in this branch of production. That was an advantage for Christian communism, which had community of consumption as its starting point. In the monastic institutions on the land this communism was compelled to tie up with communism of production, which gave it uncommon resistance and capacity for development.

Modern utopian communism started from community in producing and had a very solid foundation there; but the close ties between consumption and production in its small settlements forced it to add communism of consumption to its communism of production, with explosive effects under the existing social influences, inevitably producing endless disputes, and indeed the most disagreeable disputes over trifles.

The only elements of the population that could still successfully found communist colonies in the nineteenth century within modern civilization were elements untouched by modern capitalism, unworldly peasants. The only connection between their religion and their success is that religious enthusiasm as a social phenomenon, rather than as an individual characteristic, is only to be encountered among the most backward portions of the population.

For modern industrial segments of the population communism of production can only be put into operation on so high a level that it is compatible with a very far-reaching individualism of enjoyment, taking the word in its broadest sense.

It was not communism of production that was wrecked in the non-religious communistic colonies of the last century. This sort of communism has long been practiced by capital in the most successful manner. What was wrecked was the communism of regimentation of personal consumption, which is so contrary to the nature of modern times.

In antiquity and down through the middle ages there was no trace of individualization of needs among the masses of the people. Accordingly, monastic communism met with no obstacles in that direction, and it prospered, for its methods were superior to the prevailing ones; it was economically superior. Rufinus (345 to 410), who founded a monastery himself on the Mount of Olives near Jerusalem in 377, says that almost as many men in Egypt lived in monasteries in the country as there were in the cities. We may discount this as the exaggeration of a pious imagination, but at any rate it indicates that the number of monks and nuns was extraordinary.

Thus monasticism gave new life to communistic enthusiasm within Christianity in a form that did not have to function as a heretical opposition to the ruling clerical bureaucracy, but got along very well with it.

However, this new form of Christian communism could not become the general form of society either, and remained confined to separate units. The new communism too had constantly to change into its contrary, and the more so, the more it was technically superior, for that enabled it to raise its members into an aristocracy standing out among the rest of the people and finally mastering and exploiting them.

If for no other reason, monastic communism could not become the general form of society because in order to carry out community of housekeeping, on which it was based, it had to exclude marriage, as the Essenes had done before them and the religious communistic colonies in North America in the last century did. It is true that the prosperity of housekeeping in common required no more than exclusion of individual marriage; a sort of marriage in common could have gone very well with it, as was shown by some of the recent colonies just mentioned. But this sort of sex relations was too sharply opposed by the general social mentality of dying antiquity to be accepted and openly practised. In the general moral nausea of the period asceticism, abstinence from enjoyment, was the much more likely attitude, and one which also wove a halo of glory and special holiness about those who practiced it. By celibacy however, monasticism condemned itself in advance to being a minority. This minority might well be a large one at certain times, as the statement of Rufinus above indicates, but even his undoubted exaggeration does not venture to assert that the monasteries contained the majority. And the monastic enthusiasm of the Egyptians at the time of Rufinus soon subsided.

With the consolidation of monastic communism, the wealth of the monastery increased. The monastic latifundia soon furnished the best products at the lowest prices, since their production costs were low, thanks to their common housekeeping. Like the latifundia of the great landowners they produced virtually all the foodstuffs and raw materials they needed. Their workers were more diligent than the landowners' slaves, for they were comrades who received the entire product of their labor. Moreover, every monastery had so many workers that it could select those who were best suited for various fields of work, introducing an extensive division of labor. Finally the monastery was eternal, compared to the existence of the human individual. Inventions and trade secrets that would have been likely to disappear with the death of the inventor and his family became known to many brothers in a monastery, who handed them down to their successors. As a juridical, and so eternal, person the monastery was free of the dispersive effects of inheritance laws. It could only concentrate wealth, without ever being able to distribute it in inheritances.

Thus the wealth of the single monasteries grew and of the unions of monasteries under uniform direction and regulations, the monastic orders. But as soon as a monastery had become rich and powerful, it went through the same process that has been repeated since by many a communistic association that covers only a small part of society, as we see today in successful productive cooperatives. The owners of the means of production find it more comfortable to have others work for them instead of working themselves, as soon as they find the necessary labor power: propertyless wage-workers, slaves or serfs.

At the outset monasticism had given a new lease on life to

Christian communist enthusiasm, but in the end it fell into the same path into which the clergy had led the church previously. It too became an organization of exploitation and mastery.

It is true that it did not always allow itself to be a mere spineless tool of the rulers of the church, the bishops. Being independent of the bishops economically and rivalling them in wealth, organized internationally just as they were, the monasteries were able to stand up to the bishops as no one else dared.

In the process they sometimes helped mitigate episcopal despotism. But this mitigation too finally turned into its contrary.

After the church had split into Oriental and Occidental branches, the emperor became the overlord of the bishops in the East. In the West there was no government powerful enough to extend over the entire area of the church. Hence the bishop of Rome at first had precedence over the other bishops, thanks to the importance of his diocese; over the centuries this precedence became a domination over the other bishops. In this battle against the bishops he found powerful support in the monastic orders. As the modern absolute monarchy grew out of the class warfare between feudal nobility and bourgeoisie, the absolute monarchy of the pope grew out of a class struggle between the episcopal aristocracy and the monks, the proprietors of the monastic latifundia.

The rise of the church ends with the consolidation of the papacy. From that time on any further development in state or society signifies a defeat for it; development becames its enemy and it the enemy of any development; it becomes a thoroughly reactionary trend, harmful to society. Its usefulness after becoming the state religion had consisted in preserving and developing remnants of ancient culture which it had inherited. But when a new capitalist mode of production, far superior to the ancient form, arose on the basis which the church had saved and developed, and thereby creating the conditions for an all-embracing socialization of production, the Catholic Church could act only as an obstacle to social progress.

INDEX